COMRADES

COMRADES

A LOCAL HISTORY OF THE
BLACK
PANTHER
PARTY

EDITED BY
JUDSON L. JEFFRIES

Indiana University Press
Bloomington and Indianapolis

This book is a publication of

Indiana University Press
601 North Morton Street
Bloomington, IN 47404-3797 USA

http://iupress.indiana.edu

Telephone orders   800-842-6796
Fax orders   812-855-7931
Orders by e-mail   iuporder@indiana.edu

The paper used in this publication meets the minimum requirements of American
National Standard for Information Sciences—Permanence of Paper for Printed
Library Materials, ANSI Z39.481984.

Manufactured in the United States of America

Library of Congress Cataloging-in-Publication Data

Comrades : a local history of the Black Panther Party / edited by Judson L. Jeffries.
    p. cm. — (Blacks in the diaspora)
    Includes bibliographical references and index.
    ISBN 978-0-253-34928-6 (cloth : alk. paper) — ISBN 978-0-253-21930-5 (pbk. :
alk. paper) 1. Black Panther Party—History. 2. United States—History, Local. 3.
African Americans—Politics and government—20th century. 4. African Americans—
Economic conditions—20th century. 5. African Americans—Services for—History—
20th century. 6. African Americans—Civil rights—History—20th century. 7. United
States—Race relations—History—20th century. I. Jeffries, J. L. (Judson L.), date
    E185.615.C654 2007
    322.4'20973—dc22   2007013592

1 2 3 4 5   13 12 11 10 09 08

This book is dedicated to all those
Panthers and community workers
who served on the ground and
whose work and deeds have
heretofore gone unnoticed by
academics and laypersons alike

Regardless of their public image, the Black
Panthers need to be understood. I have worked intensively with the
    Panthers for three years and have been amazed at how few
People, black or white, have made any effort
To understand why there is a Panther Party. In the few years I have
    worked with the Black Panthers, I have become convinced that
    there is a cathartic and therapeutic element
In this revolutionary force.

I have seen their anguish, frustrations and
Undying love in their attempts to make not
Only the masses whole, but themselves as well.

I have observed that for those who became a
Part of the Panthers, life is no longer
Meaningless. They find purpose, and that
Purpose is restoring human dignity and pride
To a decadent society and world.

When one reaches this level of understanding, in most cases, it is an
    indication that one is not only in the
Process of dealing with himself but that
He has become aware that he is a part of the whole of humanity / He
has made progress in his search for identity . . .

                           —REV. JULIUS THOMAS

Contents

COMRADES

Introduction

Painting a More Complete Portrait of the Black Panther Party

Judson L. Jeffries and
Ryan Nissim-Sabat

The Black Panther Party (BPP) was different than any other radical group of its era. The BPP was not merely an organization; it was a cultural happening. Panther posters donned the walls of left-wing activists and radical thinkers all over the world, and their buttons were worn by activists in France, Sweden, China, and Israel, among other places. Although whites were not allowed to join the BPP, white supporters, sympathizers, and hangers-on were substantial in number. When Huey P. Newton was arrested for the murder of a police officer, the Party's legend appeared to grow exponentially. Released in 1970 after serving nearly three years in prison, Newton was greeted by hundreds of cheering and adoring onlookers, many of whom were white. The memoirs, newsletters, and interviews of activists around the world bear testimony to the Party's transatlantic impact. The BPP was not a mere organization, but a movement—the likes of which has not been witnessed since.

The first glimpse the country got of the Panthers was in May 1967 when the group staged its dramatic protest at the statehouse in Sacramento,

California, a spectacle that electrified the nation. Almost immediately people were transfixed by the Panthers' bold and public display of defiance. They had a swagger seldom seen before, as if they were saying to white America, "Look here, Black people aren't gonna take this s_ _t anymore. No more of this turn the other cheek stuff. We, the Black Panther Party, are here and ready to deal with you (the oppressor) anytime, anywhere." America didn't just look; it stared. In Oakland, people stared as Panthers prowled the streets intent on making police officers think twice about manhandling Bay Area Blacks—something to which they had become accustomed. People stared as Huey P. Newton, a baby-faced militant with a high-pitched voice, grew into a larger-than-life figure even before he figured out that in the minds of many he had become a savior of sorts—a cultural and political icon. People stared at and listened to Eldridge Cleaver's fiery, spellbinding indictment of the imperialist Mother Country and how her avaricious lapdogs oppressed and exploited people of color all over the world. To some whites, the Panthers were a bunch of Nat Turner reincarnates in berets and black leather jackets. Many whites erroneously thought that the Panthers wanted to do to them what whites had historically done to Blacks. On the contrary. The Panthers were not Black supremacists nor were they interested in exacting revenge on the white race for slavery or Jim Crow, but unfortunately, these are the types of images that have come to symbolize the Black Panther Party and its history. Oftentimes what gets lost in the writings and discourse about the BPP is the mundane grunt work done by local Panther activists across America. The BPP's history is robust and nuanced. What's more—it has largely been untold.

The Black Panther Party was arguably the only Black international revolutionary organization that consistently challenged the conditions of Blacks as well as poor people generally in the United States—a point too often unacknowledged. The government called the Party subversive and un-American. Not so. A close and more objective look at the Panthers reveals many of them to be patriots. Many of the Panthers served in the United States military and several fought in the Vietnam War. Some served with distinction and earned Bronze Stars and Silver Stars as well as the Purple Heart. Like many Americans, some Panthers went to war because they thought America was worth fighting for. When they returned home they fought against the practices of the U.S. government because they believed the country had lost its soul. But more importantly, they believed it could be redeemed. As Reginald Major pointed out, the Panthers were soldiers at war in "the jungle which is America," warriors "moving to bring greatness to the American Experience" by "completing the work begun by the revolution of 1776."[1]

The Panthers were not interested in destroying the country as many have argued and as some have unwittingly accepted as truth. They were interested in transforming the country into a beacon of democratic socialism, and in the process they were demanding that America live up to its promises as outlined in the U.S. Constitution, the Declaration of Independence, and the Bill of Rights. When those in power refused to take Black people's concerns seriously, then the only alternative, as the Panthers saw it, was for Blacks to take what was rightfully theirs. The Panthers believed, as did Aldous Huxley, that "liberties are not given they are taken," and they argued that doing so was well within Black people's constitutional rights as American citizens. After all, according to the Declaration of Independence, governments are created to serve people, and "whenever any form of government becomes destructive of these ends, it is the right of the people to alter or abolish it, and to institute new government, laying its foundation on such principles, and organizing its powers in such form, as to them shall seem most likely to affect their safety and happiness."

The Panthers began their struggle in October 1966 on the heels of the shooting death of sixteen-year-old Matthew Johnson by a San Francisco police officer. As one commentator put it, the murder of young Matthew over the alleged theft of a car triggered a rage in the Black community that exploded as if out of the barrel of a 12-gauge shotgun. Over the next four days stores were looted and warehouses burned, and sniper fire was traded with police officers in Hunters Point and in the Fillmore District. It did not bring the teenager back, but it did bring into being (in the Bay Area at least) a new revolutionary breed of black cat.[2] Newton and Bobby Seale capitalized on this seemingly new consciousness and established the Black Panther Party for Self-Defense. In the process, they drafted the Ten-Point Program that expressed the desires and needs of the Black community. Among these demands was Point 7, which read: "We want an immediate end to the police brutality and murder of Black people." Furthermore, "we believe we can end police brutality in our Black community by organizing Black self-defense groups that are dedicated to defending our Black community from racist police oppression and brutality," which Newton and Seale immediately put into action with police patrols in Oakland. As Point 7 suggested, the Ten-Point Program signified a taking up of arms—both literally and metaphorically—that rejuvenated the struggle for Black liberation in the United States.

Unlike many organizations that came before it, the BPP would be characterized by a national commitment to militancy that was informed by an eclectic revolutionary ideology. Writers of various backgrounds and disciplines have probed these aspects of the BPP,[3] but despite the scholarship, the existing literature is mostly repetitive. Indeed, over the past forty years, little scholarly interrogation has been done on this internationally known radical group, even though less than four years after the BPP was founded, the organization swept across the country like "wild fire," establishing chapters[4] in more than thirty cities. Yet work on the Panthers (scholarly and otherwise) has almost exclusively concentrated on the activities around the groups' central headquarters in Oakland. Even more problematic is that many writers have reduced the entire organization to the Oakland headquarters, and reduced the headquarters to the person of Huey P. Newton and perhaps a few others. Because Newton was the unquestioned leader of the Black Panther Party, he was for many the face of the organization, but it should be understood that while Newton may have been the face of the BPP, he was not the architect of the Party. In fact Newton was in jail during the organization's proliferation in the late 1960s. Bobby Seale, the Party's chairman, and David Hilliard, the chief of staff, were arguably more responsible for building the organization than anyone else during this period.

Despite the rich history of a number of Panther branches and chapters, few scholars have attempted to excavate this unexplored territory. Opened in 1968, the Los Angeles branch of the Black Panther Party, for example, was one of the first branches established outside the Bay Area, yet it has received no scholarly attention. The Illinois and New York chapters have been the subject of inquiry, but few of these pieces provide the kind of in-depth analysis that enables one to come away with a grounded sense of local Panther history. Few branches of any organization have been overemphasized the way the Oakland headquarters of the BPP has been over the years. The preoccupation with the national headquarters is both unoriginal and historically negligent. It gives the impression (intentional or not) that little of significance was accomplished or occurred outside of the Bay Area and implies further that Panther chapters and branches in other parts of the country were peripheral and unworthy of scholarly attention. Moreover, this limited Panther literature has focused almost exclusively on the often bloody confrontations between the Panthers and law enforcement officials, including local police departments and the FBI.[5] This narrow focus has in turn subliminally reinforced the dominant perception of the Party as a violence-prone organization, when in fact the Party was anything but violent. The Party's posture was defensive in nature. The Panthers did not advocate violence, but instead dared to say openly that "we will defend ourselves by arms *if driven* to that point."

At any rate, the emphasis on the Panthers' clashes with law enforcement has resulted in a missed opportunity to showcase the important and substantial community programs offered by the Panthers at the local level. This unfortunate reality has had discernible consequences. Given that the average American relies on the media and hearsay for information, it is likely that many people have an inaccurate and warped perception of the Black Panther

Party. As Judson L. Jeffries remarked in an earlier work, the media framing of a group can influence the amount of attention it is given in textbooks as well as how it is presented in the annals of history.[6] Simply put, how the media have portrayed the Black Panther Party has affected how people remember the organization, which in turn has undoubtedly had a far-reaching impact on the group's legacy. Consequently, while many are familiar with the guns and the made-for-TV Hollywood confrontations with local police departments, most are unaware of the extensive array of community survival programs that the Panthers provided poor inner-city residents throughout the country. This lack of awareness is quite evident whenever I show a Panther documentary in my upper-level African American Politics class. The overwhelming consensus among the students (regardless of race) is that they had no idea that the Panthers were so community-oriented. Said one very bright white upperclassman in 2001 after viewing the video *Power to the People,* "I had them [the Panthers] pegged all wrong." A slightly younger white student said, "I had always thought that they were the black version of the KKK." Many African American students are equally uninformed. After listening to a talk I gave to a group of elementary school kids and their parents, an African American Ph.D. candidate studying at Purdue University approached me afterward and exclaimed, "None of my teachers ever told me about the free clothing giveaways or the free sickle cell anemia testing. All I knew about was the free breakfast program." The lack of scholarly work on this dimension of the Black Panther Party has undoubtedly contributed to this unawareness.

Former Panther Jonina Abron is one of the few writers who have examined the Panthers' survival programs. Although Abron's work is useful in broadening the focus on the Panthers, it is again limited by its focus on the Bay Area; the experience of local Panthers and their particular conditions are not thoroughly analyzed. She recognizes the potential of the subject, however, as she states, "Party affiliates throughout the country possess distinct organizing styles and programs based on the qualities of the local membership and the particular needs of their respective communities."[7] Thus, in building on Abron's work, this book explores the community programs, as alternative institutions, organized and implemented by local Panthers' offices to confront the state's disproportionate allocation of resources.

The critique proffered here is not intended to minimize the significance of the Panthers' struggles with law enforcement. Much of the Panthers' time was spent dealing with the state's agents of law and order in one way or another. A cursory review of Panther history bears this out. In fact, were it not for the initial skirmishes between the Panthers and the police, the Party might have gone unnoticed by much of America, which would have impacted recruiting and the ability of the Panthers to raise people's level of consciousness, directly or indirectly. It is important to note that this critique is intended to highlight the consequences of limited historical analysis. The current literature's almost exclusive focus on the Black Panther Party's troubles with law enforcement has nearly rendered inconsequential the very essence of the Panthers' Ten-Point Program, which addressed the political, economic, and social circumstances of Black people in America. Furthermore, any study of the BPP is inadequate without some discussion of the activities and influence of the Panthers at the local level. Perhaps one of the most important reasons for studying the goings-on and inner workings of local chapters and branches is that it is vital to examine the work of the rank-and-file Panthers throughout the country in order to gain a better understanding and fuller appreciation of the organization's history. A look at various local offices gives the reader a wider and more substantive knowledge base than does rehashing the activities of the Bay Area Panthers.

Note, however, that the limitations of the existing research on the Black Panthers are not surprising. First, to some, stories about social service initiatives like free breakfast programs and tuberculosis testing are not as sexy as stories about standoffs between the Panthers and the police. Second, academics, like reporters, often write about what they believe will elicit widespread reader interest. Stories that feature drama and suspense as well as those that involve a villain and a good guy tend to attract a wide audience no matter how superficial the stories, and dramatic stories about the Panthers are in no short supply. Furthermore, it is easier to hone in on the Panthers' clashes with law enforcement because materials on the subject matter are more readily available. Materials on the Panthers' survival programs are more difficult to come by; one has to comb through hundreds of issues of the Black Panther newspaper, for which there is no index; one has to track down Panthers and hope they are willing to share their stories; and finally one has to speak with those who lived in the communities in which the Panthers served. Consequently, given the labor involved, it is not surprising that most writers choose the path of least resistance and elect to highlight the unusual and sensational aspects of the organization's history. Third, historical representations are primarily by-products of the governing codes of the hegemonic elite, and thus the foundation of the social order. Historical records cannot be separated from the intellectual framework of the recorder. Historical documentation is primarily funded through capital which has a vested interest in the dominant value system. The practical effect of this is that the results often leave out those involved in liberation struggles and confrontations with the power structure. Those that are not ignored are usually depicted pejoratively and are symbolically representative of society's other, or enemy. The depictions of the BPP fit squarely within this framework. With most of the emphasis placed on its more histrionic tendencies, the BPP has to a large extent been relegated to the status of an outlaw fringe group. Some of the more journalistic writings on the Panthers reflect this representation.

In an attempt to address this unevenness in the existing literature, this book will present a local history of the Black Panther Party by studying offices in Baltimore, Cleveland, Indianapolis, Los Angeles, Milwaukee, Philadelphia, and Winston-Salem, North Carolina. This book is not laden with academic jargon, but instead is written in layperson's terms. However, both scholars and the general reader will find the work informative and illuminating. Obviously these essays do not cover every single event that happened during the life span of each branch, but they do provide an in-depth look at the experiences of those who served on the ground as well as the work done by these unsung grassroots activists.

To a large degree, the above branches operated in the shadows of their more ballyhooed regional counterparts—New York, Chicago, New Orleans, and Oakland, respectively, and as a result they have for the most part gone unnoticed or been given short shrift in the literature about the BPP. Yet a lot of good was done by Panthers throughout the United States, and their story deserves a broad hearing. This is not to imply that the branches examined in this book were more important than those chapters and branches in New York, Chicago, New Orleans, Oakland, or elsewhere. But we contend that the work of the rank and file in Baltimore, Cleveland, Indianapolis, Los Angeles, Milwaukee, Philadelphia, and Winston-Salem was as important to the success enjoyed by the organization more generally as any of the more widely known branches situated in the same geographical region. After all, not all the West Coast Panthers were in Oakland, not all the East Coast Panthers were New Yorkers, not all the Midwest Panthers were in Chicago, and not all the southern Panthers were in New Orleans.

That said, this project analyzes the particular social forces that contributed to the creation, development, and demise of the seven branches studied in this book. The direction of this study has been greatly influenced by Charles E. Jones, who has long maintained that very little is known about the organizations' rank and file.[8] Much of the more substantive and insightful work on the BPP can be divided into two categories: exposés and memoirs. Exposés were typically written on the larger chapters and branches shortly after some dramatic or unfortunate turn of events. Panther memoirs are primarily based on the lives and experiences of national Party leaders. Few of the writings on the BPP were penned by rank-and-file Panthers. Flores Forbes's *Will You Die with Me?*; Evan Hopkins's *Life after Life*; and William Brent's *Long Time Gone* are the exceptions.[9] No one can deny that the stories told by Panther leaders offer an insightful look inside the organizations' dynamics, but the day-to-day activities and the trials and tribulations experienced by those who were on the ground have for the most part been understudied and undervalued.

The idea for this book was born out of the hope that it would inspire future rigorous examinations of less celebrated Panther branches like the ones discussed in this text. This volume recognizes the necessity for a plethora of individual studies within a larger critical analysis of the Black Panther Party as an organization. The hope is that future scholars can extrapolate the findings documented here and use them in a much broader comparative study. Only with detailed comparative studies of Panther branches and chapters in all their human variety can we expect to understand any one of them.

Through the use of archival materials, personal interviews, primary government documentation, materials from the Department of Justice, and a plethora of secondary sources, this book seeks to obtain an in-depth assessment of Panther branches in Baltimore, Cleveland, Indianapolis, Los Angeles, Milwaukee, Philadelphia, and Winston-Salem, North Carolina, as well as the specific peculiarities that influenced their development. Interview data has been collected through discussions with former Panthers, key leaders of various Black Nationalist organizations in these cities during the late 1960s, and prominent members of each city's Black community, including church and organizational leaders. Additional perspectives have been gathered through newspaper accounts of Panther activities and other important incidents. Whereas studies with a narrow focus encounter inhibiting generalizations, this book will seek to question the stigma imposed on all members of the BPP through an intensive analysis of the specific conditions and circumstances found within these seven branches.[10]

To fully grasp the significance of the BPP, it is essential to situate the organization within the general landscape of the ongoing Black Freedom struggle during the second half of the 1960s. Thus, before launching into a meaty discussion of each local branch, each author will discuss the forces that gave rise to the Panthers in each of the cities studied in this book. In chronicling the history of each branch, considerable attention will be given to the Panthers' implementation of community programs to "meet [the] daily needs" of the poor and working-class Black community.[11] We also seek to emphasize the importance of the Panthers' mobilization of the "brothers and sisters on the block," who were central to the expansion of the Party.[12]

This book will demonstrate that there are some aspects about the BPP that can be generalized, but many that cannot be. The Black Panther Party was an international phenomenon that spanned many communities, but each branch was unique, with its own history. Each branch had its own set of circumstances and should be evaluated on its own merit. As such, the development of local chapters and branches was dependent upon the specific social forces and conditions within their particular communities. Hence, it is important to discuss Black people's situation in each of the cities studied in this book in the years leading up to the opening of Panther branches there, and this work provides a social history that includes an account of matters such as housing, education, and employment conditions, to name a few. Dynamics such as these are highlighted as we set the stage for the emergence of the Panthers in these seven cities.

Building on this sociohistorical context, the authors document the genesis and growth of these local offices and their relationship to the national headquarters in Oakland. As alluded to earlier, we will also look at the composition of each branch, as it drew from Black radical circles, college campuses, high schools, and various other sectors.

To be sure, one of the most important aspects of the history of the BPP is the harassment to which the Panthers were subjected by local, state, and federal law enforcement. In *Political Repression in Modern America*, Robert Goldstein defines political repression as "government action which grossly discriminates against persons or organizations viewed as presenting a fundamental challenge to existing power relationships or key government policies, because of their perceived political beliefs."[13]

Each chapter will underscore the FBI harassment and police repression of the BPP. Whereas the existing literature might give the impression that FBI disruption was confined to the larger Panther chapters such as New York and Chicago, as well as the national figureheads, we will document the equally insidious campaign to "expose, disrupt, discredit or otherwise neutralize"[14] Panthers at the local level. Specifically, this discussion will uncover the extent to which the FBI (along with local law enforcement) collaborated to intimidate the Panther rank and file, cause dissension between local Panther branches and chapters and the national headquarters in Oakland, and instigate conflict with other groups.

Again, the literature on the BPP has often been preoccupied with the violent skirmishes between Panthers and law enforcement, and consequently the Panthers' community programs have not been assigned the significance they deserve. This work will give due consideration to the importance of these programs and their role in fostering strong community alliances and heightening the consciousness of those they served. We devote attention to the evolution of the Panthers' community survival programs and their impact on the material conditions of Black and poor people in general.

This book is not interested in exalting the Black Panther Party to a place beyond reproach. Rather, the book's objective is to paint a more complete portrait of the BPP than has been done up to this point. Consequently, following an in-depth discussion of each local office, most of the authors will conclude by highlighting the external as well as internal circumstances that led to the demise of each branch and the impact each closure had on the larger community. Moreover, a few of the authors will touch on the influence that the Party had on both the Black community and the individual members of each branch.

Finally, this project will recapitulate the implications that come from the narrow representation and selective documentation of the Party. It is necessary to understand the manifestations of the negative categorization of groups such as the Panthers in order to seriously confront the system of knowledge that produces these erroneous representations within Western society. Thus, the dominant social order—or the triadic interplay between the political establishment, the economic arrangement, and the cultural belief system— continues to reproduce its foundational ideas through the historicity of oppositional movements. The Panthers were vilified in the 1960s through their categorization as a primary enemy of the state. The documentation of these particular branches serves to challenge this image of the BPP and moderate the reproduction of the dominant order's categories. But in the end, this book is about the rank and file and the often mundane but invaluable work they performed to improve Black communities throughout America. The history of the BPP is rich with stories of unsung heroes and heroines without whom there would have been no Black Panther Party. I hope that this book is the first installment of that story.

Notes

1. Reginald Major, *A Panther Is a Black Cat* (New York: William Morrow, 1971), 280–282.

2. Earl Anthony, *Picking Up the Gun* (New York: Dial Press, 1970), 2.

3. Judson L. Jeffries, *Huey P. Newton, The Radical Theorist* (Jackson: University Press of Mississippi, 2002); Floyd W. Hayes III and Francis A. Kiene III, "'All Power to the People': The Political Thought of Huey P. Newton and the Black Panther Party," in Charles E. Jones, ed., *The Black Panther Party Reconsidered* (Baltimore: Black Classic Press, 1998), 157–176; Jim Mori, "The Ideological Development of the Black Panther Party," *Cornell Journal of Social Relations* 12 (1977): 137–155.

4. Although members of the organization make a distinction between a branch and a chapter, for the purposes of this book the words may be used interchangeably according to sound and context.

5. Examples include the murders of Panthers John Huggins and Bunchy Carter in Los Angeles, the murders of Fred Hampton and Mark Clark in Chicago, the trial of the Panther 21 in New York, the murder trial of Central Committee members Bobby Seale and Ericka Huggins in New Haven, and the harassment of various members of the central body by police in Oakland.

6. Judson L. Jeffries, "Local News Coverage of the Black Panther Party: An Analysis of the Baltimore, Cleveland and New Orleans Press." *Journal of African American Studies* 7 (Spring 2004): 21.

7. Jonina M. Abron, "'Serving the People': The Survival Programs of the Black Panther Party," in Jones, *The Black Panther Party Reconsidered*, 188.

8. Charles E. Jones, "Reconsidering Panther History: The Untold Story," in Jones, *The Black Panther Party Reconsidered*, 10.

9. Flores A. Forbes, *Will You Die with Me? My Life and the Black Panther Party* (New York: Atria Books, 2006); Evan Hopkins, *Life after Life: A Story of Rage and Redemption* (New York: Free Press, 2005); William Brent, *Long Time Gone* (New York: Times Books, 1991).

10. On the other hand, case studies are limited by their inability to make larger theoretical statements about particular occurrences or organizational structures.

11. Huey P. Newton, *To Die for the People: The Writings of Huey P. Newton*, ed. Toni Morrison (New York: Writers and Readers, (1972) 1995), 104.

12. Bobby Seale, *Seize the Time: The Story of the Black Panther Party and Huey P. Newton* (Baltimore: Black Classic Press, (1970) 1991), 60.

13. Robert J. Goldstein, *Political Repression in Modern America: 1870 to the Present* (New York: Schenkman, 1978), 64. This repression involves not only the act, but also the general message conveyed to the public. Political repression can range from the occasional police visit, arrest, or detention to widespread disappearances, torture, and killings (J. C. Scott, *Weapons of the Weak: Everyday Forms of Peasant Resistance* (New Haven, Conn.: Yale University Press, 1985)). A disappearance means a person has been seized, by either the police or a government apparatus, and placed in detention without a record. A disappearance has been called the highest form of political repression because all legal protections of the individual can be ignored. Indefinite detention and torture can then be conducted with little or no impunity and with crushing effects on individual lives (David Gutierrez, "Incarceration and Torture: The Self in Extremity," *Human Rights Quarterly* 6 (1984): 284–308). According to Student Nonviolent Coordinating Committee member Mukasa Ricks, this was a common practice used against civil rights activists (Mukasa "Willie" Ricks, personal interview with Judson L. Jeffries, May 14, 1998).

A close reading of the literature on political repression reveals three common types: legal repression, covert repression, and violent repression (see Appendix). Some argue that the use of the legal system is the most widely used means to squash dissent: Murray Levin, *Political Hysteria: The Democratic Capacity for Repression* (New York: Basic Books, 1971); Alan Wolfe, *The Seamy Side of Democracy: Repression in the United States* (New York: David McKay, 1973); J. B. Grossman, "Political Justice in the Democratic State," *Polity* 8 (1976): 358–388. Alan Wolfe defines legal repression as "when a simple law that was originally passed with no political purpose is used to harass and repress" (Wolfe, *The Seamy Side of Democracy*). Covert repression is a tactic whereby police and government officials use surveillance or put informants in place to disrupt organizational operations. Violent repression is physical aggression used to intimidate or in some cases put down those considered to be subversive or un-American.

One of the main purposes of repression is to create a climate of fear (Isaac Balbus, *The Dialectics of Legal Repression* (New York: Russell Sage, 1973)). For example, in the first half of the century, law enforcement officers in the South helped spread fear by putting pictures of lynchings in the press, ostensibly to help relatives claim their dead but actually as a warning to others (A. P. Schmid, *Political Terrorism* (New Brunswick, N.J.: Transaction Books, 1983)). Terror as a policy is so shrewd that the government does not have to do everything; terror works through personal networks based on word of mouth and rumors among the general public. Repression also involves a circle of complicity. A fully operative government apparatus for repression may come into existence and, once established, a network grows around it to maintain and protect it (A. De Swaan, "Terror as a Government Service," in M. Hoefnagels, ed., *Repression and Repressive Violence* (Amsterdam: Swets and Zeitlinger, 1977)). Beginning with the police, the FBI, and the National Guard, a repression apparatus may also include judges, lawyers, informers, and other government bureaucracies. The apparatus also tends to find a widening circle of victims (M. Ruthven, *Torture: The Grand Conspiracy* (London: Weidenfeld and Nicolson, 1983)).

14. United States Senate, "The FBI's Covert Action Program to Destroy the Black Panther Party," *Final Report of the Select Committee to Study Government Operations with Respect to Intelligence Activities* (Washington, D.C.: S.R. No. 94-755, 94th Congress, 2d Sess, 1976), 187.

1

Revising Panther History in Baltimore

Judson L. Jeffries

In 1860, the state of Maryland accounted for nearly one-fifth of the free Blacks in the United States, and twenty-six thousand of them resided in Baltimore. "Throughout the 1870s and 1880s, race relations were relatively fluid, with a fair amount of intermingling between blacks and whites in public gathering places."[1] The African American community grew steadily over the next several decades—so much so that many whites began to feel threatened by this proliferation. Consequently, by the early 1900s segregation was more pronounced in Maryland than in any other border state. By 1922 the city had established a zoning commission that effectively confined rowhouses, and by extension Baltimore's poorer residents, to poorer neighborhoods. Segregation was prominent, but there seemed to be peculiar variations of it. For example, in the 1930s, when legendary jazzman Chick Webb performed at the Hippodrome Theater, his mother and wife stood on stage to see him perform, yet Blacks were not allowed in the audience. The city's most popular spot for stage plays in the early 1950s, Fords' Theater in West Baltimore, required Blacks to sit in the second balcony, although Blacks could perform on stage. The Lyric at 128 West Mount Royal Avenue, Baltimore's main concert venue, did not allow Blacks to perform there, yet oddly had no seating restrictions for Black patrons.

As the number of Black residents in Baltimore increased, so did whites' determination to keep Blacks marginalized. Between World War II and 1960, the Black population of Baltimore increased from 194,000 to 326,000 as waves of southern Blacks were drawn by the industrial opportunities associated with the war.[2] While the number of Black residents increased, Blacks' influence remained negligible to a large extent. Schemes by whites to keep Blacks politically, economically, and socially subjugated were largely successful. An early study commissioned by the Baltimore Urban League commented on the powerlessness of Blacks in the political process:

> If ever the Negro population of Baltimore became aware of its political power, the . . . governmental, economic and racial set-up of the community would undergo a profound change. The political seers have long been aware of the presence of this sleeping giant and have handled him successfully from time to time.[3]

To those familiar with the city, it is not difficult to understand how the Urban League arrived at the conclusion it did. Baltimore is strangely unique; in many ways it is both a northern city and a southern city. Its winters can be as brutal as any city in the northeast corridor and its summers are often as humid and muggy as any in the Deep South. This peculiar characteristic of being a northern and southern city has no doubt impacted the role of civil rights there. Baltimore maintained legalized segregation until the passage of the 1964 Public Accommodations Act and was at times extremely resistant to changes in the power structure. Opponents of segregation often claimed that wholesale racism prevented integration in Baltimore, a typical southern argument. Curiously, Baltimore exhibited little in the way of a highly dramatic response to this oppression, perhaps because its political leadership and the general attitude of whites were arguably less hostile than those of a typical southern city. Like northern cities, though, Baltimore experienced an influx of Black immigrants who fled southern poverty and Jim Crow, seeking jobs and a better place to raise their children. Such interesting dynamics yielded a different local movement than that witnessed in the South generally, and the impact of these dynamics would prove to be far-reaching. For example, in 1970, Blacks constituted 46 percent of Baltimore's population, yet they were not able to convert these numbers into policy outcomes that redistributed services and goods more equitably to the Black community. In fact, it was not until 1987 that Black Baltimoreans were able to elect one of their own to the mayor's office, despite the early efforts of the Register-and-Vote campaign initiated by the Black Minister's Network that by 1957 was registering Black voters at the rate of one thousand per month. Cities like Chicago, Cleveland, Los Angeles, Oakland, and Philadelphia were able to vote Blacks into the mayor's office long before Baltimore, even though Blacks did not constitute a majority in any of those cities. In truth, the lack of empowerment of Baltimore's Blacks was in part self-induced. For a time Baltimore's Black community was sharply divided between middle-class westside Blacks and lower-class eastside Blacks, a fissure that had been widening since the end of World War II. This socioeconomic division was accompanied by deep political differences. In the early 1960s, a number of middle-class Blacks were conservative, especially with regard to civil rights protests. One reverend·commented that "middle-class black folk were just as conservative as middle-class white folks when it came to civil rights."[4] Some middle-class Blacks on the west side were not so quick to challenge the status quo that had been, from an economic standpoint, relatively good to them.

These conservative elements notwithstanding, Baltimore has a long and storied history of Black grassroots political activism that has gone largely unnoticed by many historians and students of politics. This history dates back to as early as the late 1800s when the African American community mobilized around labor disputes with immigrants who were competing for jobs. Also at that time Rev. Dr. Harvey Johnson of Union Baptist Church and some of his closest Baptist colleagues were focused on the erosion of Reconstruction Era progress and what they could do about it. The result was the founding of the Mutual United Brotherhood of Liberty of the United States of America (MUBL). The MUBL pledged "to use all legal means within our power to procure and maintain our rights as citizens of this our common country." Others like John Locks, Dr. H. J. Brown, George Lane, and Councilmen Harry S. Cummings (elected in 1890) and Warner T. McGuinn worked tirelessly to bring about better educational and housing opportunities for Blacks. Fast-forward to the early 1930s, when religious leaders and secular luminaries organized the "Buy Where You Can Work" boycotts and protests. The National Association for the Advancement of Colored People (NAACP), the second-oldest chapter in the country, played an especially prominent role in this enterprise, earning itself a reputation as one of the most powerful branches in the country. The "Buy Where You Can Work" campaign encouraged a boycott of all white-owned stores that would not employ Black people even though most of their patrons were Black.[5] In the end, the boycott brought about significant changes in the hiring practices of white-owned businesses in Black neighborhoods, ranging from small mom-and-pop stores to national chains such as A&P.

The 1940s saw more of the same kind of activism. Civil rights leaders and labor activists saw World War II as an opportunity to bring about political and social change. In 1942, Dr. J. E. T. Camper, a well-respected NAACP official, led a march in Annapolis to pressure the state to enforce equal opportunity in employment and housing. That same year, more than five

hundred people attended a rally at the YMCA on Druid Hill Avenue to protest discrimination in defense industries. Also during this time the less confrontational Urban League worked effectively behind the scenes to open up
job opportunities and training programs to African Americans.[6] In the early
1950s, the Congress of Racial Equality (CORE) made its presence felt by
leading a number of sit-ins at downtown Baltimore restaurants. These sorts
of activities laid the foundation for the rambunctious student protests of the
mid-1950s and early 1960s. In fact, by 1960, the local Civil Rights Movement
took on a new and more decisive approach to racial equality.

As early as 1955 (years before the Greensboro sit-in), Black students at
Morgan State College began protesting and demonstrating in large numbers,
targeting stores in the Northwood shopping plaza in northeast Baltimore.
Four years later, students from Morgan State College teamed with white
students from Johns Hopkins University and other area colleges to form the
Civic Interest Group (CIG). The CIG simultaneously protested Arundel Ice
Cream while they demonstrated at the Rooftop dining room at the Hecht-
May Company department store in Northwood shopping plaza. Starting in
March of 1959, students converged on Arundel Ice Cream, picketing and con-
ducting sit-ins to pressure the store's owner to end its practice of racial discrimination against Blacks. The *Afro-American* (Baltimore's Black newspaper)
reported that more than four hundred students participated in the demonstration. Five days after the sit-in began, the restaurant's manager announced to
the students that they had "as much right to be served here as anyone else.
Whenever you come here, you will be treated like any other customer."[7]
Because of CIG's successes by the early 1960s, it had become a well-known
entity and by 1963 this student movement had forced the then suburban
Northwood Movie Theater to integrate, but only after 1,500 people picketed
the theater and scores of Morgan State's student body had been arrested.

Despite these successes, whites continued to resist changes in the city's
power structure. The limited success of these civil rights demonstrations
raised both expectations and growing dissatisfaction, and many less patient
activists demanded more and faster change; they in turn reduced their commitment to nonviolent change and adopted a more militant stance.

Consequently in 1968, when insurgents across the country took to the
streets en masse in response to the assassination of Dr. Martin L. King Jr.,
Baltimore too exploded. Six persons were killed, more than seven hundred
others were injured, and numerous businesses were destroyed over a six-day
period,[8] with damages totaling more than $14 million. Many of the burned-
out stores and businesses were white-owned. Some were places that had
refused to serve Blacks in the past. A day after Baltimore erupted, Governor

Spiro Agnew declared martial law and sent in 5,500 National Guardsmen to assist 1,200 city police. Nearly six thousand arrests were made before order was restored.[9]

Several days later, Governor Agnew summoned leaders of the moderate Black community (who were exhausted from walking the streets trying to calm the insurgents) to the state capitol. Instead of thanking them, as many of the leaders had expected, the governor berated them as cowards who were secretly allied with the criminals and who shared responsibility for what had occurred. Many of those in attendance walked out, and Agnew refused to allow those who remained to explain themselves.[10] According to one of the attendees, city and state officials sat before this group of Black leaders "like a white jury sitting in judgement on the slave folk."[11] Mayor Thomas D'Alesandro issued a public statement condemning Agnew's remarks. African Americans and white liberals despised the speech, but some working-class whites throughout Maryland and indeed the country hailed it. Possessing an obvious penchant for hyperbole, the Baltimore *Labor Herald* went so far as to call Agnew's comments "one of the outstanding speeches of the century."[12]

Agnew had grown increasingly impatient with Black dissidents ever since a ruckus had broken out in Cambridge, Maryland, the previous summer. That July, violence erupted after H. Rap Brown of the Student Nonviolent Coordinating Committee (SNCC) delivered an incendiary speech that renounced nonviolence in favor of Black power. When Agnew was given a copy of Brown's speech months later, he was appalled by the rhetoric and even more dismayed that Maryland's moderate Black leadership did not share his sentiments.[13] Without any evidence, Agnew believed that Stokely Carmichael[14] was the prime instigator behind the 1968 Baltimore uprising and he accused Baltimore's Black leaders of lacking the courage to condemn him and his destructive agenda. Blaming the upheaval on "outside agitators," Agnew ignored the festering social, economic, and political ills behind the violence. His handling of this situation was indicative of the way the white establishment had historically dealt with Baltimore's Black political leadership in particular and Black concerns in general.

Moreover, by 1968 Agnew was fed up with Black protesters. Case in point: When 450 Black students from historically Black Bowie State College marched on the statehouse to see the governor, demanding improved dormitories and classrooms, Agnew refused to see them and called for the state police. More than two hundred students were arrested. To make matters worse, Agnew ordered the troops to proceed immediately to Bowie State, where they arrived at seven in the evening to shut down the college, giving the remaining students five minutes to vacate their dormitories and leave the campus.[15]

Despite the presence of the NAACP, CORE, and the Urban League, for the most part Black leaders were not taken seriously and Black socioeconomic conditions lagged significantly behind those of whites. For example, while the poverty rate for whites in Baltimore was about 10 percent in 1960, it was roughly three times that for Blacks. In 1960, 5,218 families with nearly 18,000 children were on welfare. Ten years later, 26,666 families with 77,000 children—five times as many—were on the dole. During the 1960s Baltimore was a city in disrepair. Sergeant Roger Nolan, a veteran of the Baltimore Police Department since 1967, explained that when he returned to Baltimore in 1964 after serving four years in the Marine Corps, he saw a city that had been "taken over by heroine . . . unemployment in the Black community was high, and it was the first time that I saw abandoned buildings and homes all over the place."[16]

A survey conducted in 1965 found several disturbing patterns concerning the poor and working class in Baltimore.[17] The survey found that the poor belonged to families in which undereducation was a generational pattern, as members dropped out soon after completing elementary school. They felt more oppressed by and suspicious of civilian authorities than helped by them, and they felt underserved in terms of schools, fire protection, sanitation, recreation, health care, and police protection. The point about police protection is especially noteworthy, because from March 1969 to March 1970, violent crime in Baltimore rose 7.3 percent, a development that was not lost on the rest of the country. The Federal Law Enforcement Assistance Administration ranked Baltimore highest in the nation in violent crime. In 1970, three-fourths of the crimes perpetrated in the state of Maryland took place in Baltimore.[18]

Dr. King's assassination, the inferior status to which Baltimore's Black leadership had been consigned by the white elite, and the deteriorating quality of life for the city's Black residents signaled the decline of the traditional Civil Rights Movement and ushered in an era of greater urgency. Out of this era sprang groups such as the Republic of New Africa, the Soul School, the Students for a Democratic Society (SDS), the Baltimore Defense Committee,[19] and of course the Baltimore Black Panthers.

Panthers in Baltimore

Warren Hart, a man considerably older than the typical Panther recruit, founded the Baltimore branch of the Black Panther Party in the fall of 1968, with the branch's first office located in a rowhouse on Eager Street in east Baltimore. Less than a year after Hart opened the office, he was accused of operating the Baltimore branch as a social club. The branch was experiencing financial troubles, money was disappearing from the group's coffers, and records were sloppily kept. Eddie Conway recalls being concerned about how the office was being run and reporting this to national headquarters. Conway said,

> the office was not being run in a professional manner. People were entering and roaming about the office without any supervision . . . people were having parties, playing loud music . . . all of this was taking place on Hart's watch. When I informed national headquarters about these issues, Donald Cox, Henry Mitchell, and a white lawyer named Arthur Turco came to inspect the office in the summer of 1969.[20]

Cox, Mitchell (officer of the day of the Harlem Branch), and Turco showed up unexpectedly on the Fourth of July. Mitch, as Mitchell was affectionately called, recalls the day Cox informed him that he was to accompany Cox and Arthur Turco to Baltimore. Mitch had been helping set up the Brooklyn office when he got a call and was told to return to the Harlem office. Mitch "didn't know what to think," but he kept quiet and followed orders. Mitch remembers that no one spoke for what seemed like an hour as the three drove to Baltimore; he began wondering if he had done something wrong. Halfway there, "DC [Cox] told me that we were going to Baltimore to make sure the office was running properly and that people were doing what they were supposed to be doing."[21]

Hart had given everyone in the office the day off; suffice to say the Baltimore Panthers were caught slightly off guard when the three men arrived. Steve McCutchen recalls being surprised to see Cox, Mitchell, and Turco at the front door. Nervous, McCutchen frisked all three men for weapons. "I patted them down. Every one of them was packing and I missed all their pieces." In the course of inspecting the office, Cox dressed down Hart for his lack of leadership and busted him down to Panther, and that evening Hart left the office and never returned. Days later, Donald Vaughn, a Hart loyalist, submitted a petition (supposedly given to him by Hart) to have Hart reinstated as defense captain. McCutchen then contacted the regional headquarters in New York and was told "if Hart was allowed back into the office the entire branch would be expelled." Years later some members claimed that Hart worked for the National Security Agency and that his plan was to start a branch in Baltimore with the intention of infiltrating the Central Committee in Oakland. After Hart's exit, Mahoney Kebe served as interim defense captain until August 1969, when John Clark, who had been active in the organization in Los Angeles, but was on assignment in New York at the time, was ordered to Baltimore to head up the office.[22]

The Baltimore Black Panthers brought a sense of militancy that resonated with many Blacks. According to one Black resident, "[t]he Panthers are the only brothers who can deal with the white man on any terms necessary, they're not scared to stand up and tell the honkies where to go."[23] Paul Coates,

who joined the Party after three years of military service including nineteen
months in Vietnam, said, "I began thinking about the Panthers in 1969. I set
out to join the Republic of New Africa in Washington, D.C., but discovered
that the group had moved out of the district. I also considered SNCC, but
I was never able to find their office. Ultimately I decided to become a Panther.
I felt that the Party was doing things that would have an impact on the lives of
the people."[24] Nana Njinga (Conway) Nyamekye, who had been associated with
the Soul School, explained her attraction to the Black Panthers in these terms:

> I felt the need to help my people, be involved with people who had the ability
> to teach me about myself and the plight of Black people . . . find some group
> dedicated to moving the Black community forward.[25]

The attraction most aspiring members felt toward the Panthers in
Baltimore was for the most part genuine and substantive. Connie Felder,
a graduate of Edmondson High School in west Baltimore, joined the Party at
nineteen because "I believed in the cause."[26] Where some in California may
have joined the Party because of a fascination with the gun, this was probably not the case in Baltimore. This is not to say that there weren't those who
were infatuated with the gun. McCutchen acknowledged that when he initially joined the Panthers he was naïve and did not fully understand what the
Black Panther Party was about. He remembers reading an issue of the Black
Panther newspaper and seeing the Ten-Point Program, but he also readily
admits that "seeing the illustrations of Black men with guns" appealed to
him.[27] The Baltimore Panthers did possess weapons, but only for the purpose
of protecting the Black community. Defense Captain Clark maintained that
the Panthers would use their guns "if and when confronted by the police.
We will never initiate an attack against a police officer."[28]

Where the Baltimore Panthers obviously mirrored the national headquarters
was in organizational layout. The Baltimore Panthers followed the hierarchical structure set forth by the Central Committee in Oakland. The hierarchy
included defense captain, lieutenant of information, lieutenant of education,
lieutenant of finance, communications secretary, and officer of the day.[29]
Below them were the rank and file. By midsummer 1969, Steve McCutchen
(Li'l Masai) was the lieutenant of information, Chaka Zulu was lieutenant
of education, Sherry Brown was lieutenant of finance, Reva White was communications secretary, and Larry Wallace was the officer of the day. By late
spring/summer 1970 "Baloti" had replaced McCutchen, who was at that time
performing Party functions in another state. Connie Felder replaced Reva
White as communications secretary and Paul Coates took over as defense captain, replacing John Clark, who had been abducted by bounty hunters with
the assistance of the Baltimore Police Department, and taken to Los Angeles
where he supposedly was wanted on a weapons charge.

Education was highly valued within the Black Panther Party, and political education classes were held regularly. Nana Njinga (Conway) Nyamekya explains that there were political education classes Panthers offered to the community from 5:30 to 7:30 P.M. and political education classes strictly for members of the branch that started at 8:00.[30] Special emphasis was placed on reading. Mao Tse-Tung's *Red Book* and the autobiography of Malcolm X were used to heighten the political consciousness of the organization's members. "Mao Tse-Tung had been our inspiration," said Paul Coates. "He was the symbol of achievement. Huey and Bobby read his works and used some of Mao's ideas as the basis for the Panthers."[31] The works of Frantz Fanon, Che Guevara, and Karl Marx were also required reading for new recruits. In keeping with the Party line espoused by the Central Committee, the Baltimore Panthers called for the eradication of capitalism. One Panther was quoted in the *News American* as saying that "the capitalistic system must be replaced; it must be destroyed. The present American economic system is the main factor in causing millions of blacks to suffer."[32]

The majority of the Baltimore Panthers were primarily in their late teens and early twenties, whereas members at the national level were more varied in age.[33] Nearly all the Baltimore Panthers were products of working-class families. A few were college students, but most were high school students, some of whom worked in the service, retail, and industrial sectors of the city. Several of them attended some of Baltimore's most highly regarded public high schools. At least two Panthers had been students at Polytechnic High School in east Baltimore, an institution known for science, math, and technology, while several others attended Forest Park High School in west Baltimore. The Baltimore Panthers were secretive about their actual membership. "We don't speak in numbers," said Clark. "We think all Black people are potentially Black Panthers."[34]

Some argued that the reason the Panthers would not disclose details about the membership is because the figures were not as impressive as they would have had outsiders believe. In the late 1960s, the Justice Department estimated that there were only one thousand Panthers in the entire country.[35] If true, this finding is interesting in light of J. Edgar Hoover's claim that the Black Panther Party represented the greatest internal threat to the security of the United States.[36]

In keeping with the objectives of the organization, the Baltimore branch immersed itself in community service projects, but the Baltimore Panthers did not patrol or monitor the police like their comrades on the West Coast did. This may be in part because, unlike California, Maryland law prohibited the carrying of guns openly. Moreover, police patrols were discouraged after Huey Newton was charged with shooting Officer Donald Frey in 1967. The Baltimore branch did provide the community with an array of services. Among them was a clothing giveaway. The Panthers also served as an ombudsman for many of the community's residents.[37] For example, when one lady fell ill and was unable to work, the Panthers took her to the department of social services and acted as her spokesperson, and as a result she received the necessary funds. On another occasion when an elderly woman was on the verge of being evicted from her apartment for falling behind on her rent, the Panthers provided the money. Out of this developed an initiative whereby the Panthers supplied welfare mothers and other poor residents with monies to help with rent and other subsidies. Sherry Brown remembers that sometime between late 1971 and early 1972, one of the comrades decided that residents who were short on cash or were unable to pay their bills should be able to walk into the Panthers' office and get help.[38] The Panthers also had plans to start a free health clinic, but for a variety of reasons, the project never got off the ground. However, the Panthers did provide a local coalition with medical equipment in order to help launch the founding of the People's Health Clinic, which till this day is still located at Greenmount Avenue and 33rd Street in east Baltimore.

It is also important to mention that the Baltimore branch operated a free breakfast program, which was mandated by the national headquarters. Instituted in 1969, the program was carried out with the help of local grocers who were amenable to the Panthers' request for foodstuffs. Bobby Seale made it clear that each and every branch was to have a breakfast program, and Baltimore's program operated in at least three different locations at various times from 1969 through 1971. The program briefly operated at a church on Edmondson Ave., out of Sharp Street Memorial United Methodist Church on Etting Street, and at St. Martin de Porres Recreation Hall at 901 Eager Street, where the program hit its stride. On a given day at Martin de Porres one might find more men than women cooking and serving children their meals. At about 7:30 A.M. children trickled in to eat a balanced breakfast before making their way to school. Community worker Glenda Conway has fond memories of the breakfast program. Said Conway,

> After Eddie and I got off work we would pick kids up at their home, drive them to the breakfast program where we would serve the kids cold cereal on some days and sausage, eggs, grits, fruit, milk and juice on other days. After the kids had eaten we would take them to school. We served a balanced breakfast.[39]

The Panthers claimed to have fed as many as two hundred children a day.[40] FBI documents show the number to be significantly lower than that. About the breakfast program, Clark said:

> the local merchants don't really want to do this, but we feel that since they make their living off of the poor people it shouldn't be too much to ask that they put a few dollars back into the community to feed hungry children. If they refuse to donate, we throw up a picket line and urge black people not to patronize them. They know that if blacks don't buy from them they'll have to close their doors. Eventually, they do participate in the program.[41]

The idea of picketing as a way of getting merchants to support the Panthers' breakfast program was encouraged by the national headquarters in Oakland.[42] Most of the supplies given to the Panthers were done so voluntarily without the threat of a picket. Donations of various kinds were given, including supplements and the like. On at least one occasion the Carroll Chemical Company (as reported in the *Baltimore Sun*) purportedly gave the Panthers a shipment of vitamins.[43] Picketing was not only used to pressure merchants into supporting the Panthers' survival program, but it was done to get store owners to change store policy. J. J. Brills, a store located on Pennsylvania Ave., was once the subject of a boycott when the Panthers learned that not only were customers being mistreated, but the store was selling bad meat.[44]

Soon after the breakfast program was started in Baltimore, the Panthers implemented a free lunch program during the summer months for children of grammar-school age through preteen.[45] When the Panthers started the lunch program, they served lunch and then attempted to give the children "liberation lessons." They soon learned that the children would not sit still for lectures or films after they had eaten, so the Panthers subsequently reversed the schedule so that the lessons came before lunch. According to Eddie Conway, one of the Panthers' more ambitious enterprises was the establishment of a food co-op on Biddle Street in east Baltimore. Given the state of some of the city's Black communities and the exorbitant prices charged by some of Baltimore's corner stores, the short-lived food co-op was a welcome addition.

The Panthers were always looking to lend a helping hand. Sherry Brown remembers that sometime during the summer of 1969 the Panthers received a large donation from a company that manufactured baby formula. According to Brown, "there were cases of it stacked up all over our Eden Street office. We had so much of it that it took us months to distribute it throughout the community." Among the established programs that the Panthers sponsored was the free legal clinic, which was a great way to familiarize members in the community with the law. Panthers would instruct people on how to interact with the police when pulled over or what to do when faced with an arrest. Sometimes when residents found themselves in a rent dispute with their landlord they would call on the Panthers for assistance.

The breakfast and lunch programs came under intense scrutiny. J. Edgar Hoover in nearby Washington, D.C., and officials from the Baltimore Police Department accused the Panthers of using the breakfast and lunch programs as a front for indoctrinating children with Panther propaganda. Clark maintained that nothing could be further from the truth. "They think we teach the kids to kill 'Whitey.' We try to educate the children as to what our ten-point platform is all about. It's true that we have told them that in order for the black people to survive we have to take up guns for self-defense. We see nothing wrong in that. Their minds must be prepared now so that they will understand the struggle."[46]

Like other branches, the primary source of income for the Baltimore office came from selling its newspaper, *The Black Panther*, at twenty-five cents a copy. Indeed, pressure to sell *The Black Panther* was extremely high since it was the organization's lifeblood. Once Clark took over as defense captain, the Panthers claimed to have sold five to seven thousand copies a week.[47] Nana Njinga (Conway) Nyamekye recalls hawking the paper back in the day: "I would spend nearly six hours a day on the street selling the paper. The corner of Howard and Lexington Streets was a good spot for selling the paper because of the high volume of foot traffic."[48]

Before Clark arrived in Baltimore some members were not as vigilant about hawking the newspaper. According to McCutchen, some "Panthers would take maybe twenty to thirty papers from the office and return four to five days later not having sold all the papers. All of this changed when Clark arrived."[49]

The Black Panther was not the only source of funding, but it was the most dependable. The Panthers also received donations from local businesses from time to time. The Baltimore branch also received requests to fill speaking engagements. Some within the Baltimore leadership did not view speaking engagements as a practical endeavor, especially engagements outside the metropolitan area. "We've got to get the message across to the brothers and sisters right here in the colony. It's not worth it to us to spend a lot of time traveling around to give talks. We found that four or five of our top people were killing entire days talking with people on the outside," said Clark.[50] Given the shoestring budget the Panthers had to work with, Clark's logic seems ill-founded. On occasion, when the branch was in serious need of money Professor Fred Pincus recalls that Friends of the Panthers, a group he helped create, would help arrange speaking engagements for the Panthers at major colleges such as West Virginia University.[51] The majority of the invitations, however, were from schools within Maryland including Frostburg State College, Morgan State College, Johns Hopkins University, Coppin State College, and the Community College of Baltimore as well as Catonsville Community College and the University of Maryland, College Park. High school students would try to secure Panthers as speakers, but once school officials got wind of the invitations many were rescinded. The Panthers did have enough wherewithal to use radio to communicate with the people of Baltimore. Russ Johnson at WEBB and radio station WSID were especially receptive to having the Panthers as guests. The appearance of a Panther on a radio show often elicited tremendous caller response. On occasion the exchange would become heated and in no time at all the program would be inaudible because the guest and caller would refuse to allow the other to speak, which made for good theater but did not provide a great deal of educational enrichment.

As mentioned earlier, unlike some other groups the Baltimore branch did not get consistent or substantial financial support from philanthropists. There were a few exceptions to this rule. In 1969, when the chapter was experiencing financial hardship, a group of professors at the University of Maryland, Baltimore County (UMBC), provided donations of various amounts. On another occasion the Panthers received $8,000 from the Catholic Archdiocese of Baltimore earmarked specifically for the breakfast program.[52] For the most part, the Baltimore Panthers relied on the sale of its newspaper, books, and other Panther literature.

Political Harassment in Baltimore

Like many other dissident left-wing organizations in America, the Black Panther Party was not permitted to enjoy a peaceful existence free from government harassment. In 1967 FBI director J. Edgar Hoover established COINTELPRO, a counterintelligence program designed to neutralize leftist organizations and those Hoover considered subversive. According to an internal agency memo from Hoover, "[t]he purpose of this program is to expose, disrupt and otherwise neutralize the New Left, their Leadership and adherents." Among the program's objectives was the destruction of the Black Nationalist movement in the United States. Said Hoover, "Agents are instructed to prevent coalitions from forming, to prevent 'the rise of a messiah,' to neutralize potential troublemakers," and to prevent Black Nationalist groups from "gaining respectability" by discrediting them with unfavorable publicity, ridicule, and whatever other means "imaginative" agents could think up.[53] As a result of Hoover's directive, the Panthers became the victims of manhunts, political trials, and unprovoked shootings—a search-and-destroy mission probably unprecedented in America for its scope and systematic ferocity. To give an idea of how intent the FBI was on destroying the Panthers, 79 percent of COINTELPRO's actions between 1968 and 1971 were directed against the Black Panther Party.[54]

Although Panthers in Baltimore did not walk the streets brandishing weapons like the West Coast Panthers did, they were still subjected to many of the same kinds of politically motivated scare tactics. Glenda Conway submits that she did not see any police harassment until the Panthers got serious about selling *The Black Panther* newspaper.[55]

In 1969, a group of concerned citizens (both Black and white) formed the Baltimore Committee for Political Freedom (BCPF) because they feared that the Baltimore Police Department was planning to assassinate Panther leaders in their city, as Fred Hampton and Mark Clark had been in Chicago. The committee of forty included William Zinman, an attorney for the Maryland American Civil Liberties Union (ACLU); Dr. Peter Rossi of the Department of Social Relations at Johns Hopkins University; Dr. John Mann of the School of Education; the Reverend Chester Wickwire, a chaplain for Johns Hopkins University; and others. According to Wickwire, the committee believed that Police Commissioner Donald Pomerlau (who considered J. Edgar Hoover a mentor) was engaged in a "vendetta" against the Panthers.[56] Admittedly, Dean Pappas, a professor at UMBC, at the time remembers thinking that he didn't really believe the police would go after the Panthers in Baltimore like the police had in Chicago, but as a member of the BCPF he thought it prudent to hold a vigil outside Panther offices just in case. In retrospect, "the vigil was actually a stupid thing to do on our part because we had not decided what we would do if indeed the police had come crashing down on the Panthers, we had no contingency plan."[57] In a special report on the Panthers in the now defunct *News American*, reporter John Robinson quotes policeman James K. Wells, the public information officer for the Baltimore Police Department, as saying that "there may be individual police officers who hate the Panthers, but the department itself has no vendetta against them."[58]

Pomerlau was a strict "law and order" man whose background would give some indication as to the type of reception the Panthers could expect. Pomerlau had been a U.S. Marine lieutenant colonel, a combat commander during the Korean War, and an instructor at the Marine Corps School in Quantico, Virginia, before assuming the post of Baltimore police commissioner in 1966. Incidentally, Baltimore's "red squad," formally known as the intelligence section of the Inspectional Services Division (ISD), was launched on July 1, 1966, coinciding with the date of Pomerlau's appointment as commissioner. In addition to an organized crime unit, the intelligence section housed an anti-subversive squad responsible for "gathering information regarding the activities of subversive, extremist and militant groups."[59] In 1974, two years after the Baltimore branch shut down, it was revealed that Pomerlau had compiled dossiers on the Panthers and anyone else he considered subversive.[60] These dossiers were disseminated locally to intelligence agencies of the U.S. Army, Air Force, and Navy, the Secret Service, and the United States attorney. Copies of these reports were also shared with the FBI and the mayor of Baltimore. For sixteen years (1966–1982) Commissioner Pomerlau presided over and directed a huge countersubversive operation, which he also used to intimidate his critics and repress any challenge to the political and social order in Baltimore.

Harassment laws (see appendix) were employed throughout the branch's existence. The typical harassment violations were assault, loitering, and weapons charges. For example, on February 25, 1969, six Panthers were arrested for allegedly assaulting police who were arresting a seventh Panther. The six Panthers, Gregory Ivan Fergus, Robert Ford, Charles Butler, Zeke Boyd, Charles Williams Jr., and Allen Salisbury, were accused of obstructing the arrest of Jimmy Foxworth. After witnessing the arrest of Foxworth (for trespassing on a schoolyard and possession of a .38 revolver), the other Panthers went to call a lawyer, and in a matter of seconds squadrons of police pulled up and hauled in the six. Under orders from the state's attorney's office, several policemen served as sworn witnesses to a list of eight charges against the Panthers, most notably trespassing, in an attempt to link them with arsonists who were responsible for setting a rash of school fires in Baltimore around that time. A reporter for the *Baltimore Sun* later discovered that Foxworth had been working for the police department, and at the trial eighteen months later, state prosecutors admitted that the Panthers were not guilty and dropped all charges.

In the spring of 1969, a Panther rally for which a permit had been obtained was being held in a city park when suddenly there appeared on the scene ten buses loaded with four hundred policemen.[61] Fortunately, the officers were persuaded to leave the scene and position themselves where they would not be visible. Such a show of force may have been an attempt to intimidate Panthers and their supporters. This type of psychological warfare on the part of the police was not an uncommon occurrence at Panther rallies around the country.[62]

Psychological games were a common tactic of the Baltimore Police Department.[63] A similar event occurred on October 13, 1970, when several Panthers participated in a rally protesting the conditions and the substandard medical treatment received by political prisoners in Baltimore and the Maryland State Penitentiary. During the rally the police again stood by in an apparent attempt to intimidate those in attendance, and, recognizing what the police were trying to do, the people held the rally in an orderly and peaceful manner. When the rally began to attract large numbers of passersby, the police became infuriated and began snatching signs away from people. When this did not provoke anyone, the police singled out one participant and demanded that he stop the rally. When the gentleman explained that "it was not his rally to stop," the police started clubbing him with nightsticks. Upon seeing this, the crowd began to disperse. By the end of the night nineteen persons were arrested, three of whom were Panthers. The following day three more Panthers were arrested and charged with disorderly conduct and inciting a riot, and held on $25,000 bond.[64]

There is some evidence that the police tried to stunt the development of the Baltimore branch by arresting and incarcerating its members. Early on, a few members of the Panthers wore the signature uniform of the organization, which included a black leather jacket and beret, but they discontinued the practice because the police could easily identify them. John L. Clark was arrested five times between September 1969 and July 1970. Paul Coates says he was arrested at least fifteen times "for everything you can imagine—from parking tickets to attempted murder."[65] On other occasions, the FBI would arrange for police to release one of a group of Panthers that had been arrested together or single out one Panther for special treatment, then spread the rumor that the beneficiary had cooperated.

One of the most noteworthy arrests of a Panther occurred in August of 1970 when Clark was taken to Los Angeles and charged with illegal possession of a deadly weapon.[66] Sherry Brown remembers the day Clark was picked up. "Although I did not witness the actual event I learned shortly thereafter that bounty hunters walked up to Clark while he was in the courthouse and snatched him up in the presence of some other Panthers. When I heard this I was angry at my comrades for allowing this to happen. I think and have always thought that bounty hunters are the scum of the earth."[67] Will Joyner, who was present when Clark was picked up, can appreciate Brown's position, but maintains that there was nothing that he and his comrades could do. Recounting that day's events, Joyner explains: "Clark got called down to the court house for something minor. Myself and a few other comrades accompanied him along with Attorney William Kunstler.* Out of nowhere came three bounty hunters who grabbed Clark as we were passing through the lobby. Just as we were coming to Clark's defense, police officers intervened on behalf of the bounty hunters. Kunstler looked at me and said, 'Don't let this go down.' But there was nothing we could do."[68] According to one former Panther, the arrest of the Panther leader left a leadership vacuum that proved to have a far-reaching impact on the branch during the remainder of its existence. All of the Panthers with whom I spoke thought Clark was a strong leader. Connie Felder believes that the chapter was never the same after Clark was shipped back to California. The police went to great lengths to put the Panthers out of business. No tactic was too underhanded and no infraction was too minor.[70] On one occasion, as a Party member walked toward his car several police cruisers converged on him, arrested him, and charged him with failure to have a driver's license and registration card in his possession, a questionable charge since he was not driving. In addition, in the winter of 1969 as several police officers looked on, the Baltimore Gas and Electric Company turned off gas service to a Panther house by digging up the street and shutting off the main valve.[69]

---

*Paul Coates maintains that Joyner's version is slightly off. Coates submits that it was local attorney Harold Buchman, not the famed New York attorney William Kunstler, who was there that day.

It turned out that the dwelling was not a Panther residence but the home of Malika Aigroz, a private citizen and mother of a seven-month-old child. Aigroz maintained that her service was cut off as part of a plan to neutralize the Black Panthers. A company spokesperson said her electricity was disconnected after it was learned that her home was being used for Panther activity and not exclusively as a private home, a direct violation of the terms specified in her agreement with the company. The same spokesperson admitted that information on the use of Aigroz's house was gathered from newspaper reports, a Black Panther free breakfast poster affixed to her door, and information from company employees. Another company official claimed it had no problems with the Panthers per se; the issue was the breach of contract. Aigroz acknowledged that she was not a Black Panther but did allow members of the group to use her house, which was in the same block as the Party's headquarters.[70]

When *Baltimore Sun* reporters suggested that there might be an ulterior motive on the part of the gas company, a spokesman for Baltimore Gas and Electric commented that "there might be some feeling that we are picking on the Black Panthers, but this is not correct. We are not engaged in an effort to put the Black Panthers out of business."[71] The fact that four days earlier service had also been disconnected at an apartment where several Panthers were known to frequent cast serious doubt on that claim.

The second type of law employed extensively to repress the Baltimore branch was the public order law that, simply put, prohibits disturbing the peace. Numerous Panthers were arrested for allegedly violating public order laws, which was relatively easy because police possess an enormous amount of discretion in enforcing these laws.[72] A perfect example was the arrest of a Panther charged with disorderly conduct, assault, and resisting arrest when he refused a policeman's order to stop selling the Panthers' newspaper in front of the Baltimore Civic Center. On another occasion, several Panthers were arrested on suspicion of killing a police officer after patrolman Donald Sager was killed and his partner Stanley Sierakowski was wounded in a deadly sniper attack. No gunman was identified at the scene, but Baltimore police officials suspected the Panthers on general principle.[73] The police commissioner admitted that although he had no evidence, "the persons who would commit this crime must belong to some sort of radical group."[74]

One important incident of repression by a political law was the securing of a ten-day injunction on May 1, 1970, against the distribution of the Panthers' newspaper. The state attorney general and the police department's legal adviser, Bernard L. Silbert, argued that the newspaper advocated the killing of police officers. In an accompanying affidavit, the two state officials claimed that the Panther newspaper played an important part in the "ambush" of two policemen and "will continue to present an immediate danger to the lives, health and well-being" of members of the department. Refusal to comply with the order, Attorney General Francis Burch said, can result in imprisonment for contempt of court.[75]

Forty-five "high-echelon officers" of the police department were deputized to enforce the injunction, a number which Sheriff Frank J. Pelz admitted was a bit unusual. "I don't know of any time previously that this has been the case in Baltimore," he noted.[76] David L. Glenn, executive director of the city's Community Relations Commission, criticized Commissioner Pomerlau for seeking the injunction. Said Glenn:

> There are plenty of right-wing groups in the city whose literature tells people to "kill Niggers" and I don't see the police going after them. We have been bothered by hate literature for years and years. I don't see any difference between literature that urges people to kill policemen and literature that wants Negroes killed.[77]

In response to the assertion that the Panthers represented a threat and an immediate danger to the well-being of the police department, national CORE Leader Roy Innis submitted:

> Black Panthers are no threat in Baltimore. You have never heard of them burning police stations or threatening the police. Law enforcement agents all over the country consistently have involved themselves in a massive conspiracy. At present they are using the Panthers as a foil to increase their power to suppress.[78]

Sergeant Nolan, a veteran of the Baltimore Police Department for nearly forty years, remembers that "the Panthers were nonviolent . . . they were more interested in community service programs not in committing crimes or provoking the police like some Panthers in other parts of the country."[79] On the issue of covert intelligence, a number of incidents were uncovered in which political intelligence mechanisms were employed to neutralize the Baltimore branch. In December 1969, investigative reporting by the *Baltimore Sun* and the *News American* revealed that the police had installed a movie camera in a building across the street from Panther headquarters and had engaged in round-the-clock surveillance.[80] When this discovery was made, police admitted photographing Panthers and placing their pictures on bulletin boards in precinct stations, but they denied any use of videotape. Chester Wickwire says that "when the Panthers learned of this surveillance, it put many of them on guard and fostered paranoia within the chapter."[81] McCutchen disagrees with Wickwire's assessment and states that "we were not necessarily paranoid. Rather police activities simply made us more aware of our external circumstances."[82]

The role of government surveillance of leftist groups is well documented. Sociologists Doug McAdam and Kelly Moore[83] submit that it is difficult to overestimate the divisive internal effect that government surveillance had on insurgents. Oftentimes, suspicion reduced morale and led to unfounded accusations. Over the course of the branch's existence, as far as this author could ascertain, local, state, and federal law enforcement infiltrated the branch by strategically placing at least four informants/agents provocateurs within Panther offices in Baltimore.[84] The use of informants and infiltrators by law enforcement has proved to be an effective way to neutralize radical groups. Police infiltrators are afforded the luxury of behaving extremely militantly and even engaging in illegal activity because they know that for the most part they will be protected from prosecution. Basing their actions on this assumption and hoping to please their superiors, agents/informants often concoct outrageous schemes, foment dissension, provoke others to commit crimes, or commit crimes themselves in order to disrupt an organization or provide testimony in court.[85] The job of one informant was to disrupt what was already a tenuous alliance between the Baltimore Panthers and the Students for a Democratic Society (SDS). This informant was instructed to portray SDS as an "elite corps of chauvinistic whites who wanted to exploit the BPP." These efforts must have succeeded. An August 26, 1969, memo reported that "BPP members have been instructed not to associate with SDS members or attend any SDS affairs." Another memo reported that "an officer of the Baltimore chapter [name deleted] was expelled from the chapter for his association with an SDS member."[86]

Because the business of espionage is a clandestine one, it is difficult to determine exactly how many informants infiltrated the local branch. A study by Frank J. Donner would seem to suggest that this work has conservatively estimated the number of informants used to foil Panther activities. Donner notes that of the police departments he studied, no department placed so heavy an emphasis on informers as a way of neutralizing dissident groups as did Baltimore's Inspectional Services Division.[87] The extent to which large sections of FBI documents on the Baltimore branch have been redacted suggests that the office may have been infested with agents provocateurs, adding further weight to Donner's findings. According to Gary Marx, "the use of agents can be seen as a device whereby police may take action consistent with their own sense of justice and morality, independent of the substantive or procedural requirements of the law."[88] Because intelligence operations are by nature secret, considerable damage can be done to an unpopular yet legal group without necessarily evoking legal sanctions.

While the Baltimore branch may not have been infiltrated to the degree other branches were, the infiltration that did occur was made possible by two factors. Because new recruits are the lifeblood of most organizations and because Panthers were constantly being jailed, the branch was forced to accept new members as a way of replenishing membership. Second, because being a Panther was an extremely dangerous undertaking, few individuals were overly zealous to join an organization where they would be risking their lives on a daily basis. Indeed, Michael Newton notes that coming out of the Civil Rights Movement many Blacks were still too conservative—or too afraid—to adopt the Panther Party as a vehicle for reform.[89] Hence, in some ways the Panthers could not be as selective and discerning when it came to reviewing applications as other left-wing or civil rights organizations could be, for the applicant pool was never an abundant one.

In 1969, Panther leaders began to purge members who were thought to be working against the interests of the Party. This purge was apparently in part related to infiltration of the organization. The names of purged members were subsequently printed in the Party's newspaper with the admonition that "[t]hey are not to be associated with or let into any Black Panther office anywhere."[90] Later, the organization took a more serious approach to curtail infiltration; it placed a moratorium on new members. While this tactic undoubtedly prevented agents provocateurs from gaining entry into the Party, it did little to thwart the efforts of those informants already in the organization.

Infiltration proved valuable in creating mistrust and dissension within the branch. Fear of informers was sufficient, in many cases, to generate a climate of mistrust needed to precipitate serious internal problems. Sociologist Gary Marx cites a 1970 memo in which "FBI agents were instructed to plant in the hands of Panthers phony documents (on FBI stationery) that would lead them to suspect one another of being police informers." Subsequently, several Panthers were expelled (justly or unjustly) because they were suspected to be police informants.[91]

Despite the small size of the Baltimore branch, it was subjected to an excessive amount of *violent* repression, and not even children were spared harassment by the police. One morning breakfast was interrupted at the Martin de Porres Hall by police officers who entered with guns drawn. "They walked around with their guns drawn and looked real mean. The children felt terrorized by the police. They were like gangsters and thugs," said a Panther spokesman.[92]

Raids, which are the primary method of violent repression, seldom occurred, but when they did they were carried out en masse. Most notably, on May 1, 1970, police staged numerous raids on known Panther offices and homes. According to the Baltimore Police Department's own newsletter, seventeen Baltimore homes, offices, and nightspots were raided, with approximately 150 heavily armed policemen wearing bulletproof vests participating.

By comparison, according to one study, only five raids were carried out against the Oakland office from 1966 to 1971. The Baltimore May 1 raids resulted in four party members being arrested on weapons charges and six members arrested for the murder of Panther Eugene Lee Anderson, a suspected informant[93] who, according to reports, had been tortured by having boiling water poured on him before he was driven to Leakin Park in west Baltimore and shot to death. Fortunately, the 1248 N. Gay Street office went unscathed. During this time groups of local youths (both Black and white) as well as members of the ACLU held a vigil in front of the Panther's Gay Street office as a show of support and with the hopes that their presence might discourage additional police repression. Paul Coates recalls that "during this period when we were under siege there were groups of people who slept on the sidewalk for two weeks, creating a barrier between the police and our house." Whether or not the presence of these Panther sympathizers is the reason the Gay Street dwelling went unharmed is difficult to say for certain, but their actions didn't hurt.

Several days later in a bail hearing, police detectives indicated that all evidence in the Panther murder case had been assembled three months prior to the arrests. Curiously, detectives refused to give reasons for the delay in conducting the raids. The presiding judge inexplicably refused to entertain any argument that the police may have been seeking to avenge the recent death of a fellow police officer for which Panthers Marshall Eddie Conway, James Powell, and Jack Johnson were eventually convicted.[94] Donald Vaughn, Arnold Loney, and Mahoney Kebe were alleged participants in Anderson's slaying, and all three were produced by the FBI as witnesses to the crime and turned over to the Baltimore's "red squad."[95] The police named Arthur Turco as the mastermind behind Anderson's execution.

The main discrepancy in the case concerned the identity of the body suspected to be that of Anderson. After a skeleton was discovered buried in a park, a local examiner determined it was that of a white man, aged twenty-five to thirty,[96] who had died of a drug overdose. But when the remains made their way to the FBI laboratory in Washington, the body became that of Eugene Lee Anderson, a Black man, aged twenty, killed by a shotgun blast.[97] The final indictments, delayed for half a year after the discovery of the disputed skeleton, came after U.S. Attorney General John Mitchell huddled with ranking Baltimore officials. Prosecutors sought federal advice on "how to deal with Panther cases," but what they learned from Mitchell was that the FBI had done more harm than good for the state's case. When finally hauled into court, witness Mahoney Kebe lied so outrageously that the trial judge ordered him removed from the stand and his testimony stricken from the record. The Panther named as Anderson's executioner was promptly acquitted, whereupon the state offered compromise deals to the remaining defendants. All refused, forcing the district attorney to admit in open court that there was insufficient evidence to prosecute seven of those accused. Paul Coates remembers that "attorney Larry Gibson demolished the state's case by exposing it as a conspiracy." All charges were dismissed against the seven and drastically reduced charges were substituted for the remaining defendants. Not everyone escaped the government's wrath, though. Irving Young, a community worker, was eventually convicted of first-degree murder and sentenced to jail, where he served five years.[98]

That a small branch like Baltimore was subjected to such excessive acts of violent repression is interesting for three reasons. One, while relations between the police and the Black community in Baltimore were by no means amicable, the relationship was not as volatile as it was in places like Los Angeles, Chicago, and Oakland. Unlike the police departments in those cities, Baltimore did not have a long-standing history of corruption or a reputation for excessive force and brutality against Blacks, although these things did occur. Two, repression in the United States is primarily legalistic. Given the relatively small size of the branch, the use of massive amounts of violent repression against the Baltimore Panthers was probably unnecessary, as other tactics could have proved just as effective. Third, as Isaac Balbus argues, in the United States, elites are constrained by certain norms and procedures,[99] one of which is that repression is typically implemented when there is massive intolerance of the minority group on the part of the majority. When intolerance becomes widespread, there are demands for repression, demands to which policy makers usually accede. For example, during the 1950s, the Communist Party and its suspected sympathizers were subjected to significant repression, and there seemed to be a great deal of support among the general public for such actions.[100]

Another norm is that repression is usually employed only when there is a clear and present danger to that society's way of life. Even then, conventional wisdom holds that repression is meted out in proportion to the perceived or actual threat. In other words, the amount of repression should not exceed the level of threat posed by the minority group. When government officials fail to adhere to these norms and procedures, unwanted attention is drawn to their efforts to squash dissent, which in turn increases the number of sympathizers for the subjects under attack.[101] Such was the case in the raid and shootout in Los Angeles and the raid in Illinois that resulted in the deaths of Chicago Panther Fred Hampton and Mark Clark of the Peoria branch. A major segment of the public became outraged at these overt acts of political repression and began to question government actions against the Panthers.

The same held true in Baltimore. When the community heard about the May 1 raids, Blacks and whites alike were furious at the indiscriminate manner in which those raids were carried out. As a result, a group of concerned citizens under the auspices of the Interdenominational Ministers Alliance issued the following statements:

1. Persons who are to be apprehended should be approached and arrested without fanfare.
2. There should be no attempt to attribute the actions of a few to the total black community.
3. There should be an end to the harassment and intimidation of whole neighborhoods in searching for alleged law violators, and
4. The Mayor and the Governor should impress upon the Commissioner the fact that the black community is to be treated equally and fairly in matters related to police activities.[102]

There are perhaps four reasons that could account for the excessively violent tactics levied against the Baltimore branch. First, there is the possibility that raids were launched because the purge and moratorium put in place by Panther leadership proved to be an effective countermeasure against government infiltration, leaving law enforcement without any clue as to what the Panthers were doing or planning. Second, law enforcement may have feared that the Baltimore Panthers, with their program for creating public awareness and heightening people's level of consciousness, were politicizing those who for many years accepted the status quo and remained docile. There is some evidence that support for the Black Panther Party was transcending racial, class, gender, and to some extent ideological lines. Said one white businessman: "White people must stop evading the fact that we are to blame for the conditions that produced the Panthers."[103] It should also be noted that the Panthers often held colloquia and workshops with members of the community to discuss problems with the police and other matters. On December 20, for example, the Open Meeting to Help Stop Political Repression of the Panthers convened at a local venue, where attorney William Zinman, Nancy Henley (a psychologist from UMBC), and Steve McCutchen were the featured panelists. When Henley (now a retired professor) was asked why she participated in this forum, she responded, "I saw what the police were doing to Panthers in other cities. I wanted to make others aware so that it wouldn't happen in Baltimore."[104] Students of repression argue that governments are more likely to repress those groups that give the impression of making inroads into other communities as opposed to groups whose support is confined to those that consider themselves outside the mainstream.[105] Third, at the very least there may have been some concern on the part of the powers that be that with Baltimore's Black population steadily increasing, the number of Panthers, as well as their allies, supporters, and sympathizers, might also increase. Indeed, a 1970 poll of African Americans living in New York, San Francisco, Detroit, Baltimore, and Birmingham revealed that 62 percent of Blacks polled admired what the Black Panthers were doing.[106] Clearly Black attitudes about the Panthers were not monolithic, though. Some were leery of the Panthers. Said one Black schoolteacher when asked her opinion of the group, "I think the Panthers are jiving and I'll tell you why. They have too many white women following them around. I went to one of their trials and every one of them seemed to have a white woman on his arm and even their lawyer was white. If they rap about black, then live black. Soon as they get in trouble they yell for Mr. Charlie."[107]

Fourth, unlike California, Maryland did not have a state law that permitted individuals to carry guns openly. Hence, some police officers may, strangely enough, have assumed that because Panthers in Baltimore did not carry weapons openly also meant that they did not have weapons, thereby viewing raids of Panther offices in Baltimore to be considerably less risky than in California.

An Analysis of Political Repression Against the Baltimore Panthers

Legal harassment helped to stymie the Baltimore branch in several different ways. One major result of the abuse of the law was to cause the dissipation of organizational funds and the disruption of its day-to-day activities. When Panthers were arrested, the organization was forced to meet the cost of bail and legal assistance. Anthony Oberschall perceptively notes that the government's strategy appeared to be to tie down movement leaders of the 1960s in costly and time-consuming legal battles which would impede their activities and put a tremendous drain on financial resources regardless of whether the government was successful in court. Between 1967 and 1969, total bail for all those arrested across the country was $4,890,580.[108] The Baltimore Panthers incurred at least $350,000 in bail alone in 1970. These funds could have otherwise been used for community service programs and organizational expansion.

A second way in which law enforcement neutralized the Panthers was by repressing the ideology of the Black Panther Party. Here, the government attempts to manipulate the public's consciousness so that they accept the ruling ideology and distrust and refuse to be moved by competing ideologies. If the government can convince the overwhelming majority of the people in the United States that left-wing ideologies are evil and un-American, then dissident groups will gain few adherents and eventually die out. The idea that a form of repression could be ideological has its major expositor in the Italian Marxist Antonio Gramsci. According to Gramsci, those in power keep themselves there not only forcibly, but also by developing a certain set of ideas that become part of the culture, thereby making their rule seem just and inevitable.[109]

In the case of the Baltimore Panthers, law enforcement achieved this by engaging in character assassination, which created adverse publicity for the branch. On at least one occasion a Panther was fired from his job as a parking attendant after an FBI agent spoke to his employer.[110] In *The Police and the Ghetto*, J. C. Cooper notes that "undercover police officers acting as informants were responsible for feeding the news media discoloring information about the Black Panther Party; with the result that to this day, most white and black Americans do not know the message that the Panthers were trying to deliver."[111] Moreover, when news reports told of Panthers being arrested for assaulting police officers or torturing and murdering suspected informants, a segment of the public understandably began to view the Panthers as little more than small-time thugs. The alleged torture and murder of a suspected informant months earlier by Panthers in Connecticut did little to make Baltimore residents less suspicious of Panthers in their city. But the public was often not aware of how government officials used negative media campaigns and criminal laws as a pretext to arrest Panthers and suppress organizational activities.

The consequence of these practices was that the branch lost support from some segments of the community—both Black and white. "The Black Panthers are nothing but a bunch of misfits, murderers and rapists," one white Baltimorean said. "The Panthers act too much like a Black Ku Klux Klan. I cannot support them," said one longtime African American veteran of the Civil Rights Movement.[112] To convince the public that the Panthers were the victims of malicious governmental repression, the branch was forced to devote a lot of time and energy to finding ways of garnering sympathy and support. The Panthers believed they had to expose the injustices and atrocities of the system by "educating" Black people.[113] Consequently, weekly meetings were held where Party members discussed Panther objectives with residents of the local community, like the one on March 20, 1970, where attorney Joseph Forer gave a talk titled "A Lawyer Looks at the New Repression." Speakers from the legal community undoubtedly gave the Panthers some credibility in the eyes of the public.

From what this author can ascertain, the extent to which the local police and other law enforcement agencies employed covert tactics against the Baltimore branch paled in comparison to what other Black Panther Party chapters and branches across the country experienced, but it was still disproportionate to the threat posed by the Baltimore Panthers. The national headquarters was the target of a smear campaign whereby government officials would send letters to merchants discouraging them from donating goods and services to the Panther's breakfast program. The FBI also sent anonymous letters to members in the Bay Area with the purpose of exacerbating existing problems or creating new ones. Communications secretary Kathleen Cleaver recalled that "we did not know who to believe about what ... it was a very bizarre feeling."[114] It is well known that the FBI fueled tensions between the Panthers and other Black organizations like the Black Stone Rangers in Chicago and Us in Los Angeles. In one memo, Hoover wrote: "The BPP and Us, two Black extremists groups, are currently feuding. . . . It is important that Black extremist groups be kept divided so that their strength is not increased through united action."[115] The police shot at Us and pretended the Panthers did it, then shot at the Panthers and pretended it was Us. Before the FBI launched its counterintelligence program, the Black Panther Party and Us had an amicable relationship and were allies on a number of projects. Dr. Maulana Karenga, leader of Us, recalls that "we used to do community patrols together."[116]

As far as this author can tell, the Baltimore branch was spared this kind of assault, although on November 25, 1968, J. Edgar Hoover sent a letter to an FBI field office in Baltimore stating the following:

> In order to fully capitalize upon BPP and Us differences as well as to exploit all avenues of creating further dissension in the ranks of the BPP, recipient offices are instructed to submit imaginative and hard-hitting counter intelligence measures aimed at crippling the BPP. Commencing December 2, 1968, and every two-week period thereafter, each office is instructed to submit a letter under this caption containing counter intelligence measures aimed against the BPP. The bi-weekly letter should also contain accomplishments obtained during the previous two-week under captioned Program.[117]

The letter to the Baltimore field office is interesting because it is not clear that the Us organization had a chapter in Baltimore. Nevertheless, almost all the covert activity that the Baltimore branch encountered was surveillance. This involved monitoring Panther activities, tracking the whereabouts of certain members, and staking out Panther headquarters. This may have put some Panthers on guard and made for some tense moments, but it did not disrupt the Panthers' everyday activities in any meaningful way.

Although the Baltimore branch may have experienced fewer incidents of repression than other branches, they may have proved to be more crippling given the size of the branch. The countless and frequent arrests of Party members served to intimidate potential members as well as current ones.[118] Unlike some other cities like Oakland, San Francisco, Detroit, and Cleveland, Baltimore was not the most radical of urban enclaves. Therefore, it is possible that the list of potential Panther recruits was never as long in Baltimore as it was in some other cities. Because of the government's abuse of power, the Baltimore branch was unable to devote the time and resources needed to build a long-lasting vehicle for social change.

Political Repression as Containment Policy

What the Baltimore Panthers were subjected to by local, state, and federal law enforcement jibes with what Fred D. Homer calls containment, which often means intrusion by the government to protect the majority from real or perceived violence and anarchy. Containment does not mean that all people of minority or out-groups will be repressed and harassed at all times. Supposedly, the government is intrusive only when minorities pose a threat (real or imagined) to the social peace of the majority. To a newly recruited Panther stopped for the first time, strip-searched and detained, government intrusion is an instrument of harassment. An activist's tenth trip to the police station and release without charges filed is an act of repression by the government. Thus, from the dissident's perspective, harassment becomes repression when such incidents become more frequent. Constant detention, threats, physical violence, and false accusations may all constitute tactics of repression used to reinforce containment. Whether performed on the innocent or guilty, on an individual for the first time or for the tenth time, the government practices selective random harassment by singling out members of certain minorities and out-groups for mistreatment to prevent contamination of the masses by a subversive antiestablishment minority.

Police Commissioner Pomerlau's words and actions represented the epitome of containment policy. Pomerlau saw himself as the savior of Baltimore, the embodiment of righteousness. In addition to Black militants, he also targeted antiwar activists, the ACLU, and journalists who were critical of police department procedure. Indeed, radio and television broadcasts were selectively screened for comments or criticisms of the commissioner or the department. Pomerlau viewed his office as a pulpit, and from it he denounced such evils as Black militancy, judicial laxity, communism, and lack of patriotism, such as in February 1971 when the commissioner lashed out against participants in a broad-based antiwar demonstration, denouncing them in a hastily called press conference as part of "a revolutionary movement which is communist-oriented." Pomerlau viewed the world through Manichean lenses: the good Americans (under his leadership) doing endless battle with evil and unpatriotic subversives like the Black Panthers.

In January 1975, in response to a stream of press disclosures of widespread surveillance practices and abuse of power by Pomerlau's unit, the Maryland

Senate Committee on Constitutional and Public Law conducted a series of preliminary public hearings to determine whether an investigation was warranted. On February 18, the scheduled date of Pomerlau's appearance before the committee, the panel received a letter announcing his refusal to appear on the grounds that "the Senate is being used as an instrument to disrupt the last bastion of order in Baltimore." Ironically, the letter further charged that the entire investigation was not only illegal but "immoral," amounting to "a daily rehashing of past activity solely based on the statements of those who would like to change *our* system of government other than by the lawful process of the law [my emphasis]."

Discussion and Conclusion

This chapter has discussed the history and inner workings of the Black Panther Party in Baltimore and how the government sought to render it ineffective. Along the way this study has helped to both undermine and give strength to a number of long-standing arguments surrounding the Black Panther Party in general.

First, as in other cities across the country, factors such as high Black unemployment, a poor school system, inferior health care, lack of effective Black representation, and a desire for Black empowerment helped give rise to the emergence of the Black Panther Party in Baltimore. Second, this study weakens the argument made by some that the Black Panther Party was a loosely run outfit that lacked a solid infrastructure.[119] The Black Panther Party was equipped with a firm infrastructure, starting with its Central Committee, and the organization of the Black Panther Party displayed many of the characteristics of the classic cadre party. Third, the support given to the Baltimore branch by segments of the community, both Black and white, further undermines the misguided perception that the Black Panther Party was an organization that did not enjoy even moderate support from either the Black or white community.[120] The various antirepression committees formed to assist and protect the Baltimore branch from police harassment and the donations of various kinds given to keep the branch afloat belie that notion. Some of the support the Panthers engendered seemed to have been based on the belief that the Panthers could not be bought off. Law professor Harold A. McDougall writes that "the Panthers were seen by many as the only black leaders who had not in some way been co-opted by Baltimore's white city fathers."[121] Fourth, the socioeconomic makeup of the Baltimore Panthers contradicts the notion that the Black Panther Party consisted mainly of thugs and criminals as opposed to high school, college-educated, and working-class individuals engaged in a legitimate search for solutions to the ills that plagued Black America in particular and America in general.

The major sources of political violence in America have arisen out of government attempts to suppress left-wing groups. There is little doubt that because of law enforcement's abuse of authority, the Black Panther Party was unable to devote the time, resources, and manpower needed to build a long-lasting political organization. Robert J. Goldstein submits that "the fact that the Panthers were black unquestionably added to the repression they faced." Perhaps the most lasting impact of state repression of the Black Panther Party was the effort of the FBI, in conjunction with state and local law enforcement, not only to disrupt the organization but to kill and imprison many of its key members. Between 1968 and 1971, forty Panthers were supposedly killed by local police around the country. Moreover, there are more Black Panthers in prison than there are from any other left-wing group. Michael Parenti argues that many activists remain in prison not for what they did but for the political beliefs they still hold.[122] Baltimore Panther Marshall Eddie Conway, who continues to maintain his innocence, remains in prison thirty-seven years after he was convicted of killing patrolman Donald Sager. When the author interviewed the son of the other officer shot that day, Stanley Sierakowski, he remarked, "Even if Conway is indeed guilty of murdering Officer Sager, it would seem that he has more than paid his debt to society."[123]

Although repression took its toll on the Black Panther Party, it was not the sole reason for the organization's demise. Other factors include the recruiting of individuals with criminal records and a history of violent behavior, attrition at both the leadership and rank-and-file level, infighting, and waning community support.[124] Individuals with criminal records were especially susceptible to government coercion. For instance, some individuals who happened to be on parole would be pressured by law enforcement to divulge inside information about Panther activities, and in turn law enforcement would agree not to sabotage their parole status. Admittedly, this issue was more problematic for the national office where a number (but certainly not all) of the members were ex-cons, former gang members, and petty criminals. Still other factors include depleted resources and inexperienced leadership.

Clearly, political repression played an instrumental role in undermining the activities of the Baltimore branch of the Black Panther Party. The harassment of the Baltimore branch reflected the irrational fear of those in positions of political and economic power that their way of life would end if Black rage resulted in the realization of Black advancement. In 1972 the organization's Central Committee in Oakland decided to close most of its branches around the country, including the Baltimore office. This decision was made in large part to marshal support for the political candidacies of Bobby Seale for mayor of Oakland and Elaine Brown for city council. Consequently, members of the closed branches were ordered to relocate to Oakland, where they were expected to assist in this effort. Some went to Oakland, but many did not, choosing instead to resign from the Party. Sherry Brown remembers going to Oakland hoping to convince the Central Committee to allow the Baltimore office to remain open. His pleas fell on deaf ears, as he was told in no uncertain terms to close down operations in Baltimore and report to duty in Oakland. Brown followed orders, and after all these years he still believes that the decision to consolidate the ranks had more of a crippling effect on the Party than did government repression.[125] Years later when Baltimore Panther Paul Coates was interviewed about his experiences as a Panther in Baltimore and the repression that he and his colleagues were subjected to, he offered a reflective response: "Pomerlau was a soldier, like me," he observed. "We were in a war. The people he represented felt threatened by me and people like me. He had the advantage because he had more men, who were better trained. We were young, didn't have a large arsenal, and didn't have a lot of combat experience. The outcome was predictable. In the Panthers, we understood that going in. And we did it anyway."[126]

Notes

I wrote an earlier work on the Baltimore Black Panthers that contained more errors than I care to admit, hence the reason for said title.

1. Harold A. McDougall, *Black Baltimore: A New Theory of Community* (Philadelphia: Temple University Press, 1993), 38.

2. McDougall, *Black Baltimore.*

3. Urban League, *The State of Black Baltimore* (Baltimore: Urban League, 1935).

4. David Milobsky, "Power from the Pulpit: Baltimore's African-American Clergy, 1950–1970," *Maryland Historical Magazine* 89 (Fall 1994): 275–289.

5. Andor Skotnes, "'Buy Where You Can Work': Boycotting for Jobs in African-American Baltimore, 1933–1934," *Journal of Social History* 27 (1994): 735–61.

6. George H. Callcott, *Maryland & America: 1940 to 1980 Baltimore* (Baltimore: The Johns Hopkins University Press, 1985), 149.

7. Robert M. Palumbos, "Student Involvement in the Baltimore Civil Rights Movement, 1953–63," *Maryland Historical Magazine* 94 (Winter 1999): 449–492.

8. W. E. Peterson and A. J. T. Zumbrun, *A Report of the Baltimore Civil Disturbance of April 1968* (Baltimore: The Maryland Crime Investigating Commission, 1968).

9. Susan H. Olson, *Baltimore: The Building of an American City* (Baltimore: The Johns Hopkins University Press, 1980).

10. Ibid.

11. *Baltimore Sun*, April 7, 1969.

12. *Baltimore Labor Herald*, April 19, 1968.

13. Callcott, *Maryland & America*, 163–64.

14. Stokely Carmichael was a member and one-time chairman of the Student Nonviolent Coordinating Committee. Later he joined the Black Panther Party for approximately six months.

15. Callcott, *Maryland & America*.

16. Sergeant Roger Nolan, telephone interview with Judson L. Jeffries, September 2005.

17. Health and Welfare Council of the Baltimore Area, *Survey of Action Area Residents* (Baltimore: Health and Welfare Council, 1965).

18. Nancy Gabler, "Who Are These Black Panthers and What Do They Really Want?" *Baltimore Magazine*, August 1970.

19. The Soul School promoted Black pride and a sense of consciousness. The Baltimore Defense Committee, founded in September 1968, was a small body of students, professors, and laypeople who worked on housing issues and pushed for police review boards, but mostly focused on antiwar movement activities.

20. Marshall Eddie Conway, telephone interview with Judson L. Jeffries, March 2006.

21. Henry Mitchell, interview with Judson L. Jeffries, May 2006.

22. Steve D. McCutchen, personal interviews, June 11, 1992, April 2006, May 2006.

23. John Robinson, "Black Panthers: Revolution and Social Change," *The News American*, September 6, 1970, 1.

24. Paul Coates, personal interview with Judson L. Jeffries, September 2007.

25. Nana Njinga (Conway) Nyamekye, telephone interview with Judson L. Jeffries, March 2006.

26. Connie Felder, telephone interview with Judson L. Jeffries, May 2006.

27. McCutchen, interview, April 2006.

28. Robinson, "Black Panthers," 1.

29. McCutchen, personal interview, April 2006; Steve D. McCutchen, "Selections from a Panther Diary . . .," in *Black Panther Party Reconsidered*, ed. Charles E. Jones, 115–31 (Baltimore, Black Classic Press, 1998).

30. Njinga Conway, telephone interview with Judson L. Jeffries, May 2006.

31. Coates, interview.

32. Robinson, "Black Panthers," 2.

33. Douglas Emory, personal interview, June 15, 1992; McCutchen, interview, 1992.

34. Robinson, "Black Panthers," 3.

35. Kenneth O'Reilly, *Racial Matters: The FBI's Secret File on Black America 1960–1972* (New York: Free Press, 1989).

36. U.S. House of Representatives. *Committee On Internal Security (1971) Gun Barrel Politics: The Black Panther Party*. Washington, D.C.: HR 92-470, 92nd Congress, 1st sess.

37. Al Amour, personal interview, July 6, 1993; Wayne Pharr, personal interview, June 20, 1993.

38. Sherry Brown, personal interview, March 2007.

39. Glenda Conway, personal interview, March 2005.

40. Chester Wickwire, personal interview, January 9, 1993.

41. Robinson, "Black Panthers."

42. Huey P. Newton, *To Die for the People* (New York: Random House, 1972).

43. John Pappenheimer, "Eggs Not Politics Served At Panther Breakfast," *Baltimore Sun*, 1970, C28.

44. Sherry Brown, personal interview, February 2007.

45. Wickwire, interview.

46. Nancy Gabler, "Who Are These Black Panthers and What Do They Really Want?" *Baltimore Magazine*, August 1970, 1–15.

47. Ibid.

48. Njinga Conway, interview, March 2006.

49. McCutchen, interview, May 2006.

50. Ibid.

51. Fred Pincus, telephone interview with Judson L. Jeffries, January 16, 2007.

52. Robinson, "Black Panthers."

53. Nelson Blackstock, *Cointelpro: The FBI's Secret War on Political Freedom* (New York: Vintage Books, 1975); Gary T. Marx, "Thoughts on a Neglected Category of Social Movement Participant: The Agent Provocateur and the Informant," *American Journal of Sociology* 80 (1974): 402–442.

54. Robert J. Goldstein, *Political Repression in Modern America: 1870 to the Present* (New York: Schenkman, 1978).

55. Glenda Conway, telephone interview, March 2006.

56. Wickwire, interview; Frank J. Donner, *Protectors of Privilege: Red Squads and Police Repression in Urban America* (Berkeley: University of California Press, 1990).

57. Dean Pappas, telephone interview with Judson L. Jeffries, January 22, 2007.

58. Robinson, "Black Panthers," 1.

59. Donner, *Protectors of Privilege*.

60. McDougall, *Black Baltimore*.

61. Warren Hart, "Free Huey Rally," *The Black Panther Intercommunal News*, May 25, 1969, 9.

62. Bruce M. Tyler, "Black Radicalism in Southern California, 1950–1982" (Ph.D. diss., University of California at Los Angeles, 1983), 321.

63. Wickwire, interview; "Professors Help to Form Anti-Repression Group," *Baltimore Committee for Political Freedom Newsletter*, January 30, 1970, 6.

64. "Pigs Run Amuck in Baltimore," *Black Panther Party Intercommunal News*, November 14, 1970, 1.

65. M. A. Tibbs, "Ex-activists recalls days of Black Panthers," *Virginian Pilot & Ledger Star*, n.d.

66. G. Fitzgerald, "Los Angeles Jails Panther Seized by Bail Bondsman," *The Baltimore Sun*, August 4, 1970, A1.

67. Sherry Brown, interview with Judson L. Jeffries, February 9, 2007.

68. Will Joyner, interviewed by Judson L. Jeffries, March 17, 2007.

69. P. H. Chutkown, "Panther's Power Restored As Citizens' Group Pays Bill," *The Baltimore Sun*, December 19, 1969, C8.

70. John Pappenheimer, "Power Cut Off from Home," *Baltimore Sun*, n.d.

71. Ibid.

72. D. A. Smith and C. A. Visher, "Situational Determinants of Police Arrest Decision," *Social Problems* 29 (1981): 167–177; Michael Lipsky, *Street-Level Bureaucracy* (California: Sage Press, 1980).

73. Michael Newton, *Bitter Grain* (Los Angeles: Holloway House, 1980).

74. Nancy Gabler, "Who Are These Black Panthers and What Do They Really Want?" *Baltimore Magazine*, August 1970, 1–15.

75. G. Fitzgerald, "Panthers Barred From Spreading Anti-Police Flyers," *The Baltimore Sun*, May 1, 1970, A1.

76. "U.S. Judge Alters Injunction Against Panther Literature," *The Baltimore Sun*, May 3, 1970, 17.

77. "Governor Denies Literature," *The Baltimore Sun*, May 15, 1970, A10.

78. Elizabeth Oliver, "CORE Leader Says Panthers No Threat," *Afro-American*, May 5, 1970, 2A.

79. Knowland, interview.

80. Donner, *Protectors of Privilege*. The *News American* was the second-largest circulating newspaper in Baltimore until it shut down in 1981.

81. Wickwire, interview.

82. McCutchen, interview, May 2006.

83. Doug McAdam and Kelly Moore, "The Politics of Insurgency, 1930–1975," in *Violence in America*, ed. Ted Gurr, 255–285 (Newbury Park, Calif.: Sage Press).

84. Coates, interview.

85. Edward J. Escobar, "The Dialectic of Repression: The Los Angeles Police Department and the Chicano Movement," *The Journal of American History* (Spring 1993): 1483–1514.

86. James K. Davis, *The FBI & The Sixties Anti-War Movement* (Westport, Conn.: Praeger, 1997).

87. Donner, *Protectors of Privilege*.

88. Marx, "Thoughts on a Neglected Category of Social Movement Participant," 402–442.

89. Newton, *Bitter Grain*.

90. "Purged Panthers," *Black Panther Party Intercommunal News*, January 4, 1969, 12; Bobby Seale, *Seize the Time* (New York: Random House, 1970), 370.

91. Gary T. Marx, *Racial Conflict* (Boston: Little Brown, 1971); David Hilliard, personal interview, March 10, 1993.

92. Nancy Gabler, "Who Are These Black Panthers and What Do They Really Want?" *Baltimore Magazine*, August 1970, 1–15.

93. "Police Assessment of Recent Baltimore Police Activities," *Baltimore Police Department Newsletter*, May 1970, 1–8; Charles E. Jones, "The Political Repression of the Black Panther Party 1966–1971: The Case of the Oakland Bay Area," *The Journal of Black Studies* 18 (1988): 415–434; "Police Claim Victim Sinned," *Afro-American*, May 5, 1970, 20.

94. "Pigs Railroad Panther Eddie Conway to Life in Prison," *Black Panther Intercommunal News*, February 6, 1971.

95. Michael Newton, *The FBI Plot: How the FBI Fought Against Civil Rights in America* (Los Angeles: Holloway House, 1981).

96. Ibid.

97. Frank J. Donner, *The Age of Surveillance: The Aims and Methods of America's Political Intelligence* (New York: Alfred A. Knopf, 1980).

98. Newton, *The FBI Plot*.

99. Isaac Balbus, *The Dialectic of Legal Repression* (New York: Russell Sage, 1973).

100. John L. Sullivan, J. Piereson, and Greg E. Markus, *Political Tolerance and American Democracy* (Chicago: University of Chicago Press, 1982).

101. Balbus, *The Dialectic of Legal Repression*.

102. "The Community Talks About the Panthers Arrests," *Afro-American*, May 5, 1970, 27.

103. Robinson, "Black Panthers."

104. Nancy Henley, telephone interview with Judson L. Jeffries, June 12, 2006.

105. Alan Wolfe, *The Seamy Side of Democracy: Repression in America* (New York, David McKay, 1973); Michael Stohl, *War and Domestic Violence: The American Capacity for Repression and Reaction* (Beverly Hills, Calif.: Sage, 1976); Goldstein, *Political Repression in Modern America*; James L. Gibson, "Political Intolerance and Political Repression During the McCarthy RED Scare," *American Political Science Review* 82 (1988): 512–529.

106. Philip S. Foner, *The Black Panthers Speak* (Philadelphia: Lippincott, 1970).

107. Robinson, "Black Panthers," 1.

108. Anthony Oberschall, "The Decline of the 1960s Social Movements," in *Social Movement, Conflict, and Change*, ed. Louis Kriesberg, 277–278 (Greenwich, Conn.: Jai Press, 1978); Wolfe, *The Seamy Side of Democracy*.

109. J. M. Cammett, *Antonio Gramsci and the Origins of Italian Communism* (Stanford, Calif.: Stanford University Press, 1967); G. Fiori, *Antonio Gramsci: Life of a Revolutionary* (London: New Left Books, 1970).

110. Stephen J. Lynton, "Black Panthers Step Up Activity," *Baltimore Sun*, n.d.

111. John C. Cooper, *The Police and the Ghetto* (Port Washington, N.Y.: National University Publications, 1980).

112. Robinson, "Black Panthers"; Elizabeth Oliver, "Mrs. Mitchell Does not Condone Hate Literature," *Afro-American*, May 5, 1970, 1A.

113. Robinson, "Black Panthers."

114. Emory Douglas, personal interview; James K. Davis, *Spying on America: The FBI's Domestic Counterintelligence Program* (New York: Praeger, 1992).

115. Federal Bureau of Investigation, *Director to Special Agent in Charge, San Diego, December 27, 1968, "Black Nationalist Hate Groups File,"* 100448006, section 6.

116. O'Reilly, *Racial Matters*; Us is a radical Black cultural nationalist organization founded by Dr. Maulana Karenga in 1965 in Los Angeles, California. Contrary to popular belief, Us does not stand for United Slaves.

117. O'Reilly, *Racial Matters*.

118. Robert S. Collier, personal interview, November 15, 1992.

119. D. Healey and Maurice Isserman, *Dorothy Healey Remembers: A Life in the American Communist Party* (New York: Oxford University Press, 1990).

120. Ronald Walters and Robert C. Smith, *African American Leadership* (New York: State University of New York Press, 1999).

121. McDougall, *Black Baltimore*, 74.

122. Stohl, *War and Domestic Political Violence*; Goldstein, *Political Repression in Modern America*, 524; Michael Parenti, *Democracy for the Few* (New York: St. Martin's Press, 1995).

123. Stanley Sierakowski, telephone interview with Judson L. Jeffries, July 2005.

124. D. Moore, "Strategies of Repression Against the Black Movement," *The Black Scholar* (Spring 1981): 10–16; Chris Booker, "Lumpenization: A Critical Error of the Black Panther Party," in Jones, *The Black Panther Party Reconsidered*, 337–362; Ollie Johnson, "Explaining the Demise of the Black Panther Party: The Role of Internal Factors," in Jones, *The Black Panther Party Reconsidered*, 391–416.

125. Sherry Brown, personal interview, February 2007.

126. McDougall, *Black Baltimore*, 75.

2

Picking Up Where Robert F. Williams Left Off: The Winston-Salem Branch of the Black Panther Party

Benjamin R. Friedman

Precursors: Greensboro and Charlotte

The history of white resistance to Black advancement in North Carolina made the state ripe for a Black Panther unit in the late 1960s. The Ku Klux Klan was active in Tar Heel country, and strict segregation mores were firmly entrenched in the state's culture. When Blacks initially began to act in North Carolina, their targets were almost always specific stores or restaurants. While Dr. Martin Luther King Jr. had attacked specific businesses in Birmingham and Selma, the goal of his struggle was to attain equal rights for Blacks throughout the South. Undoubtedly, North Carolinians also desired Black liberation, but their protests were often spontaneous, whereas King-led demonstrations had always been planned. King's goal was to gain the attention of white northerners through the use of the media and mass action. The goal of Black North Carolinians was constant local progress.

The Civil Rights Movement in North Carolina began (according to many scholars) in Greensboro on February 1, 1960, when four North Carolina

A&T students sat down at the local Woolworth's whites-only lunch counter and asked for service. Within two months the sit-in protest had spread
to fifty-four cities in nine states. Later that year in Raleigh, students from
across the region created the Student Nonviolent Coordinating Committee
(SNCC), which secured varying levels of desegregation in one hundred cities
by the end of 1960.

Greensboro had always been considered a "progressive city." It had been
one of the first southern cities to announce plans to comply with the *Brown v.
Board of Education* decision in 1954. But in reality Greensboro failed to live
up to its progressive image, and, along with the rest of the state, had by 1967
instituted policies to circumvent the *Brown* decision. With the election of
Luther Hodges as governor in 1955, North Carolinians had opted for resistance to desegregation. Hodges, although widely considered a moderate at
the time, ferociously attacked the National Association for the Advancement
of Colored People (NAACP) and instituted the Pearsall Plan, which would
close public schools if integration was mandated by the federal government.[1]
By 1960 tensions in the state were at an all-time high. Greensboro, with its
rich Black educational tradition (it had perhaps one of the best all-Black high
schools in the country and several acclaimed Black colleges), became a focal
point for protest.

The sit-in protests revolved around the legality of segregation in privately
owned public accommodations (restaurants, hotels, stores, etc.). The next governor of North Carolina, Terry Sanford, was widely regarded as more moderate than Governor Hodges, but like Hodges, Sanford viewed the protest
movement and its aims with disdain. A report initiated by Sanford in 1964
stated, "It is impossible for the Negro to do his full part to control delinquency
and crime while obsessed with a sense of unjust treatment."[2] The report, titled
North Carolina and the Negro, documented the progress on desegregation city
by city and showed that most cities had become less segregated, but that nearly
all these cases were the result of Black protest. Clearly, Sanford's conclusion
that protest and civil disobedience were not necessary for Blacks to gain equal
access was dubious. On the contrary, an outsider might deduce that if Blacks
would engage in further protest they would make further gains.

By the mid-1960s, North Carolina A&T College (later University) in
Greensboro became the focal point of the radicalization of the Civil Rights
Movement in the state. Massive demonstrations became nightly occurrences
in the summer of 1963, as A&T and high school students became frustrated
with the slow pace of reform. Between May 11 and June 7, 1964, more than
two thousand Black youths marched in the evenings through downtown
Greensboro. The marches had a new militancy that had been conspicuously
absent before, and many were arrested; at one point there were nearly 1,400

protesters in jail.[3] It was during these marches that a young A&T football player and student government president named Jesse L. Jackson emerged and became the leader of the Greensboro movement.

Although the protests in Greensboro were always well attended, there was a lack of adult participation, which was problematic for two reasons. First, it gave the protest an air of illegitimacy. Because the leaders were students, regardless of where they came from (most were native North Carolinians), they were dismissed as "outside agitators" by the media and the local government. The second problem was the lack of assistance and support from institutions such as the church or the YMCA that would make their struggle more effective. By the end of May 1964, adults had seen their children suffer enough abuse and were forced to act because of police neglect and violence. The stories recounted by Black youths who had been imprisoned were appalling: the students reported that they were provided little food and water and had been housed in substandard buildings with little or no plumbing. Parents were also moved to act by James Farmer of the Congress of Racial Equality (CORE), who spoke to Black audiences in Greensboro over a four-day period from May 19 to 22, 1964. On May 22, parents acted en masse. Nearly two thousand Black adults, including every Black principal, most of the city's Black teachers, and nearly all the Black ministers, marched silently through downtown Greensboro in a demonstration of support for the protesting youths. The impact was overwhelming, but the results can only be described as mixed. While most of Greensboro's businesses desegregated within a year of the 1964 protests, Greensboro remained a segregated city full of racial animosity. The protests had changed Greensboro's business practices, but not its racial attitudes, and the bitterness that lingered among whites in Greensboro resulted in a sharp increase in Ku Klux Klan membership.[4]

The KKK had a long history of intimidating Blacks in North Carolina. Cross burnings, acts of vandalism, and lynchings were not uncommon in the Tar Heel state. But not all the Klan's terrorist acts went unanswered. In the mid-1950s Robert F. Williams, a former U.S. Marine and the head of the Monroe chapter of the NAACP, became fed up with the violence against him and other Blacks and began speaking out publicly about Klan activities as well as urging Blacks to stand up for themselves. In 1957, after Williams led a demonstration to desegregate the local public swimming pool, the KKK began threatening him and other Black protesters. Since the KKK had hundreds of members and perhaps even more supporters in the city, Williams took the threats seriously and responded by arming himself and training other local NAACP members in self-defense. The small group of armed NAACP members began acquiring military equipment (helmets, gas masks, sandbags, etc.), joined the National Rifle Association (NRA), and began drilling.

The KKK, confronted with the real possibility of a Black militia, curtailed its "nightly motorcades" through the Black part of town and sought to avoid confrontations with Blacks.[5]

Williams's act of defiance was a bold statement for 1957, and it raised many of the issues that the Black Panthers would later bring up. In 1959 Williams made a statement in reference to a case in which a pregnant Black woman was savagely raped. The statement could easily be mistaken for a comment by a Black Panther ten years later. Williams stated:

> We cannot take these people who do us injustice to the court. . . . In the future we are going to have to try and convict them on the spot. We cannot rely on the law. We can get no justice under the present system. If we feel that injustice is done, we must right then and there, on the spot, be prepared to inflict punishment on these people. Since the federal government will not bring a halt to the lynching in the South, and since the so-called courts lynch our people legally, if it's necessary to stop the lynching with lynching, then we must resort to that method. We must meet violence with violence.[6]

Williams's rhetoric was not well received by many people, Black or white. Dr. King denounced Williams, and Williams was subsequently suspended by the national office as head of the Monroe chapter of the NAACP. Williams would later flee the United States in 1961 for Cuba after being indicted on trumped-up kidnapping charges,[7] but his act of picking up the gun made a difference in the day-to-day lives of Black people in Monroe County. He had upped the ante on the KKK and other racists in the city so high that the Klan was willing to curb its provocative activities. This lesson was surely not lost on the next generation of radicals in the state.

By 1968 Blacks at North Carolina A&T, perhaps the most radical Black campus in the state during the 1960s, saw that their civil rights predecessors had not substantially altered the reality of Black life in North Carolina or the country. In February 1968, three students were killed at a protest in Orangeburg, South Carolina, and in April, Martin Luther King Jr. was assassinated. Shocked by these events, a small group of A&T students began organizing around a "Black Power" agenda.

For all intents and purposes, King's murder signaled the end of direct nonviolent action in North Carolina. On the evening of King's assassination Greensboro turned into a war zone. Widespread violence rocked downtown Greensboro, as Blacks took their frustrations to the streets. On the A&T campus students threw rocks and bottles at police officers, and the violence escalated as a sniper began shooting at passing police cars.[8] A curfew was declared and the National Guard was called out. The violence subsided quickly, but simmering tensions remained.

It was about this time that groups of Blacks began to seek affiliation with the Black Panther Party. Blacks radicalized in the Greensboro protests and revolts were the first to seek affiliation, but these individuals were never officially sanctioned by the national Panther organization. Led by A&T student Eric Brown, they were mostly college students or overachieving high school students who were already deeply involved with local issues and had developed their own leaders and causes. The local police and the FBI resorted to labeling these individuals Panthers because of Brown's supposed connection to the Party and because their rhetoric and actions mimicked the Oakland-based group. The FBI and local police used this label as a tool in suppressing the group, much as they had used the communist label to attack activists in the past.

Eric Brown claimed to have been associated with the Panthers in his home state of New York during Christmas break in 1968. There he met Harold Avant,[9] who according to the FBI was a full-fledged Panther either with the New York or New Jersey chapter,[10] and he convinced Avant to accompany him back to A&T in early 1969. With Avant's assistance, Brown and a small group of individuals began organizing. While the FBI portrayed Avant as the "outside agitator" responsible for the turmoil in Greensboro during 1969, the trouble had begun on campus before Avant arrived. On December 9, 1968, an already radicalized A&T student body gathered to listen to the impassioned Stokely Carmichael, who spoke to the crowd of more than four thousand about radicalizing the struggle for freedom. According to William Chafe:

> Carmichael exhorted Blacks not only to be willing to die for freedom but to be willing to kill for it as well. Asked who he had voted for in the recent election, Carmichael replied "I didn't vote, I stayed home and cleaned my guns."[11]

Later that evening Calvin C. Matthews, A&T Student Government Association president, called for a boycott of classes on December 11th.[12]

The next day an incident involving a small skirmish occurred in one of the campus dining halls. As with so many events involving Panthers, suspected Panthers, and the police, there are two distinctly different versions of what happened. The Black Panther Party, in a document titled "Fact Sheet on the Case of Brother Eric Brown," claimed that Brown had only been a witness, not a participant in the disturbance. The A&T administration and the FBI saw things differently. The administration claimed that Brown had instigated the whole incident, and shortly before the Christmas break, he was suspended for his role in the incident.[13]

Once school resumed, events began to move quickly. On February 5, 1969, A&T students, led by Nelson Johnson, head of the Greensboro Association of Poor People (GAPP), occupied the administration building on the A&T

campus. The students' demands ranged from the ridiculous to the impractical, from the elimination of pop quizzes to the dismissal of certain professors. The event symbolized a turning point in the A&T movement. The students were now significantly organized to close the college, and their demands would only get more outlandish.

As students became more rambunctious, local authorities braced themselves for a confrontation. While jail conditions during the 1964 protest had led Blacks to question the local police, the Greensboro police had shown restraint in their handling of protesters. City officials did not want to have their city associated with the violent repression of Birmingham or Selma. This restraint had worn thin by 1969. The image of the new "revolutionary" protester gave authorities—not just in North Carolina but across the country—a pretext to go after protesters, calling them communists and insurrectionists. Police in Greensboro were no different. GAPP had its first standoff with police during a Malcolm X memorial service in late February, during which the police harassed the protesters and fired tear gas.[14] While only a minor incident, the standoff increased tension between A&T students and the police.

A few weeks later these tensions were tested. On March 13, 1969, A&T campus cafeteria workers walked off their jobs to protest unfair labor practices. The strikers, mostly Black, were upset because they worked for below minimum wages and received no compensation for overtime. Nelson Johnson organized the A&T students to respect the picket line and boycott the cafeterias, and, energized by their success, twenty-five hundred students marched on the residence of the school's president to further display support for the strikers. The scene turned ugly as the students were attacked by the police. Stone throwing and gunfire erupted as police sought to disperse the crowd, resulting in the wounding of one protester.[15]

Some of the protesters, including Eric Brown, took out their frustrations on Sid's Curb Market, a store that had refused to assist students during their protest. According to a leaflet from the "Ministry of Information—Greensboro Chapter—Black Panther Party" obtained by the FBI:

> Stemming from the March 13 incident when the people dealt with an enemy of the community (Sid's Curb Market), in a revolutionary manner, the pig power structure has tried to exterminate the leadership of the Greensboro Chapter of the Black Panther Party. Eric Brown is a victim of this attempt to stop the movement for allegedly stealing three cartons of cigarettes. We would like to inform the masses that a bootlicking Uncle Tom, pork chop lackey of the power structure by the name of Charles Atchison (1130 Scott Hall, MT State University Campus) testified against Eric Brown.[16]

Brown was later arrested and convicted on a larceny charge stemming from the incident, but Avant, who according to FBI files was the most dangerous individual involved with the protests, managed to avoid trouble with the police.

The FBI identified everyone involved in the local Black militant movement as a Black Panther because of chains of association leading back through Brown to Avant. Because of this FBI misconception, nearly every protest, rally, or meeting by Blacks in Greensboro after 1968 came under heavy surveillance. It is apparent from files obtained from the Department of Justice that the FBI kept close tabs on the whereabouts of Brown, Johnson, and Avant, and any information obtained by the FBI was embellished and forwarded to the local Greensboro police. This forwarding of information, and the FBI's conception of the breadth of Panther activity in the city, increased the already high tensions between the police and the students.

Tempers again flared into violence in early May 1968. The disruption initially broke out at all-Black Dudley High School, where Claude Barnes, a junior at the school, was barred from running for student government president by the school's administration. Barnes was an honor roll student and highly regarded in the community, but he was also a member of GAPP, which the school's administration, like much of the city, considered to be a Black Panther front organization. Barnes's support in the school was so strong that he received more than six hundred write-in votes in the SGA election on May 2, enough to win the election. Barnes, along with several hundred students, walked out of school in protest of the decision on May 9. Violence erupted two weeks later on May 21, as more than seven hundred student protesters began tossing bottles and rocks at the school building and police. Officers used tear gas and billy clubs to restore order.[17] Students at A&T saw the struggle at Dudley High School as their struggle as well, and not long after the police were able to disperse the students at Dudley, students at A&T began to act.

Rioting began as the sun set at A&T that night. White motorists were attacked as the students lashed out in rage. The police were unable to handle the escalating situation, so at 10 P.M. a state of emergency was declared, and National Guard troops were mobilized to clear the campus. Shooting broke out soon after this declaration, and one student, Willie Graves, was killed. The next day the campus was closed while National Guard and police swept through the campus looking to weed out snipers and confiscate weapons. Finding an already empty campus, the National Guard and police proceeded to shoot holes in the walls and doors in frustration.[18] Shortly after the event, Brown was convicted of the Sid's Curb Market incident, Nelson Johnson was convicted of misdemeanors relating to the Dudley incident, and Harold Avant, according to FBI reports, disappeared. Soon after, radicalism dwindled in Greensboro.

The incidents of 1968 and 1969 in Greensboro exemplify the problems of North Carolina, which even Greensboro, with its tradition of excellent Black education, was unable to change. Greensboro, the first city to announce school desegregation plans in 1954, was ironically one of the last to integrate. It was not until 1972, and then only under court order, that Greensboro desegregated its public schools.[19] Black civil rights workers and radicals learned from the Greensboro events that North Carolina would not radically change without being forced. Blacks in Greensboro had raised the stakes in the protest movement, but they were still unable to secure real change. It seemed that interference in the day-to-day lives of whites, whether through sit-ins, boycotts, or violence, was the only technique that worked.

Blacks throughout North Carolina were captivated by the events in Greensboro. Some of those who began organizing in other cities in the state had witnessed the events firsthand. Larry Little of Winston-Salem credited A&T students with piquing his interest in the Black Panther Party,[20] and Ben Chavis of Charlotte had actually participated in some of the Greensboro meetings and rallies. These two cities, Charlotte and Winston-Salem, would become the two major centers of Black Panther–related activity in the state.

Radical activity in Charlotte took off and burned out quickly. In late 1968, Ben Chavis and Jerome Johnson of Charlotte set up the Afro-American Unity Organization (AAUO), which was organized along the lines of the Black Panther Party and hoped to become the North Carolina branch of the BPP. In December 1968 Chavis contacted the national headquarters of the Black Panther Party and asked what was required to become a branch. Chavis was informed that a sum of $300 would have to be forwarded to the national office so a representative could come out and "indoctrinate the new members."[21] The Charlotte group immediately began organizing to raise this money.

The FBI began watching the Charlotte group almost from the day it organized and again created a Panther hysteria in Charlotte. On May 19, 1969, the planning of a small protest rally by the group became a top priority. The FBI sent information regarding the planned rally to local and state police, the Secret Service, military intelligence, the attorney general, and the president. Even the FBI field offices were overcome by what one author referred to as "Panthermania."[22]

Despite these efforts, the Charlotte group continued organizing in hopes of obtaining a charter. The group was able to raise the necessary money, but by that time the Black Panther Party was undergoing a purge and had instituted a moratorium on membership. The group continued its activities and began collecting weapons and making public appearances claiming to be Panthers. Members began selling *The Black Panther* newspaper and holding organizational rallies in and around the campus of the University of North

Carolina. On March 4, 1969, Chavis led a rally on campus at which the American and North Carolina flags were removed from a centrally located flagpole on campus and replaced by a black flag.[23]

A few weeks later Johnson and Chavis were arrested for the first time for their involvement in radical protest. Chavis and Johnson led a rally at all-Black Second Ward Senior High School protesting the unequal distribution of the city's school construction money, an issue that had been a source of anguish for Blacks across the United States, especially in the South. Chavis and Johnson were arrested and charged with several misdemeanors, including trespassing and disrupting classes.[24]

In May of 1969 the would-be Panthers of Charlotte sought to strike back against law enforcement agents. The FBI had been closely monitoring the group's activities, and on May 27, 1969, this surveillance led to a raid on the AAUO's office. The raid, which occurred in the early evening, was carried out to search for illegal weapons on the premises. According to the FBI, the raid was conducted by the Bureau of Alcohol, Tobacco, and Firearms (ATF), the Internal Revenue Service (IRS), and local police officers, not the FBI.[25] During the course of the raid, two AAUO members, Michael Laney and Crant Covington, were arrested for firearms violations.

The AAUO saw the May 27 incident differently. The AAUO accused FBI Special Agent Dean Paarman of organizing and participating in the raid. Assisted by American Civil Liberties Union (ACLU) lawyer George Daly, the group filed a complaint, calling the raid an illegal search. Daly also filed restraining orders against specific and unknown FBI, ATF, IRS, and local police officers on behalf of the AAUO. Paarman claimed that he was not at the raid and had only interviewed the two arrested AAUO members after the fact. In addition, the local police and FBI claimed that the raid was legal because the police were serving a warrant against an individual believed to be in the house for involvement in an armed robbery. Paarman was served with a summons relating to the legal action on June 6, 1969, and Chavis, Jerome Johnson, and the remaining members of the group were named as plaintiffs in the civil case. J. Edgar Hoover's office became personally involved in the matter in June 1969,[26] when Hoover's office sent an official memo to the assistant attorney general denying that Paarman had been involved in the raid or in conducting surveillance on the members of the group. However, the FBI files show that surveillance had been conducted by the FBI on the AAUO since late 1968, but the names of the agents involved in this surveillance were withheld. The civil case lingered in court for some time, but was eventually dismissed in late 1970.

The Charlotte group may have been overly concerned with the FBI surveillance and not concerned enough about their own actions. The AAUO eventually found itself in deep trouble with both the law and the Black Panther Party leadership in Oakland. On August 3, 1969, nine AAUO members were arrested and charged with "[g]oing armed to the terror of the people" after a shooting incident involving four white teenagers. AAUO members were accused of chasing and shooting at some youths who had apparently yelled a racial slur at the AAUO members.[27] While the exact events of the shooting are somewhat murky, it is clear that the AAUO overreacted. A group that desired affiliation with the Black Panther Party should have exercised more discretion in its handling of the situation.

The AAUO's next violent confrontation came two weeks later when the group got involved in a personal conflict with the owners of a drive-in restaurant in Charlotte. Otis Blackmon and his son Otis James Blackmon, both Black, caught two AAUO members, James Black and James Prather, prowling around their delivery truck at three o'clock in the morning on August 16, 1969. When Otis James asked the two to leave, an argument and scuffle ensued, and Prather was stabbed. A few hours later Prather and Black returned with about five other AAUO members, all of whom were dressed in the Panther uniform and some armed with shotguns. The Blackmons were also armed; Otis James still had the knife he had used earlier and the elder Blackmon had gotten his shotgun. The elder Blackmon shot Black in the hand, and Otis James was shot in the arm. Veronica Hagens, an AAUO member, was stabbed by Otis James as she tried to enter the restaurant, and a bystander was grazed by an errant bullet. Black was arrested and charged with "[a]ssault with a deadly weapon with intent to kill."[28]

The Black Panther Party's central command in Oakland, concerned about being blamed for the actions of the Charlotte group, publicly chastised the Charlotte outfit and disavowed itself from the group's actions. On September 13 the Black Panther Party's newspaper, *The Black Panther*, denounced the Charlotte group in an article titled "Panthers, Pigs, and Fools." The article stated that the Charlotte group was not connected to the national group, and it warned the AAUO to stop calling themselves Panthers. Five days later Chicago Black Panther Party field secretary Robert "Bobby" Lee spoke at Counter-Orientation Week at the University of North Carolina–Charlotte. During his speech Lee publicly attacked the Charlotte group, stating:

> There is no Panther charter in North Carolina or South Carolina. . . . And in August 16, 1969, a shootout at Chick-N-Ribs restaurant (was) unnecessary, and see this will cause Panthers to be killed nationwide. They're not Panthers, period.[29]

The group got the message and disbanded within days of this rebuke by the national Party. The Charlotte group had moved too quickly and without direction, something the national Black Panther Party would not tolerate. Larry Little said of Ben Chavis and the Charlotte group:

> Early on he [Ben Chavis] was trying to get some stuff started in Charlotte. And the way they went about it, the Party did not care for that, it looked like it wasn't quite organized the way the national organization wanted it. . . . And so he sort [of] got off on the wrong foot. They [were] trying to do the best they could.[30]

Ironically, the Charlotte group exemplified the internal problems of the national organization at that time. The Party grew too fast, and the central leadership had difficulty managing the direction of individual branches. The purge of 1968 and 1969 was designed, among other things, to slow this growth so that the organization could more easily manage its activities.

The rising tensions in Greensboro and Charlotte demonstrated the growing anxiety among Blacks in North Carolina. There was a sense of frustration among those who participated in the disorders, rallies, and protests. Life for Blacks in North Carolina had only superficially changed. Blacks could eat at lunch counters and in restaurants, but they were still relegated to second-class citizenship. Police and FBI activities also led to widespread frustration. Local police forces could be more brutal in their tactics against protesters because the new protesters were not nonviolent middle-class adults. The new protester claimed to be more radical than reformist, and in Winston-Salem, young activists calling themselves militants were in no short supply. This changing mind-set did not occur overnight, but had its origins in the layoffs, walkouts, and pickets of the tobacco companies in the 1940s.

Black labor–white management issues were not atypical in Winston-Salem during the 1940s. Until 1947 Blacks had for the most part kept their gripes to themselves. That spring, negotiations between R. J. Reynolds and Local 22 were under way for a new contract to start on May 1, 1947. The union asked for a wage increase of twenty-four cents an hour; the powers at Reynolds suggested an hourly increase of five and a half cents. The union responded with a counteroffer of fifteen cents across the board, a ten-cent night hourly wage differential instead of five, changes in labor grades, adequate health and group insurance paid by the company, union security via a checkoff system, release of liability for breached contracts and wildcat strikes, and overtime for all work over forty hours for leaf house workers and seasonal employees.

Seasonal workers were not included under the federal laws, which regulated the hourly workweek. Seasonal employment was from August to December for the handling and storing of tobacco in warehouses or for summer work involving canning vegetables and fruits for the company cafeterias.

At Reynolds, there were 10,308 regular employees and 1,056 seasonal workers. Of the regular employees, 4,999 were white while 5,309 were Black. Of
the seasonal workers, 29 were white and 1,027 were Black.[31]

Winston-Salem and Its Potential for
Black Radicalism

On April 27, 1947, thousand of Blacks decided they would no longer sub-
scribe to the notion that Blacks should just go along in order to get along. On
that day thousands of Blacks converged on the grounds of Woodland Avenue
School and voted to strike at midnight April 30th if Reynolds did not accept
union proposals. Until that time Blacks had been virtually invisible to whites.
Blacks had helped build the city, but most of them were prohibited from
voting, and as a result, Blacks had virtually no representation. Without the
use of the vote, many Blacks felt powerless. Glenn Jones would change that
mind-set forever. Like nearly everyone else at Woodland that day, Jones was a
member of Local 22 of the Tobacco Workers International Union. Organized
in 1944, the union had been haggling with the company over a new contract
for more than two months. It was high time that the company was put on
notice, Jones told the crowd. The time to strike had come. The motion was
seconded and applause erupted.

On May 1 the strike started, and it lasted a little more than a month. Few
can deny that the strike unified Winston-Salem's Black community, perhaps for the first time in recent memory. Those in power were surprised that
Blacks could be so organized. Rallies were held on Sundays at Shiloh Baptist
Church, where the Reverend Robert Pitts, considered the most electrifying
pulpit orator in the city, inspired the audience. Over the next few years, Black
voter registration increased from three hundred to three thousand due to vig-
orous voter registration drives initiated by Local 22.[32] By 1950, allegations
that communists had infiltrated the union's leadership had been published in
the city's newspaper. That there was no evidence of this was beside the point.
These charges rang out at a time when Senator Joseph McCarthy's red scare
tactics had reached a fever pitch. Any charge of communist influence was
enough to bring unwarranted and intense harassment by local police departments as well as state and federal law enforcement agencies.

Over the next three years, the union, hounded by federal investigations and
eventually discredited, lost its power and was decertified in 1951. Nonetheless
the union served its purpose. Because of its aggressive voter education and
registration efforts, Reverend Kenneth R. Williams was elected alderman the
year of the strike, making him the city's first Black elected official in the twentieth century. Soon afterward Blacks were elected to the school board and

were appointed to various other positions. This Black politicization resulted in the integration of public schools and the dismantling of Jim Crow.

While life for Blacks in Winston-Salem was no crystal stair, Blacks there fared far better than did Blacks in many other southern cities. The R. J. Reynolds Tobacco Company was not a champion of Black causes, but it did provide steady employment to thousands of Black residents, which provided them a relatively decent standard of living and a good Black public school system. The city also had a few semiprogressive politicians who were not afraid to adopt Black causes. The tone was set by Mayor Marshall Kurfees, who made several Black appointments and encouraged slum clearance to make way for affordable housing for low-income residents.

By the end of the 1940s attitudes appeared to be changing, which may explain why there were some tense moments but no violence when young Gwendolyn Y. Bailey integrated Reynolds High School in 1957, becoming the first Black in a white public school in Winston-Salem. Integration of schools continued slowly though the 1960s, and by 1969, forty-five of the sixty-six schools in the city had integrated to some degree. By 1960 Winston-Salem was in some ways very different from the city that had emerged from World War II. First, it was larger, with a population of more than 100,000. Second, it was also younger, thanks to the baby boom that dropped the median age to under twenty-eight years of age. Third, North Carolinians had always made up more than 90 percent of Winston-Salem's population, but their percentage fell nearly ten points by 1960.[33] For the first time since the city's early days, outsiders were moving to town. Fourth, whites would see Blacks exert themselves in a way they had not witnessed before. Only a week after the famous Woolworth sit-ins in nearby Greensboro, demonstrators filled Winston-Salem's segregated lunch counters, and the voices of Black protest reverberated through the city's streets.

As the decade grew old, racial violence would flare up in Winston-Salem on three separate occasions. However, the only one that could be considered a noteworthy disorder occurred between November 2 and November 5, 1967. On Sunday morning, October 15, thirty-two-year-old James Eller was approached by two white police officers who believed he was drunk. Mace was used to subdue him and place him in the police car. Once at the station, Eller was struck about the head by Patrolman W. E. Owens with a blackjack and lost his speech, forcing him to use sign language to communicate. After Eller was released, his wife took him to the Baptist Hospital and to Forsyth Memorial Hospital, a predominantly Black facility, where it was discovered, after a lumbar puncture, that he had sustained a fractured skull. Eller underwent surgery on October 20th but died on October 28th. The coroner's office reported that Eller had died of brain damage and a fractured skull.

On the day of Eller's death, Patrolman Owens was arrested on a murder warrant signed by Eller's mother. He went before the municipal court on Monday, October 30th, and the charge was dismissed. The situation grew tense as Black leaders protested that too much was unknown for the court to have made such a swift decision. Within minutes after Eller was interred, violence erupted and buildings were set ablaze and looted. The insurgents set approximately a hundred fires and did roughly $750,000 in damage. The diplomacy of Mayor M. C. "Red" Benton and the force of a thousand National Guardsmen eventually restored order.

Eller's death, coupled with the developments of the preceding years, albeit in different ways, helped foment a climate that would give rise to what one writer calls "a burst of nationalist-tinged radicalism."

Brace Yourself Winston-Salem: The Panthers Are Coming

"It's [the center of Black Panther activity] gonna be the South."[34] Many Blacks in North Carolina were convinced of the validity of this statement. They were younger than the protesters of the previous generation, and much more determined and committed. Many of them were typical "Panther material." Some were college students, and many had grown up in the mostly Black, government-sponsored housing projects. They knew exactly how racism and police brutality had affected the lives of Blacks with whom they had grown up, and they had seen the frustration of the A&T and Dudley High students explode into violent outbursts. Larry Little, among others in the group, had become politically aware during the A&T uprising. In 1968 a group of Black youths began to meet and talk seriously about the goings-on in the local community and what needed be done to meet Black people's needs. Led by Nelson Malloy and Robert Greer, they called themselves the Organization of Black Liberation, hoping to eventually become affiliated with the Black Panther Party.

The actions of the hopeful members were more deliberate and restrained than those of their Charlotte and Greensboro counterparts. They did not get involved in counterproductive activities such as shootouts that created bad press for the national organization. It took a year of meticulous work before a National Committee to Combat Fascism (NCCF) charter was granted to the group. The Winston-Salem contingent's success in gaining an official charter led to intense police and FBI scrutiny during its early existence, which largely prevented the type of community service that had endeared the Black Panthers to so many Blacks in cities across America. Donations and money raised through the sale of *The Black Panther* newspaper, instead of being used for community service, had to be used for bail and legal fees. Little said of the community service programs: "We wanted to do it earlier, but hell we were standing in court all the time."[35]

Although the Winston-Salem group began organizing in late 1968, it was not officially sanctioned by the national office as a full-fledged BPP branch until April 1971. Still, the group, with its roughly twenty members and more than fifty regular volunteers, was under surveillance by the FBI. The outfit's original membership included Robert Greer, head of the organization, William Rice, Julius Cornell, Thurmond DuBoise, Jessie Stitt, Nathaniel Shelf, Harry Tyson, Nelson Malloy, and Larry Little.[36] The group began by organizing to raise $300 to pay the transportation costs of an official from BPP central headquarters to travel to North Carolina to indoctrinate the group. On October 10, 1969, the FBI special agent in charge (SAC) at the San Francisco field office provided information from a taped phone call regarding the status of the Winston-Salem group. The memo, delivered to the SAC Charlotte and FBI headquarters, stated that the Winston-Salem cell was officially recognized as a branch of the National Committee to Combat Fascism (NCCF) by the national Black Panther organization, an event subsequently reported in the November 22, 1969, edition of *The Black Panther.*[37]

The group's activities were limited during its first year, and at first it appeared as though their antics would result in their being rebuffed by the national office in the same way the Panther wanna-bes in Greensboro were. They defied the city's establishment by openly carrying weapons while parading around in Panther regalia. Picking up where the militant NAACP leader Robert F. Williams had left off, the group implored the Black community to organize for self-defense in the face of persistent police brutality. On a few occasions members of the group picked up the gun to prevent the evictions of Black tenants.

At first the group mainly sold *The Black Panther* newspaper and provided breakfast for school kids, with the bulk of the food donated by local businesses. The breakfast program was a simple but popular program that fed children from poor families every morning during the school year. Because of its success across the country, it also became a target for the FBI. Little remembers:

> With the breakfast program the police would follow our van as we picked up kids [to] bring them to the office. And we would blow the horn buwump-buwump-wump-wump-wump, and the police would arrest the party members for unnecessary use of the horn.[38]

The other main activity, the selling of the paper, spread the message of the Black Panthers and provided the branch with its main source of income.

The branch would buy papers from central headquarters and sell them for a small profit. This venture became a major endeavor as the group regularly sold several thousand papers per week, as reported by the FBI.[39] Through these efforts the branch sought strong ties with people in the community and became involved with local issues, but this early success with community service work proved short-lived. By the middle of 1970, legal problems and constant harassment by law enforcement agencies forced the branch to curtail its activism.

Community support of the Party was not monolithic. The poor who were the beneficiaries of the chapter's community survival programs could relate to what the Panthers were doing. A sector of the Black middle class, on the other hand, while appreciating the assistance given to the indigent, feared that the Panthers' rhetoric and style would make things worse for the Black community as a whole.

Before legal problems became a central concern, the branch was able to address local issues such as housing. The Panthers used the case of Polly Graham to display their displeasure with unfair housing practices within the city. Graham was evicted from her home on March 4, 1970, for nonpayment of rent. She immediately went to the NCCF office and requested assistance. Two armed NCCF members went with Ms. Graham to her home and proceeded to move her belongings back into the house, and her rent was paid by a third party seeking to prevent violence between the police and the NCCF.[40] The incident was a small one, but it brought the group a substantial amount of press. Articles appeared in all the local daily newspapers, and several opinion pieces appeared regarding the incident. One such piece was a letter to the *Twin City Sentinel*, from Jerry Newton Jr., a "Republican candidate for mayor" and local landlord. The letter stated:

> It will be a darker day in Winston-Salem than a total eclipse of the sun and a most mournful time if a small group of seeming insurgents start shooting. This type of conflict between people would be more horrible than international war as there are rules of war that nations abide by when they are in conflict.[41]

In his letter, Newton went on to speak about a woman named Minnie Bellamy whose family had been evicted by Newton's real estate company and had, like Graham, sought NCCF assistance in the matter. Newton said of the Bellamy family: "I will see that they [local public agencies] get on the move and teach such people as the Bellamy family to learn to budget their money, prepare proper nutritional meals for themselves, do better housekeeping, and make themselves better citizens."[42] Clearly the idea of the "white man's burden" had not died in Winston-Salem. The publicity, however, was good for the branch.

The branch used this community activism to build excitement around the NCCF, holding a large rally on May 3, 1970, in support of Bobby Seale, who was then facing murder charges in New Haven, Connecticut. The NCCF requested that a member from the national headquarters speak at the rally. A member of the New York chapter was sent instead. Held at Tower Auditorium, the rally was a big success, and it provided Little with a forum to position himself as the leader of the group. At the rally, Little stated:

> You know, you don't know how long we're going to be on the set because this American Government is moving into open fascism. You got to understand they aren't just attacking Chairman Bobby Seale in Connecticut. They're attacking Black people period. And see, that's what you got to understand. Ralph Abernathy, head of the Southern Christian Leadership Conference, said that the government is now dealing with the Black Panther Party and pretty soon they'll be dealing with the SCLC and the NAACP.[43]

New York Panther "Dhoruba" (Richard Moore) spoke at the rally as well, but his speech was overly violent and lacked the subtlety and sophistication of Little's oratory. Dhoruba made extremist statements such as: "We have to get out here in these communities and we have to exterminate these faggots [police, local authorities, FBI, etc.]."[44] Robert Greer, the titular head of the branch, did not speak at the rally. It was Little's show, and it helped to introduce him to the Black community and in turn establish him as the eventual head of the local branch.

Greer's failure to devote himself fully to the work of the branch led to Little's rise as leader of the group. It was Little, not Greer, who had by mid-1970 traveled to the Panthers' central headquarters in Oakland several times. Little confronted Greer and demanded that he quit his job and devote himself full time to the branch. When Greer refused, Little, with the backing of most of the other members of the group, purged Greer and his close supporters from the group.[45]

Little, only twenty years old when he took over the branch, had moved quickly from complacency to social activism. Little had been a high school basketball star who grew up in the Kimberly Park housing project in Winston-Salem. Prior to graduation he had listened to a group of self-proclaimed Panthers from A&T speak at a rally in Winston-Salem and knew he "wanted to be a part of that."[46] Little had read Black history and felt frustrated with the condition of Blacks both in the nation and in Winston-Salem. His determination to act made him an extremely effective leader and assured the group a certain amount of success.

Under Little's leadership, the group became more thoroughly involved in local issues. While maintaining a small arsenal, in its first year of activity the branch acted as a nonviolent organization mainly concerned with access issues. The NCCF, for instance, received much media attention for its participation in a boycott of an A&P store located in the predominantly Black Carver community. The protest revolved around the mistreatment of Sara Alford, a Black shopper, by the store's management. Alford was injured in the store by a broken jar and sought medical attention. She was told by doctors that she would need an operation that would cost approximately $300, and she insisted that the manager of the A&P store pay her medical bills. The manager refused. The NCCF responded with a boycott and picket of the store. The boycott gave the NCCF and the Carver community the opportunity to speak out about other store policies that concerned them. The NCCF demanded that the store hire more Blacks and contribute to the NCCF breakfast program. In an article appearing in the June 20 issue of *The Black Panther*, Larry Little summed up the feelings of many Blacks in the community when he said, "Either you make the A&P relevant to the needs of the Black community or get out."[47]

In response to the NCCF's growing community influence, the FBI stepped up its harassment and monitoring of the group. In October 1970, under Hoover's direction, Robert M. Murphy, the divisional director of the FBI in Charlotte, concocted a counterintelligence plan that would be the envy of his FBI colleagues across the country. He authorized letters to be sent to more than two hundred Panther sympathizers and supporters (financial and otherwise) in Winston-Salem with the intent of defaming the local office. Letters were mailed under the heading "The Committee of Twenty-Five," a fictitious group made up of religious-oriented and respectable Blacks that was formed anonymously, it stated, to avoid retribution from the NCCF. The committee labeled the NCCF as "Chinese-styled" communist-inspired thieves, homosexuals, and snake oil salesmen adept at preying on unsuspecting bleeding-heart liberals.[48] Indicating that there were no depths to which the FBI would not stoop, in a perverted and desperate move to discredit the Panthers, the FBI sent follow-up letters suggesting that inappropriate behavior was taking place between the male Panthers and young girls in the breakfast program.

The FBI's smear campaign was buttressed with a similar effort to foment dissension among the Winston-Salem activists themselves. The FBI's objective was to manufacture a beef between Winston-Salem and the national headquarters in Oakland by pitting so-called supporters of Huey Newton, who stressed the importance of the community survival programs, against those of Eldridge Cleaver, who favored escalating the struggle by waging urban guerrilla warfare against the state. In the spring of 1971, at the height of the Newton-Cleaver feud, the Winston-Salem office supposedly sent a letter to the national office indicating it was time for Newton's "cheap, meaning-less talk" and lavish lifestyle to end. It called for his ouster—to be replaced by Cleaver. The Winston-Salem office wanted action, the correspondence implied. "Come home, Comrade. Come home, Comrade Cleaver," the NCCF pleaded. To support Cleaver and his position on the direction the BPP ought to be headed was in direct ideological conflict with the national office. The FBI had hoped that such an outward display of insubordination on the part of the Winston-Salem cohort would result in internecine warfare that would bring about the swift annihilation of the Winston-Salem group.

The office of the NCCF was staked out by agents at all hours of the day and night. Members were followed, and the finances of the group were closely monitored. Little remembers the FBI's tactics well: "They would shine lights in my girlfriend's house at two or three in the morning to let me know that they knew where I was."[49] The FBI also meticulously tracked the newspaper, noting who sold copies and where they were sold. In addition, the San Francisco FBI field office dispatched information to the Charlotte SAC concerning the delivery schedule of the paper, recording the number of copies, the airline, the flight number, and the airway bill number of the shipment. Little also accused the FBI of trying to incite gang violence against the NCCF. As stated earlier, one of COINTELPRO's favorite schemes was to drive a wedge between the Black Panther Party and other groups in order to foster violence. In fact, Little claims that one of his friends was offered money by the FBI to shoot him.[50]

This FBI scrutiny led to problems for the chapter. Any activity, even remotely illegal, was transformed into a major problem for the group, and, like the national group, the branch was unprepared for the severity of the attack by the FBI. The assumption of most of the Panthers was that their activities would lead to confrontations with law enforcement agencies, but that these confrontations would be overt in nature. The Panthers had prepared them-selves to combat the open hostility that had been experienced by civil rights activists in the South during the 1950s and 1960s. But they were simply not fully aware or ready for the covert tactics that were employed against them by the FBI. The FBI seized every opportunity to investigate the branch. When Party members were evicted from a residence (this occurred often—see below), the FBI was presented with an occasion to search the premises. On one such occasion the FBI found an alleged Marine Corps deserter. An FBI document states:

> A deserter from the Marine Corps, was apprehended July, Eight, Seventy, by agents of the FBI at Winston-Salem, N.C., where he was observed in the company of two members of the Winston-Salem National Committee to Combat Fascism, a Black Panther Party affiliated group. This occurred as agents were observing officers of the Forsythe County evicting a group

of former members of the Winston-Salem NCCF from an apartment on
Cleveland Avenue for non-payment of rent.[51]

On other occasions weapons and office equipment were confiscated. Quite
naturally this type of constant harassment disrupted the group's daily activities.

One of the actions the branch was able to maintain was the selling of the
Black Panther newspaper. The group regularly submitted articles for publication in the newspaper, giving themselves an outlet for their passion about
local politics. The articles also served to publicize the group's activities.
Many of these pieces documented police harassment of Blacks in Winston-
Salem. The purpose was to show that all Blacks, not just Party members,
were victims of brutality and that the most effective way of fighting back was
by supporting or joining the NCCF. "Ernest Scales Was Clubbed Viciously
for Being Black," an article written by Nelson Malloy appearing in the
August 29, 1970, edition of *The Black Panther*, was an example. The article
documented the police attack on a middle-aged, handicapped Black man.
Malloy writes: "They [the police] clubbed Ernest Scales, age 42, across the
arm and head inflicting a wound that required 14 stitches to close."[52]

Other articles written by Winston-Salem NCCF staff members dealt
with public policy issues that affected Blacks. One article, "Racist Winston-
Salem School Board Plan for School Desegregation Means Terror for Black
Children," is an excellent example. The article attacked the local school
board's desegregation plan, which included the closing of two of the three
Black high schools and the busing of those students to several all-white
schools. The article reads:

> We think you [the school board] should know Black people DO NOT want
> Carver and Anderson [the Black high schools] closed and we ARE NOT going
> to place our kids lives in jeopardy as we did last year—for those mad KKK's to
> try to intimidate and murder. If you persist in your mad scheme we will make
> you see the folly of your stupid plan.[53]

The article's focus on a local issue served both the national and local group
well. The national group could show, with articles similar to this one from
branches across the country, that it was first and foremost concerned with the
lives of Black people. The local group could also show that the power of the
national Black Panther Party was fully behind the projects of the local branch.
It was for this reason that the FBI saw the paper as such a danger and worked
hard to destroy it.

Again, the FBI and local law enforcement agencies' determination to
destroy the NCCF resulted in harassment, arrests, and legal problems for the
group. Little had his first run-in with the police on July 28, 1970, when he got
into an argument with a group of police officers after they ripped down some

posters bearing the slogan "I'm Black and I'm Proud" he had put up around the city. Little was arrested for disorderly conduct and attempting to incite a riot. According to Little, at his trial the judge gave him a choice: quit the Black Panther Party or go to jail. Little went to jail and served thirty days.[54]

The NCCF began to take defensive actions to prevent future arrests and problems with these law enforcement organizations, fortifying its headquarters with sandbags and collecting a cache of arms.[55] The group also began lashing out in frustration. The police and FBI effectively drained the NCCF's resources, and the group became discouraged at the prospect of making real change. When interviewed, Little talked about the FBI incessantly. He recounted that when "Nancy Smith said, 'Why you all [the FBI] taking my picture?' the FBI replied, 'So we can more clearly identify your body later on.'"[56] The anger felt by the NCCF members culminated in adventurism by a small group of Panther associates who were trying to establish a NCCF branch in nearby Lumberton, North Carolina. This clique, according to FBI records, disrupted a meeting of the Lumberton Urban Redevelopment Commission, and one member of the group, Sam Williamson, was accused of threatening to chop off the head of the speaker at the meeting. Later that night gunfire erupted outside the commission building.[57] Williamson, according to an article in *The Black Panther*, was later arrested for public drunkenness. Upon his arrest it was determined that he was insane, and he was sent without trial to Dorothy Dix, a public mental institution, for sixty days.[58]

The arrests of Little and Williamson were only the beginning of the legal problems the group would experience. Anthony Cain, a prominent Party member who had written articles for the newspaper, was charged with trespassing on July 28, 1970. Cain failed to appear for his trial, and a bench warrant was issued for his arrest. Though Cain was expelled by the NCCF for his counterrevolutionary antics, the NCCF headquarters was raided at 5:30 A.M. on August 18 in an attempt to locate him. Another member, James Cato, was arrested in August 1970 on a larceny charge, and in December, Forest White was charged with "failure to return rented property" after failing to return a rented truck. Finally, Joe Waddell, a member from High Point, North Carolina, was charged in January 1971 with armed robbery.[59]

The NCCF's problems were further magnified by the actions of Blacks claiming to be members of the group. This had been a problem for other chapters around the country, and it proved to be for the Winston-Salem group as well. Richard Carter and Ronald Carnes from High Point, who claimed affiliation with the NCCF, were arrested for armed robbery on September 11, 1970. An anonymous phone caller, believed to be the sister of one of the two arrested, advised "that if the two Negroes held on armed robbery charges were not released by 10/14 seven unidentified plants in High

Point would be bombed."[60] No bombs were ever placed, but the damage to the Panthers had been done.

The group tried to maintain its normal operations, but even "normal operations" sometimes led to trouble. By late 1970, the Black Panther Party had arguably become the most preeminent radical group in the country. The Party decided to unite other radical groups under its leadership by organizing the Revolutionary People's Constitutional Convention (RPCC). The convention was scheduled to take place from November 27th through the 29th in Washington, D.C., close enough to Winston-Salem that most of the chapter's members as well as a large group of supporters were able to attend. For some time, the chapter organized and planned their attendance at the convention, and they rented a small truck (the same truck Forest White later failed to return) to accommodate all the people making the trip.[61] Everyone was anticipating a history-making event. But these high hopes were dashed as the convention was a complete failure. Poorly planned and lacking any real purpose or mission, the convention was barred from Howard University, and many of the speeches and discussions were held outside in Malcolm X (Meridian) Park. The convention broke up into small workshops designed to tackle specific issues (women's rights, gay rights, police brutality, etc.). The documents produced by these workshops were hastily prepared. The students' rights workshop came up with the novel idea that "[s]tudent government should be controlled by the students."[62]

The RPCC proved to be a double disaster for the Winston-Salem NCCF. The departing members left Winston-Salem at about noon. Mysteriously, less than an hour later the NCCF headquarters was ablaze. The fire burned out of control for nearly an hour and completely destroyed the headquarters. The FBI was quick to appear on the scene, searching the debris for weapons and noting the serial numbers of several pieces of printing equipment.[63] In an article appearing in *The Black Panther*, the NCCF said that "eyewitnesses [sic] reports state that something had been thrown into the fire." In addition to the office being understaffed (there were only three NCCF members left behind), the rest of the membership ran into mechanical problems on their way to Washington. Before the conventioneers could even cross the state line into Virginia, the truck broke down. According to the NCCF, soon after they pulled to the side of the road "the FBI, state, and local pigs converged on the truck" and proceeded to search the truck for weapons.[64] After spending hours repairing the truck, the group continued on to Washington for the convention.

A few months later, in January 1971, the Panthers experienced another incident, this one involving the theft of a meat truck. As with so many incidents involving the Panthers, the stories vary. According to the FBI and local police, the meat truck was stolen by unknown thieves from the Chatam Meat Company on January 12. About ten minutes after the theft, the "owner" located the truck 'in front of the new NCCF headquarters, and within the hour a search warrant had been issued. The house was immediately surrounded, and the police gave the occupants three minutes to exit.[65] When no one exited the house, the police fired tear gas canisters at the lower-level windows, but the canisters were stopped by sandbags fortifying the house. The police then shot tear gas into the upper-level windows. Shooting between the police and those in the house ensued, which sparked a fire in the house. Fortunately, no one was injured, but two NCCF members, Willie Coe and Grady Fuller, were charged on the scene with larceny and several other felonies.[66] Little and Julius Cornell, although not inside the house, were also charged with larceny of the truck. A week later, on January 19, the police apprehended Little and Cornell during another eviction. The police arrested the two after Coe, a fifteen year-old high school student, "identified Cornell and Little as being the two people who brought the truckload of meat to the Panther house." Little and Cornell were charged with accessory after the fact, a felony. Their bail was set at $2,000 each.[67]

The NCCF had a different version of what happened on January 12, 1970. According to Larry Little:

> They [the FBI] set up a meat truck robbery. They used an informer to bring a meat truck to our office . . . the Black informer said this company, Chatam Meat Company, was contributing food to the breakfast program. Within two minutes of that meat truck coming to our office . . . our office was surrounded by the FBI and police department—probably about 100 people. They set the whole thing up to destroy the breakfast program.[68]

Regardless of what happened, Little was not at the house during the raid and probably had little knowledge of the robbery (if in fact it was a robbery) or shootout until after the events had transpired. The case lingered in court and became quite a controversial issue a year later.

The NCCF experienced a series of financial setbacks as a result of the fire and the meat truck incident. As stated earlier, the chapter members devoted all of their time to the Party. They did not hold jobs and had to rely on donations and sales of the newspaper to pay their expenses. The arrests not only depleted much of the group's financial resources, but they also removed members from the streets who would normally be selling *The Black Panther* or soliciting donations. In October 1970, the FBI estimated the NCCF's monthly income at $937.50 and their expenses as $1,027.50 (this latter figure excluded food and clothing).[69] The branch was also expected to call Oakland regularly to keep the national headquarters abreast of the goings-on in

Winston-Salem. While the branch had shown surpluses in income at various times, it rarely had "extra" money to operate community programs. Although the branch did receive donations, they were erratic and for the most part meager. In fact, things got so bad that for a period during late 1970 and early 1971 the branch was unable to secure telephone service at their headquarters.[70]

The branch's financial trouble led to evictions of party members from rented houses and apartments. These evictions were done with dispatch. Most of the time the eviction took place within a few days of the eviction court hearing and only a few weeks after the rent had been due. On some occasions NCCF members were evicted even though they had in fact paid their rent. The FBI and local police in one instance "advised [a landlord renting to the NCCF] of the fact [that] the Panthers are now located in his building." The landlord immediately sought to evict them.[71] In a four-day stretch between February 12 and 16, two groups of members were evicted and eviction hearings were held on a third group. In one instance when a landlord was asked in court to explain the reason for eviction, his attorney exclaimed, "What's the reason? We don't have to have a reason." Various city agencies appeared to be in collusion against the Panthers. More than one insurance company informed property owners that their insurance would be cancelled if any of their tenants were Panthers. Other times Southern Bell Telephone and Telegraph Company abruptly disconnected service to Panthers' dwellings or the residences of people believed to be associated with the Panthers.

All told, there were at least five evictions between November 1970 and March 1971.[72] The Winston-Salem NCCF was forced to move five times in the span of six months. One of these evictions led to a shootout with police. On February 10, 1971, police served an eviction notice on a group of NCCF members in High Point, North Carolina. The eviction was "ordered by Mendenhall-Moore Realtors as the house had been rented under false pretense with the claim it was to be occupied by a family."[73] The Guilford County sheriff's office, led by Laurie Pritchett (notorious as police chief in Albany, Georgia), surrounded the house and gave the inhabitants ten minutes to exit. One woman, Diane Mock, exited the house. After ten minutes had elapsed and no one else had exited, the police fired tear gas into the house, and the occupants returned the fire. Three officers and one NCCF member were wounded before those inside were forced to exit because of the tear gas. Four members, Larry Medley, Randolph Jennings, George Dewitt, and Bradford Lilley, all of whom were in their teens, were arrested and charged with conspiracy to commit murder, with bond set at $50,000 each.[74]

The raid in High Point was a typical example of the type of misunderstanding and fear local police had of the Black Panther Party. The police, imbued with FBI-created hysteria, overreacted out of fear of the Panthers.

The Panthers had been evicted perhaps a dozen times before and had not created any serious trouble, but the police, by surrounding the house with armed officers and giving the group only ten minutes to leave the premises, was provoking the NCCF, and the shootout was inevitable given the circumstances. The eviction itself was based on flimsy grounds; the group had paid their rent. Medley, Lilley, and Jennings were found guilty of assault with a deadly weapon with intent to kill and in February 1972 were sentenced to seven to ten years in prison.[75]

The branch's problems worsened in March 1971. Little had been charged on February 5, 1971, with carrying a concealed weapon. On March 8 he was found guilty and sentenced to four to six months in prison. His attorney gave notice of appeal, and Little was released on $2,000 bond. As Little was exiting the courtroom he let his temper get the best of him and yelled an obsenity at the judge. The judge immediately slapped Little with a thirty-day contempt of court sentence.[76] The concealed weapon conviction was later reversed.

It is a testament to the members' courage and fortitude that the group survived past 1971. The violence and legal problems experienced with the police and the FBI had largely prevented the branch from undertaking massive community service programs; only the breakfast program could be maintained during the branch's first two tumultuous years. Forced to reevaluate its tactics, the Winston-Salem office altered its image by avoiding armed confrontations and focusing its attention on community service, and during the next four years the branch was able to accomplish things that it had only dreamed of earlier.

Changes in the FBI also enabled the NCCF to become increasingly involved with community service and less involved in conflicts with law enforcement agencies. In 1971, COINTELPRO ostensibly officially came to an end after it was discovered by the media.[77] The discovery of COINTELPRO, coupled with the death of J. Edgar Hoover in May 1972, led to a less politicized FBI. Under new media scrutiny, the FBI toned down its public contempt toward the Panthers, investigations for Smith Act violations ceased, and the FBI began to employ less intrusive measures to undercut the Black Panther Party's influence. This relaxation by the FBI allowed the Winston-Salem branch to pursue its endeavors without the harassment and scrutiny of the FBI, but this did not mean that the FBI ceased its surveillance of the group. The FBI continued to watch the Winston-Salem office until it disbanded.

Revolution or Bust: 1971–1976

In April 1970 the Winston-Salem NCCF was officially recognized as a full-fledged branch of the Black Panther Party, a change in status that was an important turning point for the Winston-Salem group. The branch, having endured FBI and local police repression, was able to begin rebuilding strong community service programs that led to a new respectability for the group. The group's finances also stabilized. The amount and frequency of donations dramatically increased and the group's membership had fewer legal problems, which meant that the branch's legal expenses decreased. But the vitality of the Winston-Salem group was not mirrored by the national Black Panther Party, which was thrown into turmoil by internal problems. By 1971 the Party was no longer "fashionable" and had ceased to be considered the "vanguard" by many leftists. Drug abuse, criminal activity, and ongoing petty feuds among the remaining Party leaders tore the Party apart. The problems with the national group eventually affected the Winston-Salem chapter and caused disenchantment among the members; this disillusionment brought about the end of the Winston-Salem group just as its members were moving into positions of authority within the city.

The legal problems of the High Point four (Medley, Jennings, Dewitt, and Lilley) and those accused of the meat truck robbery (Little, Cornell, and Fuller) gave the branch issues around which to rally. In particular, the meat truck case focused community attention on the ills of the justice system. Little, Cornell, and Fuller were tried twice on the charges, with the first trial proving to be a resounding victory for the branch. During pretrial motions, the members were given an opportunity to publicize FBI harassment. A subpoena obtained by the group's attorney, Jerry Paul of the ACLU, against Special Agent David Martin, the FBI agent heading the investigation into the Winston-Salem branch,[78] sent the FBI into turmoil. A flurry of teletypes and memos was sent between the director's office and the SAC of the Charlotte field office.[79] Martin was called to testify on September 20, 1971. When asked if he had participated in surveillance of the Panthers, he declined to answer, citing "FBI departmental order 381-67," an order that instructed agents not to testify in court regarding FBI operations without instruction from the U.S. Attorney General.[80]

On September 22, 1971, Martin was given a list of questions that Paul intended to ask. The list was immediately furnished to the director's office. The questions were:

1. Have you, in your capacity as an FBI agent done any electronic surveillance regarding defendant Larry Little?
2. Have you, in your capacity as an FBI agent done any electronic surveillance regarding defendant Julius White Cornell?
3. Have you conducted any electronic surveillance regarding defendant Grady Fuller?

4. Mr. Martin, has any information come into your possession by means of electronic surveillance that any of these defendants might have committed any of these crimes upon which they stand?

5. Prior to today, a few minutes ago, when you went out with the United States Attorney and the State Prosecutors, had you discussed electronic surveillance with any person involved in the investigation and/or prosecution in this case?[81]

Martin was instructed to answer "No" to the first four questions and "No, not with regard to this particular case" to the last question, answers which were only partly true. From the FBI files it is clear that the group's most important phone calls, namely those to the Party's headquarters in Oakland, were recorded by the San Francisco field office. Martin had not himself placed or made the decision to place the phone taps in Oakland. Therefore he was technically telling the truth. However, Martin had access to all the transcripts of phone calls made to Panther headquarters and was using these transcripts to build his "Smith Act" case.

While the subpoena of Martin during pretrial hearings had put the FBI on the defensive, it was another pretrial motion that led to victory in the first trial. Paul argued that Little could not receive a fair trial in the district in which he was being tried because Black representation on potential juror lists was disproportionate to the percentage of Black citizens in the district. James N. Long, superior court judge for Forsythe County, agreed and quashed the indictment.[82] While the charges were not dismissed, the fact that a superior court judge agreed that Little could not receive justice bolstered the case made by the Panthers against law enforcement agencies. When the criminal charges were reinstated in 1973, Fuller, Cornell, and Little pled no contest to misdemeanor larceny charges. Fuller was sentenced to ninety days in prison and was fined an amount equal to one-third the price of the stolen meat. Little and Cornell were sentenced to six months in prison, suspended for two years, and were fined for the remaining two-thirds of the price of the meat. Little and Cornell never served any time under the conviction.[83]

In early 1972, the Winston-Salem branch and the national Black Panther Party began instituting policies to alter the public image of the Party. The national Party leadership suggested that Black Panther Party members join churches and build coalitions with parishioners.[84] The Winston-Salem branch was instructed to become active with traditional Black community leaders, small business owners, and ministers, and they began courting groups like the Southern Christian Leadership Conference (SCLC) and Ben Chavis's North Carolina–Virginia Council for Racial Justice (NCVCRJ). Both the SCLC and the NCVCRJ spoke at Panther rallies in support of Panther projects.[85]

The coalition with these less radical, religiously oriented groups represented a fundamental shift in Panther policy. While Chavis had always been radical and the SCLC under Ralph Abernathy had moved leftward, the Panther coalitions with these groups displayed a new outlook. The Panthers still advocated revolution, but they conceded that this might be more effectively accomplished by working through traditional legal institutions.

The branch's first endeavor to alter its image involved an old discontent. Blacks in Winston-Salem had known for some time that city services were often distributed on a racial basis rather than on the basis of need. When this service meant the life or death of a Black citizen, it was particularly galling. As early as October 1970 the branch had raised the issue of emergency health services, especially ambulance services, which was a sore point among Blacks. On October 17, 1970, *The Black Panther* ran an article titled "Pig Responsible for Death of 15 Year Old Brother," which recounted the events after the shooting of Alan "Snake" Dendy. According to eyewitnesses, the ambulance arrived on the scene half an hour after being called and the technicians found Dendy still alive but seriously injured. The article stated that "they [the ambulance technicians] refused to give the brother [Dendy] medical attention and refused to take him to a hospital." The police, instead of trying to help Dendy, began questioning people who had gathered at the scene. Dendy died within two hours. When asked why they had not helped Dendy, the ambulance technicians stated, "We didn't have permission to move him."[86] According to Little, this incident was not out of the ordinary. He stated, "We had people who died because these ambulance employees, who were county employees, determined these people were not in an emergency situation."[87] The Panthers felt compelled to act, and by 1972 it was financially able to do so.

In June 1971, the group obtained an old hearse and began outfitting it for use as an ambulance.[88] Members also began attending first aid and emergency medical technician (EMT) classes at Surry Community College.[89] The FBI, which still perceived the branch as a threat, continued harassing the group. Little remembers:

> We sent our members to Surry Community College to be trained to become emergency medical technicians. The president of that college told me that when we enrolled there they were visited by David Martin of the FBI and that they [the FBI] were trying to get them [the school] not to let us enroll in the emergency medical technician program because they wanted to stop our ambulance program from getting started.

The members were able to attend the college and were certified by the end of summer 1971. The ambulance service was begun by the end of the year, and it proved to be one of the branch's most effective endeavors. It offered a service that the community had long wanted. In May 1973 the success of the program led the National Episcopal Church to give the Panthers $35,700 so that the program could be continued and expanded. The branch bought a new ambulance and several other vehicles with the money.[90] The program transformed Little into a major political player in the city. He frequently appeared on television and was the subject of numerous newspaper articles.

The chapter instituted several other inexpensive yet highly effective community programs designed to help the city's poor residents. Among these programs was a free pest control service. Pest control was beyond the financial means of some Blacks in Winston-Salem, and the program offered a much-needed service to the poor of Winston-Salem while costing a relatively small amount of money. A similar effort was a program to bus people to visit their loved ones in prison, who were often incarcerated a considerable distance from Winston-Salem.[91] The chapter also collected clothes and shoes for the poor and set up a sickle cell anemia testing program that was also relatively inexpensive. According to Larry Little, "you could train people to do that test."[92]

While the North Carolina branch had altered its image, many members and former members of the organization had not. The members loyal to the Cleaver faction of the Party were especially dangerous and problematic for the more respectable chapters and branches, and their actions reflected poorly on the rest of the organization. Robert Brown and Daniel Johnson, New York Party members, were the first of these so-called "renegades"[93] to cause problems in North Carolina. On November 11, 1971, Brown and Johnson, wanted for bank robbery in New York, were stopped on Highway 64 in Catawba County, North Carolina, by Deputy Sheriff Ted Elmore. Brown shot Elmore three times, and the two drove off. They later fled the car after having been spotted by another police officer, but they were apprehended shortly thereafter. Inside the stolen car were eight guns, two walkie-talkies, rope, guerrilla warfare books, several knives, and a large quantity of ammunition.[94] The incident, along with information from an FBI informer in Detroit,[95] led to speculation that the radical Cleaver faction was contemplating relocating to North Carolina to set up an underground organization. While no further evidence of an underground faction in North Carolina was ever observed, the possibility that such a group might exist was supposedly seen as a serious threat by the FBI.

In early 1972, Little returned to Oakland for nearly six months of training, and in his absence Nelson Malloy served as acting head of the branch. Upon Little's return the branch was rejuvenated. The group embarked upon several new community service ventures, and members became increasingly involved in local politics. But the success was short-lived. The national party was in decline, and its emphasis on community service was an attempt to save the Party from completely dissolving. The events of late 1972 and 1973 represented a last-ditch attempt by the branch to make the Black Panther Party a force in Winston-Salem, but what the group discovered was that their personal ambitions were outgrowing the decaying Party. The successes of the final years of the charter's existence led directly to the branch's end.

Shortly after Little's return from Oakland in June of 1972, Panther Joe Waddell, who had been convicted of armed robbery, died in prison. On June 13, Waddell complained of a stomach ache shortly after lunch and died soon thereafter. An autopsy determined that the cause of death was a heart attack brought on by coronary heart disease, even though Waddell was only twenty-two years old and did not have a history of medical problems. Medical records and a routine physical examination taken days before his death showed that Waddell was in excellent health. According to Page Hudson, the state medical examiner, he was very muscular and his low body fat suggested that he exercised regularly. Suffice to say his death was a shock to many in the community, and, given the inconsistencies in the various reports, some suspected that Waddell had been murdered. On June 21, 1972, Waddell was buried in full Panther regalia before a large crowd of Panther supporters and members. The eulogy was given by Bobby Seale, who had taped his message a few days earlier.[96] If he had been murdered for being a Panther, Waddell got posthumous revenge. He had bought a sizeable life insurance policy that named the Winston-Salem branch as the beneficiary. The branch received $7,000, which it used for the ambulance program.[97] The group acknowledged its debt of gratitude to Waddell for his service by renaming the ambulance program the "Joseph Waddell People's Free Ambulance Service."[98]

Waddell's name was again commemorated on July 30, 1972, with the Joseph Waddell Free Food Program. The event, attended by two thousand people, was a huge success. The branch donated a thousand grocery bags of food to the residents of the Kimberly housing project, and in addition to free food, people in the housing project were given free sickle cell anemia tests as well as free shoes for their children. The branch also launched a voter registration drive that, according to the FBI, registered five hundred people to vote. The branch used the event as a forum to display its new outlook. Little spoke at length about working within the system and announced that he would run for local office in the future.[99] The FBI conceded that the rally was the "most ambitious project undertaken by the NC chapter to date." Two more free food rallies, smaller but still successful, were held in August and December.[100]

Members of the Winston-Salem branch were always aware of FBI surveillance of them, but they had not known the extent of that surveillance. In

August 1973, Wilbert Allen, an FBI and police informer, became displeased with the police's treatment of local Black nightclubs and came forward publicly to reveal the investigation into the branch. The FBI and local police had been investigating the clubs for some time, supposedly as centers for drug distribution. In July 1973 tensions between police and the patrons of the nightclubs snapped and the police used tear gas and billy clubs to clear the street after several people refused to disperse. The Panthers claimed that the police had provoked the whole incident. The Black community, upset by the police action, demanded a public hearing at the Public Safety Committee of the city's Board of Aldermen regarding the event. At the hearing, Allen, apparently "no longer [able] to bear the guilt and shame of his working for the police, publicly confessed that he had been a police informer."[101]

Allen's revelation did not surprise the Panthers. They had always assumed that informers existed but never really knew who they were. According to Allen, the police had been trying to link Little to narcotics distribution at the clubs.[102] Allen further stated:

> In my undercover dealings with the Winston-Salem Police Department,
> I found that, a lot of information they received was misinterpreted through
> other informers. This led to a lot of harassment of individuals whom the police
> had under surveillance and were spying on. Anything that was loose talk was
> taken to be fact. Information I gave was often misused through their own
> department.[103]

Allen's decision to come forward helped improve the image of the Panthers at a critical time. Little parlayed the issues of police brutality and surveillance into an opportunity to enter the political arena. Buoyed by Bobby Seale's campaign for mayor of Oakland and the election of Panthers to various boards and offices in Oakland in 1972 and 1973, Little decided to run for alderman.

The Democratic primary for alderman was held on May 7, 1974, when Little squared off against incumbent Richard N. Davis, also an African American.[104] Little's foray into politics coincided with the organization's shift from revolutionary politics to a more palatable approach to activism. Said Little in an interview with the left-wing publication *Anvil*, "Our goal to transform the system is still there, but our methods have changed." Little said the Black community needed streetlights "for the neighborhood, a hospital accessible to blacks, a police review board and other citizen participation programs." The election was marred by controversy. The original results showed that Little had lost the election by a vote of 646 to 566.[105] Little was highly disappointed since the Panthers had registered more than five hundred voters to ensure victory. But the chairman of the county board of elections challenged four hundred of these newly registered voters, and nearly three hundred were removed from the registration rolls. This purge may have cost Little the election, as many of those who were disfranchised had been registered during a Panther voter registration drive. When Little challenged the results, the election board chairman updated the number of votes received by the Panther leader. The new results had Little losing by a mere eight votes.[106] Although many in the community, including the *Winston-Salem Journal*, called for a new vote, the state Board of Elections refused to hold a new election. The Republican-controlled board found no irregularities during the election.[107]

To many, the election was clearly fraudulent. Irregularities that should have nullified the results existed in numerous areas. According to Little:

> The Republican chairman [of the Election Committee] said he came in and saw these stacks of cards that people had been registering. [He] picked them up, saw that they were Democrats, and he checked to see if he thought these people had been registered properly. He called [up some] of them on the phone. Some of them didn't remember putting their hand on the Bible, so he purged 546 people; just like that, off the books. [He] just threw the cards out. . . . Then they had just refused to give us credit for seventy-two votes out of one machine, and proved that in court. Then they said I lost by eight votes. And the state law says you can't purge people off the books [registration rolls] within ten days of an election. They purged them [the voters registered by Little] two days before the election.[108]

It was clear that even though the Panthers had toned down their rhetoric and shown a willingness to work within the system, they were still perceived as a threat by many people.

The branch was poised on the brink of political legitimacy. Little had narrowly been defeated in his bid for alderman, the Panthers' rallies were regularly drawing sizeable crowds, and the ambulance program was a big success. But the national Black Panther Party was moving in the opposite direction. Newton had expelled or driven out many capable comrades in the Party before he fled to Cuba. The Winston-Salem branch had simply outgrown the national organization, and Little realized that the national organization was no longer an effective vehicle for his personal goals. When the national leadership began recalling entire branches and chapters to Oakland, Little knew the Party was dead. He stated

> They moved everybody out of Baltimore, [Washington] D.C., [New] Jersey, New York, Atlanta, Connecticut. And we had these programs, and ultimately, you know . . . David [Hilliard] would never [have] deplete[d] these chapters like that. Quite frankly that's my real disillusion with the whole thing. . . . And Elaine [Brown], as conniving as she was, played a major role. . . . [She] gets

the Party off track. And then the negative things that evolved with the drug usage and things of this sort. That was just shocking to me.[109]

Little resigned from the Black Panther Party in early 1976. His resignation, for all intents and purposes, represented the end of the Winston-Salem Black Panthers. The remaining members interested in continuing their affiliation with the Panthers moved to Oakland.[110]

Legacy

The death of the Black Panther Party did not end the activism of the people who made up that organization. While some of the most notable Panthers faded away into obscurity, many others continued their public service work. Those who some consider perhaps most responsible for the demise of the organization, Newton and Cleaver, continued the socially deviant activities that had caused the group's descent. Others continued the evolution to respectability that the Party had experienced in the 1970s. Some members of the Winston-Salem branch became quite substantial figures in the city. These Panthers, like Little, continued in public life and demonstrated a determination to keep some of the Panther ideas alive.

For many members of the Winston-Salem branch, life brought tremendous success. Little again ran for the Board of Aldermen, and this time he won. He also began attending Winston-Salem State College (now Winston-Salem State University). At twenty-six he was a freshman in college and alderman of Winston-Salem's North Ward. Little was reelected to the board in the early 1980s, and during his second term he began doing graduate work in public administration at the University of North Carolina–Greensboro. Upon completion of his second term as alderman, Little decided not seek reelection. Instead he enrolled in Wake Forest University Law School. When Little stepped down from his political position to practice law, Patrick Harrison, a member of the NAACP, became the North Ward alderman. After Harrison's term was completed, former Panther Nelson Malloy assumed the position. According to Little, people in Winston-Salem started calling the North Ward alderman position the "permanent Black Panther seat." When Malloy was elected alderman, it marked sixteen out of twenty years a Panther had held that seat.[111]

By the early 1980s the Panthers' legacy was firmly cemented in the annals of Black North Carolina history. Winston-Salem's daily newspaper referred to Larry Little as the area's most influential African American citizen, and the *Winston-Salem Chronicle* (the city's Black newspaper) tabbed him for its first-ever Man of the Year Award.

The legacy of the Winston-Salem branch of the Black Panther Party is more than simply the effect it had on its members. The branch gave a voice to the rage of a dispossessed community: the Black poor. Even Winston-Salem police chief Tom Surratt begrudgingly acknowledged the BPP's impact, commenting that the Panthers were a "good source of conflict management" and their programs were a "good public service."[112] The nonviolent direct action movement led by Dr. Martin Luther King Jr. rarely addressed the economic and social concerns of this segment of society. Bobby Seale remembers his attitude toward the Civil Rights Movement:

> Before I went to college, when I was in the service [the early 1960s], I wasn't aware of civil rights; I'd been hearing about civil rights through the papers but not focusing on it that much. I was personally more concerned with getting some kind of education. . . . I was trying to get some clothes, and I bought a set of encyclopedias. I'd gotten myself a $600 set of drums, which I was also making payments on.[113]

Seale was more interested in his drums than in civil rights. This lack of interest succinctly displays the indifferent attitude of many Blacks who later joined the Panthers. The civil rights struggle was not their struggle. Some Blacks felt that the movement was not working to solve the economic problems many Blacks were experiencing. David Hilliard, who grew up in extreme poverty, often fantasized about white life. Like Seale, Hilliard was indifferent toward the Civil Rights Movement. Hilliard remembers discussing the freedom riders with a group of whites at a Youth for Jobs party (run by the Communist Party):

> I don't share everyone's admiration for the demonstration—me and my buddies think these people are crazy to let themselves be brutalized. But I keep my opinions to myself: I enjoy the talk, and, besides, I'm here for a job, not a debate.[114]

Again economic concerns overrode political interests. Hilliard's comment about the nonviolent tactics of civil rights protesters is also very telling. Nonviolence simply did not make sense to many inner-city poor Black youth. The Black Panther Party acted as the voice of the poor and oppressed, regardless of race, and it addressed the needs of the poor inner-city Black. Like the Nation of Islam, the Black Panther Party sought to use the rage of the criminal and street tough to further political demands, but with a greater sense of urgency and more aggressively.

Members of the Winston-Salem branch also found fault with the traditional Civil Rights Movement. Fighting back was a natural reaction to the violence they had experienced. When Little was asked what the most important accomplishments of the branch were, he did not talk about the ambulance program or the free food program. Instead he talked about the new attitude the Panthers instilled in people. Little stated:

> The major accomplishment I think, though, is the attitude we instilled. Dr H. . . . Malloy, who is a well-known Black surgeon who has been written up a lot for some of the surgery he has done, said that it used to be that the Ku Klux Klan he would hear would ride down his street. And his wife and kids, he would put them on the floor and they would hide. And they would lay down on the floor under the bed because he did not want to be a victim. He said that when he saw what we did with the Panthers—and picked up weapons—he said he immediately went to a sporting goods store and bought him a rifle. [He] told the man there I'm going to buy me a rifle because the Klan is supposed to ride down my street. . . . He said he went from putting his family on the floor to be willing to stand up and fight. I think that's a major accomplishment because often people in the South just accepted whatever happened. . . . The Panthers instilled in Black people a pride of fighting back and standing up for your rights.[115]

One major change in American society has been the acceptance of many of the programs of the Black Panther Party. The free breakfast and lunch programs were adopted later by the Forsyth County/Winston-Salem School Board. The attitude of public service that the Panthers promoted has also been adopted by many cities in hopes of improving the lives of poor people. But the most important Panther idea to receive wide support is community policing. The Panthers were originally organized to monitor police activity in hopes of preventing brutality. Blacks had long complained about the police, and many saw the police as an agent of repression. The Panthers called for an end to outside control of Black communities and demanded that police live in the community in which they served. Today the same idea has been welcomed by many large cities as a technique to minimize problems between the police and the community and as a better way of reducing crime. If a police officer knows the people in the community personally, he is more likely to be in a position to know who the criminals are. He is also less likely to harass or beat people because of his personal relationship with them.

The Panther legacy, however, is not all positive. The early years of the Party were marked by violence. Most of the events described above were incidents involving armed conflict with police. The Party attempted to be disciplined about its use of firearms, routinely conducting firearm safety seminars, but the Party did not have control of the use of firearms by those outside the organization. The use of the gun as a symbol of liberation is double-edged. The improper use of firearms was directly responsible for undermining the Charlotte group's attempt to secure a charter.

The Winston-Salem branch's evolution from a poorly organized, some-what adventuristic group into a force for community action and political change is in direct contrast to the path taken by some of the other Panther chapters. Of all the Panther branches in the South, the Winston-Salem branch was arguably the most effective at implementing the community service approach as outlined by the national office and using it to expand their influence in local affairs. For a brief period, it was the model of what the national organization wanted and envisioned.

The Black Panther Party should be seen as a training ground for Black leaders. The members, while clearly fascinated by the image of the gun-toting Panther during the early months of the Party, quickly became effective community servants. Little's and Malloy's hard work and dedication as Panthers directly led to their success as politicians. Black Panther Party membership demanded courage and sacrifice, important traits of the successful politician, and it introduced its members to the most strenuous and difficult arena of politics/revolution. It is no accident that some former Panthers have become successful politicians and leaders.

Notes

1. William H. Chafe, *Civilities and Civil Rights: Greensboro, North Carolina and the Black Struggle for Freedom* (New York: Oxford University Press, 1980), 5, 72–74, 99.

2. North Carolina Mayors' Cooperating Committee. *North Carolina and the Negro*, 12.

3. Chafe, *Civilities and Civil Rights*, 166–167.

4. Ibid., 173–180, 228.

5. Herbert Shapiro, *White Violence and Black Response: From Reconstruction to Montgomery* (Amherst: University of Massachusetts Press, 1988), 457–458.

6. Ibid., 459, quoted from James Forman, *The Making of Black Revolutionaries* (Washington, D.C.: Open Hand Publishers, 1985); Robert F. Williams, *Negroes with Guns* (Chicago: Third World Press, 1973), 175.

7. Rhoda Lois Blumberg, *Civil Rights: The 1960s Freedom Struggle* (Boston: Twayne, 1991), 141.

8. Ibid., 250–251.

9. William Chafe, in his work *Civilities and Civil Rights*, discusses Harold Avant in detail. At the time of Chafe's writing, the FBI North Carolina–Black Panther Party files had not been fully released, and Chafe could only refer to Avant as "Mister X." Much of the key information in the files, including specific names and dates, has since been released. Chafe speculates about Mister X (Avant) in an extensive footnote. He states:

> Oral testimony suggests that Mr. X acted in a provocative way proposing illegal activities such as bombing, arson, ambush of police, and the use of drugs—any one of which would have made Black insurgents liable to arrest. According to oral sources, Mr. X espoused these activities in a reckless fashion. He offered to teach other participants in the group how to detonate explosives and bragged of

his previous exploits. [Nelson] Johnson and others became suspicious of Mr. X. According to FBI documents, Mr. X portrayed himself as a section chief of the Black Panther Party sent to organize new chapters in North Carolina. . . . Other FBI documents, however, raised questions about Mr. X's authenticity as a Black Panther Party member. [A] Memo notes that Mr. X was suspended by the national Black Panther Party for calling himself a field marshal when in fact he had no rank within the party. . . . On the basis of this oral and written testimony, there seems to be good reason to suspect: (a) that Mr. X never was a Black Panther, and (b) that he was acting as an agent provocateur. It would seem that Avant acted as the conduit through which Brown and others became associated with the Black Panther Party, and that his direction led directly to actions that would get Brown and others in trouble with the law. However, the cafeteria incident for which Brown was expelled appeared in official Panther files. This inclusion leads one to believe that the Party's national leadership was aware of Brown's and Avant's activities, and tacitly approved of them. It is impossible to determine for sure what Avant's role was; however, it must be remembered that the Party's purge in late 1968 and 1969 was begun because the party had attracted too many hangers-on, agent provocateurs, and con-men.

10. From FBI Black Panther Party–North Carolina files (hereafter BPP–NC), file number 105-165706-8, section #1. "Racial Matters" case report of Charlotte FBI field Office, document number 105-165706-8-31, p. 11.

11. Chafe, *Civilities and Civil Rights*, 257.

12. "Fact Sheet on the Case of Eric Brown." Black Panther document secured by the FBI from Party members arrested on January 23, 1969, at JFK airport. FBI BPP–NC, file number 105-165706-8. "Racial Matters" case report of Charlotte FBI field office dated May 23, 1969, document number 105-165706-8-31, p. 13.

13. Ibid., p. 11.

14. Chafe, *Civilities and Civil Rights*, 258.

15. Ibid., 259, 260.

16. Leaflet distributed in Greensboro on March 13, 1969, by unknown individuals. Stamped as being from the "Ministry of Information—Greensboro Chapter—Black Panther Party." Obtained by FBI. Reproduced in FBI BPP–NC, file number 105-165706-8, section #1. "Racial Matters" case report of FBI Charlotte field office dated May 23, 1969, document number 105-165706-8-31, p. 18.

17. Chafe, *Civilities and Civil Rights*, 261–265.

18. Ibid., 266–275.

19. Ibid., 313–314.

20. Larry Little, interview, January 26, 1994.

21. FBI BPP–NC, file number 105-165706-8, section #1. Airtel from Special Agent in Charge (SAC) San Francisco to FBI Director and SAC Charlotte dated December 16, 1968, document number 105-165706-8-1.

22. Ibid.; teletype from FBI Charlotte to Director FBI dated May 19, 1969, document number 105-165706-8-30. Stamped at the bottom of the document is the following information "Included in summary to White House and Attorney General"; Gail Sheehy, *Panthermania: The Clash of Black against Black in One American City* (New York: Harper & Row, 1971).

23. Ibid.; FBI "Racial Matters" case report of FBI Charlotte field office dated May 23, 1969, document number 105-165706-8-31, pp. 6–9.

24. Ibid., 10.

25. Ibid.; Airtel from SAC Charlotte to FBI Director dated May 29, 1969, document number 105-165706-8-33.

26. Ibid.; Airtel from SAC Charlotte to FBI Director dated June 10, 1969, document number 105-165706-8-40.

27. "Panthers Charged in Local Shooting," *Charlotte Observer*, August 4, 1969.

28. FBI BPP–NC, file number 105-165706-8, section #3. Teletype from SAC Charlotte to FBI Director dated August 16, 1969, document number 105-165706-8-63.

29. Ibid. Speech made by Robert E. Lee, September 18, 1969, at University of North Carolina Counter-Orientation Week. Taped by the FBI. Transcript appearing in Airtel from SAC Charlotte to FBI Director dated November 11, 1969, document number 105-165706-8-110, p. 102.

30. Little, interview.

31. Fran V. Tursi, *Winston-Salem: A History* (Winston-Salem, N.C.: John F. Blair Publishers, 1994).

32. Ibid.

33. Ibid.

34. Little, interview.

35. Ibid.

36. FBI BPP–NC. Memo from SAC Charlotte to FBI Director dated July 24, 1969, document number missing.

37. Ibid. Airtel from SAC San Francisco to FBI Director (care copy sent to SAC Charlotte) dated October 2, 1969, document number 105-165706-8-92; Airtel from SAC Charlotte to FBI Director dated December 1, 1969, document number 105-165706-8-113.

38. Little, interview.

39. See FBI BPP–NC. Monthly reports submitted to FBI Director from SAC Charlotte estimated the total newspaper sales for that month in order to calculate the chapter's income.

40. "People of the Community vs. the Slumlords and Fascists of Winston-Salem," *The Black Panther*, March 26, 1970, 2.

41. Jerry L. Newton Jr., "Newton Speaks Out," Letters to the Sentinel, *Twin City Sentinel*, March 8, 1969.

42. Ibid.

43. Larry Little, from FBI transcript of taped rally, May 3, 1970.

44. Ibid.

45. Several FBI documents refer to this incident. Some of them say that Greer quit, while others say he was forced out. The latter seems more plausible. By the time Greer was kicked out of the Party, Little had already been acting as the real leader for several months. Greer's expulsion is no doubt related to his inability to act as a true leader. The FBI first reported the split in an Airtel from SAC Charlotte to FBI Director dated June 5, 1970, document number 105-165706-8-209.

46. Little, interview.

47. "Ms. Alford Victim of A&P Racism," *The Black Panther*, June 20, 1970, 4; "Carver Community Wants Changes at Food Store," *The Winston-Salem Journal*, June 2, 1970; "Black People of Winston-Salem, N.C., Boycott Avaricious A&P Grocery," *The Black Panther*, June 20, 1970, 4.

48. Fran V. Tursi, *Winston-Salem: A History* (Winston-Salem, N.C.: John F. Blair Publishers, 1994), 249–250.

49. Aingred Chislayne Dunston, "The Black Struggle for Equality in Winston-Salem, North Carolina, 1947–1977" (Ph.D. dissertation, Duke University Department of History, 1981).

50. Little, interview.

51. FBI BPP–NC. Teletype from SAC Charlotte to FBI Director dated July 8, 1970, document number 105-165706-8-228.

52. "Ernest Scales Was Clubbed Viciously for Being Black," *The Black Panther*, August 29, 1970, 3.

53. "Racist Winston-Salem School Board Plan for School Desegregation Means Terror for Black Children," *The Black Panther*, August 21, 1970, 4.

54. Little, interview.

55. FBI BPP–NC. "Racial Matters: Smith Act 1940: Seditious Conspiracy: Rebellion and Insurrection," case report of SAC Charlotte dated November 25, 1970, document number 105-165706-9-341, p. 20. It should be noted here that these "Smith Act" reports were part of a broader effort initiated by the San Francisco field office to prosecute the national leadership of the Black Panther Party for advocating the overthrowing of the U.S. government. The reports were divided into several sections: "Revolutionary Program and Policies as Expressed by Black Panther Party Leaders," "Acts in Furtherance of the Revolutionary Program or Policies," "Teaching of the Revolutionary Program," and "Evidence of National Unity." The idea was to prove that all actions undertaken by the Black Panther Party across the country were the direct responsibility of the national leadership. It should also be noted that these reports from Charlotte were provided to the anti-Klan unit of the FBI. At this time, according to Kenneth O'Reilly, perhaps as many as 50 percent of active Klansmen were informers for the FBI. One can only wonder how this information was used by the anti-Klan unit.

56. Little, interview.

57. FBI BPP–NC. "Racial Matters: Smith Act of 1940; Seditious Conspiracy: Rebellion and Insurrection," case report of Charlotte SAC dated November 25, 1970, document number 105-165706-8-341.

58. "Southern City of Racist Exploitation and Oppression," *The Black Panther*, October 17, 1970, 7.

59. FBI BPP–NC. Airtel from SAC Charlotte to FBI Director dated September 4, 1970, document number missing; NCCF flyer obtained by FBI on August 26, 1970; "James Cato of Winston-Salem Subjected to Fascist Frame up," *The Black Panther*, September 5, 1970, 7; Airtel from SAC Charlotte to FBI Director dated January 4, 1971, document number 105-165706-8-417; teletype from SAC Charlotte to FBI Director dated January 18, 1971, document number 105-165706-8-389.

60. Ibid. Memorandum from (blacked out) to Mr. C. D. Brennan dated October 15, 1970, document number 105-165706-8-305.

61. Ibid. Teletype from SAC Charlotte to FBI Director dated November 27, 1970, document number 105-165706-8-345. It should be noted that this document listed the color, make, model, and license plate numbers of the vehicles departing for Washington.

62. FBI BPP–NC. "Racial Matters: Smith Act 1940: Seditious Conspiracy: Rebellion and Insurrection," case report of SAC Charlotte dated November 25, 1970, document number 105-165706-9-341, p. 20; Revolutionary People's Constitutional Convention "Students' Rights Workshops" statement. Document seized by FBI during raid on NCCF Winston-Salem headquarters and reprinted in FBI files. Title, date, sender, and recipient of FBI document withheld, document number 105-165706-8-366.

63. FBI BPP–NC, cover page withheld dated December 18, 1970, document number 105-165706-8-366. Airtel from SAC Charlotte to FBI Director dated December 4, 1970, document number 105-165706-8-363. This document gives the approximate time of departure of the conventioneers. Teletype from SAC Charlotte to FBI Director dated November 27, 1970, document number 105-165706-8-352.

64. "Pigs Burn Down Winston-Salem NC Office in an Attempt to Sabotage the R.P.C.C.," *The Black Panther*, December 5, 1970, 6.

65. It is unclear if the owner owned the truck or the meat company. In addition, no mention of the owner's name is made in any of the FBI documents; FBI teletypes from January 12, 1970. The Charlotte field office sent three teletypes regarding the incident on January 12, 1970: one at 12:30 P.M. (document number 105-165706-8-383), one at 2:20 P.M. (document number 105-165706-8-392), and one at 6:12 P.M. (document number 105-165706-8-385).

66. Ibid.

67. Ibid. Teletype from SAC Charlotte to FBI Director dated January 19, 1971, document number 105-165706-8-396.

68. Little, interview.

69. FBI BPP–NC. Airtel from SAC Charlotte to FBI Director dated November 20, 1970. The Charlotte field office submitted monthly reports concerning the financial situation of the NCCF.

70. Ibid. Airtel from SAC Charlotte to FBI Director dated December 2, 1970, document number missing.

71. Ibid. This particular document notes a $1,000 donation from Jane Fonda for legal fees associated with Little's previous legal problems. Teletype from SAC Charlotte to FBI Director dated February 16, 1971, document number missing.

72. Ibid. See documents number 105-165706-8-405, 105-165706-8-424, 105-165706-435, and 105-165706-8-426.

73. Ibid. Airtel from SAC Charlotte to FBI Director dated February 12, 1971, document number 105-165706-8-436.

74. Ibid. Teletype from SAC Charlotte to SAC San Francisco dated February 14, 1971, document number 105-165706-8-434.

75. Ibid. Airtel from SAC Charlotte to FBI Director dated March 2, 1971, document number 105-165706-6-628.

76. Ibid. Teletype from SAC Charlotte to FBI Director dated March 8, 1971, document number 105-165706-8-454.

77. Nelson Blackstock, *Cointelpro: The FBI's Secret War on Political Freedom* (New York: Vintage Books, 1975), vii.

78. FBI BPP–NC. Teletype from SAC Charlotte to FBI Director dated September 18, 1971, document number 105-165706-8-568.

79. Ibid. See documents number 105-165706-8-568, 105-165706-8-567, 105-165706-8-574, and 105-165706-8-576.

80. Ibid. Teletype from SAC Charlotte to FBI Director dated February 16, 1971, document number 105-165706-8-567.

81. Ibid. Teletype from Charlotte SAC to FBI Director dated September 23, 1971, document numbers 105-165707-8-577 and 105-165706-8-575.

82. FBI BPP–NC. Teletype from SAC Charlotte to FBI Director dated September 27, 1971.

83. Ibid. Airtel from SAC Charlotte to FBI Director dated March 22, 1973, document number 105-165706-8-709.

84. Ibid. Transcripted phone calls from Charlotte to BPP headquarters in Oakland. Airtel from SAC San Francisco to FBI Director dated January 15, 1971, document number 105-165706-8-515.

85. Ibid. Airtel from SAC Charlotte to FBI Director dated July 29, 1971, document number missing.

86. Ibid. Airtel from SAC Charlotte to SAC San Francisco dated March 2, 1972, document number 105-165706-6-628; "Pig Responsible for the Death of 15 Year Old Brother," *The Black Panther*, October 17, 1970, 2.

87. Little, interview.

88. Blackstock, *Cointelpro*, vii.

89. Little, interview; FBI BPP–NC. Airtel from SAC Charlotte to FBI Director dated July 7, 1971, document number 105-165706-8-534.

90. FBI BPP–NC. Airtel from SAC Charlotte to FBI Director dated June 29, 1973, document number 105-165706-8-714.

91. Little, interview.

92. Ibid.

93. *Renegades* was the term used by members of the organization to refer to anyone who had been expelled from the Party but still claimed to be a Panther and carried out work in the name of the Party.

94. FBI BPP–NC. Teletype from SAC Charlotte to FBI Director dated November 12, 1971, document number 105-165706-8-*** (final three numbers missing).

95. Ibid. Airtel from SAC Charlotte to FBI Director dated November 5, 1971, document number 105-165706-8-591.

96. Ibid. FBI "Extremist Matters" case report of SAC Charlotte dated October 31, 1972, document number 105-165706-8-682, p. 10.

97. Ibid. Airtel from SAC Charlotte to FBI Acting Director dated November 17, 1972, document number 105-165706-8-687.

98. Ibid. FBI "Extremist Matters" case report of SAC Charlotte dated April 2, 1974, document number 105-165706-8-733.

99. Ibid.

100. FBI BPP–NC. Airtel from SAC Charlotte to FBI Director dated June 19, 1973, document number 105-165706-8-714; Little, interview.

101. "Winston-Salem Police Informer Confesses," *The Black Panther*, September 1, 1973, 5; "Tension Mounts in Winston-Salem: Police Attack 300," *The Black Panther*, August 26, 1973, 7.

102. Little, interview. Little indicated that he knew of no people that he could say for sure were informers even after having seen the FBI files.

103. "Winston-Salem Informer Confesses: Conclusion," *The Black Panther*, September 18, 1973, 6.

104. The Democratic primary election in the North Ward usually determined the outcome in the general election.

105. FBI BPP–NC. "EM" (Extremist Matters) case report of SAC Charlotte dated September 30, 1974, document number 105-165706, p. 11.

106. "In the System," *The Winston-Salem Journal*, May 10, 1974, 1.

107. "Little's Bid for New Vote Is Denied by State Board," *The Winston-Salem Journal*, June 14, 1974, p. 1.

108. Little, interview.

109. Ibid.

110. Ibid.

111. Ibid.

112. "In the System," *The Winston-Salem Journal*, May 10, 1974, 1.

113. Bobby Seale, *Seize the Time* (New York: Random House, 1970).

114. David Hilliard and Lewis Cole, *This Side of Glory: The Autobiography of David Hilliard and the Story of the Black Panther Party* (Boston: Little Brown, 1993).

115. Little, interview.

3

Panthers Set Up Shop in Cleveland

Ryan Nissim-Sabat

The history of the Black Panther Party (BPP) in Cleveland, Ohio, cannot be fully understood unless one has knowledge of the conditions under which Blacks lived during the preceding decades. It was the specific cultural and economic climate of Cleveland that provided the impetus for Black militancy during the late 1960s. A significant portion of Cleveland's Black population was imprisoned in dehumanizing conditions, ranging from rat-infested housing in overcrowded Black neighborhoods to inadequate educational facilities and opportunities for Black children. Blacks in Cleveland additionally found themselves either disproportionately unemployed or working in the most undesirable and lowest-paying jobs. Yet these conditions also had a role in the development of the Black community's consciousness; individuals are not disconnected from the social and economic relations that produce the context of their existence. Since the creation of the Americas, Blacks have symbolically represented the conceptual other as white people have defined themselves as the standard human. Through these role allocations, society has legitimated the brutality it has imposed on Blacks, categorizing them as inferior rather than as part of the larger human species. The documentation below will demonstrate the ways in which the dominant order was actualized within Cleveland's Black community. Furthermore, these social and institutional circumstances provided the foundation for militant resistance, namely the Black Panthers, who moved to confront the social order and real-locate the city's material resources.

Cleveland's Black Community during the Twentieth Century

Cleveland's growth as an industrial stronghold attracted scores of European immigrants during the early twentieth century and led to the designation of the city as the "melting pot of nationalities." Cleveland was the world's leader in the lighting industry, second in the production of machine tools, and a forerunner in the production of paints and varnishes, motor fuel, trucks and buses, electrical goods, and metal products. Its position as a leader in industrial production crossed into other fields of labor as well, including copper, aluminum, brass, hardware, household appliances, and clothing, to name a few. As William G. Rose notes, Cleveland was tapped as "the best location in the nation" in terms of industrial overlapping.[1] Yet the distinction as the best location seemingly only panned out for members of the white community. Even with a bustling economy at the turn of the century, specifically the expanding steel industry, only a handful of laborers were Black.[2]

However, some historians have argued that Cleveland was a liberal city in regard to race relations. These scholars point to the 1910 election of Thomas W. Fleming to the City Council, the first Black to hold such a position in a major northern city, as a reflection of Cleveland's tolerance and liberalism.[3] Others highlight the successes of numerous Blacks who held early positions as judges and state legislators. But such achievements among an elite group of Blacks within Cleveland did not translate into progress for the larger Black population.

Of the 8,448 Black people living in Cleveland at that time,[4] 60 percent resided in the central area, west of East 55th Street and north of Woodland and Cedar Avenue.[5] The early formation of what Kenneth L. Kusmer calls a "Black enclave" set the boundaries and zones for the location of African Americans.[6] This physical isolation transcended into the social and economic sphere as well. Typically employed in the unskilled or service sectors and denied access to the influential power of the labor unions, Blacks in Cleveland continually found themselves on the bottom of the economic totem pole. Even as theaters segregated the Black population and hotels refused to accommodate Blacks, Cleveland was still often perceived as one of the best places for "the Negro."[7]

Trickle-down equality hardly resulted in economic or social parity for the Black masses. As the few digested petty rewards from the power structure, the vast majority of Black Clevelanders endured deplorable conditions. Furthermore, the advances and rewards of the few reinforced the dominant paradigm of the Protestant work ethic, which argued that anybody could rise above social discrimination and obtain elite status. Aside from the economic disparity, Blacks, who constituted a mere 1.5 percent of the population in 1910,[8] were not seen as a threat to the resources controlled by white people. But as the Black community grew, the city's elite attempted to further safeguard their own social and cultural standing, as well as their own economic possessions. As such, the numerical increase in the Black community was met with a clearer articulation of the position that Blacks were to assume within the hierarchical order. In other words, the growth in population was used to justify high rates of Black unemployment, increased rents for deteriorating housing in an already overpopulated East Side, and unequal educational facilities.

The exodus of southern Blacks to northern industrial centers was fueled by a combination of factors, most notably a need for cheap labor, low wages down South, untenable land, and southern white repression. From 1915 to 1919, a sharp drop in European immigrants affected industrial employers who depended on their cheap labor.[9] Thus, during and after World War I, the Great Migration of Blacks from the South cashed in on the opportunity to fill vacant job openings, mostly in unskilled labor.[10] As the North highlighted an ostensibly liberal social and political environment, Blacks had few misgivings about leaving the South in search of both employment and an escape from white supremacist brutality. In addition, southern mechanization of human labor required Black workers to find other means of subsistence. The transformation in the South of cotton farming from a labor-intensive economy to a capitalist, machine-oriented economy, a movement initiated and subsidized by political coalitions between organized farm operators and the federal government, eliminated the need for cheap Black labor.[11] Finally, migration by southern Blacks was instigated by natural disasters such as the boll weevil plague and the floods of 1910–1915, which paralyzed the southern agricultural economy. Rose summarizes the movement of Blacks to the North, and specifically Cleveland, with a quote from State Senator Harry E. Davis, a lone Black legislator in the Ohio House in 1920:

> War industries . . . induced a mass movement of colored workers into Cleveland which almost completely submerged the older elements of the colored population. Industry sent agents into the South to recruit labor, and they were brought to Cleveland in carloads. Many of them came with only the clothing they were wearing, with no preparation for housing, and with little idea of the problems they must inevitably encounter.[12]

There were few social institutions or organizations established to support newly arrived Blacks, and the government fulfilled its role by squeezing the Black population into smaller colonies.

Following World War II, Cleveland, like other northern cities, saw another influx of Blacks migrating from the South. In 1930, the Black population was 72,469 people (8 percent). By 1940, the Black population had risen to 147,847 residents (16 percent) and the percentage continued to increase as whites fled to the suburbs.[13] Although Blacks spread into new domains, by 1950 the housing shortage remained a problem, and school construction in Black neighborhoods lagged behind the growing number of children.

During the 1960s, the movement of Blacks within the city challenged the territorial possession of whites. The 1960 census reported that Cuyahoga County's Black population increased from 87,145 in 1940 to 255,310 in 1960. As the white population continued to move to the suburbs, Cleveland's Black population was centralized within the inner city, largely around East Cleveland and the Ludlow area of Shaker Heights. In fact, 90 percent of Blacks in Cleveland resided in the eastern side of the city.[14] Blacks increasingly began to migrate northeast along St. Clair Avenue toward East Cleveland, and southeast down Lee, Miles, Harvard, and Kinsman toward the city limits. The movement away from the dense inner city was an attempt by Blacks to obtain better housing and schooling for their children. The Black middle class had the means to make the first move, migrating to Glenville, then to Mt. Pleasant, and farther into Lee-Seville and Lee-Harvard. The small group of Blacks who left the inner city were middle-aged and rarely had children under fifteen years of age.[15]

By 1960, Cleveland was the eighth-largest city in the United States with 250,818 Black residents (29 percent of the total population in Cleveland[16]). The Urban League reported that "[b]etween 1950 and 1960, the city's white population declined from 765,300 to 622,900, that is, lost one-fifth of its 1950 total. From 1960 to 1963, an estimated 44,500 white residents left the city."[17] Furthermore, Cleveland's Black population became more youthful as the white population grew older. Cleveland's Black population found itself increasingly segregated into the restricted areas of the East Side. In what looked like an American apartheid city, 98.2 percent of all Black people lived within East Cleveland, which follows the pattern set in April of 1910, when 97.6 percent of Black Clevelanders lived in the inner city.[18] The Urban League reported that "[i]n 1963, an estimated 277,600 out of 287,000 Negro county residents lived in the eastern third of the central city in contiguous census tracts covering about 15 square miles."[19] Segregated within St. Clair Avenue, Broadway, Corlett, Lee Road, Harvard, Miles, and the eastern suburbs, Blacks were relegated to a specific location, both physically and ideologically. As one Black man facetiously remarked, it was as if "[w]e are liable to contaminate someone."[20]

The areas of Central, Hough, Glenville, Mt. Pleasant, and Kinsman contained 90 percent of Cleveland's Black population. Lost within these figures, however, is why these areas were the enclaves, the ghettos. Consistent with the dominant order, Black people were relegated to the oldest and most dilapidated sections of the city. For instance, the Hough community's development is representative of the larger situation in Cleveland's Black neighborhoods. In 1950, only 3.9 percent of the Hough population was Black. By 1960, as buildings wore down, the Black population of Hough increased to 73 percent.[21] As the population increased in the Black community, so did the demand for work.

Employment and Unemployment

Whether employed in the most dehumanizing jobs or not employed at all, Blacks were rarely given any breaks. As discussed above, the industrial expansion associated with defense spending in World War II created increased job openings in northern cities. With no other choice, employers turned to the newly arriving southern Blacks for jobs. As Russell Davis notes, many employers looked to the Urban League for advice on integrating Blacks into the organizational structure. Yet Davis again misses the philosophical stance of white employers when he states, "[t]o be sure [the Black worker] was first assigned the simple tasks of machine operation but the ice was broken and he had entry into a field that heretofore had been denied to him."[22] In actuality, Black workers were assigned those jobs because they were the least desirable and white employers needed a new pool of labor to exploit. This ice-breaking ceremony was not an attempt to be kind to Blacks; it was done out of economic necessity. Furthermore, the fact that Blacks were relegated to the most demeaning forms of labor reaffirms the conceptual notion of the dominant order, which defined Blacks as lesser human beings.

In addition, Davis fails to take into consideration the employer's interest in creating worker dissension rather than worker solidarity. Blacks who moved into the labor force were quickly depicted as invaders of white work as they took less pay for the same jobs, and white workers thus directed their frustration toward Black workers rather than toward their white employers. Kusmer discusses the earlier use of Black laborers as strikebreakers, hiring them on a temporary basis and paying them less.[23] The perpetuation of this division within the surplus labor pool has been fundamental to the white property owner's maintenance of the cultural and economic order. Furthermore, the unions in Cleveland rarely represented Black people. For example, in 1966, statistics were given to the Civil Rights Commission in Cleveland on the numbers of journeymen and apprentices in each union.[24] Collectively, the unions had 7,122 journeymen who were white and 51 who were Black; of the apprentices, 609 were white and only 4 were Black.[25]

As noted above, Black workers predominantly occupied the unskilled and undesirable labor ranks. Whereas whites often worked as managers with salaries, Blacks always found themselves in the worst-paying jobs.[26] In addition, Herman Stein noted that "[o]f employed Negro women [in 1965], 56 percent hold menial service jobs, of which half are in private households."[27] The Urban League confirmed the predicament, stating that "as a rule, Negroes are given jobs in the lowest occupational categories."[28]

Even as Blacks began to make headway into industrial positions, technological advances in manufacturing quickly eliminated them from the payrolls. As the Urban League reported, "[s]ince 1953, manufacturing industries have declined in the total number of workers employed. Some 80,000 factory blue-collar jobs, mainly in heavy industry—steel mill, foundry, machinery—have disappeared from the Cleveland area, while, at the same time, some 30,000 non-factory white-collar jobs were making an appearance on the labor market." Following World War II, the Black labor force found itself the most affected by the downsizing in the industrial employment sector. The Urban League stated, "[i]n 1960, nearly two-thirds of the Negro employed labor force worked as semi-skilled operatives (26% mostly in manufacturing), service workers (26%) and laborers (12%)."[29] Furthermore, as increases in technological automation eliminated the need for the lowest-skilled workers, Blacks found themselves in the unemployment lines. Although Davis remarks on the advances of laborsaving machinery and the rise in unemployment in 1960, he neglects to mention who was hardest hit by such measures.[30] As construction and manufacturing jobs evaporated with the advancement of technological automation, so did employment for Blacks.[31] Employment downsizing normally meant that Blacks, as the unskilled laborers, lost their jobs first.

The corollary to Blacks having the worst jobs is that Blacks would also be paid the least. The income of Blacks was considerably less than that of whites; 56 percent of the Black population was receiving an income of less than $3,000, compared to only 40.2 percent of the white population.[32] Income limitations meant limited choices in housing for members of the Black community and, in turn, affected the quality of schools for Black children. Yet with no income, these choices were almost nonexistent. In December 1963, Blacks constituted over a third of the unemployed, or 11,900 out of a total of 34,000. Within the Black community, 10.5 percent of the population was unemployed, as opposed to 3.2 percent of the white population.[33]

Housing Conditions

Velma Jean Woods and her husband moved into the Clevelander Apartments on East 93rd in June 1957. The Woodses were only the second Black family to move into the seven-story, seventy-two-unit apartment complex. As the Cleveland Black population expanded and entered into new territories, white people first resisted, then eventually fled. Some white families departed as quickly as the Woodses moved in; others were forced out as rent escalated with the new Black tenants. Whereas the elder white tenants had a fixed rent which rarely fluctuated, the arrival of Black tenants provided the impetus for landlords to maximize profits. As elder white occupants disappeared, so did decent landlord service. By 1964, the Clevelander had deteriorated as rents continued to escalate. The elevator had not worked in two years, roaches and rats made daily appearances, and maintenance workers rarely showed their faces.[34]

Mrs. Woods's story was similar to the experiences of many Black people in Cleveland. Overcrowding, high rents, and shoddy maintenance were typical of the dwellings located in the Black community. Davis notes that in one census tract of the Black community, "99 percent of the approximately 1,200 dwellings had serious deficiencies in 1950." He continues, "[h]ousing fifty or more years old, [was] occupied by a succession of families of poorer and poorer circumstances and by absentee owners."[35] White landlords ignored the situation and refused to upgrade living facilities. The response from the city of Cleveland was to invoke programs of "slum clearance." Lawrence Brisker notes that as families were forced out of one neighborhood, they would double up with relatives or friends in another community, contributing to its increasing deterioration.[36] In addition, home owners eagerly converted family homes into smaller apartments and profited off Black residents who had been forced out of overcrowded "slum" areas.

With little choice of where to live, Blacks were usually segregated into central Cleveland and East Cleveland, which in turn created immense overpopulation. However, like the situation at the Clevelander Apartments, as Blacks moved into the city, whites flocked to the suburbs. This provided some working-class Black families the opportunity to purchase decent housing in areas such as Glenville and Mount Pleasant during the later 1950s. In time, the Black population would swell to where neighborhood expansion was inevitable, regardless of white resistance. The shortage of low-income housing for the majority of Blacks initiated public housing construction by the Cleveland Metropolitan Housing Authority in 1944. Projects such as Carver Park and Outwaite Homes alleviated some of the shortage, but had little effect on the overall density problem.[37]

In 1957, the government constructed the Longwood apartment complex between East 33rd and East 40th Streets, with 836 units. In addition, along 79th Street south of Kinsman in the central area, the government built the Garden Valley public housing project.[38] Davis argues that the surroundings of these public housing projects, notably poor schools and "slums," led to rapid turnover of residents.[39] Furthermore, the establishment of public housing units contributed to an escalating frustration and hopelessness as Blacks were partitioned into specific segments of the city. In combination with the social issues previously mentioned, the poorer sections of Black Cleveland were waiting for an organization to confront the resource allocation of the dominant order and challenge the inferior status of Blacks.

Overcrowding within Cleveland's residential Black communities overshadowed the increase in Black home ownership during the 1950s, as the Urban League reported a home ownership jump from 8,782 to 19,621.[40] Far from being dispersed throughout the Black community, this growth was restricted to the older segments of the Black community, who most often only moved to the outer boundaries of the original Black Cleveland. As middle-class Blacks attempted to move outside of Glenville, Hough, and Mt. Pleasant, white property owners were not hospitable. Protests erupted in the Lee-Harvard area in 1953 as white residents stoned and smeared paint on a house being pursued by a Black buyer. Likewise, one home constructed for a Black family in the Ludlow area was bombed in 1956. But not all white residents shared this hostility. Whites and Blacks united and formed the Ludlow Community Association in 1957 in support of an integrated neighborhood.[41]

In general, the housing situation in Cleveland was deplorable. An official for the U.S. Commission on Civil Rights testified that "[h]ousing conditions have not changed substantially since the 1960 Census and at that time 9,000 Negro families in the city lived in substandard dwellings, over 13,000 were in overcrowded houses, and among renters nearly 24,000 paid a quarter or more of their total income for rent."[42] In 1960, 28.2 percent of all housing occupied by Blacks was below the minimum standard, either dilapidated or deteriorating, compared to only 7.4 percent of white people's housing.[43]

Effects of De Facto Segregation in the Public School System

Glenville's Patrick Henry Junior High was a typical public school in Cleveland's Black community. The facilities were inadequate to accommodate its 2,100 students. Overcrowding burdened teachers and inhibited the learning potential of the students. Mrs. Percy Cunningham, a science teacher at Patrick Henry, explained, "I teach in a science room that is in the basement. There is very little, if any, as far as facilities, as far as pictures on the wall, and microscopes and equipment that can be used."[44] To no surprise, she continued to say that most of the students' achievement was lower than it should have been.

For Blacks, the experience in the Cleveland public school system was no different from the experiences in employment and housing. The racial polarization noted earlier in the population figures created two different educational systems in Cleveland—one for Blacks and one for whites. As the Urban League reported, "[s]ixty percent of all public elementary schools in the Cleveland school district [were] either all-white or all-Negro." Likewise, they documented that 40 percent of public junior high schools and 58 percent of public senior high schools in the city were completely segregated.[45] But these figures are extremely conservative when compared to the U.S. Commission on Civil Rights' document "Staff Report, Education, Cleveland, Ohio."[46] Testifying on behalf of the commission, Richard Bellman stated that "[i]n the 169 schools considered, it was found that 82.6 percent of the children are attending schools with a population either 95 to 100 percent white or 95 to 100 percent Negro." White teachers predominantly taught at white schools and Black teachers were assigned to all-Black schools.[47] Furthermore, the expenditure per child was less in the inner city than in white school districts, and the ratio of teacher to student was also considerably different: 60 per 1,000 students in the white community, 39 per 1,000 in the Black community.[48] Integrationists organized around the public school arrangement to confront the institutionalized white racism.

Murray Hill, Cleveland's "Little Italy," and Collinwood were the settings for confrontation over the schooling of Black children in Cleveland during the early part of the 1960s. In the summer of 1963, a new coalition was born called the United Freedom Movement (UFM), uniting Black ministers, Jewish leaders, traditional Black leaders, and the new militants of Cleveland.[49] The UFM was formed to protest the deployment of Black children to overcrowded Black schools while white schools had vacant spaces. The UFM also criticized the construction of two new schools within Cleveland's run-down Black enclaves, seeing them as steps that inhibited integration. At a planned protest in Murray Hill in January 1964, Black demonstrators and passersby were beaten by a mob of white residents, with little police intervention. After Mayor Ralph Locher refused to intervene, he quickly became the target of a sit-in in February.[50] Police forcibly removed Black ministers and community activists who were occupying the Board of Education building, and the images of community members being dragged out by the police remained in the consciousness of the Black community.

The situation of children in public schools mirrored the larger situation of the Black community in Cleveland. In 1964, the report by the Cleveland Urban League stated that if the disparities between Blacks and whites were not rectified, the city would be on the verge of destruction. Two years later, on July 18, 1966, Cleveland erupted.

The Rise of Black Militancy and Political Power

As the student sit-ins began in the South, the Cleveland National Association for the Advancement of Colored People (NAACP) followed with a persistent picketing of white companies in the early 1960s to protest against unfair hiring practices. Out of this protest, Lewis Robinson and the demonstrators formed the Freedom Fighters, first to monetarily assist students and communities of Black sharecroppers in the South, then focusing on discriminatory practices within Cleveland.[51] Through the support of the NAACP, the Freedom Fighters pushed the Cleveland civil rights agenda during the early part of the 1960s, targeting the practices of Cleveland's banks, department stores, and public offices to deny certain privileges to Black people. As Robinson described in his memoirs, "[t]hese were Freedom Fighters! A group of factory workers, not peoples with degrees; not the bourgeois, but hungry ex-southerners like me who came north looking for equality and brotherhood and discovered that you had to fight even harder than in the South."[52] Robinson and the Freedom Fighters laid the groundwork for a new militancy within the Black community.

During the early months of 1966, hostility between white and Black youths escalated to a boiling point. Roving gangs of white youths provoked Blacks walking by Cleveland's Little Italy.[53] As the police made excuses for their inability to charge the perpetrators, militant organizations like Robinson's new JFK House began to mobilize opposition. Following a series of meetings with Black youths, Robinson and fellow Black Nationalist Harllel Jones attempted to contain the general youth frustration with the police's inadequate response and the behavior of the white youths. Meetings, however, could not calm the response following the shooting of a Black woman on a bus in a white neighborhood. On July 18, 1966, tensions escalated and finally boiled over at the Seventy-Niner's Café on East 79th Street and Hough Avenue, when the white owner refused to serve a drink to a Black customer and then placed a sign outside reading "No Water for Niggers."[54] The crowd that had gathered in front of the café became furious, hurling rocks and initiating four nights of rebellion in Hough that left four dead and ten wounded.

Cleveland's political establishment was unable to recuperate in the aftermath of the rebellion. Thus, Hough set the stage for Cleveland's most tumultuous political change. As the incumbent Democratic mayor Ralph Locher lost support from his political power base, the door opened for a new political machine. After defeating Locher in the Democratic primary, Carl B. Stokes became the first Black mayor of a major industrial city as he squeaked out a victory over the Republic Seth Taft in the 1967 election.[55] Some considered the victory a gift from the white establishment, which hoped Stokes would contain the "hostility" of the Black youth. As City Council member Leo Jackson stated, the business community was purchasing security when they elected a Black mayor in 1967.[56]

With Stokes in office, sectors of the Black community looked for answers to their lack of employment, substandard housing, and inadequate education. In response, Stokes initiated his Cleveland: NOW! campaign to confront the conditions of the city's poor. The government mobilized businesses and foundations to donate more than $5.5 million toward community projects such as day-care and recreation centers, drug-treatment centers, and expansions of public housing facilities.[57] In advocating the increased expenditure of federal programs, however, Stokes perpetuated the flawed liberal ideology that government and profit-oriented enterprise could bring an end to poverty. Without seriously deconstructing the cultural system which allows for the existence of poverty, or the structure of economic production and exchange, Stokes had no chance of arriving at the solution. William Nelson further argues that Stokes refused to confront Cleveland's economic structure and thus could not alleviate the poverty imposed on unemployed Black workers.[58] The election of Stokes did, however, open the door for members of the Black middle class, who flowed into positions of government authority.

Stokes prided himself on uniting Black militants and accommodating white conservatives. His relationship with Afro Set leader Harllel Jones was often noted in the criticism of his administration's support of militants.[59] Yet Stokes was only in support of militancy or Black Power when it directly bene-fited him and his base of power. If Jones could keep the Black Nationalists in line, then Stokes had room for him in his circle of friends. In addition, Stokes relied heavily on the funding of the white establishment and "couldn't afford to do anything to aggravate the white voter."[60] Thus, when Dr. Martin Luther King Jr. visited Cleveland in 1967, Stokes informed him that "if you come here with those marches and what not, you can see what the reaction will be. . . . You're going to create problems that we do not have now and may not be able to handle. I would rather that you not stay."[61] Stokes had no intention of being criticized by the nation's leading civil rights leader.

As noted earlier, the situation in Cleveland had reached a boiling point during the mid-1960s with the Hough rebellion. Likewise, as the promises of a Black mayor faded, segments of Cleveland's Black community again geared up for resistance. Black Nationalists expressed their concerns to deaf ears as the police continued to harass political activists. Police were often perceived as an occupying army in the Black community, and they harassed Black residents with no repercussions. Suffice to say that the police department was never seen as an ally of Black residents. The situation that unfolded in Glenville established the tone of Black militancy and of Stokes's position.

On July 23, 1968, an abandoned Cadillac on Beulah Avenue was scheduled to be towed by the Cleveland Police Department. As two civilians dressed as police officers, William McMillan and Roy Benslay, began removing the Cadillac, shots rang out from the bushes and from the area in front of the car, the first shots in a rebellion supposedly initiated by Fred Ahmed Evans. McMillan later recounted: "The snipers set up the ambush and used the tow truck as a decoy to bring the police in. They had their crossfire all planned. We were sitting ducks." The ambush theory was widely accepted throughout Cleveland, but Louis Masotti and Jerome Corsi, in their government-commissioned investigation, cast doubt on the theory after gathering additional information from individuals who had spoken with Evans that evening.[62]

On the night of the shootout, Ahmed Evans had Councilman George Forbes and others at his house.[63] The Cleveland Police Department had given Forbes and other Cleveland officials information from the FBI that Evans and his organization, the Black Nationalists of New Libya, were planning an attack on July 24th in conjunction with organized riots in Akron and Canton.[64] Furthermore, the Masotti and Corsi report listed Stokes, Councilman Leo Jackson, William Walker (publisher of the Black newspaper the *Call and Post*), community activist Baxter Hill, and patrolman James Payne as assassination targets. With shaky information from the informants, police decided to institute a mobile surveillance of Evans's apartment with Black police officers. However, when Forbes arrived at Evans's apartment, two cars full of whites were stationed in front of the building.[65]

During Forbes's stay, Evans expressed concern about the potential of seemingly harmless police surveillance. He had just witnessed a police raid on a Black Nationalist headquarters in Akron, where police had tear-gassed and clubbed the organization's members. Forbes, however, was unsuccessful in removing the police vehicle stationed across the street from Evans's residence, and he soon left the premises. Shortly after, shots rang out and the Glenville rebellion began. The following hour, from 8:30 to 9:30 P.M., twenty-two people were either killed or injured.[66] Masotti reconstructs the events to show that the police officers who were on surveillance became targets only after Evans became threatened. Rather than a planned ambush, Evans and his organization claimed to have acted in self-defense.

Stokes's decision to take all the white members of the National Guard, police force, and nonresidents out of the Glenville area created a situation in which Black people finally had community control. The shooting halted after Stokes placed Black community leaders and police officers directly in the community. Stokes, however, was not interested in the grievances of the Black community who were caught in the gunfire of the Glenville rebellion.[67] His primary concern was establishing law and order in the Glenville area.

The prominence of Black Nationalism and the election of Stokes in 1967 sparked an elevation in consciousness. Members of Cleveland's Black community whose political awareness was developing began to join a variety of Black Nationalist organizations. Others who were not content with the ideological direction of Black Nationalism made plans to establish a local chapter of the Black Panther Party.

The Beginnings of the Cleveland Black Panthers

As gunshots rang out in Glenville on the evening of July 23, 1968, the murder trial of BPP leader Huey P. Newton, who was being tried for the alleged murder of Officer John Frey in Oakland the previous year, was only one week old. Just as Newton's trial was galvanizing the consciousness of Blacks on the West Coast, the summer rebellion in Glenville elevated the consciousness of Cleveland's Black communities, spurring greater political activity and Black militancy. The timing of the Glenville riots and the "Free Huey" campaign represents not only a symbolic convergence, but also a practical one—one that set the stage for the growth of the BPP into a national movement.

The initial appearance of the Panthers in Cleveland came by way of two avenues: first through the activities of unofficial, self-declared Panthers; and second through the activities of criminals who were labeled Black Panthers by the state. The first sightings of Panthers surfaced in late September 1968, when the Young Socialist Alliance at Case Western Reserve University (CWRU) organized a meeting with a group that called itself the Black Panthers. Dressed in full Panther regalia, the self-appointed Panther Marvin Wolf-Bey and five others addressed the crowd of 140, most of them students, with the standard Panther rhetoric. Wolf-Bey recited the BPP Ten-Point Program and demanded justice for minister of defense Huey P. Newton, stating that "Panthers will protect other Blacks by any means necessary."[68] Over the course of that year, numerous newspaper articles declared Wolf-Bey the leader of the Black Panthers in Cleveland and listed their headquarters as East 78th Street and Hough Avenue. The *Cleveland Press* reported, for example, that the "Black Panthers, formerly an unrecognized group here, last week were officially chartered as a member of the national Black Panther Party."[69] Yet the national BPP leadership continually denied the existence of an official branch of the Party in Cleveland until the winter of 1970. In the meantime, Wolf-Bey's tenure as a self-styled Panther ended behind prison bars. In July 1970, he pled guilty to both the murder of James Ferguson Jr. and to shooting at firefighters.[70]

Even though the national BPP never recognized Wolf-Bey as a Black Panther, Cleveland law enforcement seized the opportunity to connect him with officially recognized Black Panthers. Assistant County Prosecutor Charles Laurie remarked, for example, that Wolf-Bey's plea was significant because it was "the first time Black Panthers admitted shooting at safety forces."[71] The state's labeling of criminals as Black Panthers proved to be effective in influencing popular sentiment, and the media's negative depiction of the Panthers also influenced the public's perception of the Party. For example, the alleged shootout between the Afro Set (the largest Black militant outfit in Cleveland) and Black Panthers was publicized as a war between the two organizations.[72] Although the individuals involved were never official members of the Black Panther Party, the Cleveland media followed the story circulated by the police and stigmatized the image of the BPP before its local inception.

Other "Black Panthers" made headlines in the Cleveland papers, primarily for murder or other violent crimes.[73] While these criminal activities reinforced the dominant representation of the BPP, it is also quite possible that the self-appointed Panthers saw themselves as real Party members after they dressed in the black garb and tossed on a beret. They may have even thought that killing an alleged CIA agent was a revolutionary act.[74] Cleveland during this time was flooded with cultural and political organizations, and the identity of a Black Panther commanded respect and prestige, with or without official approval from national headquarters. These youths were the "brothers on the block" whom Newton and Bobby Seale hoped to organize for political action.[75] The BPP attempted to funnel the collective frustration of the inner city into the workings of a revolutionary political machine. Yet without a local political organization in Cleveland to coordinate the activities of Black youths, revolutionary criminal activities were sure to be met with state violence.

Lindsay Maddox proclaimed to head a separate group that identified itself as the Cleveland Black Panther Party. In the summer of 1969, Maddox announced that the group had organized during the summer and had established an office at 7809 Superior Avenue with "about 500 members or applicants at one time."[76] After continual harassment from white vigilantes and the police, their funds were drained on bail, and by December the group had disintegrated. According to Maddox, the group had applied to national headquarters for a charter but disbanded before hearing back from the BPP leadership.

According to *The Black Panther* newspaper, there was no official chapter or branch of the BPP in Cleveland through 1969.[77] As will be discussed, every visit by the national Party leadership to Cleveland resulted in a denunciation by the leadership of the self-styled Panther activity in Cleveland. Furthermore, as most branches of the Party reported on their community programs or police repression in the weekly issues of *The Black Panther*, the alleged Panthers in Cleveland never had an article published through 1969.[78]

The Real Cleveland Panthers:
The Early Years

The emergence of the official Cleveland Panthers came after the BPP leadership established a strong alliance with leaders of Cleveland's anti-war movement—the "mother country radicals," as Newton labeled them.[79] Donald Freed, a playwright who organized a group called "Friends of the Panthers" in Los Angeles to raise funds for the Party, connected the Panther leadership with white liberals in Cleveland.[80] The BPP utilized the contacts with the progressive white movement in Cleveland to speak out on the unauthorized local Panther activities as well as to publicize the national activities and repression of the Party.

One of Freed's friends in Cleveland was Dr. Paul Zilsel, a professor at CWRU and head of the United Front for Political Defense. In association with Wilbur Gratton, minister of state and foreign affairs for the Republic of New Africa, they organized a series of speakers in May 1969 to focus on the state of American political prisoners.[81] Among the featured speakers was "Masai" Hewitt, the minister of education for the BPP, who made it clear that there were no legitimate BPP chapters in Cleveland.[82] Another progressive white was Sidney Peck, a sociology professor at CWRU, who was instrumental in organizing two visits by David Hilliard in October and December 1969.[83] During Hilliard's first visit to Cleveland, a radio interviewer informed him about "a lot of misinformation about the Party" in Cleveland.[84] Hilliard took advantage of the opportunity to "counteract the bad atmosphere caused by lies" and to reiterate that there was no official branch of the Party in Cleveland.[85]

In addition to denouncing the activities of unofficial Panthers, Hilliard used his speaking engagements to establish connections with local Black radicals who could possibly carry out a plan to mobilize segments of the Cleveland community around the tenets of the Party. One of those individuals was Ernest Watts, who was selling issues of the BPP newspaper, *The Black Panther*, with a small, integrated leadership core that included Robert Jackson, Wolf Raymer, and Wolf's wife, Debbie.[86] In December, Hilliard promised Watts he would send some organizers from Oakland or Detroit to coordinate the framework for a Panther operation in Cleveland.[87]

In July 1969, the BPP held a national conference from which emerged a new organizing bureau of the Party called the National Committee to Combat Fascism (NCCF).[88] The following year, individuals interested in establishing a BPP branch were told that the only operations being authorized were NCCF branches,[89] so Hilliard's promise to coordinate a Panther operation in Cleveland took the form of an NCCF branch in 1970. As the literature from the Cleveland Panther office later stated: "The NCCF Ohio Chapter is a social and political organization of the Black Panther Party. Our goals are to educate the masses of people in Cleveland as to the correct ideology of the Party."[90] In addition to these goals, the NCCF offices were used to incorporate white people into the BPP. For practical purposes, however, there was no difference between the two: the NCCF followed the Panther doctrine and instituted the same community programs as BPP branches and chapters.[91]

The Panthers in Cleveland were originally given the status of an NCCF branch for two possible reasons. First, the BPP closed ranks in 1969 in order to "cleanse" all agents provocateurs who had infiltrated the local branches and chapters.[92] New Panther operations were first given the title of NCCF as a method of screening potential Panthers. Once they proved their worthiness to the Party, national headquarters granted a branch or chapter. A second reason was because Hilliard was aware that Watts had connections with whites from the West Side. Although these individuals had actually left Cleveland before the spring of 1970, when the Cleveland Panthers began to make headway, it's likely that Hilliard and the BPP assumed that this leadership core was still an integrated coalition.

In any event, the distinction between the NCCF and the BPP branches was not always maintained, particularly in the minds of local members. One Cleveland NCCF member stated, "[Regardless of what we were called,] I always considered myself a Black Panther."[93] Given this fact, the title Cleveland Panthers will be used throughout this chapter to signify all official Panther activities in Cleveland, including both the early Cleveland NCCF and the later Cleveland Branch of the BPP.[94]

Despite their status as the Cleveland NCCF, the early Cleveland Panthers started on rocky terrain. Early on, dissension had crept into the small core of organizers, which included Watts, the Raymers, Jackson, and Jerry Lindsey.[95] Lindsey had initiated the strife in January 1970 when he phoned the national headquarters. He was adamant about banning white people, including the Raymers, from participating on the steering committee. Masai Hewitt's response to Lindsey was unsupportive, however, and Hewitt went so far as to state that "we control the NCCF from [Oakland] and if we can't control it, we will shut it down."[96]

Lindsey's antics continued to frustrate the BPP leadership.[97] Locally, Watts and the other core members were fed up with Lindsey as well. They too had contacted the national headquarters and informed them that Lindsey had solicited funds in the Party's name for personal use and had stolen Party literature. The BPP leadership found these observations to be credible and Lindsey was soon purged from the Party.[98]

Following the elimination of Lindsey, the Cleveland Panthers began to move in a more stable direction. Like other inexperienced Panther organizers, Watts visited the national headquarters in Oakland for a short time to become familiar with the BPP Ten-Point Program and the Party's organizational structure.[99] He returned to Cleveland and continued to sell *The Black Panther* in front of City Hall and Public Square. The paper proved to be a valuable organizing tool. In addition to serving as the Party's primary instrument of information, it gave local Panthers the opportunity to recruit new members.[100] During the late winter months of 1970, Ron Robinson, a former Black Nationalist, approached Watts and stated that he was interested in instituting some of the Panthers' community programs. Soon after, Robinson introduced Watts to Norman Peery and the three began to organize a series of community meetings to solidify the direction of the Party in Cleveland.[101]

Initially, the group began meeting at the Friendly Inn Settlement House, and later at the Garden Valley Neighborhood Community Center. Although the Panthers eventually obtained office space of their own, working in these venues provided the opportunity to interact with various other community institutions. In particular, Rev. Herman Graham, director of the Garden Valley Neighborhood Community Center, was impressed with the Panthers and their early organizing techniques. He stated, "We gave the NCCF office space because we looked on them as a community service agency. It didn't take long to realize they were doing something we couldn't do—reaching people we couldn't reach."[102]

By spring 1971, a collection of Panthers, including Robinson, Peery, and Watts, became attracted to the idea of establishing an office in the lower Kinsman neighborhood, where Robinson had grown up. It was important to establish the Panther office in a Black neighborhood, and according to Peery, the area was ideal because there were no established organizations and plenty of work to be done. The Afro Set had dominated the political activity in Hough, and the remnants of Ahmed Evans's Black Nationalists of New Libya controlled Glenville. This left lower Kinsman wide open.[103] Moreover, 79th Street was a main thoroughfare and would provide the Panthers with plenty of traffic. By June, the Cleveland Panthers' core group of fifteen (a number significantly smaller than the seventy-five that the FBI credited the Panthers with having) had moved their office to the corner of 79th and Rawlings.[104]

Years of Growth

The new recruits for the Cleveland Panthers came primarily from three camps: (1) committed and experienced Black radical activists; (2) college students; and (3) neighborhood high school teenagers.[105] As mentioned earlier, the political consciousness of Cleveland's Black community was heightened after the rebellions in Hough and Glenville. A number of organizations mobilized around the strong sentiments of Black Nationalism, and from these organizations emerged a core group of committed radicals. However, not all politically conscious insurgents were satisfied with the ideological tenets of the popular resistance movement in Cleveland. The maturation of the Black Panthers in Cleveland largely came as a result of this frustration, as a small cadre of Black radicals searched for a new avenue to confront the conditions in the Black community.

Peery was among this cadre. He had attended some Afro Set meetings before he committed himself to the Panther vision of self-defense.[106] Uninterested in the cultural nationalist foundation of the Afro Set, Peery explained that he "especially liked the fact that [the Panthers] were willing to pick up the gun and organize to defend themselves and their community."[107] The BPP's revolutionary assertiveness gave frustrated Black radicals a different approach to confronting the social order. In addition, the BPP stimulated a new form of insurgency by blending the principles of armed self-defense with the establishment of community institutions that addressed the material needs of local Blacks.

Essex Smith, who joined the Cleveland Panthers after graduating from Kennedy High School, was also influenced by the alternative vision of the Party. He stated, "I was disillusioned with the Black Nationalists and I was looking for an organization that was more progressive, . . . that was doing some education and some teaching and also had social programs, which the Panthers did."[108] Likewise, Robinson was a former Black Nationalist who was frustrated with the limited philosophy of the movement. The BPP provided him the opportunity to dig into the works of international thinkers.[109]

Complementing the discontented Black radicals who joined the Cleveland Panthers, the Party also drew heavily from the various local college campuses. Panthers such as Al Hayes, Fred Clark, Richard "Mike" Dowell, and Curtis Johnson were taking classes at Cuyahoga Community College (Tri-C) as they participated in the daily operations of the Party.[110] Some of these students were involved in political activities before they joined the BPP. Cleveland Panther Bill Davis, for example, was active in organizing the Black Student Union at Cleveland State University and joined the Panthers after he witnessed Bobby Seale shackled and gagged in the Chicago Seven trial.[111] Other students were recruited into the organization from the audience after the leadership of the Cleveland Panthers made speeches at the campus meetings of Black organizations.[112] A particularly effective member in this effort was James "Rock" Todd, the deputy chairman of the Cleveland Panthers. One Cleveland Panther recalls, "I remember hearing Rock talk. I was so impressed with him. He could get up and rap the Party line—he was saying things I had never heard."[113]

As the Cleveland Panthers recruited students from college campuses, they simultaneously mobilized the final component of their core: the teenage youth in the Kinsman and Central areas. The new Panther office quickly enticed neighborhood high school students like Allan "Red" Gaines, Danny Solomon, Daryl "Mad Dog" Harris, and the Hall brothers.[114] Initially attracted to the confidence surrounding the Panther image, these youths were organized by the Party into a social and political force in the community. The teens actively participated in political education classes and worked in the community programs. As Robinson recalls, "[the teens] were taught that this is part of what it means to be a part of the Black Panther Party. . . . You didn't become a Panther to wear a beret and a jacket. You came to work in the community to help people with the problems they had daily."[115]

Older Panthers like Bill Davis stressed the importance of the Kinsman youth in the success of the Cleveland Panthers: "[T]hey were willing to work. They had the energy. They were willing to organize, go downtown, and stand on the corner for eight hours a day selling papers."[116] Likewise, when the Panthers moved locations and opened the free breakfast program, it was the youths who were instrumental in these transitions.[117] The Cleveland Panthers utilized the new recruits in the Kinsman neighborhood in a variety of community political institutions, including the free breakfast program, a reading program, and basic political education classes for Party members and for the community as well.[118] In addition, the Cleveland Panthers carried out the first phase of their community health program, going door to door with volunteer doctors and doing routine health checks and blood tests. As the Cleveland Panthers expanded and became more effective in the surrounding community, local and federal law enforcement took notice and initiated their campaign to eliminate the Party's local operations.

In late June 1970, the Cleveland Panthers caught the attention of the popular media and residents outside the Kinsman area after a shootout with police at their office. The incident defined the context of hostility between the Cleveland Panthers and the Black political establishment, namely Mayor Stokes and his public safety director, Gen. Benjamin Davis Jr. As the Panthers were categorized as a threat to the established order, they swiftly became legitimate targets to be eliminated.

The Repression of the Cleveland Panthers

Clashes with Local Law Enforcement

When the BPP picked up the gun in October 1966, the leaders of the social order moved swiftly to label them as the primary enemy. The Panthers were stigmatized as the prophets of hate, brainwashing children and seeking to "off the pigs." With these public descriptions, police and federal officials could justify the force they used to squash the Party.

Just as the FBI's campaign worked nationally to intimidate leaders of the Party, Cleveland officials attempted to fuel confrontations between the Panthers and other Black Nationalist organizations in Cleveland as well as between Blacks and the police.

To no one's surprise, in July 1968, Cleveland erupted again. This time, Fred Ahmed Evans and the Black Nationalists of New Libya were involved in a shootout with Cleveland police officers. After five days of rebellion in Glenville, seven were dead and fifteen others were wounded. What resulted from this insurgency was a more repressive environment where organizations like the Panthers were subject to intensified harassment and hostility. Stokes took full advantage of the opportunity and set the stage for the eventual elimination of the Cleveland Panthers.

The Black Panthers in Cleveland never had any lofty ideas about the direction of the Black community during the mayorship of Stokes. Public-speaking appearances by Cleveland Panthers usually contained fiery criticism of Stokes and his political machine.[120] They accused him of serving the interests of the white establishment and withholding support for organizations in the poor Black communities.[121] In Panther terms, Stokes was a "traditional white-endorsed, black-faced candidate."[122] In response, Stokes simply ignored the Panthers and attempted to create the illusion that they never existed in Cleveland.[123] This tactic disappeared, however, in January 1970, when Mayor Stokes appointed General Benjamin Davis Jr. as the city's new safety director. Davis immediately began a campaign against crime and "enemies of law enforcement." The Cleveland Panthers proved to be an easy target.

In the early afternoon of June 29, 1970, Cleveland Panthers Fred Clark, Mike Dowell, and Curtis Johnson were driving to the Panther office on 79th and Rawlings from the Cuyahoga Community College campus. Clark recalls being nervous the whole ride over, a sense that "something just didn't feel right." After the three arrived at the Panther office, Clark went upstairs in the front room and sat down at the typewriter to finish some paperwork. Johnson and Dowell were downstairs and the rest of the office was empty. Clark peered out the window and saw a few white cars pass in front, but thought nothing of it. Minutes later, both sides of the street were filled with police officers and federal law enforcement officials. Clark heard one shot. Then a barrage of bullets flooded the room he was in. One ricocheted and struck him in the back of the head, and Clark fell to the floor. Partially dazed, he wandered into the hallway, only to be shot again in the abdomen. Police stormed the office and dragged him outside, half-conscious with blood flowing everywhere.[124]

The raid on the Cleveland Panther headquarters was officially to serve warrants that had been requested by Thomas Avery, the owner of Avery's Pharmacy, located across the street from the Panther office. Avery contended that Cleveland Panthers had threatened his life and demanded money from him.[125] He contacted the police, who jumped at the chance to instigate a confrontation. Between fifty and seventy-five police officers from the Cleveland Tactical Squad arrived at Panther headquarters that afternoon to serve "peace warrants" on Johnson and Robert Hall.[126] The squad was dressed in full battle gear: dark steel helmets, bulletproof vests, carbines with plastic grips, and no badges. As the Panthers later stated, these are "familiar sights in the Black communities across the country of Babylon."[127] The police alleged that they were greeted with gunfire upon their arrival and had returned shots. Clark was the only Panther wounded; Officer Heinrich Ortag was shot in the jaw and a resident in the area, Mary Smith, was injured when an officer struck her in the foot with the butt of his rifle.[128]

The Cleveland Panthers denied demanding money from Avery and accused the police of using the feud as an excuse to execute a military assault on the Party. Consistent with the declaration of the BPP in *The Black Panther*, "[e]ach raid that has been pulled on all of our offices and homes has been . . . to kill and/or jail as many Panthers as possible."[129] The police walked away with Clark, Dowell, and Johnson in handcuffs, arrested for allegedly shooting with the intent to kill a police officer. In addition, the tactical squad illegally confiscated tape recorders, cameras, office machines, and files from the Panther office, even though these items were not listed on the warrants.[130]

In support of the Panthers, neighborhood residents retaliated and looted Avery's store that evening, forcing him to move out the following week. They spray-painted "Avery Killed Fred" and "Avenge Fred's Death" on his storefront after seeing Clark carried away on a stretcher with blood flowing from his head.[131] In addition, a coalition of white clergy, peace groups, and college groups denounced the tactics of the Cleveland police, stating:

> the police raid on the [Panthers] is consistent with the police practice in this city for the past five or six years. It is also consistent with the national wave of violent political repression that is sweeping this country with national guard and police bullets.[132]

In a similar and surprising tone, Cleveland's Black newspaper, *Call and Post*, criticized Davis and the police tactics, stating that "[s]omeone needs to answer whether or not it has become Cleveland police policy to resort to massive show of force when seeking to apprehend suspects in the Black community."[133]

The force exhibited in the raid was just the beginning of a police harassment campaign against the Cleveland Panthers. Panthers and residents of the Central area complained that police drove by day and night with their guns pointed at the Panther office.[134] The director of the Legal Aid Society's Kinsman office, Ramon Basie, had an office a half—block away from the Panthers'. He asked police on numerous occasions to avoid bringing guns in the area and pointing them at the Panthers.[135] As soon as the Panthers set up shop, he said there was an "increased police presence in the area. . . . I heard from neighborhood youths of weekend visits by policemen, 40 strong and pointing guns at people."[136] Moreover, Basie noted that this was an area that normally got delayed or inadequate responses from the police when their assistance was requested.

Following the raid, the Cleveland Panthers were quick to demand Davis's resignation. They also rallied protesters for the indictment hearings of Clark, Dowell, and Johnson at the Criminal Courts Building on July 21, 1970.[137] Similar to the Panther tactics at the trial of Huey P. Newton, the Cleveland Panthers distributed flyers stating that they would pack the courtroom hearing and picket the building.[138] However, the hearing was canceled after Clark, Dowell, and Johnson were indicted by a county grand jury earlier in the morning.[139] A month later, as the Cleveland Panthers organized again for the preliminary hearings, common pleas judge Frank Gorman canceled the session, stating that "[u]ndercover city detectives informed us that friends of the defendants had been conducting a widespread campaign to pack the courtroom with the Black Panthers. There might have been trouble." In response, Cleveland Panthers' lawyer Frederic Ferrell informed the judge that they would plead not guilty and have their day in court.[140]

The trial against the three Panthers did not start until June of the following year, and Clark remained imprisoned the entire time.[141] During the trial, Ferrell argued that police had harassed the Party in the weeks before the incident and had used the "peace warrants" to launch a military assault on the office. The state presented no evidence that any of the five weapons in the Panther office had been fired, and in particular never presented a clear case that the bullet in Ortag's jaw came from a Panther gun. Still, a twelve-person jury, consisting of ten whites, convicted all three Panthers.[142]

Although the trial was successful in the eyes of Stokes and other establishment figures, the coalition of Black leaders in City Hall was not as solid as it appeared. A month after the raid on the Panther headquarters at 79th Street, General Davis resigned as safety director, citing Mayor Stokes's inadequate support for his programs. In particular, Davis stated that Stokes was supporting certain "enemies of law enforcement," including the Cleveland Council of Churches, the *Call and Post*, and the Friendly Inn Settlement House.[143] For the most part, the accusations were ludicrous, and the mayor made Davis look foolish in front of the press. Stokes, however, agreed with Davis on the lawlessness of one organization, the Friendly Inn. The issue was not so much the house as it was the individuals who were using it, namely the Cleveland Panthers. As Stokes said, "I shared [General Davis's] dismay at [the Friendly Inn Settlement House's] being used as the meeting place of the National Committee to Combat Fascism." After Stokes was repeatedly criticized in the Panthers' literature, he saw no problem in declaring the Panthers an enemy and taking measures to eliminate them.[144]

The most disturbing plan Stokes and Davis initiated involved dum-dum bullets. Following the raid on the Panthers, General Davis placed an order for thirty thousand hollow-point cartridges, or dum-dums, which expand after they hit a target and cause serious damage to internal organs. When the issue went public, Stokes presented himself as the virtuous one. He quoted the Geneva Conventions that outlawed the bullets and quickly demanded that Davis withdraw the bid. Yet the meetings Stokes had behind closed doors on the issue connect him with a larger campaign, one that uncovers his abhorrence of the Cleveland Panthers. Although Stokes had publicly decried the use of "any hollow point cartridges," he appeared to have one exception.[145] During an internal meeting, Stokes jotted notes down about both the ammunition and the existence of the Black Panthers in Cleveland, implying that the bullets would be justifiable for groups such as the Panthers. Days after publicly rejecting Davis's idea of the police carrying dum-dum bullets, he wrote "use Super-Vel hollow-point," right above his notes on establishing a "[f]und for informers" to infiltrate the Cleveland Panthers.[146] The threat presented by the Panthers was great enough for him to consider violating the same laws he was elected to uphold.

Stokes and Davis, however, were not alone in their hatred of the Panthers. Frank J. Schaefer, president of the Fraternal Order of Police in Cleveland, stated that "the Panthers need to be wiped out in the public interest." Thus, despite Davis's resignation, the harassment of the Cleveland Panthers continued. Twenty-five members were arrested and charged with forty felonies during a three-month time span in 1970[147] in an obvious attempt to limit the group's effectiveness. As the organization devoted time and resources to court hearings, numerous bail bonds, and defense strategies, the community service operations of the Party suffered.

Among the many arrested were Panther leaders Tommie Carr, Danny Solomon, and Essex Smith, who were put on trial for allegedly inciting a riot.[148] After they wrote down badge numbers and questioned plain-clothes officers, the three were arrested under a new law aimed at curbing riots. As Carr recalled the incident, "I started hollering to the people of the neighborhood to look out their windows and see what the police were doing. It looked like they were headed for our office."[149] He didn't want a replay of the shooting that had occurred only three months earlier. Prior to the officers' arrival, the Panthers' medical unit was upstairs conducting laboratory tests following a week of blood sampling from the community. As the police approached armed with machine guns, the team quickly exited the building and neighboring residents ran for cover. One bystander called the incident a combination of "Keystone cops and Hitler's Gestapo."[150] The trial of the three Panthers was again delayed for a year. After a mistrial, Smith was finally acquitted at a second trial, only to be convicted on charges stemming from another incident with police.[151] The jury could not reach a verdict on Carr during the second trial, and he finally skipped town before the start of the third trial. The establishment's tactics of tying Panthers down in long court battles was successful in neutralizing them.[152]

In another set of arrests, Panthers Smith and Daryl Harris were charged with the abduction, armed robbery, rape, and attempted murder of a Cleveland State University couple. The Cleveland Panthers set up the "N.C.C.F Political Prisoners Defense and Bail Bonds Committee" in the hope of freeing their comrades, who each had their bail set at $100,000.[153] After common pleas judge John T. Patton read the guilty verdict, Smith stated, "I feel I was not tried by a jury of my peers. There is no justice in America for a Black man."[154] During the proceedings, the Rev. Dewey Fagerburg of the East Cleveland Congressional Church, or the People's Church, attempted to submit the deed of the church as collateral for the excessive bail bonds of the defendants.[155] In bringing forth the deed, Fagerburg said that his church supported Black militants as a matter of policy. The court, however, refused to accept the deed as bail. Smith and Harris were eventually convicted after they were tried three times.[156]

Clashes with Federal Law Enforcement

In addition to repression at the hands of local law enforcement, the Cleveland Panthers also faced federal persecution. As the federal campaign against the BPP thrived nationally, federal agents in Cleveland jumped on the bandwagon to institute Hoover's mandate to "expose, disrupt, discredit or otherwise neutralize [Black Nationalist] groups and their leadership."[157] One of COINTELPRO's priorities was the disruption and elimination of the Panthers' newspaper, which was the financial bread and butter of the Party. The FBI kept detailed records of the paper's distribution schedule—how many issues were to be shipped where and when, and whose responsibility it was to pick up the shipment. A memo from FBI headquarters to field offices in May 1970 stated:

> The Black Panther Party newspaper is one of the most effective propaganda operations of the BPP. Distribution of this newspaper is increasing at a regular rate thereby influencing a greater number of individuals in the United States along the Black extremist lines. Each recipient submit by 6/5/70 proposed counter-intelligence measures which will hinder the vicious propaganda being spread by the BPP. . . . It is the voice of the BPP and if it could be effectively hindered, it would result in helping to cripple the BPP.[158]

In line with these orders, papers either disappeared or were consistently delivered around the country wet, soiled, or late.[159] The delivery of papers to Cleveland was no exception. For example, on March 3, 1970, the papers arrived twenty-seven hours late. The following month, on April 17th, two boxes were lost and the rest of the shipment was twelve hours late.[160] Keeping in mind Hoover's request for "imaginative and hard-hitting counter-intelligence measures," the Cleveland FBI field office came up with a proposal to send an impostor for Norman Peery, the Cleveland Panther who picked up papers at the airport.[161] The memo from Cleveland to FBI national head-quarters states:

> The Cleveland Office proposes the following plan which the office believes will disrupt the Ohio Chapter of NCCF at Cleveland, Ohio, and which plan might also be suitable for use against the Toledo Chapter of NCCF. The plan would consist of the use of a Negro Agent in the interception of the delivery of the Black Panther Newspaper to the Ohio Chapter. Prior investigation has shown that the Panthers receive their newspapers via Air Freight through TWA, UAL or American Airlines and that the Cleveland Office had advance information concerning the arrival of the newspapers. Cleveland proposes that when such advance information concerning the arrival of the newspapers

is received a Negro Agent proceed to the appropriate airline freight office
with sufficient other Agent personnel in the area to assure his security and
impersonate NORMAN PEERY of the NCCF who has usually picked these
papers up in the past. Investigation at the airline terminals has reflected that
the freight clerks are not familiar with PEERY and would not in all likelihood
recognize the Negro agent as an impostor. This agent would then sign
PEERY's name to the air bill. It is felt that the above tactic will disrupt the
Ohio Chapter because of prior complaints by this Chapter of not receiving
newspapers and of recent arguments between National Headquarters and this
Chapter regarding the payment for these papers.[162]

Other methods used by the FBI to destroy the Black Panthers included
the distribution of false information on the activities of local Panther leaders.
A popular tactic among local FBI field offices was to send anonymous letters
to Panther leadership to create dissension within the Party. Ward Churchill
describes the process of "snitch-jacketing" or "bad-jacketing," which refers to
"the practice of creating suspicion through the spreading of rumors, manufacture of evidence, etc., that bona fide organizational members, usually
in key positions, are FBI/police informers, guilty of such offenses as skim-
ming organizational funds and the like."[163] In Cleveland, these tactics were
used to disrupt the relationship between the Cleveland Panther leadership
and the Central Committee in Oakland. For example, in March of 1971,
June Hilliard, brother of chief of staff David Hilliard, received a phone call
from Cleveland Panther Tommie Carr concerning the upcoming speaking
engagement of Huey Newton in Cleveland. Hilliard informed Carr that his
brother "had received a letter, unsigned, accusing Carr of being a defec-
tor,"[164] which forced Carr to defend his allegiance to the Party and the legitimacy of the Cleveland Panthers. The dissemination of false information by
the FBI was to plant seeds of suspicion and create tension and distrust so that
the national leadership would be skeptical about the Cleveland Panthers.

COINTELPRO extended its activities beyond the inner workings of the
Party and worked to incite violence between Panthers and other organizations.
The most widely known case of FBI instigation involved pitting the Panthers
against Maulana Karenga's organization Us. Similarly, in Cleveland there
were attempts to divide the Panthers and popular Black Nationalists. The largest Black Nationalist organization in Cleveland at the time was the Afro Set,
founded by Harllel Jones in 1968.[165] The animosity that existed between Black
Nationalists and Black Panthers in Los Angeles was similar to the relationship
between the two differing ideologies in Cleveland. The Cleveland Panthers
found early resentment from Afro Set members because they were the new
organization in the community. After the Panthers had moved north to 79th
and Central Avenue, Afro Set members driving over from Hough started to

harass them, asking if they had "permission to be in the area."[166] Indeed FBI documents reveal that the leaders of the Federation of Black Nationalists held a meeting on June 10, 1970, at which members of the Afro Set introduced the matter of how to mitigate the BPP's attempts to organize.

The turf mentality and competitive atmosphere was also fueled by the Panthers, who resented the fact that Jones and the Afro Set were working so closely with Stokes and the political power structure. The cozy relationship between the two instigated suspicions that the Afro Set was being used to eliminate the Panthers. Panther Essex Smith remarked, "Stokes was trying to keep the Panthers out of Cleveland because he didn't want to have any problems."[167] The Cleveland Panthers considered themselves "the outcasts," whereas the Afro Set and other Black Nationalists seemed to have a direct line of communication with the city administration. Confrontations with the Afro Set eventually escalated to the point where the Panthers felt they were fighting two battles: one with the government and the other with the nationalist community.[168] However, the confrontations never descended into a war, to the chagrin of the FBI.

News of a "power struggle" between the Afro Set and the Panthers was noted in the press, which often received its information from police sources. For example, in early June 1969, each of Cleveland's newspapers labeled an alleged shootout between Panther and Afro Set members as "a war" between the organizations.[169] In response to these false and misleading stories, the two groups were forced to organize a joint press conference to explain that the incident was apparently nothing more than a botched robbery and, most importantly, that none of the individuals involved were members of either organization. Nonetheless, the illusion created by the media of an all-out war had its effects on the two groups.

This incident demonstrates how it was necessary for agents of the social order to represent a disunified Black militancy with trigger-happy, renegade members. This of course had a twofold purpose: (1) it reduced the possibility of widespread popular support for the groups, and (2) it was used to justify the state's methods of repression. Despite these intentions, however, there were examples of unity among the Black militant groups in Cleveland. For instance, the Panthers marched in solidarity with a spectrum of Black Nationalists in July 1970, which marked the second anniversary of the Glenville rebellion. Since many of the Cleveland Panthers had come from the various organizations within the Black Nationalist community, organizational contacts had already been established.[170]

In some rare cases, the "divide and conquer" strategies even backfired. One example of this occurred on August 18, 1971, when the Panthers' new and expanded free health clinic was bombed. Well trained by the media, the public's eyes immediately turned to the Afro Set, who seemed just as upset by the incident as the Panthers. In the end, the bombing brought the two groups together. Afro Set gathered in solidarity with the Cleveland Panthers, and Omar Majied, minister of Afro Set, declared a new coalition between the two organizations to combat the persistent harassment of law enforcement officials. Majied stated that "[t]he Afro Set is Black and we look out at a Panther and he is Black. We have different ways of coming to a solution, but we can work together." Along with the Nation of Islam and several other Black Nationalist organizations, the BPP and the Afro Set spearheaded a fund-raiser picnic with the Afro Set donating a portion of the proceeds to the rebuilding of the People's Free Health Center.[171] Assistance also came from a local glass company, which offered to replace the broken windows in the building.

The tactics used by local and federal law enforcement in Cleveland fit squarely within the national COINTELPRO campaign to eliminate the Panthers, a project that was legitimated when the Panthers were relegated to the status of trigger-happy criminals. As the BPP was conceptualized as the primary enemy of the state and symbolically representative of society's other, agents of the social order could move quickly to plot their destruction.

The Panthers' Alternative Institutions

In the current literature on the Panthers, the confrontations between armed Panthers and law enforcement are often invoked as evidence of the Party's *revolutionary* struggle. However, what is missing from these works is a focus on the Panthers' *revolutionary* struggle to improve the material conditions of Black people.

As the Panthers articulated the problems inherent in the American system of order, they also moved toward the establishment and control of just institutions that transformed the consciousness of their local communities and exposed the contradictions of the state. To borrow from Lenin, the Panthers wanted to establish a structure of "dual power," in which their community programs competed with the institutions of the dominant power structure.[172] Newton wrote, "You have to set up a program of practical application and be a model for the community to follow and appreciate."[173] The BPP was interested in overthrowing the dominant superstructure of the social order and replacing it with their own forms of community institutions. As Seale described, the Panthers wanted to establish "a broad, massive, people's type of political machinery" that served the needs of their respective communities.[174]

The Black Panther: Funding Programs and
Distributing the Message

Despite the state repression that inhibited the development of the BPP's community programs, the Party was successful in raising money and soliciting donations to support their agenda. Cleveland's community programs were far-ranging and successful. Panthers there instituted a free breakfast program for children, handed out free clothing, provided free medical care, organized free trips to prisons for relatives of inmates, and conducted political education classes in the community.

The cornerstone of the Panthers' financial stability came through the distribution and sales of *The Black Panther,* "an organ which lumpen proletarian brothers and sisters produce[d]."[175] Initiated after the April 1967 police murder of Denzil Dowell in northern California, the weekly paper expanded and had an average distribution of 100,000 in Panther branches and chapters across the country between 1968 and 1972.[176] In addition to providing the financial bedrock for the Party's community programs, the paper served two additional roles: (1) it allowed Panthers to organize and recruit during their selling shifts; and (2) it educated community members about both the practices and philosophy of the Party, and the experiences of Black people throughout the country.

Although vital to the funding of programs, a relatively small number of papers were delivered to the Cleveland Panthers in comparison to other Panther operations in Ohio. For instance, testimony by an investigator with the Committee on Internal Security reported that in 1970, Cleveland received an average of 1,500 papers a week, whereas Toledo was shipped 2,400 and Dayton 2,250.[177] The Cleveland Panthers reached their peak in July 1971 when they had more than 2,350 papers delivered.[178] Regardless of the number of papers received in Cleveland, it was of utmost importance to sell the entire stock to provide funding for local community programs or legal defense. At twenty-five cents a copy, the paper brought the Cleveland Panthers a decent weekly income which contributed directly to the advancement of the BPP's revolutionary agenda.

Beyond the financial importance of the paper, the BPP used the instrument to mobilize support for the Party. As Lenin argued, "the role of the paper is not confined solely to spreading of ideas, to political education and to procuring political allies. A paper is not merely a collective propagandist and collective agitator. It is also a collective organizer."[179] The youthfulness of the Cleveland Panthers, like most branches in the Party, provided an easy avenue for organizational activities on college campuses. Al Hayes and Billy Brock, Cleveland Panthers and students at Cuyahoga Community College and Cleveland State University, respectively, sold papers on campus and enticed students to attend a Panther political education class.[180] Other Cleveland Panthers took *The Black Panther* downtown to generate support from the older generation.[181] Cleveland Panther Essex Smith stayed in the Kinsman neighborhood where the Panther office was located and hawked the paper in the middle of 79th Street.[182] The sales of the paper downtown or on campuses fueled the local growth of the Party.

In addition to utilizing *The Black Panther* to organize community members, the BPP also used it as an instrument for their own discourse and communication. As Emory Douglas, minister of culture, stated, "[t]he Party needed to have a newspaper so we could tell our own story."[183] Complementing the regular flow of information from the national level to the local branches, there were also communications moving in the other direction. Local branches and chapters throughout the country took advantage of the opportunity to write about the conditions in their specific communities or to report on the developments of their community programs. As Seale stated, "[a]ll the people who get the Black Panther Party newspaper can read about what is really happening, about the thousands of black brothers and sisters who are murdered, shot, and brutalized in the black communities and the wretched ghettoes throughout the country."[184] Among the regular contributors were the information officers of the Cleveland Panthers, who consistently published articles about the impoverished conditions of Black people in their community, including inadequate housing and improper health conditions, as well as issues of police brutality.[185]

The Cleveland Panthers also tapped into the skills of their rank and file to publish their own local newsletter called the *People's Community News*, which they inserted into the weekly issues of *The Black Panther*.[186] Complementing the newsletter, the Cleveland Panthers also had a small radio transmitter which they used to broadcast messages throughout a two-block radius around the Panther office. Davis and Smith remember how Panthers would talk all day, even though it was heard only around the block.[187] The Cleveland Panthers recognized the importance of having the story of the Black community told from their own perspective. This emphasis could also be seen in the development of political education classes, which were conducted within the Party as well as in the larger community.

Political Education Classes and the
Liberation School

Panthers who hawked the newspaper were proud of the Party and the image it represented. The pictures of bold Black youths confronting the agents of the dominant social order and instituting programs that addressed the needs of the Black community meant a great deal. There had never been a national organization of Black people who were so assertive in promoting a particular program. The BPP developed, nourished, and transformed the raw energy of Black youth through their political education classes. An internal institution that addressed the inadequacies of the state's educational system, the weekly sessions were required of every Panther. Panthers engaged the thoughts of Malcolm X, Frantz Fanon, Mao Tse-Tung, Che Guevara, and Robert Williams, as well as the Party leaders' weekly theoretical pieces, in *The Black Panther.*

The political education classes instituted by the Cleveland Panthers were similar in structure to those of other branches: each Panther was required to read two hours a day and be familiar with the current issue of *The Black Panther.*[188] The political education classes were attractive to college students and local teens because they provided an alternative base of knowledge, separate from the hegemonic educational system. "These guys never would have picked up a book if it hadn't been for us," remembers Peery.[189] For those younger than fourteen, the Cleveland Panthers organized a liberation school in the summer months of 1970, using the facilities at the Friendly Inn and the League Park Center.[190] In addition to providing food for more than twenty-five children, they conducted ten hours of instruction during four separate classes per week.[191] In accordance with Point 5 of the Panthers' Ten-Point Program, the Cleveland Panthers instituted an "education that teaches us our true history and our role in the present-day society."[192]

The external component of the political education classes was the general community meetings, held one night a week at the Friendly Inn and the Garden Valley Neighborhood Community Center, only to later move to the office on 79th and Rawlings. As JoNina Abron states, "[t]he Party's community political education classes were the educational counterpart for adults. In addition to listening to lectures about the Party's ideology, goals, and activities, community adults were taught basic reading and writing skills."[193] Articulate Panther leaders, such as Smith or "Rock" Todd, led the weekly discussions and mobilized the participants around the BPP Ten-Point Program. The early programs had a quick effect on the surrounding community. Rev. Herman Graham, director of the Garden Valley Neighborhood Community Center, stated "[w]ith less resources and in a shorter time, the Panthers have done more for the black community than we have."[194]

Complementing the general community political education classes, the BPP also had community members organize smaller sessions at their homes. Frank Stitts, a member of the St. Adalbert Church and chair of the Cleveland Black Lay Catholic Caucus, regularly gathered a small group of community residents at his home to hear Tommie Carr discuss the politics of the Party and its local community programs. As Stitts explained, it allowed them to understand the Panthers through the voice of the Panther leadership rather than through the sensationalism of the popular media.[195] He recalls how militants and organizations like the BPP first intimidated him and other members:

> We didn't know enough about them. All we knew was what we read in the papers and watched on TV. They were all painted as violent and vicious groups. But really, when you got to know something about their philosophy, they really weren't. . . . They were doing some good things locally for people.[196]

This was no surprise. As Essex Smith observed, "everybody associated the Panthers with guns, but they never associated the Panthers with all the community programs."[197] The establishment of alternative institutions and political education classes was successful in confronting the negative representations of the Party as well as in mobilizing the community around a political agenda. Through the combination of community discussion and active programming, the Panthers envisioned the eventual removal of the dominant institutions and agents in power.

The Community Health Program

In 1969, Chairman Seale issued a directive for local Panther operations to begin the construction of free health clinics. The first institution, the Bobby Hutton Community Clinic, opened its doors in Kansas City in August 1969.[198] Other Panther chapters followed the example, providing sickle cell anemia testing, prenatal care, and a variety of other health services. The particular community needs drove the composition of the Panthers' alternative institutions generally, and the health programs were no exception.[199] Likewise, the Cleveland Panthers responded to the city's closure of its health facilities in the Black neighborhoods on the East Side by devising their own institutions to meet the medical needs of the affected residents.

During the early summer of 1970, the Cleveland Panthers sent a delegation to Chicago to meet with Ronald "Doc" Satchel, the minister of health for the Chicago chapter of the BPP, and to observe the functioning of the People's Free Medical Care Center.[200] Emphasizing the idea of an oppositional institution, Satchel explained that the health clinic served as "an alternative to the existing health care system."[201] Armed with the knowledge and skills to run a fully operational clinic, the Cleveland Panthers soon organized the Community Health Program in the Kinsman neighborhood surrounding their office on East 79th and Rawlings.

During the late summer of 1970, with the assistance of Richard Wright, a medical student in his first year of residency at the Cleveland Metropolitan

Hospital, the Cleveland Panthers compiled a team of medical students, nurses, and doctors from both the hospital and the Medical Council for Human Rights. The Panthers' health program thus started simply, with the Panthers and medical volunteers going door to door to inquire about the health of neighborhood residents. They quickly learned that relatively few people had ever seen a doctor.[202] Austin Jones, coordinator for the Cleveland Panthers' health program, stated that "[f]or this society to deny a person medical care because he doesn't have enough money is to deny that person the right to live . . . and that too is violence."[203] By responding to the needs of their community, the Cleveland Panthers had extended the revolutionary concept of self-defense to include health care. As Newton stated, "when we used the words 'Self-Defense,' it also meant defending ourselves against poor medical care, against unemployment, against poor housing and all other things that poor and oppressed people of the world suffer."[204]

Three nights a week, the Panther health team tested residents for medical conditions such as tuberculosis, diabetes, high blood pressure, and sickle cell anemia. Following the free tests, the volunteers checked the samples at their respective laboratories and the Panthers reported the results to the residents. If a further visit was necessary, the Panthers either had an additional doctor visit the home or they arranged for transportation and accompanied the person to a nearby clinic. In the summer of 1970 alone, the Panthers treated close to 450 people.[205] Yet the programs organized by the BPP were not only intended to provide for members of the community, but also to organize politically. Elaine Brown, former chair of the BPP, discussed the importance of the community programs in the revolutionary process:

> We had to elevate our Survival Programs to models for alternative institutions, as the Mozambicans had. [Samora] Machel had emphasized that the mass of their people had been inspired and educated and ultimately, incorporated in their armed liberation struggle primarily because of FRELIMO's establishment of schools and hospitals. . . . We had to do everything possible to embrace more and more of our people, if we were to become a serious revolutionary force in the world.[206]

The Cleveland Panthers utilized their community programs to meet and speak with members of the neighborhood and to educate them about the philosophy of the BPP.

Following the positive feedback from the community, the Cleveland Panthers planned to expand their health program into the People's Free Health Center during the summer of 1971. Despite the incessant arrests and imprisonment of the local leadership, Wright continued his recruitment of medical students and doctors, amassing twenty volunteers and several physicians to operate the clinic. In addition, the Panthers continued to obtain in-kind gifts such as laboratory equipment.[207] The Cleveland Panthers reported that "[i]t was the community that provided the labor and much needed donations and materials in order to build the clinic."[208] Community volunteers assisted in painting and plastering the upstairs of the Panther office in hopes of opening the clinic on August 23, 1971. But in the early morning hours of August 18th, two sticks of dynamite exploded, leaving the People's Free Health Center in disrepair and nearly killing Panthers Willie Slater and Alton Delmore. The Panthers were quick to accuse the government, noting that the police had arrived on the scene too quickly.[209] Beyond this observation, however, they had no evidence to support their claim.

As explained earlier, the Afro Set came to the aid of the Cleveland Panthers after the bombing. A group of fifty Afro Set members and leaders of the Federation of Black Nationalists marched to the site of the ravaged clinic and made a cash donation to assist the Panthers in their repairs.[210] The Cleveland Panthers continued their vision of opening a free health clinic. Three weeks following the explosion, they organized a public picnic "to provide funds to repair and reschedule the health center services for the poor," said Davis.[211] The Afro Set again assisted the Panthers, directing the event's traffic at the Midway Lake Park.[212] Coalition efforts such as this, rare as they may have been, were the product of a general consensus about the treatment of Black revolutionaries by the state. As Carr stated, the greater the repression, the greater the unity.[213] Although the Cleveland Panthers dissolved before the clinic was instituted, their efforts exemplified the Party's program of addressing community needs.

Breakfast and Clothing Programs:
Community Resources at Work

One of the Panthers' most publicized and effective programs was the free breakfast program, first instituted in 1968 in the Bay Area.[214] Feeding hungry children early in the morning drew widespread community support and provided another opportunity for Panthers to establish local alliances. The government, however, took a different perspective, asserting that "the Panthers use the free breakfast time as an opportunity to indoctrinate the youngsters with their philosophy of hate."[215]

The initial free breakfast program in Cleveland began during the early summer months of 1970 at the Friendly Inn Settlement House and on the roof of the Panthers' office at 79th and Rawlings. By November, they had expanded their operation and were serving breakfast five days a week.[216] Panthers like Gail Walters, Jimmy Slater, and Estella Smith awoke each morning before dawn to prepare the youngsters' meals. Walters, a program coordinator, said, "We serve the hot meals so the children will get the nutrition they need to learn without the distraction of an empty stomach." The breakfast program was feeding meals of eggs, grits, and ham to an average of fifty children a day.[217] Like other Panther endeavors, the level of community support for the breakfast program fueled its expansion.[218] As the community health program used the expertise of medical volunteers, the breakfast program depended on the facilities of the churches in Cleveland's Black community. According to Slater, the Cleveland Panthers "had the best relationship with the churches of any Panthers that I have been around, anyplace."[219]

One afternoon Carr, who was attempting to mobilize churches to assist in the various Panther programs, contacted Father Gene Wilson, pastor of the St. Adalbert Church, only a few blocks west of the Panther office.[220] From the start, Father Wilson supported the free breakfast program and assisted in the development of the Panthers' programs by providing space and support.[221] Frank Stitts, a member of the church, reaffirmed the necessity of the Panthers' program: "When I look around our community where [the Panthers] were feeding kids . . . there was a great need, and they meet the need." Yet Panthers were not the only community workers "meeting the need." In fact, they encouraged and recruited members of the community to become involved in the maintenance and development of their alternative institutions. These interactions between community residents and the "super-militants," as Stitts called the Panthers, allowed for a breakdown of the demonic image depicted by the media and agents of the social order.[222] The sharing of resources between the Panthers and local organizations, such as the Cleveland churches, ensured the success of the community programs.[223]

Likewise, the Party was dependent upon local businesses to donate food for the breakfast program. Among his other duties, Luke McCoy was responsible for the food collection. He would empty the trunk of his own car and visit numerous local businesses that the Panthers considered potential allies. The markets on both the East and West Sides provided eggs, grits, cheeses, meats, and other breakfast items. Some businesses, like the meat packaging warehouses on the predominantly white West Side, provided boxes of food each week, whereas others were sporadic in their donations.[224] Sometimes, the Cleveland Panthers experienced good fortune. Bill Davis, the Cleveland Panther information officer, remembers when another Panther, Danny Solomon, obtained some food for the breakfast program: "Danny pulled up to the office one time and said 'I got a whole truck of potatoes that won't chip.' So we called WABQ and WJMO and they announced it on the radio. . . . A whole truck. A great big 40-footer full of potatoes."[225] As the

Panthers distributed the potatoes for free, they also educated the community about the Party and its programs. Similar to the use of *The Black Panther* to mobilize the community, the Cleveland Panthers organized the community through their programs. Following the thoughts of Newton, the Cleveland Panthers "recognized that in order to bring the people to the level of consciousness where they would seize the time, it would be necessary to serve their interests in survival by developing programs which would help them meet their daily needs."[226]

Whether it was serving food at the free breakfast program or distributing sweaters at the free clothing program, the Cleveland Panthers used the alternative institutions to educate and organize politically. The implementation of the free clothing program was less consistent, but it was still supported through the efforts of members of the Kinsman community. The Panthers again utilized the facilities of the St. Adalbert Church and distributed clothes and shoes "to all who asked for them," said Carr. Since some of the clothing for the program was secondhand, the Cleveland Panthers made efforts to provide newer items. McCoy, for instance, made contacts with a business on 55th and Superior that was manufacturing sweaters. After he described the merits of the program, they gave him boxes of brand—new sweaters and knit dresses.[227] Likewise, Slater and his brothers Frank and Willie would visit the department stores in Cleveland and collect discontinued lines of clothing. Merchants and community residents donated clothes and local dry cleaners assisted in the cleaning. As Carr stated, the program intended to "show people how successfully a so-called small organization [could] come up with the necessities of life [while] the city, state, and Federal Governments failed."[228] The Panthers intensified their creation of community institutions to challenge the ideology and organization of the state apparatus.

Busing to Prisons: Exposing the State and Uniting Families

The community programs discussed thus far have been grounded in the BPP's models of alternative institutions. In addition to cultivating the consciousness of the people directly served, these programs were designed to transform the social order and embody the principles embedded in the Panthers' Ten-Point Program. The Free Busing to Prisons program added an additional feature to this design by exposing one of the state's internal mechanisms that perpetuated the dehumanization of poor people.

Abron states that the BPP's busing to prisons program was first established by the Seattle branch in July 1970.[229] Shortly thereafter, the Cleveland Panthers organized a free busing program of their own and on December 27,

1970, made the first trip to the Ohio penitentiary with relatives and friends of inmates, in hopes of easing the "financial and transportation difficulties."[230] Cleveland Panther Jimmy Slater discussed the development of the program:

> [A]fter so many comrades and Black Nationalists and people we knew were in prison, . . . we knew we had to organize something to get families out, you know, to see their loved ones. And so the busing program sort of stemmed from so many of us going to jail, really.[231]

As Slater suggests, the demand for the Panthers' program grew as the incarceration of Black men increased. In three months, the Panthers expanded to the Chillicothe, Marion, and Mansfield State Reformatories.[232] A collection of primarily elderly gray-haired mothers and younger women with their children loaded onto a borrowed church bus or minivan each Saturday and made the trek to see imprisoned friends and family members. Within half a year, Carr reported that the Panthers had transported more than 1,000 people since the inauguration of the program.[233]

Like the other community programs launched by the Cleveland Panthers, the busing program was dependent on the donations of local organizations and businesses. Luke McCoy, the initial program coordinator, stressed the importance and variety of the contributions from the community: "The churches used to give us their buses because they thought it was a great idea. The gas station gave us gas and food. All we had to do was remember to bring copies of *The Black Panther* so that we could read articles on the way back from the prison." Other community members who did not consider themselves "supermilitant" also had the opportunity to participate in the Panthers' programs. Volunteers, usually brothers or cousins of imprisoned inmates, drove the bus back and forth to the prisons and became an integral part of the Panthers' alternative institution. "It was really a community-oriented program," McCoy recalls.[234]

Again, the Cleveland Panthers used their programs to educate the community about the BPP and to attract new members. For instance, McCoy was assisted in his efforts by Cecile McBride, a co-worker from his earlier days at the Hough Federal Credit Union. After McBride's husband was incarcerated, she took advantage of the opportunity to work with the Panthers and to visit him.[235] In addition, the Party got new recruits from groups of inmates freshly released from prison. With so many Cleveland Panthers imprisoned, it was inevitable that new recruits would find their ways from the cells to the Party. While he was in jail, Cleveland Panther Essex Smith remembers organizing cell mates and having classes on the BPP and then "getting word out [to the Party] when a brother was released." His dedication inside the state's penal institutions was only possible because of the support he received from the Party. The busing to prisons program was organized not only for community members to see their families, but also for Panthers to visit imprisoned comrades. Every visiting day, Smith and fellow Panther Daryl Harris spoke with Panthers. "I couldn't have asked for anything more," Smith said. Even the younger Panthers like Alton Delmore, who were juveniles and could not visit the county jail, wrote weekly letters to Panthers on the inside. In addition, the Cleveland Panthers made sure that Smith and Harris always had money and the latest edition of *The Black Panther*.[236]

The descent of the Panthers in Cleveland, which will be further addressed later, can be attributed to two factors: the continual imprisonment of local members and the national movement to consolidate operations in Oakland. In 1972, Newton envisioned a Panther city, with members throughout the country closing their local offices and moving to Oakland to assist in the election of Seale for mayor and Elaine Brown for city council. Members like Jimmy Slater and Bill Davis left Cleveland, but Panther JoAnn Bray remained in her hometown.

Before the Panthers, Bray was alone in East Cleveland. She was confined to a wheelchair at the age of fifteen after contracting rheumatoid arthritis when she was six. By the time Bray was twenty-five, she lived by herself and had a lot of time to think. Most of her early education was through tutors, until she finally graduated from a predominantly white high school. Her experiences as a youth influenced her feelings toward the Black militancy of the late 1960s. Bray despised the rhetoric and tactics of the Black liberation movement, and the images of Black Panthers "made her sick."[237]

In the early part of 1971, however, Bray began to engage some political texts. She started with the *Autobiography of Malcolm X*, then Eldridge Cleaver's *Soul on Ice*, and finally the history of the BPP in Seale's *Seize the Time*. After thinking about her situation and the conditions within her community, she wrote a letter to Newton in August 1971, saying she wanted to take advantage of her mind and donate her skills "to awaken the Black community." She wanted Newton to write her back for inspiration and guidance, but most importantly, she wanted to be a Black Panther and recruit in East Cleveland.[238]

A month later, Bray received a letter from Huey's assistant, suggesting that she contact the Black Panthers in Cleveland and become active in the community programs. However, Bray had already become engaged in political action. After the execution of Panther George Jackson at the Soledad Prison, she wrote a letter to the editor of the *Call and Post* stating that "Jackson's death is just a carbon copy of what happens to any black that refuses to compromise his integrity."[239] Bray wrote Newton again three weeks later to inform him that she had taken his advice and had begun to work with the

Cleveland Panthers' Free Busing to Prisons program.[240] She initially organized the passenger list and made reservations with the appropriate prisons, while McCoy picked up the buses and food for the visits. Once McCoy left Cleveland and the local Panthers disbanded, Bray took over full operation of the program.[241]

Without the financial resources of the Cleveland Panthers, Bray found it difficult at first to operate the busing program. Out of necessity, Bray changed the name to the People's Busing Program and began to charge passengers for the weekly visits.[242] She still had the support of local organizations such as the Inner City Protestant House and League Park, but without the income from the sales of *The Black Panther*, Bray was forced to make changes, such as renting vans for liability reasons instead of using church buses. Ironically, Bray's home was robbed while she visited the Chillicothe Correctional Institution in October 1972, and she lost more than $1,000 worth of personal possessions. The community responded to her misfortune and donated a television, records, and clothes to replace the stolen items. Yet the most inspirational donation came from prisoners at Lucasville, who sent cash to assist Bray and the busing program.[243]

Bray continued to provide busing services to prisons around the state, and she joined with prison rehabilitation groups and became a member of the Ohio Ministers' Penal Task Force.[244] Bray expanded trips to the Ohio Reformatory for Women at Marysville and in 1975 acquired a $16,000 grant from the Law Enforcement Assistance Administration, which enabled her to obtain an additional minibus.[245] Prison visits were expanded even further to include the correctional facilities in Lucasville, as well as Ohio's juvenile detention centers in Lancaster and Columbus. This increased the number of monthly riders to 300 people traveling to nine penitentiaries.[246] This tremendous expansion, which occurred over a span of five years, was eventually threatened in May 1976. For the first time since Bray had taken over the busing program, she was forced to cancel trips after being unable to meet the payments for a new insurance policy.[247] Nevertheless, Bray's maintenance of the free busing program, long after the Panthers dissolved in Cleveland, is a testament to both her dedication and the effectiveness of the Panthers' alternative institutions. The Cleveland Panthers' strong community programs depended upon durable community alliances, committed leaders, and a framework for revolutionary change.

Final Thoughts on the Invisibility of Panther Programs

The BPP organized their political action around the Ten-Point Program, and as Elaine Brown said, the Party "was underwritten by the gun." It is undeniable that the initial program of the Panthers was carrying weapons and patrolling the police. Likewise, the image of the Panther as a revolutionary who stood against the agents of the white power structure was highly influential in mobilizing scores of young Black men and women in the Party. This study does not refute the importance of the Panthers' original purpose and the importance of their group identity construction. The problem evolves when the discussion on the Party ends with these militaristic aspects. As Newton stated, "[t]he image of Blacks armed for self-defense against police brutality catapulted the Party nationally into the public consciousness and gave an erroneous impression that it advocated armed confrontation."[248] Rather than furthering the assessment of the Panthers, the literature on the BPP has simply reflected the narrow categorization of the Party as mere thugs.

Yet the Panthers had a larger goal: the destruction of the American social order and the rebuilding of a society to address the needs of its citizens. To that end, the Panthers initiated community programs to compensate for the inadequate institutions of the state and to raise the consciousness of people in their local communities. Newton stated, "[a]ll these programs were aimed at one goal: complete control of the institutions in the community."[249] The Cleveland Panthers were an important local contribution in the revolutionary movement of the Party. Through their programs, the Cleveland Panthers developed strong community alliances and permanently changed the consciousness of those who participated in the Party's development. Their labor, like the work of all the other Panther operations, is too often placed on the back burner in favor of the symbolic representation of the Panthers as a violent organization. Unless that representation is challenged, it will become the paradigm that will doom future revolutionaries to suffer the same fate.

The Demise of the Cleveland Panthers and
Future Implications

The demise of the Cleveland Panthers was triggered during the later months of 1971, as the leadership began to thin and rank-and-file members increasingly found themselves behind bars. Although enjoying some contact with Party members, imprisoned Panthers were disconnected from the Party's daily community programs and their Panther experiences quickly became distant memories. Others refused to sit in the state's penal institutions. Sensing a lack of support from the BPP national headquarters, Carr jumped bond and left the Party during his third trial on charges of inciting a riot.[250] He never resurfaced and the Cleveland Panthers suffered through organizational changes and instability.

As the leadership thinned, the fate of the Cleveland Panthers ultimately rested in the hands of the BPP Central Committee. In 1972, the Party decided to gradually close all its chapters and branches and consolidate Party activities in Oakland, the "base" of the next stage of the revolution.[251] The new direction of the BPP was initiated by Newton, who envisioned political control in Oakland as a feasible step in the process of self-determination. This divergence from the BPP roots obviously changed the Party's revolutionary framework, as the Panthers entered the social order's political arena rather than continuing their direction of organizing alternative institutions with the community programs. Several members of the Central Committee initially resisted the plan, objecting to the removal of Panthers from their local communities and changing the political activities of the Party.[252]

Newton won however, and Panthers from around the country descended upon Oakland and began to organize around the mayoral campaign of Bobby Seale and the city council campaign of Elaine Brown. The eventual defeats in both races demoralized the Party. With so much invested in the two elections, many Panthers were left physically and mentally drained. As Professor Ollie A. Johnson III argues, "the decision to invest almost all of its political and material resources in the 1973 elections proved to be a critical strategic mistake by the Party leadership."[253] Cleveland Panthers who made the trip, like Bill Davis and Jimmy Slater, had mixed feelings on the experience. On one level, the opportunity to work with so many Panthers from various geographical locations was invigorating and educational. Yet it was also difficult to work in an alien community with a different political context.[254]

The example of the Cleveland Panthers' demise is most likely applicable to other branches who had established strong roots in their community. The successful local community programs were simply ended or taken out of the Party's name after Newton directed all Panthers to cease their operations. Thus, the labor that went into the development of strong community alliances and programs was simply eliminated. Local Panthers had struggled to find their niche in the community, and the unfortunate consequence of being connected to a hierarchical organization was that local experiences were second to the decisions made at the upper levels of leadership.

Party Impact on the Community and on Local Members

Despite the elimination of the local community programs initiated by the Cleveland Panthers, the spirit of the Panthers existed long after they disbanded. As was discussed earlier, JoAnn Bray continued the free busing program until 1976. Likewise, members of the St. Adalbert Church continued to distribute free clothes to the community "with no strings attached," directly influenced by the initial free clothing program of the Cleveland Panthers.[255] As Frank Stitts stated, "one of the important things is [their] continuing influence. There are Panthers out there who need to know that what they did back in the 60s is still influencing people today, thirty odd years later."

The effects of the BPP extended beyond the particular local community; it also impacted the members involved. Bill Davis takes the same message of the Panthers to a different platform with a new philosophy. As a minister, he preaches in prisons and keeps the church's commitment to the outside community strong. "A lot of the same principles and all, I'm still doing those, as an ordained minister," says Davis.[256] Other Cleveland Panthers remain active in the Cleveland community today, carrying on the principles of the BPP. The experiences in the Party are ones that will not be forgotten, as they created an idea of a better society and a vision to keep on struggling.

In sum, the selective documentation on the national leaders and larger chapters has silenced the experiences of rank-and-file Panthers and the development of local Panther operations. To ignore those experiences is to give an incomplete account of the Party. The story of the Black Panther Party extended beyond the confines of Oakland, New York, or Chicago and had a tremendous impact on local communities and individuals. As Cleveland Panther Luke McCoy said, "[t]he ideas that we got as a Panther will be with us all of our lives."[257]

Notes

1. William G. Rose, *Cleveland: The Making of a City* (Cleveland: World Publishing, 1950), 966–967. Rose's mammoth history of Cleveland is the renowned narrative of Cleveland, and one cannot talk about the city without referring to his documentation. Published in 1950, the book provides excellent illustrations of Cleveland's industrial expansion and the individuals of economic and political importance. Unfortunately, that's where its usefulness ends. Rose's neglect of the Black community in Cleveland is disturbing and renders even his colossal work incomplete. Yet this disregard of Black people is no surprise, even among intellectuals. As the dominant order conceptualizes Blacks as the other, historical demography will likewise reflect the belief system and pay little attention to Black people's experiences.

2. Kenneth L. Kusmer, *A Ghetto Takes Shape: Black Cleveland, 1870–1930* (Chicago: University of Illinois Press, 1978), 66. Kusmer's work on the development of Cleveland's Black ghetto at the turn of the century is clearly unmatched. His comprehensive data is coupled with a rich analysis that digs deep into an undocumented urban history of Cleveland. Kusmer explores both the dynamics among the different leaders within Cleveland's Black community and their relationship to the white power structure. In

addition, he touches on the interaction between the Black community and the influential immigrant community, encompassing economic, political, and social circles. Even though Kusmer provides an excellent starting point for this study, his analysis ends before the start of World War II and thus leaves out important information about the social conditions that birthed the Black militancy of the 1960s. His work lays the foundation, but it does not bring us full circle.

3. Rose, *Cleveland: The Making of a City*, 690.

4. There was a total population of 360, 633.

5. Russell H. Davis, *Black Americans in Cleveland from George Peake to Carl B. Stokes 1796–1969* (Washington, D.C.: Associated Publishers, 1972), 14. Davis's documentation of Black Cleveland begins with the founding of Cleveland as a city in 1796 and concludes with the reelection of Carl Stokes in 1969. In contrast to Kusmer's analytical insight, Davis simply gives a dry chronological account of the achievements of Black people in Cleveland, which very well may have been his intent. Often focusing on the success of political and business leaders, his text serves its purpose of providing factual information on Black people in Cleveland. Furthermore, he contributes to the larger history of Cleveland through his recording of important geographical locations in Cleveland's Black community.

6. Kusmer, *A Ghetto Takes Shape*, 41.

7. Davis, *Black Americans in Cleveland*, 15.

8. Kusmer, *A Ghetto Takes Shape*, 10.

9. Davis, *Black Americans in Cleveland*, 159.

10. Kusmer, *A Ghetto Takes Shape*, 158–173.

11. Neil David Fligstein, "Migration from Counties of the South, 1900–1950: A Social, Historical, and Demographic Account" (Ph.D. diss., University of Wisconsin–Madison, 1978), 28.

12. Quoted in Rose, *Cleveland: The Making of a City*, 686.

13. Davis, *Black Americans in Cleveland*, 46, 305–307, 329.

14. Lawrence Brisker, "Black Power and Black Leaders: A Study of Black Leadership in Cleveland, Ohio" (Ph.D. diss., Case Western Reserve University, 1977), 66.

15. Davis, *Black Americans in Cleveland*, 356; Brisker, "Black Power and Black Leaders," 62; Cleveland Urban League, Roger Mitton, Research Director, *The Negro in Cleveland, 1950–1963: An Analysis of the Social and Economic Characteristics of the Negro Population, The Changes Between 1950–1963* (Cleveland: Urban League, 1964), 6. The Urban League's report on the condition of Black people in Cleveland contributes to an accurate depiction of the social forces that led to the emergence of the Black Panther Party during the later part of the 1960s. Although their documentation is brief and rarely analytical, the Urban League does provide a wealth of statistical information on Cleveland's Black community, ranging from figures in education, employment, and housing. The Urban League's information contributes to the local data within the following narrative.

16. U.S. Bureau of the Census, *U.S. Censuses of Population and Housing: 1960 Census Tracts*. Final Report PHC(1)-28 (Washington, D.C.: U.S. Government Printing Office, 1962), 14; Urban League, *The Negro in Cleveland*, 1.

17. Urban League, *The Negro in Cleveland*, 2.

18. This contributed to the composition of the potential work environment: unskilled Black employees vs. trained white management. Urban League, *The Negro in Cleveland*, 2; Kusmer, *A Ghetto Takes Shape*, 10.

19. Urban League, *The Negro in Cleveland*, 3.

20. U.S. Commission on Civil Rights, *Hearing in Cleveland, OH, April 1–7, 1966* (Washington, D.C.: U.S. Government Printing Office, 1966), 201.

21. Urban League, *The Negro in Cleveland,* 15.

22. Davis, *Black Americans in Cleveland,* 305–326.

23. Kusmer, *A Ghetto Takes Shape,* 69.

24. The unions that responded were the Electricians Local 38, Sheet Metal Workers Local 65, Ironworkers Local 17, Plumbers Local 55, and Pipefitters Local 36.

25. Commission on Civil Rights, *Hearing in Cleveland,* 443, 444.

26. Of all Blacks who worked in 1950, 26.9 percent were in manufacturing jobs, 19.6 percent in the service industry, 18.2 percent in labor jobs (including farm), and 10.8 percent in private household work. By 1960, the numbers had changed only slightly, to 25.9 percent, 18.4 percent, 12.1 percent, and 7.8 percent, respectively. In contrast, of all whites who worked in 1950, 22.2 percent were in manufacturing jobs, 6.8 percent in the service industry, 4.6 percent in labor jobs (including farm), and 0.9 percent in private household work. In 1960, the numbers for whites had changed to 19.2 percent, 6.8 percent, 3.5 percent, and 0.9 percent, respectively. Census, *U.S. Censuses of Population and Housing,* 14.

27. Herman Stein, *The Crisis of Welfare in Cleveland* (Cleveland: Case Western University Press, 1969), 50.

28. Urban League, *The Negro in Cleveland,* 12.

29. Ibid.

30. Davis, *Black Americans in Cleveland,* 337.

31. *Public Welfare in Metropolitan Cleveland* (Cleveland: Cleveland Metropolitan Services Commission, 1959), 8.

32. U.S. Census of Population, Ohio: 1950 and 1960.

33. Ohio Bureau of Unemployment Compensation—Total Figures Released February 1964.

34. Commission on Civil Rights, *Hearing in Cleveland,* 107–111, testimony of Velma Jean Woods.

35. Davis, *Black Americans in Cleveland,* 330, 333.

36. Brisker, "Black Power and Black Leaders," 70.

37. Davis, *Black Americans in Cleveland,* 308–309.

38. Brisker, "Black Power and Black Leaders," 70.

39. Davis, *Black Americans in Cleveland,* 331.

40. Urban League, *The Negro in Cleveland,* 16.

41. Davis, *Black Americans in Cleveland,* 331.

42. Commission on Civil Rights, *Hearing in Cleveland,* 96.

43. U.S. Census of Housing, Ohio: 1960.

44. Commission on Civil Rights, *Hearing in Cleveland,* 296.

45. Urban League, *The Negro in Cleveland,* 8.

46. Richard Bellamy, an attorney for the U.S. Commission on Civil Rights, testified that the staff study considered 135 elementary, 21 junior high, and 13 senior high schools in Cleveland. He said that "[u]sing 1963 statistics, 1965 census data, and data gathered on interviews with school officials, it was possible to determine with substantial accuracy the racial composition of the 1965 Cleveland public school population." Commission on Civil Rights, *Hearing in Cleveland,* 274.

47. Commission on Civil Rights, *Hearing in Cleveland,* 274, 276.

48. Urban League, *The Negro in Cleveland,* 8, 9.

49. Louis H. Masotti and Jerome R. Corsi, *Shoot-Out in Cleveland: Black Militants and the Police, A Report to the National Commission on the Causes and Prevention of Violence* (Washington, D.C.: U.S. Government Printing Office, 1969), 33.

50. Masotti and Corsi, *Shoot-Out in Cleveland*, 34.

51. Lewis Robinson, *The Making of a Man* (Cleveland: Green & Sons, 1970), 58.

52. Ibid., 59.

53. Estelle Zannes, *Checkmate in Cleveland: The Rhetoric of Confrontation During the Stokes Years* (Cleveland: Case Western Reserve University Press, 1972), 23.

54. Ibid., 25.

55. William E. Nelson Jr. and Philip J. Meranto, *Electing Black Mayors: Political Action in the Black Community* (Columbus: The Ohio State University Press, 1977), 162.

56. Zannes, *Checkmate in Cleveland*, 17.

57. Carl B. Stokes, *Promises of Power: Then and Now* (Cleveland: Friends of Carl B. Stokes, 1989), 129–130.

58. Nelson and Meranto, *Electing Black Mayors*, 385.

59. The Afro Set, founded by Jones in 1968, was the strongest Black Nationalist organization in Cleveland and centered its activities around the Hough area. Harllel Jones, personal interview, November 18, 1998.

60. Stokes, *Promises of Power*, 102.

61. Ibid., 102.

62. Masotti and Corsi, *Shoot-Out in Cleveland*, 26–34, 44.

63. Ibid., 44.

64. Ibid., 44; Stokes, 208.

65. Masotti and Corsi, *Shoot-Out in Cleveland*, 44–46.

66. Ibid., 46, 49, 50, 57.

67. Stokes, *Promises of Power*, 216. Stokes was struck with a heavy political blow when it was later learned that Evans had bought his weapons with funds from a Cleveland NOW! project. Masotti and Corsi, *Shoot-Out in Cleveland*, 46.

68. "CWRU Audience Given Black Panther Credo," *Cleveland Press*, September 28, 1968, C2.

69. "Panthers, Afro Set Battle," *Cleveland Press*, June 4, 1969, A3.

70. "'Wolfe Bey' Enters Manslaughter Plea," *Call and Post*, July 18, 1970, 7A.

71. Ibid.

72. "Black Nationalists War on Each Other: 1 Dead, 2 Wounded, 3 Beaten in Park Fight," *Call and Post*, June 7, 1969, 1A, 16A; "Panthers, Afro Set Battle," *Cleveland Press*, June 4, 1969, A3; "Officials Probe Fights, Shooting," *Cleveland Plain Dealer*, June 5, 1969.

73. "Five Local Black Panthers Face Murder, Arson Charges," *Call and Post*, February 1, 1969, 1A, 12A; "Five Blacks Charged in Glenville Murder, Fire-Bombing," *Cleveland Press*, January 23, 1969, A4.

74. Walter Brown and Darryl Payne, two of the five "admitted members of the Black Panthers," were charged with first-degree murder after they allegedly stabbed Willie T. Davis, an individual they declared was a CIA agent. "Five Blacks Charged in Glenville Murder, Fire-Bombing," A4.

75. In some ways, the lumpen awe attached to the Panther mystique generated its own problems. Clarence Munford argues that the lumpen sector lacks the loyalty necessary to be a revolutionary force and are prone to continuing their old habits of violence in solving problems. "The Fallacy of Lumpen Ideology," *Black Scholar* 4 (July–August 1973): 47–51.

76. "Black Panther Party Is Dead Here," *Cleveland Press*, December 9, 1969.

77. The Party issued a list of all its official chapters and branches in November 1969, without noting the activities in Cleveland. *The Black Panther*, November 1, 1969, 20.

78. Although some suggest that this void was the result of the FBI's seizure of Cleveland Panther articles, this argument holds little merit considering that two articles were written on Fred Ahmed Evans. One of these articles was written by Wilbur Gratton, a Cleveland Black Nationalist who assisted the BPP leadership in organizing speaking engagements. See Wilbur Gratton, "Legal Lynching and More of the Same: Fred Ahmed Evans," *The Black Panther*, September 13, 1969, 9; "Ahmed Evans' Story," *The Black Panther*, October 18, 1969, 5.

79. David Hilliard and Lewis Cole, *This Side of Glory* (Boston: Little, Brown & Co.), 123.

80. In one case, Freed attempted to persuade Bobby Seale to speak in Cleveland, stating that "it's still 1966 to them, both black and white, but especially the blacks, and you could turn the tide" (March 24, 1969). Stanford University Libraries, Department of Special Collections, Newton Foundation Inc. Collection: Series 4, Box 1, Folder 20; Hilliard and Cole, *This Side of Glory*, 285–288.

81. "Rallies Here Seek Funds for Activists," *Cleveland Plain Dealer*, May 9, 1969, 7D; "Biracial Crusade Under Discussion," *Cleveland Plain Dealer*, May 10, 1969, 11A; FBI Teletype from SAC San Francisco to Bureau and Cleveland, May 8, 1969, "Week of Political Prisoners Rally, Cleveland, Ohio." Stanford University Libraries, Department of Special Collections, Newton Foundation Inc. Collection: Series 4, Box 7, Folder 3.

82. D. Hilliard and Emory Douglas, minister of culture, were originally scheduled to accompany Hewitt to Cleveland. Zilsel had purchased the tickets for all three, but after some complications at national headquarters, only Hewitt made the trip.

83. In late 1969, the BPP attempted to negotiate the "Pilots for Panthers" trade—an exchange of American prisoners of war in Vietnam for imprisoned Panther leaders Newton and Seale. As Eldridge Cleaver mobilized Vietnam's National Liberation Front (NLF) contact in Algiers, the BPP had Peck and other antiwar activists pressure the American government. Kathleen Neal Cleaver, "Back to Africa: The Evolution of the International Section of the Black Panther Party (1969–1972)," in *The Black Panther Party Reconsidered*, ed. Charles E. Jones, 233, 234 (Baltimore: Black Classic Press, 1998); Stanford University Libraries, Department of Special Collections, Newton Foundation Inc. Collection: Series 4, Box 4, Folder 18.

84. Peck continually presented opportunities for the BPP leadership in Cleveland. Hilliard's visit to Cleveland included an appearance on the Allen Douglas Show after Peck had suggested him to the producer, Bill Baker. Stanford University Libraries, Department of Special Collections, Newton Foundation Inc. Collection: Series 4, Box 3, Folder 8.

85. FBI Phone Log, San Francisco, October 2, 1969, pages 4, 5. Stanford University Libraries, Department of Special Collections, Newton Foundation Inc. Collection: Series 4, Box 3, Folder 40.

86. Jackson had created a community information center on the East Side whereas the Raymers organized a Neighborhood Information Center on the predominantly white West Side. "A Look at City's Black Panthers," *Cleveland Press*, July 23, 1970, A1, A4.

87. FBI Phone Log, San Francisco, January 21, 1970, page 2. Stanford University Libraries, Department of Special Collections, Newton Foundation Inc. Collection: Series 4, Box 4, Folder 47.

88. Floyd W. Hayes III and Francis A. Kiene III, "'All Power to the People': The Political Thought of Huey P. Newton and The Black Panther Party," in Jones, *The Black Panther Party Reconsidered*, 167.

89. FBI Memo from SAC San Francisco to FBI Director dated April 11, 1970. Stanford University Libraries, Department of Special Collections, Newton Foundation Inc. Collection: Series 4, Box 12, Folder 3.

90. "Policeman Shot in Raid for Weapons," *Cleveland Press*, June 29, 1970, A1, F3.

91. Interestingly, some of the BPP leadership were initially confused about the whole purpose of the NCCF. In October 1969, three months after the conference, Masai Hewitt asked June Hilliard, "What's this stuff about 'National Committees?'" According to June Hilliard, "David (Hilliard) wanted the new chapters to be called National Committee to Combat Fascism." The NCCFs were to replace all new Panther branches and chapters. Stanford University Libraries, Department of Special Collections, Newton Foundation Inc. Collection: Series 4, Box 3, Folder 46.

92. During an October 1969 phone conversation with Don Cox "DC," the field marshal of the BPP, about a new Panther organizer in Texas, Hilliard stated, "he can work through the National Committees [NCCF] but he can't work in the Party because the Party is closed and it might not be opened again until after the revolution." Stanford University Libraries, Department of Special Collections, Newton Foundation Inc. Collection: Series 4, Box 3, Folder 51.

93. Luke McCoy, personal interview, April 24, 1999.

94. The Cleveland Panthers were declared an official branch of the BPP in April 1971. On the national headquarters communications sheet for the week of April 4–April 8, 1971, it states, "Toledo, OH was informed that they are now a chapter of the BPP and Mike Cross is the coordinator of the entire state—establishing Dayton and Cleveland as branches." Stanford University Libraries, Department of Special Collections, Newton Foundation Inc. Collection: Series 2, Box 5, Folder 2.

95. The early Cleveland Panthers ran their operations out of two homes, it seems. One was Robert Jackson's at 4096 E. 139th St., and the other was Watts's at 2734 Hampshire #302. "Black Panther Party List of All Recognized Chapters, Branches, and NCCFs," *The Black Panther*, May 9, 1970, 10.

96. Phone Log, San Francisco, January 13, 1970, page 2. Stanford University Libraries, Department of Special Collections, Newton Foundation Inc. Collection: Series 4, Box 4, Folder 43. Demonstrative of the Party's organizational principle of "democratic centralism," the local Panthers had little power and autonomy in the Panther hierarchy. Elaine Brown, *A Taste of Power: A Black Woman's Story* (New York: Pantheon, 1992), 320.

97. FBI Airtel from SAC San Francisco to FBI Director dated January 23, 1970, "Black Panther Party—Cleveland Division." Stanford University Libraries, Department of Special Collections, Newton Foundation Inc. Collection: Series 4, Box 12, Folder 1.

98. Phone Log, San Francisco, January 21, 1970, page 2. Stanford University Libraries, Department of Special Collections, Newton Foundation Inc. Collection: Series 4, Box 4, Folder 47; "Wanted: By the People, Yahoo Bandit Running Amuck," *The Black Panther*, March 15, 1970, 15.

99. Ron Robinson, personal interview, April 24, 1999. Before heading to Oakland, Watts seemed unsure of his ability to organize the Panthers, asking Hilliard how they could get more people on their side. Watts ranted about the "pork chops" and Afro Set, "approved by the pigs and financed by it." Phone Log, San Francisco, January 21, 1970,

page 2. Stanford University Libraries, Department of Special Collections, Newton Foundation Inc. Collection: Series 4, Box 4, Folder 47.

100. Hilliard and Cole, *This Side of Glory*, 154.

101. Robinson and Peery had known each other for a while, working together on various community projects in the Black community. Norman Peery, personal interview, April 24, 1999.

102. "Police, Black Community Split on Panthers," *Cleveland Press*, July 24, 1970, A1, A4. The comments of Graham demonstrate that despite the popular negative representation of the Panthers, there were still local organizations and community leaders who chose to work with the Party. The interplay between the generations in the Black community also sheds light on the uniqueness of the BPP; they mobilized young people to press an agenda that positively influenced the daily living conditions of the older generation, or the entire community at large.

103. Peery, interview.

104. "Panthers Tell of Play Lot, Free Breakfast Programs," *Cleveland Plain Dealer*, June 30, 1970, 15A.

105. Like other BPP branches and chapters, the majority of Panthers were young college students and teenagers. Louis Heath, ed., *The Black Panther Leaders Speak: Huey P. Newton, Bobby Seale, Eldridge Cleaver and Company Speak Out through the Black Panther Party's Official Newspaper* (Metuchen, N.J.: Scarecrow Press, 1976), 133.

106. Peery, interview. Likewise, Luke McCoy was interested in the Panthers' attention to the class analysis rather than the cultural nationalist tendencies of the Afro Set. He lived in Hough, the stronghold of Afro Set, yet was more intrigued by the ideas and programs of the BPP. McCoy joined the Cleveland Panthers after spending some time working with CORE and the Hough Development Corporation. McCoy, interview.

107. Peery, interview.

108. Essex Smith, personal interview, April 25, 1999.

109. Robinson, interview.

110. Fred Clark, personal interview, April 17, 1999; Bill Davis, personal interview, April 24, 1999; "Attempt to Railroad People's Servants," *The Black Panther*, July 4, 1970, 16.

111. Before joining the Party, Davis had met David Hilliard during his speech at Case Western Reserve University in December 1969. Davis, interview.

112. For instance, Clark, a rank-and-file Panther, was recruited at Tri-C after a Cleveland Panther attended a collective meeting of white radicals and Black revolutionaries. Clark, interview.

113. McCoy, interview.

114. Peery, interview; McCoy, interview; Robinson, interview.

115. Robinson, interview.

116. Davis, interview.

117. Peery, interview.

118. Robinson, interview.

119. See Robinson, *The Making of A Man*; Scott Jelen, "Race Riot in Cleveland, July 1966: A Sociological Examination" (honors paper, Department of Sociology and Anthropology, Kent State University, 1983).

120. "Stokes 'Myth' Is Fading, Says Black Panther Leader," *Cleveland Press*, March 9, 1971; "Woodland Hills Church: 'The Misery of Blackness' Is Theme of Youth Sunday," *Call and Post*, March 6, 1971, 8A.

121. Jimmy Slater, personal interview, August 31, 1998.

122. Brown, *A Taste of Power,* 323.

123. In his autobiography, Stokes incorrectly refers to "Afro Set, a group so strong locally that they were able to keep the Black Panthers from even establishing a local chapter." Stokes, *Promises of Power,* 198.

124. Clark, interview.

125. Avery was the president of the Kinsman Multi-Service Corporation and received $30,000 from Cleveland NOW!, a project initiated by Mayor Stokes where wealthy businesses would contribute to a fund which would be used for community projects. Avery claimed to have been harassed and threatened for six weeks by Panthers after he refused to give them government funds to build a playground on a nearby vacant lot. Panther lawyer Frederic L. Ferrell argued that the Panthers wanted no more than $500 to build a playground on the land. "One Year Later: Panthers Trial Opens in Shooting of Policeman," *Call and Post,* June 19, 1971, 1A, 6A; "Police, Black Community Split on Panthers," *Cleveland Press,* July 24, 1970, A1, A4.

126. Like the U.S. Park Police count of participants at the Million Man March, members of the establishment and police stated that only twelve police cars and forty to fifty officers arrived on the scene. The Panthers and members of the left stated "75–100 strong." See "Policeman Shot in Raid for Weapons," *Cleveland Press,* June 29, 1970, A1; "Fascist Storm Troopers Wage Cowardly Attack on N.C.C.F Office . . . Ohio," *The Black Panther,* July 11, 1970, 3.

127. "Raid Victim?" *Call and Post,* July 25, 1970, 18A; "Fascist Storm Troopers Wage Cowardly Attack on N.C.C.F Office . . . Ohio," *The Black Panther,* July 11, 1970, 3.

128. "Panthers Go On Trial for Gun Battle Here," *Cleveland Press,* June 15, 1971; "Raid Victim?" *Call and Post,* July 25, 1970, 18A.

129. "Repression of the Black Panther Newspaper," *The Black Panther,* August 8, 1970, 11.

130. "Director Says He Wants Stop and Frisk Law," *Call and Post,* July 11, 1970, 1A, 18A.

131. "Source of Anger," *Cleveland Press,* July 1, 1970.

132. "Group Assails Raids on Blacks by Police," *Cleveland Plain Dealer,* July 2, 1970, A5.

133. "Hot or Cool?" *Call and Post,* July 11, 1970, 10B.

134. Clark, interview.

135. "Panthers Claim Police Fired First," *Call and Post,* July 4, 1970, 1A, 16A.

136. "Police, Black Community Split on Panthers," *Cleveland Press,* July 24, 1970, A1.

137. Other organizations that united with the Panthers were the Case Western Reserve University Strike Community, Youth Against War and Fascism, United Front for Political Defense, Youth International Party, Cleveland Resistance, and Artists for Peace. "Panthers to Demand Resignation of Davis," *Cleveland Press,* July 20, 1970, D1.

138. In regard to the Panthers' presence at the trial of Newton, Hilliard said, "Opening day and throughout the trial; it's part of our strategy—we pack the courtroom: we want to impress the jury that a movement, not only an individual, is in dock" (Hilliard and Cole, *This Side of Glory,* 205).

139. "Protesters, Panthers Jam Municipal Court Hearings," *Cleveland Press,* July 22, 1970, G1.

140. "Trouble Feared, Panther Hearing Canceled Here," *Cleveland Press,* August 18, 1970, A4.

141. "Panthers Go On Trial for Gun Battle Here," *Cleveland Press,* June 15, 1971.

142. "Jury Convicts 3 Panthers in Shooting of Policeman," *Cleveland Plain Dealer*, July 8, 1971, 1A, 10A; "3 Panthers Guilty of Shooting Police," *Cleveland Press*, July 7, 1971, A1. As it later became clear, the Cleveland Panthers were convicted before they were even tried. Robert Horner, chief investigator for the Committee on Internal Security, testified before Congress in 1970 concerning explosives and "law enforcement officers killed or wounded by gun shots fired by Black Panther Party members." His compilation listed one officer wounded in Cleveland, Officer Ortag. The Panthers had yet to have their day in court, at which time they argued that police gunfire wounded Ortag. Regardless, Horner and the U.S. government convicted them. As Ferrell argued in court, their crime was not firing at police, it was being a Black Panther. United States House of Representatives, Subcommittee of the Committee on Internal Security, *Black Panther Party, Part 4: National Office Operations and Investigations of Activities in Des Moines, Iowa, and Omaha, Nebr.* Committee Exhibit No. 3, "Law Enforcement Officers Killed or Wounded by Gun Shots Fired by Black Panther Party Members," 4721, 4985.
    143. Stokes, *Promises of Power*, 194–199.
    144. The Western Reserve Historical Society. Papers of Carl B. Stokes. Container 81, Folder 1574. Cleveland Panther James "Rock" Todd agreed with this assessment and willingly accepted the label of enemy of law enforcement, stating:

> We definitely consider ourselves enemies of those racists and those fascists that wear badges and carry guns. . . . What we're working for is the total liberation of Black people in the colonies and revolution in the oppressed section of America, and the way we view these policemen—we feel they should be removed from the communities, and the communities should be policed by the inhabitants of the communities. We feel we have to work on the enemy of all mankind, which is these capitalists-exploiters of our people. We are the oil of the well-run machinery of imperialism and colonialism.

Quoted in Zannes, *Checkmate in Cleveland*, 224.
    145. "Dum-Dum Bullet Order Backfires," *Call and Post*, August 1, 1970, 1A, 18A.
    146. The Western Reserve Historical Society. Papers of Carl B. Stokes. Container 29, Folder 519.
    147. "Free Darryl and Essex," *The Black Panther*, May 1, 1971, 17.
    148. Smith, interview.
    149. "Asks Inspector for ID, Will Face Riot Charge," *Call and Post*, October 3, 1970, 10A.
    150. "Police Pull Machine Gun Raid and Find Office Empty," *Call and Post*, September 26, 1970, 14A.
    151. "Jury Frees Panther in Riot Trial," *Cleveland Press*, August 6, 1971.
    152. "Ex-Panther Doesn't Arrive for Riot Trial," *Cleveland Press*, November 2, 1971. Cleveland Panthers were not always blameless for the police surveillance and fear. For instance, in October 1970, Officer Joseph P. Tracz Jr. was killed in his cruiser and his partner, Frederick R. Fulton, was wounded by an assailant's bullets. With Point 7 as his foundation, Charles "Amokoea" Faison described the incident in *The Black Panther*: "After a scuffle with this pig, the lumpen (in the correct manner) knocked the pig down, took his gun and fired into the pig, bang, bang, dead pig!" He continued to glorify the acts of these seemingly unknown revolutionaries: "This and other revolutionary acts will continue to happen until community control of police is implemented throughout racist,

fascist Babylon." "One Pig Dead One Pig Wounded at the Hands of the Lumpen," *The Black Panther*, October 3, 1970, 5.

153. "Pair Charged in Assault and Shooting," *Cleveland Press*, October 1, 1970; "The Cleveland 2 Each Illegally Held on $100,000," *The Black Panther*, October 17, 1970, 17. The *Call and Post*, in its "Good Morning Judge" section, argued against the excessive bail within the terms of the constitutional provision requiring "reasonable" bail for individuals waiting for trial (October 17, 1970).

154. "Two Guilty in Assault on Coed," *Cleveland Press*, June 10, 1971. As Point 9 of the BPP Ten-Point Program states, "[w]e want all Black People when brought to trial to be tried by a jury of their peer group or people from the Black communities, as defined by the Constitution of the United States." *To Die for the People: The Writings of Huey P. Newton* (New York: Vintage Books, 1972).

155. "Church Deed Is Refused as Bail for Panther Trio," *Cleveland Plain Dealer*, December 17, 1970; "People's Church Fights White Racism," *Call and Post*, August 21, 1971, 8A.

156. "Two Guilty in Assault on Coed," *Cleveland Press*, June 10, 1971; "Two Face 3d Trial After Jury Disagrees," *Cleveland Press*, May 18, 1971.

157. United States Senate, "The FBI's Covert Action Program to Destroy the Black Panther Party," *Final Report of the Select Committee to Study Government Operations with Respect to Intelligence Activities* (Washington, D.C.: S.R. No. 94-755, 94th Congress, 2d Sess, 1976), 187.

158. FBI memorandum from headquarters to Chicago and seven other field offices, May 15, 1970. Quoted in Huey P. Newton, *War Against the Panthers* (New York: Harlem River Press, 1996), 83.

159. In San Diego, FBI special agents proposed spraying the newspaper printing room with a foul chemical spray. Newton, *War Against the Panthers*, 83.

160. "Repression of the Black Panther Newspaper," *The Black Panther*, August 8, 1970, 11.

161. FBI memorandum from headquarters to fourteen field offices, November 25, 1968. Quoted in Newton, *War Against the Panthers*, 71. FBI Airtel from SAC Cleveland to FBI Director, December, 4 1970, "Counter-Intelligence Program Black Extremists." Stanford University Libraries, Department of Special Collections, Newton Foundation Inc. Collection: Series 4, Box 12, Folder 14.

162. FBI Airtel from SAC Cleveland to FBI Director, December 4, 1970, "Counter-Intelligence Program Black Extremists." Stanford University Libraries, Department of Special Collections, Newton Foundation Inc. Collection: Series 4, Box 12, Folder 14.

163. Ward Churchill and Jim Vanderwall, *Agents of Repression: The FBI's Secret Wars against the Black Panther Party and the American Indian Movement* (Boston: South End Press, 1990), 49.

164. FBI Memorandum from SAC San Francisco to Director, April 6, 1971, "Black Panther Party–Cleveland." Stanford University Libraries, Department of Special Collections, Newton Foundation Inc. Collection: Series 4, Box 6, Folder 4.

165. Jones, interview.

166. Smith, interview; Peery, interview.

167. Smith, interview.

168. Peery, interview.

169. "Panthers, Afro Set Battle," *Cleveland Press*, June 4, 1969, A3; "Officials Probe Fights, Shooting," *Cleveland Plain Dealer*, June 5, 1969.

170. Slater, interview.

171. "Afro Set, Panthers Join in FBI Protest," *Cleveland Plain Dealer*, August 21, 1971, C5.

172. Vladimir Ilyich Lenin, "The Dual Power," in *The Lenin Anthology*, ed. Robert C. Tucker, 301–304 (New York: Norton, 1975).

173. Huey Newton, "We Are Nationalists and Internationalists," in *The Coming of the New International: A Revolutionary Anthology*, ed. John Gerassi, 45 (New York: The World Publishing Co., 1971).

174. Bobby Seale, *Seize the Time* (New York: Random House, 1970), 412.

175. Hilliard wrote that "the paper, throughout my membership in the Party, remains the bedrock of the organization's finances, and all monies go only to paying the ongoing Party costs" (154); Seale, *Seize the Time*, 179.

176. Huey Newton, *Revolutionary Suicide* (New York: Harcourt Brace Jovanovich, 1973), 137–144; JoNina M. Abron, "'Raising the Consciousness of the People': The Black Panther Intercommunal News Service, 1967–1980," in *Voices from the Underground: Volume I, Insider Histories of the Vietnam Era Underground Press*, ed. Ken Wachsberger (Ann Arbor, Mich.: Mica, 1993).

177. "Black Panther Weekly Sold in 5 Ohio Cities," *Cleveland Press*, November 19, 1970, E6; United States House of Representatives, Subcommittee of the Committee on Internal Security, *Black Panther Party, Part 4: National Office Operations and Investigations of Activities in Des Moines, Iowa, and Omaha, Nebr*, Appendix A, Committee Exhibit No. 6, "Production, Distribution, and Sales of Black Panther Party Newspaper and Applicability of Federal Statute Relating to it's Mailability [sic]," 4721, 4991–4995.

178. This was still minuscule in comparison to Chicago, Detroit, and Los Angeles, which received 15,000, 7,508, and 7,500 respectively for the July 12, 1971, issue. Stanford University Libraries. Department of Special Collections. Newton Foundation Inc. Collection: Series 2, Box 13, Folder 9.

179. Vladimir Ilyich Lenin, "Where to Begin?" in Tucker, *The Lenin Anthology*.

180. "Attempt to Railroad People's Servants," *The Black Panther*, July 4, 1970, 16.

181. This strategy had, after all, already proven effective because Ron Robinson and Norman Peery had themselves joined the Party after noticing the steady appearance of Ernest Watts selling papers downtown in front of Cleveland's Public Square. Peery, interview; Robinson, interview.

182. Smith, interview. Other Cleveland Panthers, such as Fred Clark, were less productive. As Clark remembers, "[t]hey were always getting on my case because I was always messing around with the ladies down at Tri-C instead of selling the papers." Clark, interview.

183. Abron, "'Raising the Consciousness of the People,'" 181.

184. Seale, *Seize the Time*, 371.

185. The following articles published in *The Black Panther* were written by the Cleveland Panthers exclusively about the conditions in Cleveland's Black community: "Mad Dog Racist Murders Young Brother" (June 27, 1970, 4); "Cleveland, Ohio-Avaricious Slumlord Evicts Black Family" (September 12, 1970, 15); "Black People Live in the Ruins of America" (September 12, 1970, 2); "Oppression is Alive and Running Amuck at Cuyahoga County Nursing Home" (October 17, 1970, 15); "Sister Murdered in Cold Blood by Rent-a-Pig" (January 2, 1971, 5); "Crippled Girl and Her Mother Denied Right to Decent Housing" (May 22, 1971, 6); "They're Even Shooting Those Who Teach Our Youth" (July 3, 1971, 4, 5); Davis, interview; Robinson, interview. Curtis Johnson,

who served as the education section leader for the Cleveland Panthers, also had a number of articles published on local events.

186. Curtis Johnson, for instance, was an editor for *The Liberator*, a radical Black newspaper published at Tri-C; "Policeman, Black Militant Shot," *Cleveland Plain Dealer*, June 30, 1970, A1; Robinson, interview.

187. A Cleveland Panther named Jeffery was the wizard with electronics. He rigged the transmitter to send the Panther voice over the airwaves. Smith, interview; Davis, interview.

188. Davis, interview.

189. Peery, interview.

190. "Another Cleveland N.C.C.F. Liberation School," *The Black Panther*, July 4, 1970, 14. Cleveland Panther Essex Smith said that the Panthers also had classes for the liberation school on the roof of their office at 79th Street. Smith, interview.

191. "A Look at City's Black Panthers," *Cleveland Press*, July 23, 1970, A1, A4.

192. Newton, *To Die for the People*, 4.

193. Abron, "'Raising the Consciousness of the People,'" 185.

194. "Police, Black Community Split on Panthers," *Cleveland Press*, July 24, 1970, A1.

195. *The Black Panther* often had branches and chapters submit small advertisements for their community programs. For an example of the structure of the northern California community discussion groups, see page 14 of the January 3, 1969 issue. Frank Stitts, personal interview, April 13, 1999.

196. Stitts, interview.

197. Smith, interview.

198. Abron, "'Raising the Consciousness of the People,'" 184.

199. The Winston-Salem branch of the BPP received a $37,000 grant from the National Episcopal Church to run a nonemergency medical transportation service, which they named the Joseph Waddell People's Free Ambulance Service, after a fallen comrade. Stanford University Libraries. Department of Special Collections. Newton Foundation Inc. Collection: Series 2, Box 6, Folder 10; Abron, "'Raising the Consciousness of the People,'" 185. "Winston Salem Free Ambulance Services Open," *The Black Panther*, February 16, 1974, 3.

200. "Black Panthers Organize Community Health Program," *Call and Post*, March 27, 1971, 7A; "The Free Clinics: Ghetto Care Centers Struggle to Survive," *American Medical News*, February 21, 1972, 12–14. In Stanford University Libraries. Department of Special Collections. Newton Foundation Inc. Collection: Series 2, Box 17, Folder 10.

201. "The Free Clinics: Ghetto Care Centers Struggle to Survive," *American Medical News*, February 21, 1972, 12–14. In Stanford University Libraries. Department of Special Collections. Newton Foundation Inc. Collection: Series 2, Box 17, Folder 10.

202. "Black Panthers Organize Community Health Program," *Call and Post*, March 27, 1971, 7A; "Black Panthers Here Shift Emphasis to Social Action," *Cleveland Plain Dealer*, July 12, 1971, A1, A16; Smith, interview.

203. "Black Panthers Organize Community Health Program," *Call and Post*, March 27, 1971, 7A.

204. Newton, *To Die for the People*, 176.

205. "Police Pull Machine Gun Raid and Find Office Empty," *Call and Post*, September 26, 1970, 14A; "Black Panthers Organize Community Health Program," *Call and Post*, March 27, 1971, 7A.

206. Brown, *A Taste of Power*, 303–304. Mozambique achieved independence from the Portuguese on June 25, 1975, behind the leadership of Samora Machel and FRELIMO (Frente de Libertacao de Mocambique [Front for the Liberation of Mozambique]). For a discussion on the FRELIMO programs administered following independence, see Joseph Hanlon, *Mozambique: The Revolution Under Fire* (London: Zed Books, (1984) 1990), especially chapter 14, titled "People's Power." See also Bertil Egero, "People's Power: The Case of Mozambique," in *Africa: Problems in the Transition to Socialism*, ed. Barry Munslow (London: Zed Books, 1986). A larger discussion on the history of the Mozambique struggle can be found in the work of Eduardo Mondlane, the FRELIMO president, assassinated on February 3, 1969, *The Struggle for Mozambique* (Middlesex, England: Penguin, 1969).

207. "Black Panthers Here Shift Emphasis to Social Action," *Cleveland Plain Dealer*, July 12, 1971, A1, A16.

208. "Cleveland Racists Dynamite People's Free Health Center," *The Black Panther*, September 11, 1971, 9, 17.

209. "Panther Medical Center Bombed," *Call and Post*, August 21, 1971, 1A, 6A; "Cleveland Racists Dynamite People's Free Health Center," *The Black Panther*, September 11, 1971, 9, 17.

210. "Afro Set Marches to Aid Panther Clinic," *Cleveland Plain Dealer*, August 22, 1971, A16. The Cleveland Panthers also extended their "revolutionary appreciation and solidarity" to the Emmanual Episcopal Church, Out Reach Community Program, The People's Church, and the House of Israel, all of whom rallied to support the Panthers. "Cleveland Racists Dynamite People's Free Health Center," *The Black Panther*, September 11, 1971, 17.

211. "Panthers Invite You to Picnic," *Cleveland Press*, September 9, 1971.

212. "Panthers Hold Open-Air Party," *Cleveland Plain Dealer*, September 13, 1971, A6.

213. "Black Panthers Here Shift Emphasis to Social Action," *Cleveland Plain Dealer*, July 12, 1971, 1A, 16A.

214. For an in-depth look at the impact of the Party's free breakfast program, see *The Black Panther*, April 27, 1969.

215. United States House of Representatives. Committee on Internal Security. Ninety-First Congress, *Black Panther Party, Part 1: Investigation of Kansas City Chapter*; *National Organization Data*, Committee Exhibit No. 5, "The Black Panther Party (Staff Study)" (Washington, D.C.: U.S. Government Printing Office, 1970), 2808.

216. Robinson, interview; Clark, interview; Smith, interview; "Panthers Tell of Play Lot, Free Breakfast Programs," *Cleveland Plain Dealer*, June 30, 1970, 15A. The Cleveland Panthers advertised their program and stated that "[a]ll children in grammar schools and growing young adults in junior high school can receive free, full breakfasts in the morning before they go to school." "Cleveland Breakfast for Children Program to Expand," *The Black Panther*, April 17, 1971, 9; "Opening of the Cleveland NCCF Free Breakfast Program," *The Black Panther*, November 7, 1970, 3.

217. "Black Panthers Provide Eggs, Grits to Hungry Kids," *Cleveland Press*, October 15, 1971; "Black Panther Party Sponsors Breakfast Project," *Call and Post*, October 5, 1971, 5A.

218. Even Harllel Jones, leader of the Afro Set in Cleveland, said that "one of the greatest programs of the 1960s was the Black Panthers' free breakfast program." Jones, interview.

219. Slater, interview.

220. Carr often did the "church circuit," speaking at various locations to initiate support for the Party. For instance, teenage members of the Woodland Hills Community Presbyterian Church organized a Youth Sunday service that featured Carr and four other Cleveland Panthers. Carr elaborated on the programs instituted by the Cleveland Panthers and stressed the need for Black churches to open their facilities "to respond to the needs of the poor." "Woodland Hills Church: 'The Misery of Blackness' Is Theme of Youth Sunday," *Call and Post*, March 6, 1971, 8A; Gene Wilson, personal interview, April 28, 1999. St. Adalbert Church, located in the Fairfax neighborhood next to Kinsman, was active beyond the boundaries of Cleveland. In September 1970, they organized the first Ohio Conference for Black Lay Catholics, with four hundred participants, including Bishop Harold R. Perry of New Orleans, the only Black Catholic bishop in the United States. "400 Attend Conference for Black Catholics," *Call and Post*, October 3, 1970, 1A.

221. Wilson, interview.

222. Stitts, interview. Eventually, the city saw the same need. In October 1971, the Cleveland public schools announced a "Free Lunch Policy" to assist families "suffering from unusual circumstances or hardships." "Schools Announce Free Lunches for Children Unable to Pay," *Call and Post*, October 16, 1971, 3A.

223. Seale mentions that most free breakfast programs started in churches and were funded through the donations of local businesses and members of the Black community (*Seize the Time*, 413).

224. McCoy, interview.

225. Davis, interview.

226. Newton, *To Die for the People*, 104.

227. McCoy, interview.

228. "Panthers Group Holds Giveaway," *Cleveland Press*, March 26, 1971, C7.

229. Abron, "'Raising the Consciousness of the People,'" 186.

230. "Free Busing Program," *The Black Panther*, December 26, 1970, 9; "Panthers Offer Free Bus Rides for Prison Visits," *Call and Post*, April 10, 1971, 4A.

231. Slater, interview.

232. McCoy reported to the Cleveland media that "[w]e don't have enough buses or volunteer drivers to meet the total need." "Black Panthers Still Offer Bus Rides to Ohio Prisons," *Cleveland Press*, May 26, 1971; "Cleveland Free Busing Program," *The Black Panther*, March 27, 1971, 9; "Panthers Plan Buses to Prisons," *Cleveland Plain Dealer*, July 1, 1971, 7A. The Panthers added the fifth prison, the Southern Ohio Correctional Facility at Lucasville, in the early months of 1973, about the same time that they added the sixth, the new London Correctional Institute. "Dynamo Keeps Buses to Prisons Running," *Cleveland Press*, April 13, 1973.

233. "Black Panthers Here Shift Emphasis to Social Action," *Cleveland Plain Dealer*, July 12, 1971, 1A, 16A. The number of people transported each week depended on the particular institution. Mansfield, for instance, was for first-time offenders and usually required a large school bus. McCoy, interview.

234. McCoy, interview.

235. Ibid.

236. Smith, interview.

237. JoAnn Bray to Huey Newton, Stanford University Archives, Department of Special Collections, Newton Foundation Inc. Collection: Series 2, Box 12, Folder 5.

238. Stanford University Archives, Department of Special Collections, Newton Foundation Inc. Collection: Series 2, Box 12, Folder 5.

239. JoAnn Bray, letter to the editor, *Call and Post*, September 4, 1971, 3B.

240. Stanford University Archives, Department of Special Collections, Newton Foundation Inc. Collection: Series 2, Box 12, Folder 5.

241. McCoy, interview.

242. "Invalid Now Runs Bus to Prisons That Black Panthers Ran Free," *Cleveland Plain Dealer*, March 31, 1972.

243. "She Got More Than She Lost—More Than Money Could Buy," *Cleveland Press*, November 18, 1972.

244. "She Lost Her Stereo But Kept Her Smile," *Cleveland Press*, October 14, 1972.

245. Other sources of income assisted the program as well. Bray once received a watch from an inmate who told her to sell it and use the money to finance a bus. "She Lost Her Stereo But Kept Her Smile," *Cleveland Press*, October 14, 1972.

246. "Dynamo Keeps Buses to Prisons Running," *Cleveland Press*, April 13, 1973; "Keeping Families Together Is Goal of Jail Visitation Busing Program," *Cleveland Plain Dealer*, January 25, 1975; "People's Busing Program Lacks Insurance," *Cleveland Press*, May 19, 1976; "Bus Rides That Bring Togetherness," *Cleveland Press*, March 18, 1974.

247. "People's Busing Program Lacks Insurance," *Cleveland Press*, May 19, 1976.

248. Newton, *War Against the Panthers*, 32.

249. Newton, *Revolutionary Suicide*, 167.

250. Davis, interview; "Ex-Panther Doesn't Arrive for Riot Trial," *Cleveland Press*, November 2, 1971.

251. Brown, *A Taste of Power*, 276–282.

252. Ollie A. Johnson III, "Explaining the Demise of The Black Panther Party: The Role of Internal Factors," in Jones, *The Black Panther Party Reconsidered*, 404, 405.

253. Ibid., 406.

254. Davis, interview; Slater, interview.

255. Stitts, interview.

256. Davis, interview.

257. McCoy, interview.

Harllel Jones (far left), leader of the Afro Set, stands outside their headquarters in the Hough. (CP)

(*above*) Mayor Carl B. Stokes (right) swears in General Benjamin Davis, Jr. as Safety Director. (CP)

(*below*) Jones (center left) and Mayor Stokes observe the Afro Set drill. (CP)

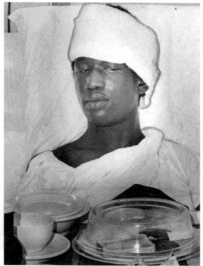

Cleveland Panther Fred Clark before and after the police shoot-out. (CP)

Protesters march for the release of the Cleveland Panthers pictured in previous photo and the removal of General Davis as Safety Director. (CP)

(*right*) Charles "Amokoea" Faison worked with the Cleveland Panthers' clothing program and later headed the communications section. (LM)

(*left*) Austin Jones served as the coordinator for the Cleveland Panthers' health program during the late summer of 1970. (LM)

(*right*) Typical of the youth within the Black Panther Party, Allen "Red" Gaines started working with the Cleveland Panthers when he was sixteen years old. (LM)

Luke McCoy served as the coordinator for the Cleveland Panthers' Free Busing to Prisons Program. (LM)

Bill Davis was the Cleveland Panthers' information officer before he moved to Oakland and served on the Party's Central Committee. (LM)

Panther Charles Faison (left) looks through the shoes with some community members during the Cleveland Panthers' free clothing program at the St. Adalbert Church. (LM)

Community members and Cleveland Panthers Tommy Tuck (far left); Allen "Red" Gaines (second from the left); "Sleepy" (third from right), Diane Carr (second from right), wife of Cleveland Panther leader Tommie Carr; and Charles "Amokoea" Faison (far right) stand in front of the St. Adalbert Church before the opening of the Panthers' free clothing program. (LM)

Cleveland Panther Curtis Johnson (standing) reads over the Party's newspaper, *The Black Panther*, with children during the Panthers' Liberation School. In addition to summer reading, the Cleveland Panthers provided a free lunch during each class. (CP)

(*above*) Family and friends of inmates board a bus to the Mansfield Prison as part of the Cleveland Panthers' Free Busing to Prisons Program. (LM)

(*left*) Cleveland Panther Luke McCoy (far right), coordinator for the Free Busing to Prisons Program, poses with the family members of inmates after a trip to Marion Prison.

The Cleveland Panthers hold a press conference outside their Kinsman office. From left to right: Tommie Carr, Ron Robinson, James "Rock" Todd, and Mike Cross, a Panther from the Toledo chapter. (CP)

Father Gene Wilson, who assisted with the Cleveland Panthers' community programs, gives the salute with Panthers Tommy Tuck (left) and Charles Faison (right). (LM)

Harold Taylor and Talibah Shakir from the Los Angeles office of the Black Panther Party.

Talibah Shakir from the Los Angeles office of the Black Panther Party.

Steve McCutchen from the Baltimore office of the Black Panther Party.

From left to right, Connie Felder (Baltimore office of the Black Panther Party), Steve McCutchen (Baltimore office of the Black Panther Party), and a relative of Steve's.

Marvin Jackson of the Los Angeles office of the Black Panther Party. Photo taken while in the U.S. Army.

Keith Parker of the Indianapolis branch of the Black Panther Party. Photo taken while a student at Indiana University.

M. Eddie Conway of the Baltimore Black Panthers, jailed since 1970.

M. Eddie Conway as U.S. serviceman.

4

Nap Town Awakens to Find a Menacing Panther; OK, Maybe Not So Menacing

Judson L. Jeffries and Tiyi M. Morris

The Indianapolis Black Panthers have been as mischaracterized, misread, and rigorously understudied as the organization itself. The Indy Panthers were part of the political fabric of Indianapolis, if only fleetingly. Yet in books about Indiana in general and Indianapolis specifically, the Panthers have received scant attention. In the past ten years both the state of Indiana and the city of Indianapolis have been the subject of numerous theses and dissertations. Moreover, since 2000 at least two scholarly books have been published on African Americans in Indiana. Of the two, only Emma Lou Thornbrough's *Indiana Blacks in the Twentieth Century* devotes more than one page to the Panthers.[1] In *Polite Protest: The Political Economy of Race in Indianapolis 1920–1970*, the more recent of the two books, historian Richard Pierce devotes less than one full sentence to the Indianapolis branch.[2]

On those occasions when the Panthers are mentioned in the literature, the statements are more often than not inaccurate, puzzling, and unsubstantiated. For example, news articles in the *Indianapolis Star* repeatedly referred to Panther leader Fred Crawford as a California native when in fact he was born and raised in Indianapolis. Most scholarly as well as quasi-scholarly works are equally unpolished. In *Bitter Grain*, Michael Newton makes the dubious statement that some observers have called the Indianapolis chapter the "most successful Panther organization east of Oakland." However, the author does not provide a citation; hence it is difficult to ascertain the identity of those observers. Three paragraphs later Newton claims that the key to the Indy Panthers' success lay in their ability "to avoid the financial shortages which plagued other party units."[3] Former Indy Panthers recall that while the chapter did receive a one-time gift of $3,000, donations were on the whole small and sporadic. In other words, the Panthers' coffers were not as impressive as Newton suggests. Most Panther branches and chapters operated on a shoe-string budget. To say the same of the Indy office would be too generous a characterization.

Although the Indy Panthers were in no way, shape, or form the most effective branch east of California or among the better-financed, they also were not among the least effective offices as Pierce insinuates. In his dissertation (later expanded into a book), Pierce implies that the Indy branch was not very political—that the branch was a Panther office in name only. As proof he submits that the Indianapolis Panthers never had an article published in the Black Panther newspaper during their existence. Our examination of *The Black Panther* reveals something very different. At least ten articles written by Panthers in Indianapolis were found in *The Black Panther* in 1968 and 1969 alone. This type of carelessness does little to elicit the kind of interest and serious inquiry into the Panther organization that is necessary in order to gain an accurate, substantive, and nuanced understanding of this multifaceted, community-oriented organization.

In fact, the Indianapolis branch of the Black Panther Party (BPP) was very political and quite active; the lengths to which law enforcement went to neutralize the branch and the fact that both the local police department and certain federal agencies felt compelled to act within six months of the branch's formation are suggestive of that. For instance, FBI documents reveal that on December 18, 1968, Indianapolis police officers, accompanied by agents from the Internal Revenue Service's Alcohol and Tobacco Tax Unit, arrived at Black Panther Party headquarters with a federal warrant to search for unregistered automatic weapons under the new U.S. Gun Control Act. In some respects the raid mirrored the proposition rejected by Mayor Wes Uhlman in Seattle, with the FBI standing in for IRS agents.[4] According to the FBI, based upon information gathered by the Indianapolis Police Department, the bureau had reason to believe that the Panthers had been stockpiling machine guns at their local office. Security officers on duty that day, Michael Cannon and Dan Ginns, refused to permit the agents to enter without seeing the warrant. As a result, the office was tear-gassed and Cannon and Ginns were subsequently arrested. Lawrence Roberts, who was called to the headquarters during the incident, was arrested as well and charged with interfering with a federal officer. To the dismay of the authorities, the search failed to turn up any weapons.

America's heartland, once considered a bedrock of ultraconservatism, did not seem a likely host to a Panther office, but the Black militants put down stakes there all the same. And like every other chapter and branch of the Black Panther Party, the Indianapolis Panthers could not escape police repression. Even though, according to deputy minister of information Robert O'Bannon, they were "the most non-violent chapter in the country," Indianapolis Panthers endured their fair share of harassment.[5] Opened in the summer of 1968 by deputy chairman Fred Crawford, the Indianapolis office would expand the organization's Midwest base, claiming members in the capital city as well as in Bloomington and Muncie. The Panthers' arrival brought a contrasting political view to the conservative midwestern city for both Black and white residents. Given the political and social consciousness of many Black Hoosiers, it is a wonder that the Panthers were able to muster enough support for a branch.

Early Black Activism and the State of Black Indiana

Black political activism in Indianapolis prior to the Panthers can be characterized as genteel. Although Indiana was by no means considered an epicenter of civil rights activity, Black Hoosiers did participate in the nationwide activism that made up the Civil Rights Movement. National organizations made their way into Indianapolis's communities, allowing the city to mimic movement trends. For example, Black youths sat in at their local Woolworth stores. Furthermore, the establishment of these various organizations allowed for the implementation of a wide array of civil rights tactics, ranging from lobbying for civil rights legislation and voter registration drives to nonviolent direct action.

As in many other places, the principal civil rights organization in the city was the National Association for the Advancement of Colored People (NAACP). Since its founding in the Circle City in 1913, the NAACP had been at the forefront of measures taken to protect and advance the rights of Black Hoosiers. The NAACP was particularly active in the 1920s in response to threats from the Ku Klux Klan. Membership in the Indiana Klan increased dramatically during the post–World War I era partly in response to the influx of Black residents during the Great Migration. During this period, Blacks more than quadrupled their numbers in some midwestern cities. Like cities such as Chicago, Detroit, and Cleveland, Indianapolis also experienced a significant increase in its Black population. From 1910 to 1920 Indianapolis's Black population grew 59 percent, from 21,816 to 34,678.[6] By 1930, this number would rise to 43,967. Other cities throughout the state, such as Gary, East Chicago, South Bend, and Fort Wayne, would experience even more dramatic changes, with Gary's Black population increasing by 1,283 percent. Despite such increases throughout the state, Indianapolis retained the largest number of Black residents.

The proliferation of Blacks magnified racial tensions. Job competition and increased housing needs put some whites in greater contact with Blacks, and as Blacks sought political representation in these areas, many whites resisted. Securing a stronghold in city and state politics, largely by dominating the Republican Party, the Klan instigated racial tensions through such efforts as forced segregation in the school system.[7] In this political predicament, the NAACP became a primary organizing force for the Independent Voters League, which was established to defeat "Klan-backed candidates."[8] Moreover, Blacks drifted away from the party of Lincoln for the Democratic Party—a relationship that would be strengthened by the New Deal policies of Franklin D. Roosevelt. From efforts in the 1920s to resist Klan intimidation to the 1930s' "don't buy where you can't work" campaigns and school segregation in the 1940s and 1950s, the NAACP was instrumental in raising awareness and spurring both Blacks and whites to action.

During the 1960s, a solid network of civil rights organizations was being established. Leading the fight for Black equality, the local NAACP maintained the organization's traditional approach to civil rights activity, filing lawsuits and lobbying for civil rights legislation. Other civil rights organizations in Indianapolis included an affiliate of the Southern Christian Leadership Conference (SCLC) and Operation Breadbasket, established by Rev. Andrew Brown (pastor of St. John's Missionary Baptist Church) after Dr. Martin Luther King Jr.'s visit to the state capital in 1958–59. In 1963, Rev. Brown founded the Social Action Council. This organization was designed to be the "action arm of the NAACP," engaging forcefully in voter registration efforts that would yield positive results, such as producing the city's largest Black voter turnout for the November 1963 elections.[9] Additionally, the Congress of Racial Equality (CORE) joined the scene in 1964 under the leadership of John Torian. Young Black Hoosiers welcomed the arrival of CORE, for many of them were less patient with the incremental progress being made by organizations like the NAACP and SCLC. The NAACP and SCLC tended to shy away from direct confrontation. But CORE had a reputation, dating as far back as the 1940s, for being more bullish in its approach to civil rights than the aforementioned groups. Consequently, given the exuberance displayed by many Black youths, it is not surprising that many of them gravitated toward CORE. In addition to participating in voter registration, CORE organized a sit-in at the Indianapolis School Board building in the summer of 1964.

Civil rights, however, did not concern only African Americans. In 1965, prominent Blacks and whites joined forces to launch a chapter of the National Urban League. The Urban League had been an important vehicle for social change in other Indiana cities—promoting positive race relations and providing necessary social services to Black residents, particularly new migrants to the city. The formation of an Urban League chapter in Indianapolis came much later than in other midwestern and northern cities of comparable size. This was due in part to resistance from the prominent Black and white leaders who ran the Flanner House. Established in 1898 by Frank Flanner, a white Indianapolis mortician, the Flanner Guild (later House) began as a segregated component of a local settlement house.[10] With the support of both white and Black philanthropists, it grew to become the most important social service center for Blacks in Indianapolis.

Governed by a biracial board and guided by a philosophy of self-help, the Flanner House comprised three divisions—"social service, vocational aid, and self-help services."[11] Similar to settlement houses characteristic of the Progressive Era, services included training classes, nursery schools, extracurricular activities through boys and girls clubs, and a music department, as well as medical services. Unable to escape the racial bias of the time, however, and with limited financial recourses, training classes were often focused on preparing Blacks for the few jobs that were open to them, such as domestic service for women. According to the 1960 census, more than half of Black women in the workforce were employed as domestic servants of some kind. Although not challenging the status quo, the Flanner House did assist these women in finding employment and also sought to ensure that they received an adequate wage and fair treatment. Those securing employment through the Flanner House in the 1920s, for example, could expect to receive wages of $2 or $2.35 per eight-hour day, depending on one's work experience, significantly more than the typical domestic who earned a mere four or five dollars a week.[12]

Over the years, the Flanner House experienced continual development and expansion of its services. In 1908, the "Flanner Guild Rescue Home was established to care for unmarried mothers and their children," in 1918 the Children's Development Center opened, and in the 1950s Flanner House began its "Sweat Equity" housing program (similar to Habitat for Humanity) to increase Black home ownership.[13] Thus, some perceived the Urban

League's emphasis on similar issues such as labor, education, housing, and improving race relations to be in direct competition with the Flanner House. Board members worried that the Urban League might tap into financial sectors of the community that had historically supported the Flanner House. In fact, Henry J. Richardson, the driving force behind the establishment of the Indianapolis Urban League, was critical of the Flanner House's housing program. He argued that Flanner House homes merely facilitated housing segregation by pacifying the Black community with homes for a few African Americans but did not directly challenge housing discrimination. As a result, the Urban League would immediately become involved in the push for open housing and would be another viable resource for Black Hoosiers in their struggle for equality.

In 1959, the Nation of Islam (NOI) opened a temple in Indianapolis, bringing a new level of activism to this sleepy town. By and large the temple was not well received by the Black community, let alone by the white community. Had the Muslims arrived a year or two earlier they might have been able to win over some segments of the Black community, but unfortunately for them their arrival in Indy occurred the same year as CBS correspondent Mike Wallace's story on the Nation of Islam titled *The Hate That Hate Produced.* Millions of viewers tuned in, and both Blacks and whites were floored by the NOI's rhetoric. To many white viewers, the NOI came off as a Black version of the KKK, preaching Black supremacy to anyone within earshot. As far as Blacks were concerned, the NOI was a bunch of crazy ni__ers. Some even thought the NOI was a cult. Suffice to say, the Nation of Islam was unable to generate the kind of support in Indy that existed in cities such as Chicago, Detroit, and Cleveland. This resistance to radicalism by the Black community would be witnessed again with the lack of response to the assassination of Malcolm X. As reported in the *Indianapolis Star,* some Black leaders were not only critical of Malcolm X's "extremism," but, in a gross underestimation of the extent of white racism, believed that had he followed King's philosophy he would still be alive.[14] Preferring King's viewpoint over Malcolm X's, the majority of Black Hoosiers were simply not ready for radical, Black Nationalist politics. Furthermore, incremental political gains undermined any potential for Black radicalism.

As the Civil Rights Movement gained momentum throughout the 1960s, Indiana began to undergo changes in its political landscape. Black political participation increased, and white politicians recognized the practicality of encouraging dialogue on civil rights matters and undertook efforts to improve race relations. In the 1960 governor's race, both candidates, Democrat Matthew E. Welsh and Republican lieutenant governor Crawford Parker, promised to support civil rights.[15] The platforms of high-profile statewide candidates always included civil rights planks on general principle, but most voters understood that civil rights rhetoric was just that—a ploy to avoid turning Black voters off rather than a harbinger of one's legislative agenda.

The 1960 race was a lively one. Welsh's campaign, which centered on creating a more efficient and involved state government, was highly critical of the incumbent administration of Harold W. Handley. During a speech at the annual meeting of the Indiana Democratic Editorial Association in August 1960, Welsh questioned Handley's character and accused the incumbent of being a caretaker. Furthermore, Welsh said the Republicans lacked the leadership to address the needs of the people and had demonstrated a complete inability to get the job done.[16]

Welsh's platform included eliminating government financial excesses and waste, a fairer tax system, improved schools, and better job security, especially for government employees. Regarding civil rights, Welsh admitted that while it was not a central campaign issue, it merited some attention. At a Democratic rally held at the historic Madame Walker Theatre, Welsh appealed to his Black constituency by calling for equal employment through a strong fair employment practices act, an end to housing discrimination, improved education, and equal access to public accommodations. Furthermore, he asserted that he would be the leading force behind such initiatives. He wrapped up his speech by saying, "Your Indiana government must set the moral tone with bold, imaginative action—under the leadership of a Governor who is indignant enough about the present conditions to do something about them."[17] Parker, on the other hand, who was nominated without opposition and with the support of the incumbent governor, was less vocal about civil rights. Sure, he pledged to back civil rights legislation if elected, but, interestingly, no significant piece of civil rights legislation was passed during his tenure as lieutenant governor. Therefore, few people expected him to be an advocate of civil rights if elected governor.

Addressing the mainstays of civil rights legislation—housing, employment, education, and public accommodations—Welsh was elected and endorsed at best a moderate civil rights agenda. During his tenure as governor he was able to gain passage of a meager public accommodations bill (it lacked "penalties and compulsory features"), and in 1961, Welsh established the Fair Employment Practices Commission (later the Civil Rights Commission) as an independent agency to investigate and make recommendations regarding civil rights violations that involved employment and public accommodations. In 1963, the commission was directed "to induce compliance by persuasion and conciliation if possible."[18] With this new power to enforce legislation, the commission could "issue cease and desist orders, enforced by the courts, in cases of discrimination in employment, public accommodations, and education."[19] Furthermore, the new public accommodations act allowed "the aggrieved person to go directly to the courts in a civil action for damages rather than compelling him to go through the prosecutor's office."[20]

Welsh also sought to end discriminatory hiring practices by the state with a directive for department heads to target Blacks for employment. Additionally, a December 1961 executive order required that "state government contracts include a nondiscrimination clause that made breach of the provision a basis for cancellation of the contract." Overall, Welsh's term resulted in some gains for Blacks. According to a Civil Rights Commission report on Welsh's tenure, "three Legislatures enacted a set of civil rights laws as comprehensive as any other state has enacted in a 16 year period."[21]

Citywide politics also produced some gains for Blacks. The 1963 mayoral election of Democrat John Barton had positive outcomes for Blacks although Barton was not considered a major supporter of civil rights. One such development under Barton's tenure was the creation of the Greater Indianapolis Progress Committee (GIPC), a bipartisan advisory board made up of prominent civic and financial leaders. The GIPC proved instrumental in furthering civil rights initiatives through such efforts as endorsing "federal aid for public housing" in hopes of creating more diverse communities.

Some believed that Republican Richard Lugar's election in 1967, however, turned back some of the progress made by his Democratic predecessors. In addition to ignoring the Black community's concerns, Lugar promoted a "metropolitan government" plan (commonly referred to as "Unigov") that would consolidate city and county governments and dilute the Black vote in Indianapolis. Prior to the consolidation proposal, Indianapolis elections had revealed a solid Democratic majority. The city's surrounding areas (population 300,000), however, "voted republican by a 2-1 majority." Thus, combining Indianapolis with its surrounding suburbs and rural areas would reduce the Black population in Indianapolis from 27 percent to 17 percent, shifting power away from the central city and increasing Republican strength in elections.[22] In 1969, this initiative became a reality as Indianapolis merged with Marion County, which expanded the mayor's power and strengthened the Republican vote. The gains Blacks experienced in the early part of the decade began to dissipate, creating a space for leftist ideologies to take root.

While housing segregation had historically been a problem for Blacks, increased migration to northern and midwestern cities in search of jobs during the war years caused housing problems to intensify. Increased numbers of Blacks led to more restrictions and discrimination from whites. Blacks were generally confined to certain "colored" areas of the city by the use of restrictive covenants, which prevented the sale of homes to nonwhites in certain areas, and by banks' policies of either refusing to lend money to Blacks or requiring higher down payments. Housing was also excluded from the initial civil rights bill in the early years of Governor Welsh's tenure. The 1961 public accommodations bill's provisions against housing discrimination applied only to "housing owned by cities, towns or the state."[23] Consequently, the majority of housing, which was owned by individuals or real estate companies, was unaffected by the legislation. The 1963 civil rights bill that included "enforcement provisions" also excluded housing. The election of Republican Rufus Kuykendall and Democrat Rev. James Cummings, both Black, to the city council in 1963 was the impetus behind passing a housing ordinance. With endorsement from the Indianapolis Chamber of Commerce, the city council passed an ordinance outlawing "discrimination in the sale or renting of housing" in 1964.[24]

As in other areas of civil rights, employment discrimination was a battle to be waged on two fronts—legal and social custom. In the early 1960s the majority of Black Hoosiers were employed in blue-collar jobs with little possibility of advancement, a tenuous position given increased technological advancement. Multiple factors caused a shift in employment opportunities for Blacks—the enforcement powers of the Civil Rights Commission, the Civil Rights Act of 1964, the creation of the Equal Employment Opportunity Commission, fears of "urban unrest," and the Indianapolis Chamber of Commerce's call to local businesses to hire minorities.[25] Additionally, in 1961, Governor Welsh directed departments of state government to end discrimination in hiring, urging them to employ more African Americans, "particularly at the upper levels," thereby increasing the numbers of Blacks holding civil service jobs. These efforts contributed to a slight increase in nonwhite state employees from 9.5 percent to 11.69 percent in ninety-two departments.[26] Through these efforts Black employment outside of the service sector began to reflect their population in the city.

Overall, Black Hoosiers' progress was modest during the 1960s. However, according to Emma Lou Thornbrough, "[i]n spite of the state's reputation for political conservatism, Indiana lawmakers moved earlier than Congress in enacting civil rights legislation."[27] In fact, the adoption of the 1963 law made Indiana the only state in the Midwest with enforceable legislation in three major areas of discrimination.[28] By 1968, however, Indiana appeared to be rolling back the progress that had been made up to that point. That year Hoosiers elected Roger Branigan as their governor, and to the surprise of many, upon taking office the Democrat said he favored "gradualism" in accomplishing the idea of equal rights for all and that there were penalties for "pressing beyond the point of public acceptance."[29] That a Democrat would make such a remark struck many people as a bit odd for two reasons. First, Democrats had been known to at least appear receptive to pushing civil rights as an agenda item. Second, the Black vote almost always played a critical role in the election of Indiana Democrats. But then again Indiana is an odd state in many respects.

Indianapolis was also unique in the absence of "urban unrest" that affected other cities in the latter part of the decade. Longtime state representative Bill Crawford explained the lack of racial upheaval this way:

> First Blacks could find work in Indianapolis. Sure there was unemployment in the Black community, but not like in Chicago or Detroit, places like that. Second, Indianapolis is a horizontal city, not a vertical city like the ones I just mentioned. In Indy we're not stacked up on top of each other. Everybody, rich or poor, had a lawn. We did not have the level of tension that existed in urban communities with a high population density and a high concentration of underprivileged people.[30]

Crawford's analysis seems plausible. However, not every horizontal city was devoid of racial uprisings. Los Angeles, for example, is one of the most horizontal and sprawling cities in the United States, yet two of the most infamous revolts of the twentieth century occurred there. Also, Black unemployment in Indianapolis may not have reached the level of Chicago or other cities, but Blacks were still disproportionately impacted by unemployment. In fact, according to the 1970 census the Black unemployment rate in Indianapolis was 8.3 percent while Indianapolis generally was approximately 3 percent.[31]

Even in the wake of King's assassination, Blacks in Indianapolis would follow King's nonviolent philosophy after repeated urgings by local ministers and NAACP and Urban League leaders, as well as Mayor Lugar and Robert Kennedy, who was in town making a speech when he received news of the tragedy. Kennedy, who was on the presidential campaign trail, was scheduled to make a stop in Indianapolis and was told of King's death minutes after his plane touched down at the airport. Kennedy arrived to find people in a jovial mood, anticipating the excitement of his appearance. Realizing that the audience was unaware of the assassination, he climbed aboard the platform and broke the news as women screamed and men gasped. Kennedy appealed to the crowd's sense of loyalty to King's legacy. He said,

> Martin Luther King dedicated his life to love and to justice for his fellow human beings, and he died because of that effort. . . . What we need in the United States is not division; what we need in the United States is not hatred; what we need in the United States is not violence or lawlessness; but love and wisdom, and compassion toward one another, and a feeling of justice toward

one another, and a feeling of justice toward those who still suffer within our country, whether they be white or they be black.[32]

Rev. Brown of the SCLC argued that Black people's calm response and the overall lack of racial disturbances in the area were not necessarily because of Kennedy or Lugar but because the "white power structure" and middle-class Blacks did not want to "rock the boat."[33] From the standpoint of some, the lack of Black uproar was not something to take pride in. Andrew Ramsey, president of the state NAACP conference and columnist for the *Indianapolis Recorder,* frequently criticized Black Hoosiers for their lethargy and failure to demand their rights. He specifically singled out the president of the Indianapolis NAACP chapter for her cautious approach to problems, which he characterized as saying "[l]et's not do this or that or we might get into trouble."[34]

Despite the initial peaceful response to King's death, however, this tragedy would serve as a catalyst for militancy and a sense of urgency among some Black Hoosiers. Moreover, the conservative backlash brought on by Lugar's administration and Blacks' previous sublimation of frustrations made the city a potential powder keg that could blow up if Black progress continued to move along at a snail's pace.

One issue in particular that would be a focal point of this growing frustration was police brutality. Ben Bell, director of the College Room, was quoted as saying the police department could only think of one way to "keep the niggers in their place," by using guns, mace, fists, and police dogs.[35] Police harassment of Blacks occurred not only on the street but extended into after-hours clubs. For example, on June 8, 1969, a group of police officers entered The Place, an establishment that served no liquor and was a spot where Blacks enjoyed live music. Without explanation, officers began pushing patrons out of the way as they entered and drawing guns on those who objected. Officers held one band member and his wife at gunpoint while threatening to arrest the club owner and shut the place down. Although no one was injured during the ruckus, the incident made an impression on club owner James Schaffer, who questioned in a letter to the *Indianapolis Recorder* if the police really wanted to improve race relations. In his closing, Schaffer remarked, "This place could end up like Watts, Detroit, or Newark. We Blacks are not going to take it like we have in the past. The time is now for you to use some diplomacy, and my advice is to take heed."[36]

Even before King's assassination, Blacks had been concerned about the possibility of racial violence. Black leaders warned that maintaining a city without racial disturbance, in light of the abuse and discrimination to which Blacks were subjected, was becoming ever more difficult. In the foreground of simmering militancy, unaddressed grievances like police harassment paved the way for the emergence of the Black Panther Party.

Panthers Open Office in Indy

With a Panther branch, Fred Crawford not only brought the organization's survival programs to Indianapolis, but he also provided an outlet for the city's budding militancy. When asked why he joined the Black Panthers in 1969, Keith Parker (now an assistant vice chancellor at a prestigious public university) replied, "I wanted to change the world; civil rights was not enough."[37] Crawford had gotten the idea of opening a Panther office while in Oakland, California, where he had gone after dropping out of high school. His friend, Stanford "Ox" Patton, with whom he attended Crispus Attucks High School in Indianapolis, was living in Los Angeles at the time. Patton, who would later join the Indianapolis branch, had had a storied basketball career in high school, winning a state title on a team with the legendary Oscar Robertson. It was in California that Crawford and Patton encountered Panthers for the first time.

Crawford recalls seeing Stokely Carmichael speak at a Free Huey Rally in Oakland he and Patton attended and being very impressed. Other Panther luminaries such as H. Rap Brown, Bobby Seale, and Eldridge Cleaver were present, but it was Carmichael who made the biggest impression on Crawford. "Stokely appeared to be a very dedicated activist and was very approachable," remembers Crawford.[38] Inspired by Carmichael's speech, Crawford started going to meetings and regularly attending Panther rallies. Over the course of several weeks, Crawford made the decision to remain in the Bay Area and become a Panther. He approached the organization's hierarchy about joining the Party and was told that if he was serious about becoming a Panther he should return to Indianapolis and start a branch there. Crawford, however, was not optimistic that the Black community in his hometown would be amenable to a Panther branch. After all, Indianapolis's Black community was a very religious and conservative one. As far as Crawford was concerned, "Blacks were behind in consciousness compared to others Blacks in big cities across the country."[39] Much to Crawford's surprise, when he returned to Indianapolis he found pockets of young Blacks who were receptive to the concept of Black Power. When George Wallace, former governor of Alabama and self-proclaimed segregationist, visited Indianapolis in the summer of 1968 to garner support for his presidential campaign, Wallace found a receptive audience. Crawford had always known that Indiana was a conservative state, but the notion that a candidate like George Wallace could elicit a following was eye-opening. Wallace's showing spurred Crawford into action, and by week's end he had opened a Black Panther office in Indianapolis.

Shortly after the BPP office was established, it caught the attention of the Black press and the local mainstream media, as well as the attention of several law enforcement agencies. Crawford advocated core Panther doctrines of working for political empowerment and helping Blacks gain control of their communities. In keeping with Point 7 of the organization's Ten-Point Program, one of the primary concerns of the Indianapolis office was the "defense and protection of the Black Community."[40]

The arrival of the Panthers led to "increased police surveillance in black neighborhoods," further exasperating the already intolerable circumstances of police harassment.[41] Donald "Duck" Campbell, a veteran of the Korean War and deputy minister of information, reported in *The Black Panther* of the continual harassment of Blacks, both BPP members and nonmembers. According to Campbell, in December of 1968 patrolman Steven Schatke arrested circulation manager Abram Sharrief and another member for disorderly conduct while they were advertising an upcoming rally. A month later, Officer Schatke shot a Black man and charged him with auto theft and violation of the 1935 Beverage Act, charges which were subsequently dropped. The following February, several Panthers were charged with disorderly conduct and trespassing on private property for distributing Panther literature at a local school. And in March, a Black man was arrested in downtown Indianapolis for driving too slowly.[42] These cases are representative of the surveillance and harassment to which Black residents were subjected without meaningful recourse. As a result, Panthers took on the responsibility of protecting Blacks from police harassment and other threats, such as a local white motorcycle gang called the Grim Reapers. After disturbances in the Indianapolis Eastside community by this particular gang, armed Panthers patrolled the community, vowing to "take whatever means necessary to protect black citizens."[43] Unfortunately, this vow would lead to the arrest of members Charles W. Goliah and Bill Council for violating the 1935 Firearms Act, a charge for which Goliah would serve forty-nine days in jail.[44]

In spite of their reputation as unruly militants, the Panthers did receive public accolades for their efforts in preventing a potential fracas after the "firebombing" of a Big 10 supermarket in Lockefield Gardens on June 6, 1969.[45] The incident began "when two white officers sent to the area in response to a report of a fight were jumped by a group of about twenty young blacks, one of whom grabbed the officer's revolver and badge."[46] As the crowd of community residents grew, more police arrived on the scene and were pelted with bricks and bottles. During the melee, shots were exchanged and two police officers were injured, one by a sniper. Local businesses were damaged and fire completely destroyed the Big 10 market. Peace was eventually restored as local leaders, such as Rev. Mozell Sanders and Black Radical Action Party president Charles "Snooky" Hendricks, and members of the BPP calmed the crowd and helped disperse it.[47] Even deputy police chief Raymond J. Stratton commended the Panthers for "exerting a calming influence" in the area.[48]

As a result of their instrumental role in allaying the anger and frustrations of community residents, the BPP was one of the local organizations invited to meet with area residents to address the disturbances in the Indiana Avenue–Lockefield area and to formulate solutions to present to city officials.[49] Many of these grievances centered on police harassment of residents, and proposals included a significant reduction in the number of police patrols in the area and assigning Black officers to Black neighborhoods.[50] This inclusion of Panther representation in generating grassroots activism illustrates the organization's respect and support from certain sectors of the Black community. Coverage of the supermarket incident by a local underground newspaper, the *Indianapolis Free Press*, stated, "The Black Panther Party was at the center of the rebellion both nights. They were there to save the lives of the brothers and sisters. . . . The Panthers urged people to go home, to stay off the deadly streets."[51] Their positive influence during this ordeal was also a likely factor in the Park Board's approval of their use of the Douglass community center later that month for the free breakfast program.

The Panthers' Survival Programs

In addition to advocating political empowerment and armed self-defense, the BPP supplied the community with a variety of resources intended to meet the immediate needs of its less-well-off residents. Indianapolis Panthers provided social services for the Black community that included free clothing for school kids, coal and medicine for the indigent, and keeping the streets clean.[52] They also established the core survival programs of free breakfast and food distribution. Starting in mid-summer 1968, youngsters on their way to school were able to stop in at 17th and Martindale for a tasty and nutritious meal. The Panthers took pride in the free breakfast program. "We are doing something about hunger and not just talking about it," boasted one Panther. The Panthers claimed to have fed at least fifty children a day. Said Donald Campbell, deputy minister of information, "the Breakfast Program was instigated because children were being neglected by the power structure, and unable to receive meals at home."[53] Some of the kids were so appreciative of the program that they would volunteer to help wash dishes and wipe tables clean. As a way of showing their gratitude some parents would assist with the preparation of the meals.

In early November, members of the BPP began making preparations to assist needy families during the holiday season. Aware that some families went through the holiday season without a turkey or any of the trimmings associated with Thanksgiving, the Panthers sponsored several food giveaways. With Christmas less than a month later, the Panthers also began working on a clothing giveaway and a toy drive, which proved to be a big hit with the kids. At the same time, the organization initiated plans for their first free breakfast program, to begin on Monday, December 2nd, at Porters' at 30th and Capitol Streets.[54]

In June of 1970, the Panthers proposed a collaborative effort with other Black-oriented groups such as the Black Radical Action Party, College Room, and Dignity Unlimited[55] to operate a breakfast program at the Douglass Park Community Center.[56] Despite the resistance to the Panthers from large segments of the Indianapolis community, due in part to the often unflattering portrayal of the Panthers in the white press, the Park Board approved of the use of its community center. This approval, as well as the collaboration of other local organizations, reveals some support for Panther programs. The program, which was scheduled to run through August 30th, provided meals for seventy-three children the first day and served an average of fifty children per day throughout the summer. Support from local businesses and private citizens as well as the volunteer efforts of children and parents was instrumental in sustaining the program.[57] The Indianapolis Black Coalition, made up of doctors, lawyers, business leaders, and sectors of the working class, helped fund the Panthers' breakfast program.[58] In spite of "setbacks from lying preachers and merchants" and wavering support from College Room and Dignity Unlimited, the breakfast program was a huge success. The Panthers also planted a people's garden to increase their food distribution efforts,[59] and in November 1970 put out a call for donations of food and winter clothing. These efforts enabled the Party to implement a program to provide emergency relief on a year-round basis, and the Panthers expanded their food offerings with the establishment of a free food pantry in November of 1970, housed at their 413 East 23rd Street headquarters. With donations from local businesses, the Panthers provided for those "not eligible for public assistance or who need[ed] their public assistance supplemented,"[60] regardless of race. Consistent with the Party's philosophy of empowering all individuals, the pantry was characterized as an effort to provide for "all oppressed people." The pantry was necessitated by the announcement that the Center Township trustee would no longer provide emergency food and clothing that year because of a lack of funds. Upon learning the news the Panthers issued the following statement:

> We will not sit idly by and wait for Center Township Trustee to cough up the funds for emergency food orders. We will not be pacified by the

Administration of the Department of Public Welfare when they claim the state of Indiana does not have any more funds for Public Aid, but in fact raises staff salaries.

By using social practice and implementation of free programs, the Black Panther Party will expose the Department of Welfare's cheesy "take what we give you and be satisfied" tactics. The Black Panther Party has taken the power of decision making in relationship to Public Aid from those who do not need it (salaried), and look down on those who need it, and are giving this power to those who deserve it. We set no standards or qualification on needs. One of the basic understandings is that aid should be distributed to those who express need in general, and to those who express emergency need in particular, without compromise and attachments.[61]

The Panthers undoubtedly brought sorely needed programs and resources to the city's Black community. With the opening of the Eldridge Cleaver Community Information Center in May of 1970, the Panthers had an expanded base from which to offer economic, social, and political support for Black Hoosiers. In Campbell's words, "the center's primary purpose is to provide a meeting-ground for the party and one of the city's poorer neighborhoods . . . this is a place where they can come and learn what the Party is and how it operates, and where we can learn more about the real concerns of this community, and begin to help it." In addition to providing a gathering space for community residents, the Panthers held political education classes there and a Saturday morning liberation school for children aged eight through twelve. Educating children was especially important to the Panthers. "We're educating them on the basis of truth, self-knowledge, Socialism and sharing with their brothers and sisters," said a Panther spokesman.[62] Plans were made to establish a free health clinic, but the endeavor never materialized.

Police Harassment of the Panthers

The warped representation of the Black Panther Party by the mainstream media preceded the Indianapolis branch's formation. In fact, a study of press coverage of Panther offices in three different cities shows that for the most part the Panthers were framed as small-time hoods using revolutionary rhetoric as a subterfuge for illegal activity,[63] a depiction that undoubtedly contributed to law enforcement's constant surveillance of them. Panthers around the country were subjected to repression through the oft-used tactics of harassment, arrest, and slander, an example of which was the December 1968 raid on Panther headquarters in Indianapolis. As indicated earlier, the raid and unsuccessful search for illegal weapons resulted in the arrest of Panthers Michael Cannon, Dan Ginns, and deputy minister of finance

Lawrence Roberts. As reported in the *Indianapolis Recorder*, law officials arrived at the 113 West 30th Street location and demanded that Cannon and Ginns admit them into the building. Under orders not to allow strangers to enter the premises, Cannon and Ginns refused to allow the officers entry and requested that the warrant be slid under the door. Instead of producing the warrant, and because Cannon and Ginns were allegedly brandishing shotguns, police tear-gassed the office, causing the Panthers' evacuation of the premises and their subsequent arrest. Cannon and Ginns were originally arrested on charges of disorderly conduct and drawing a deadly weapon.[64] Roberts, who had been called to the scene by Cannon and Ginns, was also arrested for purportedly interfering with the arresting party as well as for disorderly conduct. He was eventually convicted on both charges and "was fined $25 and sentenced to 10 days in jail on each charge," but the jail terms were suspended.[65] Later, federal charges were filed against Cannon and Ginns; bonds for the two were set at $20,000 and $5,000, respectively. Months later (in June 1969), Cannon changed his plea from not guilty to guilty.[66]

In June 1968 the mainstream press reported the story of a break-in at the Marine Corps Reserve Training Center, at 2830 E. Riverside Drive, by three men identified by authorities as Black Panthers. In the article "Black Panther Plot for Raid on Armory Unfolding in Court," Carolyn Pickering of the *Indianapolis Star* recounted the twisted story. Arrested on June 23, 1968, Leon Andrew Gomillia, Melvin Johnson, and Omar Shabazz (Eldridge Morrison Jr.) were charged with "conspiracy to commit murder and conspiracy burglary" for alleged plans to kill police chief Winston L. Churchill and narcotics bureau lieutenant Richard A. Jones with weapons they intended to steal from the center. According to the *Star*, Churchill believed that the Panthers plotted his death as "a status symbol."[67] Jones was targeted, he believed, because as a narcotics agent his work hindered the extracurricular activities of the Panthers, a clear implication that the Panthers were dealing drugs.

With the assistance of Allen Ray Watkins, an undercover Indianapolis police officer who infiltrated the organization and perhaps may have encouraged the plot, the men broke into the center only to find members of the FBI, Indianapolis Police Department, and the Secret Service waiting to arrest them. During the trial, Watkins testified that he worked undercover for three months and received a $450 salary "paid by the FBI and Indianapolis Police Department."[68] He provided details of conversations between himself and the defendants planning the break-in, which was initially intended for a sporting goods store but was changed because no one could disconnect the alarm system at the sporting goods store. Defense attorneys Charles E. Johnson and Donald L. Fasig (as well as certain members of the Black community) argued that the young men were victims of entrapment and a police plot against "Black Power advocates." The defense also argued that Gomillia, Johnson, and Shabazz were enticed by Watkins's "fancy car" and moneymaking schemes and lured into conversations about the burglary, conversations which were tape-recorded and used by the prosecution as evidence to support both conspiracy charges. This theory, in light of community concerns about police harassment, was not implausible, and as a result the three defendants received a fair amount of support from the Black community during their trial. Concern also centered on the credibility of Officer Watkins, who was characterized by the defense as a perjurer who had lied about his age on his job application and was subsequently "fired from the police force and rehired as a civilian employee."[69] Ultimately, Shabazz and Johnson were found guilty on charges of burglary, the murder conspiracy charges were dropped, and they were sentenced to two terms of fourteen years. Eighteen-year-old Gomillia (who waited outside as a lookout and never entered the premises) was freed.

As it turned out, none of the men arrested were actually members of the Black Panther Party as the *Indianapolis Star* had reported. But the damage had been done. Despite repeated denials by Panther leaders, the press maintained that the men were Panthers. Channel 6 newscaster Carl Stubblefield urged Fred Crawford to set the record straight, publicly. Soon after, on WGEE radio, Crawford announced that the "men who broke into the training center were not Panthers at that time or at any other time." Shortly thereafter, though, in a most bizarre move the Panthers inexplicably adopted the men, taking up their cause and providing them with moral and financial support. Although the men were not allowed to join the branch, Crawford says that some of his comrades felt that the men "were being railroaded so we came to their defense." When pressed, Crawford admitted that "in retrospect that probably was not a wise decision; if anything it undermined our credibility."[70]

Undercutting whatever cachet the Panthers may have enjoyed was seemingly a top priority for certain local institutions. Although by the late 1960s red-baiting had lost some of its effectiveness as a scare tactic, the Indianapolis Panthers, like many civil rights and leftist organizations, were labeled communists as a way of undermining their credibility and effectiveness. On at least two occasions the *Star* reported on the alleged communist influence of the Party. During the July 1970 investigations into the Indianapolis branch by the U.S. House of Representatives, one witness, self-proclaimed minister of special security Barron Howard, testified that Donald Steed, the supposed head of the Indiana Communist Party, supplied the chapter with funds to rent a hall, bail members out of jail, and attend a national convention in Chicago.[71] Additionally, Gerald W. Kirk, a Black FBI informant who infiltrated the Communist Party, stated unequivocally during a speech at the Glendale Shopping Center auditorium sponsored by the Indianapolis Truth About Civil Turmoil Committee that leftist groups like Students for a Democratic Society (SDS) and the BPP were controlled by communists.[72]

The characterization of the BPP as a "gang" and one of their rallies as a "tirade" was also an attempt by the white press to weaken the group's credibility, especially in light of the fact that many whites around the country already viewed the Panthers as hooligans. That the *Indianapolis Star* would cast the Panthers as criminals is not all that surprising given that its owner, Eugene C. Pulliam, had a reputation as a right-wing conservative and was reputedly a supporter of the John Birch Society.[73] Statements by the police claiming that the Panthers held secret target practice in wooded areas west of Rockville did little to disabuse some of the perception that the BPP was a violence-prone outfit. Needless to say, statements like these served to undermine the Panthers' ability to engender community support. Such depictions also justified law enforcement agencies' repeated infiltration and harassment of the organization. Furthermore, Chief Churchill's false claim that there was no connection between the local group and the California Panthers was also a desperate attempt to portray the Indy Panthers as renegades and to delegitimize the local branch.[74] This assertion was clearly unsubstantiated in light of the branch's activities in support of the national organization. On May 1, 1969, the Indianapolis branch held a demonstration at the federal building in support of Huey P. Newton, who was then on trial. Speaking explicitly about the branch's connection with the California-based organization, Campbell stated, "The demonstration showed solidarity of oppressed people and black people in particular. People are concerned with the racist policies and they believe in Mr. Newton and the Party."[75] In August of that same year, following a Panther convention in July concerning the establishment of a national front against fascism, the Indianapolis branch held a rally in support of the initiation of a united front to combat fascism.[76] Panthers would again gather at the federal building in May of 1970 for a memorial rally in observance of the second anniversary of the tragic death of Bobby Hutton at the hands of Oakland police. The branch also held a rally in July of 1970 protesting the white power structure and in support of "Bobby Seale and other Party members in Connecticut" in conjunction with the trial involving the killing of an informant.[77] This connection is further substantiated by the Indy Panthers' publications in *The Black Panther* and their public appeals to local Blacks to attend the national conventions. Additionally, pictures, articles, and information about the Oakland chapter, such as a petition to "Keep Cleaver out of Prison," adorned the front windows of the Indianapolis Panthers' headquarters.

Community Support for the Panthers

Despite the efforts of some to portray the Panthers as a fringe group with a penchant for rabble-rousing and criminal activity, the Panthers were not without their sympathizers. One indicator of community support was the foodstuffs and money provided by local merchants and juke joint owners. Gamblers and proprietors of pea-shake houses were often receptive to Panther solicitations. While the amounts were generally small, the support was much appreciated especially since support from national headquarters was in short supply. Says Keith Parker, "what we, as a chapter, were able to do, we did in spite of Oakland [national headquarters] not because of Oakland."[78]

The harassment and repression to which the chapter was subjected was combated to a small degree by the support the Indy Panthers received from various groups within the city, especially from religious leaders. While the clergy in Indianapolis had historically been active in advancing civil rights, most tended to shy away from radicalism and militancy. Some ministers, however, did support the Panthers, especially with fundraising. During the trial of Shabazz, Johnson, and Gomillia, the BPP joined with local religious leaders to hold a $25-a-plate freedom rally fundraising dinner at the United Methodist Church.[79] Panther leaders from Colorado flew in to help with the proceedings.

The BPP also received nonclergy support, as evidenced by the Committee to Defend the Black Panther Party that picketed outside police headquarters during the arrests of Cannon and Ginns, as well as the approximately forty sympathizers who attended their federal bond hearing threatening to "tear the joint down."[80] Community support was also evident among Black youth, some of whom were suspended from school for wearing "Black Panther garb" or distributing organizational literature. The multiplicity of support the Panthers received was bolstered by their efforts to forge alliances with other organizations working for social justice. At the July 1970 rally, for example, Panthers shared the stage with representatives from the women's liberation movement and antiwar activists.[81]

A Panther Runs for Student Government

In addition to the city of Indianapolis, the Indy Panthers would establish a small presence in the southern part of the state with the enrollment of Keith Parker at Indiana University in 1969. In March of the following year, Parker was elected president of the student body, the second Black in the school's history to hold that office. Parker ran a dynamic campaign, while his opponent, Tom Morrison, lacked his personality and tireless campaign style. Parker's running mate Mike King contends that Parker defeated his opponent because "he was well-liked, uncompromising in his principles and engaging in personality."[82]

When the votes were counted Parker garnered 39 percent (2,289) of the vote compared to Morrison's 30 percent (1,717) out of 5,830 ballots cast. Four other candidates split the remaining 1,824 votes. Turnout in the election was tremendously low as only 20 percent of the student body voted, compared to the 1967 election when more than ten thousand students went to the polls, and the 1968 and 1969 elections, at which at least eight thousand students cast ballots. According to university rules at the time, in the event no candidate received 40 percent of the vote, a runoff must be held between the top two vote getters. The runoff was scheduled for the following week, but Morrison conceded the election and Parker assumed office. As student body president, Parker found yet another outlet for his activism, which also included antiwar protests, while maintaining his activism in the Indianapolis-based branch. Furthermore, Parker was able to raise the profile of the Black Panther Party in Bloomington through such events as Bobby Seale Weekend in October of 1970, which included films, discussions, workshops, and a Defense Fund benefit.[83] Parker was also responsible for organizing a December memorial service for Fred Hampton and Mark Clark, during which he advocated "community control of police and coalitions between students and workers."[84] After the Kent State killings, Parker implored students to boycott classes, and he tried to organize pickets while students participated in a referendum on the war and various other issues. Nearly eighteen thousand students voted, and two-thirds opposed the invasion of Cambodia and wanted Congress to cut off support for the Vietnam War. About the same number backed a call for the Indiana University Foundation to open its records to public inspection, and more than half supported canceling classes to protest the Cambodian incursion and wanted the university to repudiate the war.[85]

In keeping with the national headquarters' willingness to build coalitions with revolutionary-minded whites, Parker joined forces with SDS member Mike King, a white student and editor of the local underground paper, the *Spectator*. King would serve as vice president of the student body. Dr. King (who went on to become a professor at Yale and currently is a successful journalist) later admitted that he and Parker "were stunned that they won."[86] They ran under the banner of the United Student Movement (USM) and hoped their racial diversity and radical leadership would generate a diverse coalition of activists. With the goal of empowering the student body, "the USM ran a populist campaign with radical rap." Incorporating Panther rhetoric and ideology into their campaign, "Parker and King customarily ended speeches and articles with raised fists or capital letters:

'ALL POWER TO THE PEOPLE.'"[87] They also drafted a fourteen-point platform that focused on greater student involvement in university offices and policy making, such as control of campus police and the student union. Out of that platform a student legal service was established. The USM candidates expanded their concerns beyond student issues to advocate empowerment of all oppressed people, promoting policies such as "adequate wages for all university employees." Parker and King were able to muster strong student support on a number of issues, but not all. For instance, while many called for an end to the war, most wanted officer training programs on campus such as ROTC to continue, and less than a fifth favored giving university money to Seale's defense fund. Consequently, while Parker and King were hugely popular on campus, clearly their supporters were not of one mind.

At the end of Parker's and King's terms in office, the editors of the *Indiana Daily Student*, IU's student newspaper, found little benefit from their time in office. The editors argued that their polarizing administration had done more harm than good, that Parker and King actually reduced the power of student government by antagonizing state lawmakers, school administration, and a fair number of students. Assessing the merits of this critique is not within the purview of this chapter. However, such criticisms notwithstanding, Parker and King gave future student government aspirants an "alternative" model on which to campaign for office. Indeed one could argue that both men laid the groundwork for the subsequent election of the first woman president the following year.

The Indy Panthers Are No More

The long history of Black self-help and civil rights organizations shows that African Americans in Indianapolis differed amongst themselves as to the methods to be employed in the struggle for Black equality. By and large, Black leadership in Indiana was more reserved than in other large northern and midwestern cities. Complacency and apathy on the part of middle-class Blacks, who appeared reluctant to take aggressive steps to improve conditions, were criticized by the more rambunctious members of the community. Many younger Blacks were understandably impatient with a policy of gradualism when racial discrimination was still widespread more than a hundred years after the abolition of slavery. Still, it appears that relatively few in the community seemed moved by the more militant and pro-Black organizations that appealed to so many urban Blacks in other parts of the country. For whatever reason, the Black community as a whole was not attracted to the Panthers in the way that Blacks were in cities like Chicago, Oakland, Detroit, New York, Cleveland, and others. This is not to say that the Panthers were isolated from the community, but because of the conservative mind-set of many Blacks, the branch was unable to amass a large membership and a strong following.

Barron Howard, self-professed minister of special security, testified before a House Internal Security Committee that there were three hundred members on the chapter's roster, but only sixty-five of them were active.[88] Keith Parker indicated that Howard's estimates were not in line with his experience. Moreover, Parker said, there had been no such position as minister of special security. Even if there had been such a position, Howard would have held the title of deputy minister, not minister. Parker pointed out that the title of minister was reserved for those who served on the organization's Central Committee. Additionally, "Howard was not a prominent player in the chapter; he was more on the periphery."[89] At its height the Indy chapter had one hundred names on its membership lists, but only fifteen or twenty of them were active members. The remaining eighty to eighty-five members, Parker said, were "Rally Panthers," a derisive term for those who showed up for rallies but weren't around to do the day-to-day grunt work.[90]

The Indy Panthers provided the Black community with a variety of sorely needed services that it otherwise would have gone without. But again the Indy Panthers never built the kind of following that existed in other places. The Indy office was short-lived and it never engendered the kind of support (financial or otherwise) that other chapters and branches enjoyed. On this point Keith Parker explained that "we didn't do enough to bring the Black community along . . . we were not immersed in the community in the way that we should have been." When Parker was reminded that the Panthers fed a lot of children, he shot back, "Yeah, but we didn't feed enough. We should have fed more." Furthermore, Parker submitted that "we didn't have a defining issue with which to sustain support around or rally around."[91]

It should be noted that while some Blacks might have agreed with the Panthers' programs, many were probably reluctant to come out in support of the Panthers for fear of economic, social, and political reprisal. Whereas many Black organizations accepted concessions from the white establishment and sought compromise on matters of racial equality, the Black Panther Party as an organization had a reputation for making demands, an approach that did not go over well with many Blacks. A study by Frank N. Magid Associates of Indianapolis Blacks supports this. When Blacks and whites were asked if Blacks could get equal opportunities without making constant demands on the white community, nearly 60 percent of Blacks responded yes, while only 35 percent of whites said yes.[92] Even in this environment, the Panthers did get support from certain sectors of the Black community. For example, after the Panthers' headquarters was raided in December 1968 and Ginns and Cannon were bound over to the grand jury, a small group calling itself The Committee to Defend the Black Panther Party picketed outside police headquarters.[93] During the short time they were there, members of the group passed out flyers accusing the police of racism and corruption. To be sure, support for the Panthers in Indianapolis did exist, but it was modest. Even on the campus of Indiana University (which was considered radical by many observers), while many Black students were taken with the Panthers' style and rhetoric (even though the Panthers argued that institutions like IU were creating a new group of Uncle Toms and that "the sole means, the total means, of liberation is the gun"), most Black students remained committed to nonviolence.[94]

Another point that should be considered is that while Indianapolis was not a utopia for Blacks, the conditions under which most Blacks lived were not as bad as they were in many other large urban cities. Furthermore, the absence of an ogre like Frank Rizzo in Philadelphia, Eugene "Bull" Connor in Alabama, or Richard J. Daley in Chicago against which the Panthers could mobilize Black folk made it sufficiently difficult to rally Blacks. Sure, police brutality existed, but as Keith Parker remembers, "there were instances of harassment by police officers, but people weren't getting savagely beaten or being killed by the police like they were in other places."[95] State Senator Bill Crawford goes one step further, stating that while police brutality existed in Indianapolis, it was not a major problem. In fact, says Crawford, "the IPD were like Keystone Cops more than anything else."[96] These tolerable conditions were in part attributable to the city's history of interracial cooperation dating back to the early 1900s through organizations such as the NAACP and Flanner House. These organizations had been successful in gradually improving conditions in the Circle City without the radicalism and direct action proposed by the Panthers, perhaps discounting in the minds of many the need for such strategies.

Aside from lukewarm support from the Black community, inner turmoil and attrition at the national as well as local level plagued the Indianapolis office from the outset and took its toll on the branch. Within a year after the office was established, several of the chapter's initial members had drifted away. In early 1969, deputy chairman Fred Crawford and Ox Patton expelled Bob O'Bannon and Joe Martin, two of the branch's most dedicated members. The decision to expel O'Bannon and Martin was not a popular one, and it caused dissension within the office. Not long after O'Bannon and Martin were ousted, Crawford and Patton left the Party for various reasons, which opened the door for O'Bannon's and Martin's reinstatement. Crawford resigned a year after opening the branch, citing that he could no longer accept the Panthers' ideology. Crawford later explained that he left the Party because "the Panthers' beliefs conflicted with his religious beliefs."[97] At the time of Crawford's resignation he denounced the Panthers' revolutionary rhetoric, maintaining perhaps astutely that most Blacks were not ready for a revolution but instead preferred the nonviolent approach of the Civil Rights Movement. He also criticized the Panthers for "dictating to the people what they should want." In an interview with a news reporter, Crawford remarked that "the establishment in Indianapolis would support the breakfast program if the Panthers would stop calling members of the establishment 'pigs.' "[98] Crawford's comments were interesting if for no other reason than that the approval and support of the establishment was not something the Panther organization strove for or was interested in.

Looking back, Crawford's turnabout is quite interesting. While he claimed that the Panthers' violent rhetoric turned him off, it was he who set the tone for the branch in this regard. Shortly after the office opened he was quoted in the *Indianapolis News* as saying, "I don't feel we [Blacks] can gain our freedom without a revolution. This could only happen if the white man raised his feet off the black man's neck, but I don't think he'll ever do that."[99] Some of Crawford's colleagues did not believe that his resignation adversely affected the chapter. The prevailing sentiment was that had Crawford not resigned, he would have eventually been purged from the branch because of his failure to attend important meetings and his overall lack of leadership.

The Newton-Cleaver feud of 1971 created a schism that proved to be far-reaching, and the turmoil at the national level had an effect on local branches, including the Indianapolis office. Unlike some other chapters and branches, most members within the Indy office felt no special allegiance to either Newton or Cleaver. "Huey may have been the face of the organization and Eldridge may have been the voice, but Bobby was the heart of the organization. Our loyalty was to him," says Parker. "As far as some of us were concerned, Cleaver came across as a madman and Newton appeared to be detached from the rank and file." And since the Indy Panthers refused to support either side, "the branch was just kind of left out there."[100] By 1972 several members grew disheartened as a result of the Cleaver-Newton war and simply quit the Party. Many Panthers around the country answered Newton's call to relocate to Oakland to work on Bobby Seale's mayoral campaign. Rather than relocate to Oakland, several Indy Panthers left the Party rather than uproot themselves and their families to go west.

In addition to internal strife, government attempts to squash the Indy Panthers were no less systematic or insidious than they were on the national level. The year 1969 was an especially tough one for the Indy chapter. In February, police arrested three Panthers during a raid and hit them with the dubious charge of disorderly conduct and interfering with a federal officer in the course of his duties. Each was fined $25 and sentenced to ten days in jail.

In June of 1969, Panther offices were raided twice in a two-week period, with sixteen members being swept up in police dragnets.

According to *The Black Panther*, the following spring twenty-five Panthers were arrested and charged with felonies over a three-month period. Harassment of the Indy office was so overt that a local white attorney by the name of William C. Erbecker, who had a reputation for taking on civil rights cases, felt compelled to file a motion for an injunction to restrain Indianapolis police officers from rousing, intimidating, and interrogating members of the branch.

There is no question that Panthers were harassed, followed, and arrested. Many local, state, and federal government tactics used against the Panthers were questionable and violated both the letter and spirit of the law. On the other hand, though, there were times when the Indianapolis activists were complicit in their own demise. Indeed, there were times when the Panthers engaged in what we call victim-precipitated repression. In other words, by breaking the law the Panthers put themselves in a position to be arrested, harassed, or accosted. Unlike many civil rights activists who were arrested and beaten for breaking laws they considered to be unjust, some of the infractions committed by members of the Indianapolis Panthers were reckless and apolitical. When authorities responded to various criminal activities, the Panthers printed articles in their newspaper depicting themselves as victims of unnecessary and unmerited police action. Examples of this victim-precipitated repression abound. For instance, Fred Crawford was arrested and charged with assault and battery after he struck a female meter maid who was giving him a parking ticket. Crawford claimed that he approached the meter maid and tried to explain that the meter was broken; an argument ensued and Crawford became angry and hit the meter maid about the face. He was arrested within hours of the incident. Parker remembers one incident in particular when one of his comrades tried to pick a fight with a police officer during a rally at a local park.[101] Panthers also claimed they were harassed and arrested for merely selling *The Black Panther*, but oftentimes they were doing so on private property and without a permit.

To say that some Panthers were guilty of poor judgment is an understatement. In late 1970 Charles W. Goliah was fined $85 and placed on 180 days probation for carrying a concealed weapon.[102]

As was the case with many other Panther branches across the country, law enforcement infiltrated Panther offices in Indy. In fact, our research has revealed that there were at least seven informants inside the Indianapolis office—two of whom were members of the police department. Some Panthers claim they were often the victims of entrapment. However, even if the police department was guilty of entrapment, the fact remains that some of the Panthers' actions were idiotic at worst, such as Crawford's assault on the meter maid, and misguided at best, especially since it was well known within the organization that informants had penetrated its ranks.

When the national headquarters learned the extent to which the Party had been infiltrated, Panther leaders as early as 1969 began purging members from the Party who were thought to be working against the organization's interests. In Indianapolis, the Panthers purged five members in April of 1969 alone. In a recent interview Crawford disclosed that one Panther, apparently ridden with guilt, broke down and confessed to being an informant.[103]

As was mentioned in chapter 1, the names of purged members were printed in *The Black Panther* with the admonition that "[t]hey are not to be associated with or let into any Black Panther office anywhere." Later, the organization took more serious steps to curtail infiltration by placing a moratorium on membership intake. While this tactic undoubtedly prevented agents provocateurs from gaining entry into the Party, it did little to thwart the efforts of those informants already in place. It appears, though, that to some extent the purging of members in Indianapolis undermined law enforcement's ability to monitor the goings-on within the chapter—so much so that in July 1970 a House Internal Security Committee opened hearings on the Indianapolis and Detroit branches of the BPP. Said Representative Richard Preyer, the subcommittee chairman, "The hearings are being held to develop more information about the local chapters and to help find out what the party has for its objectives."[104] Unsatisfied with previous covert operations "to further cause dissension among the black organizations and the BPP," government officials undertook overt activities to disrupt the organization.[105]

Given where the Panthers set up shop, it is surprising that some of them would behave so irresponsibly. Being in Indianapolis meant that the branch could ill-afford to give the appearance of impropriety. The Indianapolis office was one of only a few Panther branches established in a state capital, which impacted the Panthers in ways that did not play out in some other cities. Because Indy is the state capital, there was a heavy media presence in the city. Newspaper organizations typically put a premium on covering news in state capitals for many reasons. First, many of the laws and policies that govern the state are introduced and formulated in the legislative chambers of the statehouse. And many news organizations devote a fair amount of resources to covering news in the capital. More beat writers are assigned to cover the capital city than any other city in a state if the state capital is a major city and the largest in the state, which Indianapolis is. It should also be noted that the largest city within the state is often the state's largest media market.

Second, since the capital is considered the seat of power, some of the state's most influential political figures make their home there or at least spend a fair amount of time there. Suffice to say, beat reporters are on alert for any kind of story that may contain drama, intrigue, or scandal. Third, since some of those legislators are also some of the most politically important people in the state, law enforcement is often proactive about ensuring the safety and general welfare of said citizens. Fourth, in light of the stir that the Oakland Panthers caused at the statehouse in Sacramento, California, in May 1967, the law enforcement community in states across the country was primed to prevent the same from happening in their city. Given this, it was not surprising that the Indy Panthers would garner significantly more media attention than the other branches examined in this book.[106] Unfortunately, this type of media attention brought with it a level of surveillance by law enforcement that other Panther chapters and branches of comparable size did not experience. Simply put, the more information the Indy police were able to collect, the more difficult it was for the Indy Panthers to gain a foothold there.

Conclusion

The Indianapolis branch was founded in 1968; by 1972 the branch had closed its doors. Despite their nearly four-year run, the Panthers are but a footnote in Indiana history. This could be because the Circle City Panthers were not menacing nor were they theatrical. They did not prance around as their Oakland counterparts did. The Indy Panthers' efforts were at times honorable and commendable, but at other times the behavior of some individual members was curious and counterproductive. More than any of the branches examined in this book, the prospect of sustaining a Black militant organization proved to be a most daunting task. Indianapolis Blacks on the whole were not ready or willing to support the perceived hyperradical Black Panthers, and this proved to be the Panthers' biggest obstacle, one they could not overcome. Ultimately, this along with poor judgment and the residual effects of the Newton-Cleaver feud, led to the branch's closing.

Notes

1. Emma Lou Thornbrough, *Indiana Blacks in the Twentieth Century* (Bloomington: Indiana University Press, 2000).

2. Richard Pierce, *Polite Protest: The Political Economy of Race in Indianapolis 1920–1970* (Bloomington: Indiana University Press, 2005).

3. Michael Newton, *Bitter Grain* (Los Angeles: Holloway House, 1980), 136–137.

4. SAC Indianapolis to FBI Director, December 16, 1968. In February 1970, agents of the Internal Revenue Service's Alcohol, Tobacco, and Firearms unit contacted Seattle mayor Wes Uhlman about collaborating on a raid of Panther headquarters. If Uhlman would provide local police as backup units for an assault on Black Panther offices, the

ATF would manufacture the necessary probable cause in the form of warrants charging suspected possession of illegal weapons. Uhlman declined the offer publicly, denouncing the proposition of "cooperation" against the Panthers as an example of "Gestapo-type tactics."

5. "Official Says $600 Missing After Raid," *The Indianapolis Recorder*, December 21, 1968, 12.

6. Darlene Clark Hine, William C. Hine, and Stanley Harrold, eds. *The African American Odyssey*, combined volume, 2nd edition (Upper Saddle River, N.J.: Prentice Hall, 2003), 389.

7. Emma Lou Thornbrough, *The Negro in Indiana Since 1900: A Study of a Minority* (Indianapolis: Indiana Historical Press, 1957 [rpt. Bloomington: Indiana University Press, 1993]), 395.

8. Emma Lou Thornbrough, *Since Emancipation: A Short History of Indiana Negroes, 1863–1963* (n.p.: American Negro Emancipation Centennial Authority, 1964), 32.

9. Thornbrough, *Indiana Blacks in the Twentieth Century*, 174.

10. John W. Lyda, *The Negro in the History of Indiana* (Terre Haute: s.n., 1953), 77.

11. Ibid., 78.

12. Thornbrough, *Indiana Blacks in the Twentieth Century*, 38.

13. http://www.flannerhouse.com/1946.html.

14. Thornbrough, *Indiana Blacks in the Twentieth Century*, 264n.

15. Ibid., 167.

16. "speeches and releases," vol. 4.

17. Matthew E. Welsh, *View from the State House: Recollections and Reflections, 1961–1965* (Indianapolis: Indiana Historical Bureau, 1981), 43, 62–63.

18. Thornbrough, *Indiana Blacks in the Twentieth Century*, 169.

19. Thornbrough, *Since Emancipation*, 45.

20. Thornbrough, *Indiana Blacks in the Twentieth Century*, 192

21. Welsh, *View from the State House*, 193, 196.

22. Robert V. Kirch, "Unigov in Marion County," in *The Hoosier State: Readings in Indiana History*, ed. Ralph Gray, 451–453 (Grand Rapids, Mich.: William B. Eerdmans Publishing Company, 1980).

23. Thornbrough, *Indiana Blacks in the Twentieth Century*, 153, 168.

24. Ibid., 171.

25. Ibid., 181.

26. Welsh, *A View from the State House*, 193–194.

27. Thornbrough, *Indiana Blacks in the Twentieth Century*, 172.

28. Thornbrough, *Since Emancipation*, 46.

29. Thornbrough, *Indiana Blacks in the Twentieth Century*, 172.

30. Bill Crawford, telephone interview by Judson L. Jeffries, October 2005.

31. "Employment Characteristics of the Negro Population for Areas and Places: 1970." 1970 Census of the Population (U.S. Department of Commerce, Bureau of the Census, April 1973).

32. Robert F. Kennedy, "On Martin Luther King's Death," in *Ripples of Hope: Great American Civil Rights Speeches*, ed. Josh Gottheimer, 318–319 (New York: Basic Civitas Books, 2003).

33. Thornbrough, *Indiana Blacks in the Twentieth Century*, 185.

34. *Indianapolis News*, August 10, 1964.

35. "Black Leader Raps: An Interview with Ben Bell," *Indianapolis Free Press*, April 19, 1969.

36. "Police Brutality Charge Made by Showtime Prexy," *Indianapolis Recorder*, June 28, 1969.

37. Keith Parker, interview by Judson L. Jeffries, July 2005.

38. Fred Crawford, interview by Judson L. Jeffries, October 27, 2005.

39. Fred Crawford, interview by Judson L. Jeffries, October 25, 2005.

40. "Black Panthers Form Chapter in Our City," *The Indianapolis Recorder*, November 2, 1968, 1.

41. Thornbrough, *Indiana Blacks in the Twentieth Century*, 187.

42. "Pig Shoots Indianapolis Panther,'" *The Black Panther*, May 19, 1969, 14.

43. "Panthers Vow 'Protection,'" *The Indianapolis Star*, July 14, 1970, 11.

44. "Eastside Cycle Gang Raided; Seven Arrested, Weapons Seized," *The Indianapolis Star*, July 15, 1970, 21; "Local Panther Jailed 49 Days," *Indianapolis Free Press*, 14–23 September 1970, 3.

45. "Warrant Is Issued For 'Panther' Arrest," *The Indianapolis Star*, June 7, 1969, 10.

46. Thornbrough, *Indiana Blacks in the Twentieth Century*, 187.

47. Ibid.

48. "Sniper Hunted, 20 Arrested on Indiana Avenue," *The Indianapolis Star*, June 7, 1969, 25.

49. "'Avenue Disturbances' Are Topic of Public Meeting," *The Indianapolis Recorder*, June 21, 1969, 1.

50. Thornbrough, *Indiana Blacks in the Twentieth Century*, 187.

51. "The Lockefield Incident," *Indianapolis Free Press*, June 13, 1969, 2.

52. "Official Says $600 Missing after Raid," *The Indianapolis Recorder*, December 21, 1968, 12.

53. "Panthers Provide Meals for Eastside Youngsters," *Indianapolis Free Press*, July 26, 1969, 3.

54. "Black Panthers Form Chapter in Our City," *The Indianapolis Recorder*, November 2, 1968, 1; "Black Panthers Are to Sponsor Free Breakfast," *The Indianapolis Recorder*, December 7, 1968.

55. Charles "Snooky" Hendricks founded the Black Radical Action Project in 1968. The group was instrumental in helping quell the disorder that erupted in Lockefield Gardens during the summer of 1969. The College Room, led by local radical Benjamin F. Bell, was an antipoverty youth center/project designed to get youths off the street and provide them with the resources and opportunities to become productive, self-sufficient individuals. Programs included tutoring, Black studies classes, job counseling, extracurricular activities such as boxing and basketball, and providing resources, like free shoes, for the needy. The College Room also sought to instruct individuals on how to organize for community improvement, addressing issues such as traffic safety, community-police relations, and crime prevention. Under the direction of Rev. Luther C. Hicks, a Black Power advocate and native of Norfolk, Virginia, Dignity Unlimited was created in May of 1968 as a social and economic welfare program to improve local Black communities. Focusing on assisting the poor, economic self-sufficiency, and self-determination, the organization engaged in initiatives such as creating employment opportunities and assisting with entrepreneurial efforts for Black youth. Additionally, through projects such as Operation Santa Claus, which donated Christmas trees and presents to local families, Dignity Unlimited provided for the needy. Because they undertook projects similar to the BPP's survival programs, Dignity Unlimited was a natural ally of the BPP.

56. "Bulger New President of Park Board," *The Indianapolis Star*, June 25, 1969, 27.

57. "Panthers Provide Meals for Eastside Youngsters," *The Indianapolis Recorder*, July 26, 1969, 3.

58. Bill Crawford, interview.

59. "Indiana Breakfast," *The Black Panther*, July 19, 1969, 16.

60. "Panthers Open Free 'Pantry,'" *The Indianapolis Star*, November 19, 1970, 60.

61. "Indy Panthers: Panther Pantry," *Indianapolis Free Press*, 9–22 November 1970, 7.

62. "Black Panther Community Center," *Guardian*, May 23, 1970, 1.

63. Judson L. Jeffries, "Local News Coverage of the Black Panther Party: An Analysis of the Baltimore, Cleveland and New Orleans Press," *Journal of African American Studies* 7 (Spring 2004): 21–38.

64. "Official Says $600 Missing after Raid," *The Indianapolis Recorder*, December 21, 1968, 1.

65. "Found Guilty in Panther Raid Case," *The Indianapolis Star*, February 23, 1969, 7.

66. "Youth Pleads Guilty to U.S. Charges," *The Indianapolis Star*, June 3, 1969.

67. "3 Held in Plot to Slay Chief Churchill, Lt. Jones," *The Indianapolis Star*, June 26, 1968, 7; Robert N. Bell Jr., "Policeman Tells of Infiltrating Gang Bent on Stealing Firearms," *The Indianapolis Star*, June 27, 1968, 57.

68. Carolyn Pickering, "Black Panther Plot for Raid on Armory Unfolding in Court," *The Indianapolis Star*, March 6, 1969, 18.

69. "Alleged Panthers' Atty. Asks Court for New Trial, Accuse Chief, Prosecutor of 'Conspiracy,'" *The Indianapolis Recorder*, April 26, 1969, 16.

70. Fred Crawford, interview, October 27, 2005.

71. "Communist Financed Panthers In Indianapolis, Ex-Member Says," *The Indianapolis Star*, July 23, 1970, 5.

72. Monte Trammer, "Reds Influence Campus Leftists, Young Ex-FBI Informant Asserts," *The Indianapolis Star*, September 1, 1970, 15.

73. The John Birch Society was founded in Indiana in 1958; it opposed the Civil Rights Movement because it believed the Civil Rights Movement was under the influence of the Communist Party.

74. "3 Held in Plot to Slay Chief Churchill, Lt. Jones," *The Indianapolis Star*, June 26, 1968, 7.

75. "Panthers Stage March Here," *The Indianapolis Recorder*, May 3, 1969, 2.

76. "The Black Panther Party, Ministry of Information News Bulletin," *Indianapolis Free Press*, August 1969, 6.

77. "Black Panther Party Calls Rally for Today," *The Indianapolis Star*, July 10, 1970, 33.

78. Keith Parker, interview by Judson L. Jeffries, July 7, 2005.

79. "Black Panthers Schedule Dinner for 3 Black Men," *Indianapolis Recorder*, November 9, 1968, 1.

80. "Black Panthers Threaten Force," *The Indianapolis Star*, December 19, 1968, 54.

81. "Black Panther's Tirade Draws Only 150," *The Indianapolis Star*, July 11, 1970, 17.

82. Mike King, telephone interview by Judson L. Jeffries, September 2005.

83. "Jacobs Sent Cookbooks to GOP: Burton," *The Indianapolis Star*, October 9, 1970, 8.

84. "Panther's Death Called 'Murder' at State Services," *The Indianapolis Recorder*, December 20, 1969, 10.

85. Thornbrough, *Indiana Blacks in the Twentieth Century*, 214–216.

86. King, interview.

176 Nap Town Awakens to Find a Menacing Panther

87. Mary Ann Wynkoop, *Dissent in the Heartland: The Sixties at Indiana University* (Bloomington: Indiana University Press, 2002), 102–103.

Nap Town Awakens to Find a Menacing Panther

87. Mary Ann Wynkoop, *Dissent in the Heartland: The Sixties at Indiana University* (Bloomington: Indiana University Press, 2002), 102–103.

88. "Communist Financed Panthers In Indianapolis, Ex-Member Says," *The Indianapolis Star*, July 23, 1970, 5.

89. Keith Parker, telephone interview by Judson L. Jeffries, March 31, 2006.

90. Keith Parker, telephone interview by Judson L. Jeffries, August 2005.

91. Keith Parker, telephone interview by Judson L. Jeffries, January 27, 2006.

92. Frank N. Magid Associates, *The Negro in Indianapolis* (Frank N. Magid Associates: Cedar Rapids, Iowa, 1969).

93. "Free Alleged Panther On $1,000 Bond," *The Indianapolis Star*, December 24, 1968, 9.

94. Wynkoop, *Dissent in the Heartland*, 128.

95. Parker, interview, July 2005.

96. Bill Crawford, interview, October 25, 2005.

97. Fred Crawford, interview, October 27, 2005.

98. "Panthers' State Head Quits Post," *The Indianapolis Star*, September 24, 1969, 17.

99. Thornbrough, *Indiana Blacks in the Twentieth Century*, 166.

100. Parker, interview, March 31, 2006.

101. Parker, interview, March 31, 2006.

102. "Panther Draws Fine, Probation," *The Indianapolis Star*, September 26, 1970, 19.

103. Fred Crawford, interview, October 27, 2005.

104. "House To Probe Indianapolis Black Panthers," *The Indianapolis Star*, July 21, 1970, 13.

105. Letter to FBI Director, December 30, 1968.

106. The Indy branch garnered more press coverage than any of the branches studied in this book.

5

Picking Up the Hammer: The Milwaukee Branch of the Black Panther Party

Andrew Witt

In a 2003 interview, former Milwaukee Black Panther leader Michael McGee was asked what he thought was the Black Panther Party's main objective. McGee responded that the main objective of the Party was to provide community programs and services to the African American community. McGee said, "It [the Black Panther Party] was about picking up the hammer [meaning the community programs]. We used to pick up the hammer more than we did the gun."[1] Historian Arwin D. Smallwood underscores McGee's point when he states, "The Party was established with two major purposes. One was to protect blacks from abuse by the police and the other was to help feed and educate black children who were living in the inner city."[2] And according to Panther co-founder Huey P. Newton, the sole reason the Panthers existed was to "serve the people."[3] Many earlier works dealing with the Panthers have failed to recognize the importance of their services, and some people have referred to the Panthers' attempts as simply "band-aid" solutions.[4] Regardless of judgments on the success of the Party in providing for the community, the efforts to do so clearly illustrated that the Panthers fought for the betterment of the Black community, despite facing harassment, beatings, and even death.

Many white and Black Americans united in the nonviolent Civil Rights Movement during the 1950s and 1960s, struggling to guarantee African

Americans their basic human rights. The mainstream movement was led by individuals such as Dr. Martin Luther King Jr. and NAACP leader Roy Wilkins, who believed that their strategy of nonviolent tactics would be the best way to expose the brutality of the oppressor.[5] Some Blacks and whites realized that the philosophies of nonviolence were not a realistic option given the society in which they were forced to live. For instance, Panther co-founder Bobby Seale acknowledged that the Panthers respected the philosophy of non-violence, but he argued that it would be more practical for people to defend themselves and their community than to engage in sit-ins and marches.[6] Similar sentiments were echoed by some newspapers, which ridiculed the countless civil rights marches that seemed not to produce any tangible results for many African Americans. Headlines such as "The March Went on and on and on and got the Black Man Nowhere" became a more frequent complaint among newspaper columnists.[7] Author Roy E. Finkenbine states, "The boycotts, marches, sit-ins, and freedom rides had raised black awareness and expectations but could do little to ameliorate the conditions of ghetto life."[8] The traditional Civil Rights Movement had come and gone, and in 1969, 32 percent of African Americans still made less than $3,000 a year, compared to only 13 percent of whites. Median annual income for Blacks was $4,481, while whites averaged $7,517 a year.[9]

The dissatisfaction with the results of the conventional Civil Rights Movement helped lead to the emergence of a strong Black Power movement in the mid-1960s. Black Power advocates emphasized the need for African American political and economic empowerment, development of cultural pride and institutions, and the right to self-defense.[10] It was in this context that the Black Panther Party was formed. Newton and Seale recognized that large numbers of Black Americans were forced to live in intolerable conditions and that they needed immediate and tangible help.[11] Poverty, inadequate education and health care, and police brutality were all grave problems facing many Black communities.

The Party set out to address the various problems affecting lower-income African American communities with a Ten-Point Program which called for decent housing, greater educational opportunities, and an end to police brutality. By the early 1970s, the Black Panther Party had established more than thirty branches in twenty-five cities in the United States, and eventually spread outside the United States to Algiers, Algeria.[12]

Even though the Panthers won some support across the nation and throughout the world, they never received widespread acceptance because most whites, as well as a sizeable percentage of Blacks, could not get past the guns and militant rhetoric of the Panthers. As Newton stated, "Our ten-point program was ignored and our plans for survival overlooked. The Black Panthers were identified with the gun."[13] The media was exclusively preoccupied with the Panthers' weaponry, not their ideology or community programs.[14] In his study "Local News Coverage of the Black Panther Party: An Analysis of the Baltimore, Cleveland and New Orleans Press," Black Panther scholar Judson L. Jeffries buttressed this point when he found that for the most part, the press devoted significantly more coverage to gunplay and confrontations than it did to the Panthers' various survival programs.[15]

The federal government was also preoccupied with the Panthers' assertive posture. In 1969, the head of the Federal Bureau of Investigation (FBI), J. Edgar Hoover, incredulously went so far as to warn that the Black Panthers were the number-one internal threat to national security. As a result of Hoover's outlandish remarks, the FBI and local law enforcement agencies proceeded to make life difficult for the Black Panther Party, something that records from the FBI clearly illustrate.[16] Some observers of the period contend that a "genocidal war" was waged on the Black Panther Party, as evidenced by the myriad Panther-police shootouts.[17] Charles E. Jones, another Black Panther scholar, also argues that "[p]olice-Panther gun battles became a defining feature of the early Panther experience," which was shown by the six Panthers who were killed by police in 1969.[18]

In addition to the external attacks from local and federal agencies, the Party also had to face internal problems. Many individuals joined the Party for entirely the wrong reasons, from identifying solely with the gun to being a government informant, and had to be purged from the Panthers as a result.[19] In fact, Bobby Seale reported expelling roughly one thousand such members from the Party over the course of its history. For instance, seventeen Panthers were purged from the Boston branch and twenty-one were expelled from the Omaha office in the summer of 1969 for violating various Panther rules.[20]

One of the most legendary members to be expelled was former national leader Eldridge Cleaver, who was ousted in 1971 largely because he wanted to de-emphasize the community programs of the Panthers while promoting urban guerrilla warfare.[21] Another notable was William Lee Brent, who reportedly held up a gas station in California for eighty dollars while driving the Panther newspaper delivery truck. Brent's act forced the Party to state that he was either "a provocateur agent or an insane man."[22]

Despite the almost constant harassment by various law enforcement agencies, coupled with the internal fissures, the Party implemented a number of social welfare programs and community services, called "survival programs" by the Party, that illustrated a deep commitment to working-class African American communities.

One of the first issues the Panthers believed they had to address was police brutality.[23] The Black Panthers typically, though not always, tried to stem police brutality by patrolling the police in African American communities. The Party members who went on these patrols were armed so that they could adequately defend both themselves and members of their community if the need arose.[24] The Black Panthers stayed a reasonable distance from the police when they were making arrests. Their interest was to monitor the arrest as it was being made and advise the person being charged of his or her rights.[25]

The Black Panther Party realized, however, that countless other grave problems besides police brutality faced Black communities. One major crisis the Party felt it had to address was the rampant hunger that existed among many poor, young African Americans. In response to this situation, the Panthers initiated their Breakfast for Children Program in January of 1969.[26] The Panthers knew they had to provide this service to their communities, because the government was not adequately addressing the problem. In 1967, only a meager $600,000 was spent nationally on breakfast programs by all levels of government. Furthermore, an estimated 3.5 to 6 million children qualified for free government breakfasts in 1972, but only 1.18 million were actually fed.[27]

The Panthers' Breakfast for Children Program was designed to serve all children of elementary and middle school age. Regardless of whether the parents of the children were Party members or if they were Black, the Panthers fed them.[28] The breakfast programs, like all Panther programs, were run by Black Panthers with financial assistance from local white and Black businesspeople. Breakfast for Children had varying degrees of involvement throughout the country. The Los Angeles and Peekskill, N.Y., branches of the Panthers reported feeding fifty children a day, whereas the Illinois chapter of the Black Panther Party provided two hundred breakfasts daily. By the end of 1969, twenty-three branches, from New Haven, Connecticut, to Oakland, California, offered breakfast programs that served approximately twenty thousand children a week. In 1972, Bobby Rush of Chicago reported that twenty-five thousand children were fed every day nationwide by the Panthers' breakfast programs.[29]

The Panthers also addressed the lack of adequate health care facilities for poor African Americans. For instance, the entire Black community of Watts, California, did not have a single hospital until 1965.[30] In 1973, author Pierre de Vise noted that "America's black ghettoes have but one-tenth of the physicians they need."[31] Clearly, many African Americans needed better health care, and Newton and other Panther leaders dealt with this issue by establishing their own medical clinics. Free health clinics were established in 1969 in cities such as Kansas City, Philadelphia, and Brooklyn. The clinics relied mainly on monetary donations and medical professionals from the surrounding community who volunteered their services.[32]

Another illustration of the Panthers' community service orientation was their Busing to Prisons Program. In 1974, sociology professor Leo Carroll estimated that minorities made up nearly half of the prison population of the United States.[33] The Panthers believed that the highly discriminatory judicial system had incarcerated a disproportionate number of Black Americans, and Point 8 of the Black Panthers' Ten-Point Program called for the release of all African Americans held in prison, for the simple reason that they had not been tried by a jury of their peers. Realizing it was unlikely that this demand would be met, the Panthers had to deal with the situation as it stood. Panther branches and chapters, such as those in Chicago and Boston, implemented a busing program for the relatives of prison inmates that provided poor families with the opportunity to visit their loved ones.[34]

All told, the Black Panther Party offered more than thirty services and programs to African Americans at various Panther branches throughout the nation. One such branch was located in Milwaukee, Wisconsin.

Prior to the 1920s, African Americans were a tiny population in the city of Milwaukee. As of 1890, there were only 158 African Americans in the city, and by 1910, there were fewer than a thousand.[35] As the Great Migration occurred, however, Milwaukee witnessed the influx of a substantial number of African Americans in search of wartime work and greater sociopolitical freedom.[36] The Milwaukee Black population jumped 125 percent between 1910 and 1920, and by 1930, 7,501 African Americans called Milwaukee home.[37]

During and after World War II, African Americans again came to Milwaukee in large numbers, again in search of work created by the war effort and a less overtly Jim Crow society.[38] Milwaukee's general population swelled to 637,392 by 1950, with more than eleven thousand African Americans in the greater Milwaukee area. The 1950s witnessed an immense expansion of the Milwaukee African American populace, which grew to 62,458 by 1960, making up 8.4 percent of the city's population. African Americans continued to come to Milwaukee throughout the 1960s in search of the once plentiful industrial jobs that had largely been eliminated by automation or replaced by low-pay service sector jobs. By 1970, Milwaukee boasted a population of 717,099 and a Black population of 105,088.[39]

African Americans moved to Milwaukee to find opportunity and a less oppressive society, but many found a "very racist" society instead. As Joe McClain, former president of the National Association for the Advancement of Colored People (NAACP) in Milwaukee, stated, "The only difference between racism here [the North] and in the South is that the southern racist is more outspoken, [whereas] the northern racist claims, 'I'm not racist.' "[40]

Illustrating the racism present in Milwaukee was a study conducted by Peter Eisinger, an Urban Studies professor at the University of Wisconsin–Madison (UWM). He discovered that the average household income for Milwaukee residents in 1960 was $7,000, but it was only $4,000 for African American families. To put this into perspective, the 1960 Conference on Economic Progress considered an annual income of less than $4,000 as living in poverty. In fact, by 1970, 16 percent of Milwaukee's African American population still made under $3,000 annually, compared to only 7.5 percent of whites who made less than this paltry figure.[41] Black unemployment was also estimated at two to three times that of whites.[42]

Further exacerbating the situation in Milwaukee were a white mayor and police chief who were unsympathetic (at best) to the needs of Milwaukee's African American population. Henry Maier served as mayor of Milwaukee from 1960 to 1988, and during his long tenure it was clear that he cared little for Milwaukee Blacks, or any other minorities for that matter. Local journalist Frank Aukofer claimed that "Henry Maier's communication with most of the established Negro Leadership in Milwaukee was almost nil."[43] Mayor Maier even denounced local civil rights activists, such as Father James Groppi, and blamed them for worsening the racial situation in Milwaukee.[44] Maier reflected the belief systems of his largely white working-class constituency that did not prioritize the concerns of its African American citizenry, and Maier was determined to keep the support of his white voters.[45]

Unfortunately, Police Chief Harold Breier thought even less of the African American population than Mayor Maier did. Throughout Breier's career as chief, it was apparent through his actions and those of his officers that he detested African Americans or anyone else who challenged the status quo.

Breier joined the Milwaukee Police Department (MPD) in 1939 at the age of twenty-eight. He slowly worked his way up the ranks of the department before becoming chief in 1964, a position he would hold until he retired in 1984. Breier was characterized by many as an "active and aggressive officer" who would not hesitate to shoot at suspected criminals, which he demonstrated by firing his weapon at suspects on at least five different occasions.[46]

Coupled with Breier's aggressiveness was his latent bigotry, which helped to foster a highly racist environment within the MPD. For instance, in 1965, a Milwaukee organization called the Citizens Anti–Police Brutality Committee stated that "some law officers in this city constantly insult, harass and brutalize Milwaukee Negroes . . . every Negro is a second class citizen."[47] Reflecting Breier's bigotry, there were only thirty-five to forty

African Americans on the Milwaukee police force in 1968, out of two thousand total officers.[48]

The bigoted views of many Milwaukee police officers frequently manifested themselves in countless acts of police brutality against the African American residents. For example, fourteen-year-old Tyrone Dumas was allegedly beaten by Milwaukee police in May of 1967. In July of the same year, the police reportedly kicked a pregnant mother and beat her sixteen-year-old son "like he was a dog."[49]

The brutality of the Milwaukee Police Department against African Americans was a main cause of the July 29, 1967, uprising,[50] which lasted for three days. Four people were killed, more than three hundred were injured, and 186 were arrested in what was labeled the third-worst civil disorder of the exceptionally turbulent year of 1967. One of those killed was an eighteen-year-old named Clifford McKissick,[51] whose death further enraged the Black community since McKissick had been shot in the throat by a Milwaukee police officer. The death was ruled "justifiable homicide," and the officer was not reprimanded. Frank Aukofer noted, "To many Milwaukee Negroes, McKissick's death was simply another case of a white man killing a nigger and getting away with it."[52]

In 1968, the Survey Research Lab conducted a survey of 119 of the 186 people arrested in the Milwaukee uprising. Of the 119 surveyed, 95 were African American, 84 percent of whom testified that police brutality was a major cause of the disorder. Only 24 percent of white respondents agreed with that statement, however. The Survey Research Lab concluded that "blacks in the general population, as well as arrestees, are more likely to say that police 'frequently' insult Negroes, unnecessarily frisk and search Negroes, beat people up, and the like."[53] In addition, a 1970 study in Milwaukee conducted by Urban Observatories revealed that 53 percent of African Americans surveyed were dissatisfied with the local government of Milwaukee, while only 11 percent of whites were.[54]

The uprising and the reaction of the police sparked outrage in many circles in Milwaukee, but the anger did not stop similar events from occurring later. In January of 1971, a pregnant Mary Mills claimed she was kicked by a police officer while under arrest, and in April, twelve-year-old Jeffrey Harris said he was beaten by the police. And in February of 1973, one African American was beaten so badly by the police that "public officials were sickened by his appearance four days later." Actions like these by the police caused headlines to read "Black Men are being beaten to a pulp by Milwaukee's 'finest' every day" and "Police Clubs Tenderize Black Heads."[55] As these examples also illustrate, the police did not restrict their brutality and misconduct to adult males.

Beyond this level of abuse, a number of Black Milwaukeeans were reportedly killed by the police, only to have the deaths labeled "justifiable homicide."[56] The deaths of Daniel Bell in 1958, Clifford McKissick in 1967, Lee Wilson in 1968, Tommie Chesser in 1969, and Jacqueline Ford in 1972 were just a few among a larger number of African Americans who allegedly were gunned down by police.[57] These killings led additional headlines to read "The Black community in Milwaukee is tired of trigger happy policemen in Milwaukee killing Black people at whim" and that Blacks were tired of "Mississippi Justice." While all these incidents were occurring, Chief Breier maintained that police brutality did not exist,[58] and he even denied that there was "need for improvement" in African American and police relations.[59] Clearly the city of Milwaukee needed to undergo substantial changes, and a variety of individuals and organizations were eager to take the lead.

Milwaukee, in fact, has a long, rich history of African American protest. Two of the most senior civil rights activists in Milwaukee were Ardie Halyard (Clark) and Wilbur Halyard. The Halyards, originally from Atlanta, moved to Milwaukee in 1920 and helped organize the first branch of the National Association for the Advancement of Colored People (NAACP) in Milwaukee.[60]

The Milwaukee NAACP was a vigilant organization, but it remained relatively small, with only 950 members as of 1947. As the Civil Rights Movement blossomed throughout the nation in the 1950s and 1960s and as Milwaukee's Black population swelled, however, Milwaukee's civil rights groups also grew. By 1966, the Milwaukee NAACP claimed a membership approaching five thousand.[61]

One dynamic individual that helped lead the Milwaukee NAACP through the 1960s was Lloyd Barbee, an African American lawyer and Wisconsin state assemblyman for more than twelve years. Barbee and the Milwaukee NAACP took their lead from the national NAACP in the 1960s and made the desegregation of schools one of their central objectives. The Milwaukee NAACP was not alone in its struggle to end school segregation, however. They were soon joined by the Milwaukee chapter of the Congress of Racial Equality (CORE).[62]

CORE emerged in Milwaukee in the fall of 1963 and initially launched a series of sit-ins and marches protesting comments made by Fred Lins, a member of the Community Social Development Commission. The commission had been created by local officials in 1962, and one of its main objectives was to improve the conditions affecting Black people in Milwaukee. Lins, however, had been quoted as making statements like, "An awful mess of them [African Americans] have an IQ of nothing" and "Negroes look so much alike that you can't identify the ones that committed the crime."

CORE's protest efforts against Lins were successful and he resigned from the commission in December of 1963.[63] After the Lins episode, CORE turned its attention to the NAACP's school desegregation campaign.

In March of 1964, the Milwaukee chapter of CORE and the NAACP created an umbrella organization, the Milwaukee United School Integration Committee (MUSIC), to coordinate their school desegregation efforts, with Lloyd Barbee as its chair.[64] MUSIC staged massive picketing and leafleting campaigns to draw attention to the segregated school systems in Milwaukee and also conducted a boycott of Milwaukee public schools on May 18, 1964, in which eighteen thousand students stayed home from school in protest of the segregated system.[65] Barbee ultimately filed a lawsuit in federal court on June 17, 1965, challenging the school segregation in Milwaukee. Eleven long years later, the court ruled that the Milwaukee public school system was guilty of practicing de facto segregation.[66]

The Milwaukee NAACP not only had an energetic senior membership, they also had an incredibly active Youth Council. The council was formed in Milwaukee in 1947 and it took part in many civil rights demonstrations throughout the city.[67] It was under the leadership of Father James Groppi in the mid-1960s, however, that the Youth Council became a major participant in the Milwaukee civil rights struggle.

Father James Groppi was arguably the most well-known civil rights activist in Milwaukee during the 1960s and 1970s, and possibly ever. Groppi's early childhood experiences prepared him for a life of social activism. An Italian American who lived in a predominantly Irish American neighborhood, Groppi routinely had to defend himself from ethnic slurs and assaults. Groppi and his family were even prevented from worshiping at the local Catholic Church because of their ethnicity.[68]

Because of his childhood experiences, Groppi chose to become a priest so he could help change society, and the Catholic Church, for the better. In 1963, Groppi was assigned to St. Boniface, on Milwaukee's predominantly Black north side.[69]

Groppi's willingness to take on all issues of social justice appealed to most churchgoers at St. Boniface, especially younger African Americans. A number of the young African American parishioners at St. Boniface were also members of the NAACP Youth Council, and Groppi quickly emerged as the advisor to the council in July of 1965.[70]

Almost immediately, Father Groppi wanted the council to tackle highly visible issues so they could draw greater attention and support to their cause. In 1966, the council conducted widely publicized marches into Wauwatosa, a middle-class, overwhelmingly white suburb of Milwaukee, to protest the prestigious all-white Eagle's Club. Many bigoted whites in the Wauwatosa

area did not appreciate the presence of Groppi and the Youth Council marchers, and as a result, a number of Youth Council members were roughed up
during their Wauwatosa march, and the Youth Council Freedom House was
bombed by local members of the Ku Klux Klan on August 9, 1966.[71]

Amid the violence facing Groppi and the nonviolent Youth Council, the
Milwaukee NAACP Youth Commandos were formed in October of 1966. The
Commandos, a select, interracial group of roughly 150 members, played a pivotal role in protecting Groppi and the Youth Council, especially during the
open-housing marches. The Commandos were a paramilitary organization,
largely because many of their leaders had been in the United States military
at one time or another and had adopted that method of organizing and mobilizing.[72] The Commandos did not carry weapons, but they still functioned
as bodyguards for Groppi and the council and as organizers for the marches
themselves. Joe McClain claims that the Commandos were trained never to
instigate any fight or disturbance until "they [racists] put their hands on you."[73]

On August 28, 1967, Groppi and the Youth Council and Commandos
began the open-housing marches in response to the highly segregated housing market in Milwaukee. After more than two hundred nights of marching,
during which the marchers were subjected to racial epithets and violence
from bigoted citizens, and assaults and arrests from police officers, Mayor
Maier finally signed an open-housing ordinance on December 13, 1967.[74]

It was in this context of activism that the Black Panther Party also
attempted to provide realistic solutions to the various ills that afflicted
Milwaukee, particularly its African American residents. The Party emerged in
Milwaukee in 1969, coinciding with the "peak period" of the Black Panther
Party nationally.[75] The Panthers believed that marches, like those of Groppi
and the Youth Council, would not bring sufficient and timely changes to the
many problems gripping the African American community. In addition, a
number of Milwaukee Black Panthers, such as Booker Collins, Donald Young,
and Ronald Starks, also were Vietnam veterans with a sense of militancy that
could not be placated by marches and sit-ins.[76] The Panthers believed in
direct-action programs that provided immediate and tangible results for the
people, and they wanted to be more than bodyguards, which was what the
Commandos appeared to be.

The Black Panther Party made inroads into the Milwaukee community
in January of 1969 by establishing an office at 829 West Atkinson Avenue.
By June of 1969, the Party had moved to 2121 North 1st Street. The Panther
office was open seven days a week, from noon until 8 P.M., attempting to
serve the Black people of Milwaukee.[77]

The Panthers emphasized that their primary objective was "to bring the
entire black community together to work on common problems." In addition,

the branch also stressed the importance of engaging in self-defense. Panther John Trenton stated that the Party "will take no acts of aggression but we're going to defend ourselves."[78]

The Panthers also emphasized recruiting women into the Party, but the Milwaukee branch appeared to have some initial difficulty in this area. Hoping to get more women involved in the Party, in June of 1969 branch member Lovetta X made a spirited plea that urged Black women to get involved in the Party. Lovetta X did caution potential female recruits, though, when she stated, "Sisters, [you've] got to be ready. If you're scared, then you better stay where you are. We don't need you."[79]

When the Black Panthers came into existence in Milwaukee, Joe McClain of the Commandos told them that "the police were going to come down hard on them."[80] Unfortunately, McClain was very astute in his assessment of the Milwaukee police force. Almost immediately after opening their first offices, the Panthers were besieged by an aggressive police force that was determined to eliminate the Black Panther Party as a viable organization in Milwaukee.

The Panthers in Milwaukee were "outwardly confronting the power structure in the name of oppressed Black people," and the 1969 Milwaukee Panthers paid a heavy price for doing so. For example, in March of 1969, Walter Chesser, deputy minister of defense of the Milwaukee Panthers and brother of Tommie Lee Chesser, alleged that he was beaten by police for no apparent reason other than for being a Panther. In early June of 1969, Nate Bellamy, lieutenant of information of the Milwaukee branch, had his car rammed by the police, causing him to be hospitalized and arrested for allegedly carrying a concealed weapon. Bellamy was handcuffed to his hospital bed while six Milwaukee police officers guarded his room making sure no one could visit him. Later in June, four Milwaukee Panthers were arrested for carrying loaded handguns and held in jail with bail set at $350 apiece. Three of the four Panthers were then sentenced to ninety days in jail, and the fourth had the charges dismissed because he was a juvenile.[81]

The worst spell of persecution occurred in September of 1969, where within a span of forty-eight hours, six Panthers were incarcerated in two separate incidents. In the first incident, three Party members were stopped for a traffic violation, and according to eyewitnesses, they were viciously beaten during the arrest. One Panther was supposedly beaten by an officer while two other police officers held his arms. When Panther field lieutenant Felix Welch finally was able to visit the three Panthers, he "almost got sick to his stomach" because of their grotesque physical appearance as a result of the beating.[82]

The other arrest was of the locally infamous Milwaukee Three. Panthers Booker Collins, Jessie White, and Earl Levrettes had supposedly tried to murder Robert Schroder, a Milwaukee police officer, in September of 1969. According to Schroder, the three Panthers drove up behind him while he was walking his "beat" on Fond du Lac Avenue in the early morning hours. One of the Panthers supposedly pointed a shotgun at Schroder and fired. Miraculously, Schroder had the presence of mind to drop to the ground just in time to avoid the shotgun blast, but he also claimed that he saw the gun discharge. Not only did Schroder exhibit catlike reflexes, but he kept his composure long enough to write down the license plate number of the car as it sped away.[83] The three claimed they did not even have a shotgun in the car when they were later pulled over by the police for the attempted shooting of Schroder. According to the three, however, one officer, with a shotgun in hand, went over to the car, searched it, then came out of the car with the same shotgun and said, "Here, I found a shotgun."[84]

The three contended that after they were arrested they were all brutally beaten six separate times within twenty-four hours while wearing handcuffs. A reporter from the *Milwaukee Courier* who interviewed the Milwaukee Three shortly after their arrest said there was no doubt the three had been beaten, given all the bruises and swelling on their faces. In addition to the physical beating, the three were found guilty by an all-white jury. Collins and White were given thirty-year sentences, while Levrettes was given ten.[85]

Largely as a result of the external pressures placed on the Milwaukee Panthers, the branch was dissolved by the organization's Central Committee in November of 1969. Before being disbanded, however, the Milwaukee Panthers of 1969 reached a highly respectable seventy-five to one hundred active members.[86]

Even though police persecution was the primary reason the first wave of the Milwaukee Panthers disbanded, internal dissension also helped pull the branch apart. In November of 1969, shortly after the trial of the Milwaukee Three was over, Dakin Gentry requested that the Central Committee disband the local branch for what Gentry perceived as a lack of success in the community. Many Panthers, such as Lovetta X and the Milwaukee Three, were outraged because Gentry never showed the letter to the Panther rank and file nor consulted with them before making such an important, yet arbitrary decision.[87]

Shortly after Gentry issued the press release calling for the dissolution of the Milwaukee branch, the Milwaukee Three verbally attacked Gentry in the *Milwaukee Courier*. To the Milwaukee Three, Gentry's decision to ask the Central Committee to disband the Milwaukee branch reeked of sabotage. One of the three, Jessie White, went so far as to call Gentry a "pig just doing your job like a good boy."[88] The three also maintained that Gentry was to blame for many of the shortcomings of the Milwaukee branch and that the Party was entirely centered on Gentry and Felix Welch and neglected the concerns and contributions of the general Panther membership.[89]

The Milwaukee Three further claimed that Gentry and Nate Bellamy had "sold out." To substantiate their claim, the three pointed to the jobs that Gentry and Bellamy had within the city's "Concentrated Employment Office" less than a month after resigning from the Party.[90] Joe McClain, formerly of the NAACP Commandos, stated that the local government in Milwaukee frequently offered various social service jobs to Black militants of the era. For instance, a number of Youth Commandos took jobs working for the city, where they could serve the people in drug or prison rehab projects. The problem, according to McClain, was that the former Commandos had their militancy stifled because they then had to work within the confines of a bureaucracy.[91]

The Milwaukee Three also maintained that Gentry took the job with the city to avoid going to jail, the inevitable course for many Panther leaders throughout the country. Furthermore, the three alleged that Gentry stepped down from his position within the Party simply because he was beaten by the police.[92] As Jessie White, one of the Milwaukee Three, said, "When the struggle really gets tough you'll find out who's just there to find out what was going down" and who was actually committed to the cause.[93]

Lovetta X supported the claims of the Milwaukee Three in a separate interview in the *Milwaukee Courier* in January of 1970. Lovetta stated that those in leadership positions within the Milwaukee branch, such as Bellamy and Gentry, "contained and controlled the rest of the members of the party under their bullshit methods, like psyching people through the forceful manner that they had." Lovetta X also claimed that Dakin Gentry hurt the Party, and the Black community of Milwaukee as a whole, when he stated on local television that the "people in Milwaukee were forming guerilla bands to counteract what the police are doing in the community." Lovetta X maintained that it was highly destructive to say something as inflammatory and incorrect as what Gentry said. She also said his statement could potentially cause the Milwaukee police to become even more repressive toward the Black community in an effort to sift out these fictitious "guerilla bands."[94]

Gentry eventually responded to these criticisms in another interview in the *Milwaukee Courier*. Gentry reasserted that he resigned from the Party and asked that the branch be dissolved because he did not think that he or the Panthers were serving the people properly. Gentry's short rebuttal ended by labeling the critiques of his character and decisions as nothing more than "bullshit."[95]

Not only did Gentry apparently cause fissures within the Party, he also hindered the Panthers' ability to serve the people by preventing alliances with other progressive organizations. Joe McClain stated that when the Panthers became established in Milwaukee in 1969, Dakin Gentry visited the Commandos to inform them that the Panthers were "taking over" the movement. McClain, on the other hand, did not see why there was not enough room for both groups, as well as others, in the struggle. After Gentry's brash statement, McClain and other Commandos were not enthusiastic about working with the Panthers.[96]

In addition to the previously mentioned internal conflicts with the Milwaukee branch, the Black Panther Party's militant image also attracted the wrong people to the Party. According to Gentry, some individuals wanted to join the Party because they viewed the Panthers as a "gun club or some sort of guerilla outfit." Gentry stated that when the uninformed prospective members "learned that the party required discipline, study and hard work in political action, some changed their minds about joining."[97] Lovetta X substantiated Gentry's point when she claimed that some people joined the Milwaukee branch simply because it was a power trip and trendy, not because they seriously cared about the community.[98] Noncommitted Panthers, as described by Lovetta X, did not want to work in the community programs or help with the day-to-day operations of the Black Panther Party. Therefore, tensions arose between those Panthers devoted to helping the community and those who only cared about being chic.[99]

Despite all the difficulties that faced the Milwaukee Panthers in 1969, the Black Panther Party was not completely finished in Milwaukee. In April of 1972, Ronald Starks, former lieutenant of education of the original Milwaukee Panthers, and Michael McGee formed the People's Committee to Free Jan Starks. Jan, Ron's brother, was a soldier in the military who had been imprisoned in Taiwan for allegedly possessing opium.[100] There was a firm belief in many circles that Starks had been framed because of his race and low military rank; Wisconsin congressman Henry Reuss regarded the case as nothing more than a "frameup."[101]

After Jan Starks was freed thanks to efforts by the People's Committee, the larger African American community and Reuss, Ronald Starks and McGee sought to create a more permanent organization that would serve the African American community of Milwaukee. On April 22, 1972, the two helped to form the People's Committee for Survival, which was predicated on community service.[102] Although the People's Committee had no official affiliation with the Black Panther Party, the People's Committee did not hide their devotion to the ideals of the Party. As Kenneth Williamson, the committee's minister of information, stated, "We [the People's Committee] accept the ideology and follow the leadership of the Black Panther Party."[103]

After the committee became a stable organization, it applied for a Black Panther Party charter, which it received 1 1/2 years after applying. In August of 1973, a Panther branch was reestablished in Milwaukee under the leadership of Starks and McGee. The major reason it took so long to receive the charter was that the Panther Central Committee, given the past history of the Milwaukee branch, was hesitant to grant another charter in Milwaukee and wanted to wait and see if the People's Committee was a stable organization that deserved a charter.[104]

The "second wave" of Black Panthers in Milwaukee peaked at fifty members, yet reported a membership as low as ten at one point. Much like other Black Panther offices across the nation, the Milwaukee branch had a significant representation of women. In fact, according to Panther leader Michael McGee, the Milwaukee branch probably had a few more women members than male members. The membership was made up of individuals from fairly diverse backgrounds, ranging from students to city workers to ex-prostitutes.[105]

Just like the earlier Milwaukee branch, the 1973 Black Panthers also had their share of difficulties with law enforcement agencies. The MPD assigned the "Red Squad," a small, select unit that followed, harassed, and kept hidden files on local radicals, to investigate the Panthers.[106]

In addition to the constant surveillance by the Milwaukee police, especially the Red Squad, the FBI attempted to sabotage the Milwaukee branch. Much like at the national level, the FBI spread negative rumors among possible allies of the Black Panther Party, such as various Black churches as well as the Nation of Islam. Furthermore, the FBI frequently broke into the Panthers' headquarters in an effort to uncover incriminating information about the Party.[107]

The FBI also placed informants in the Milwaukee branch. Michael McGee claimed that FBI infiltration was so frequent that "you almost had to expect [sic] everyone who came in." In addition, the FBI purposely compromised the identity of one of the informants, "Barry," in an effort to get the Panthers to kill him so someone in the Party could be charged with murder. Unfortunately for the FBI, the Panthers did not kill Barry, but they did expel him.[108]

The "second wave" of Milwaukee Panthers also had to contend with internal problems, such as when McGee, who had helped reestablish the Party in Milwaukee, was expelled from the Panthers in 1974. Apparently, McGee had acted alone and without the Party's authorization when he filed a suit against the Milwaukee Police Department requesting the "Special Assignment Squad's" (Red Squad's) secret files. The Special Assignment Squad was Harold Breier's special task force, which kept files on virtually every organization and individual in Milwaukee who threatened the status quo. As a result of this seemingly minor action on McGee's part, he was denounced by others within the Milwaukee branch for "very questionable and devious activities" and forced to leave the Panthers.[109]

A factor that possibly contributed to McGee's dismissal, which further illustrates the internal problems within the Party, was his decision to place women in leadership positions in the Party. According to McGee, "Women carried 60 percent of the load" of the Black Panther Party in Milwaukee. Even though Panther women such as Doris Brown played a pivotal role in the Milwaukee branch, numerous Party males refused to acknowledge their contributions or roles within the Party. McGee reported that he had to suspend certain males, as well as expel males on occasion, for their blatantly sexist behavior. McGee was called a "wimp" or a "fag" by sexist males who resented his ideas about gender equality.[110] It is likely that McGee's gender-neutral policies hastened his removal from the Party.

The Milwaukee Panthers began to wither away by 1976, and in 1977, Huey Newton shut down all branches outside of California in an attempt to limit infiltration by law enforcement agencies. As a result, many members of the Milwaukee Panthers merged into a local umbrella organization, the United Black Community Council (UBCC). The UBCC was a fairly diverse Black Power organization, incorporating former Panthers as well members of the Republic of New Africa and the National of Islam. The UBCC existed for roughly ten years until it collapsed, largely due to the members who tried to make the UBCC adhere to only one ideology.[111]

Even though the history of the Milwaukee Black Panther Party is a sordid one because of police harassment and internal dissension, the Party did clearly illustrate that their main concern was to serve the people. The Party placed great emphasis on community control of the police as part of their larger efforts to improve police–African American relations. The Panthers also initiated a successful Busing to Prisons Program and operated their own health center, known as the People's Free Health Clinic. In addition, the Milwaukee branch of the Black Panther Party provided an array of miscellaneous services and programs to the community.

Following the national Black Panther Party line, the Milwaukee Black Panthers attempted to address the problems of police brutality without resorting to violent means. Milwaukee Panther Walter Chesser noted that the Panthers "have the gun as merely a defensive tool." Michael Walker, an assistant to Mayor Henry Maier, also wrote, "The Party has no wish to create any civil disorder in the Community, but [with] such problems as police brutality, or any problems of this nature, the Party will intervene and try to rectify the problem with the best means possible."[112]

In October of 1969, reflecting the Party's desire to stem police brutality without using violence, the Milwaukee Panthers began their push for the decentralization of the Milwaukee Police Department, with the ultimate aim of greater community control. The Panthers noted that "the trend in law enforcement by the Milwaukee Police Department has been toward arbitrary and unequal enforcement of the law to the detriment of the poor, the propertyless, minority groups, and especially Black persons." The Party and many Milwaukee citizens believed that police "king" Breier exercised too much power and this power needed to be given back to the people.[113] The Milwaukee Panthers, according to Nate Bellamy, sought to remove "all these fascist, racist storm troopers [Milwaukee Police] and, in turn, replace them with some respectable new police officers." He noted that the Panthers "realize that there are some people on the police force, fortunately, who are actually dedicated to the people's needs," but these officers could not adequately serve the people for fear of losing their jobs under Breier's racist administration.[114]

The Panthers' proposal called for the creation of separate police departments for the white, Black, and brown communities. The Party firmly believed that under its new system, the police would be more representative of the areas in which they lived and therefore more in tune with the needs of the community. Each department would be administered by a commissioner who was selected by a fifteen-member "neighborhood police control council." Ronald Starks noted that these fifteen "would choose area police commissioners, rather than one single, centralized administrator as Breier is now." Members of the neighborhood police control councils would be elected by their own communities. In addition, police officers, commissioners, and council members would be subject to recall if they did not perform their duties sufficiently for the community. As Dakin Gentry claimed, "The people should control everything," not racist and dictatorial police chiefs such as Harold Breier.[115]

Not only did the Panthers call for greater community involvement in the selection and oversight of the police, but the Panthers also wanted police officers patrolling the areas in which they lived. The Party maintained that community policing would create better community-police relations as well as lessen the caseload of overburdened courts. The Panthers claimed that many cases resulted from police officers abusing their authority and arresting people on petty or trumped-up charges. The Black Panthers logically believed that these officers would not be as likely to behave in such a fashion in their own neighborhoods. Furthermore, according to the Party's plan, the Milwaukee police force would inevitably become more ethnically diverse if police officers were chosen from all sections of the highly segregated community of Milwaukee.[116]

When the Milwaukee Black Panther Party was disbanded in November of 1969, the remaining Panther members were told by the Party's national leadership to organize under the newly formed National Committee to Combat

Fascism (NCCF). The national leadership of the Black Panther Party perceived the need for one organization that coordinated the efforts of myriad different organizations while simultaneously recognizing the autonomy of each organization. Therefore, the Party sponsored a conference in July 1969 and formed the NCCF, an umbrella organization that incorporated such groups as the Students for a Democratic Society, the Brown Berets, and Young Lords, as well as various women's and gay liberation organizations.[117] Despite varying ideologies and concerns, one constant factor that bound the groups together was that they all faced varying levels of police persecution. Therefore the NCCF emphasized community control of the police to stem police repression.

Roughly forty branches of the NCCF sprouted up throughout the United States during 1969 and 1970, including one in Wisconsin. Formed in 1970, the Wisconsin Committee to Combat Fascism (WCCF) carried on the Panthers' efforts to decentralize the police. In 1970, the WCCF circulated petitions to the Milwaukee Common Council urging the council to take power away from Chief Breier and give it to local communities.[118] The WCCF also sent out a six-page letter in 1970 to various community organizations stating their platform for community control of the police. Among the demands of the WCCF was the call for

> The establishment of neighborhood [police] districts throughout the city. The districts shall be divided to reflect the economic, cultural, ethnic, and racial makeup of the various neighborhoods of the city. Each district shall have neighborhood police control councils which will select the police commissioner from the district and will have the power to review police policy as it affects the neighborhood district, including the power to discipline police officers for breach of department policy.[119]

According to the WCCF, their proposal would remove "the one-man dictatorship of Chief Breier" and put the power where it belonged, in the hands of the people.[120]

The WCCF struggled to gain notoriety during an era of immense organizational activity, and their efforts were largely futile. Therefore, the Party once again took the lead in the decentralization campaign after they were officially reestablished in Milwaukee in August of 1973. The Black Panther Party may have led the struggle for community control of the police, but they also sought to incorporate as many different people and groups into their struggle as possible, working in concert with Westside and Eastside whites, as well as Southside Latinos.[121]

In May of 1974, the Panthers publicly announced a plan that would allow citizens to elect a multiracial governing council of fifteen people, known as the Citywide Police Commission. The elections would be "low budget" elections so that rich candidates could not buy an election. The city government would allot every candidate a small amount of funds for his or her campaign. Those elected would have to be at least eighteen years of age, not hold any other public office, and not be on the Milwaukee police force. Ronald Starks also stated that "these district citizen boards will have control over hiring and firing, promotions, citizen complaints, grievances and internal investigations of the police department." The records and meetings of the Citywide Police Commission would be easily accessible to the public, and citizens could petition for special meetings to take place.[122]

The Party set a goal of thirty thousand signatures for a 1976 petition that would request the state legislature to change the laws governing police affairs. The Panthers were not successful in 1976, but their work paid off somewhat with the passage of Assembly Bill 42 in July of 1977. Assembly Bill 42, which limited the terms of police chiefs and fire chiefs to ten years, passed the State Assembly and Senate in April of 1977, and acting Governor Martin Schreiber signed the bill into law in July of that year.[123] The Black Panther Party was not directly credited with the passage of Bill 42, but it is arguable that without the community organizing and the attention the Panthers brought to the issue, Bill 42 would never have passed.

Unfortunately, Milwaukee police chiefs and fire chiefs were omitted from Bill 42's provisions,[124] which demonstrates the power Chief Breier had. But despite the failure of Panthers to reduce Breier's power, the Party was successful in helping to make other Wisconsin communities more democratic in terms of their police and fire departments. The Party should not be judged in terms of their success, but in terms of their commitment to helping working-class African American communities. As the prolonged battle for the decentralization of the Milwaukee Police Department illustrated, the Party was devoted to helping the lower-income people of Milwaukee.

Further demonstrating their dedication to providing for the lower-income Black community of Milwaukee, the Milwaukee branch created a successful free Busing to Prisons Program. The busing program, initially created on June 9, 1972, by the People's Committee for Survival, became a Panther program when the Party formally returned to Milwaukee.[125] The Panthers, and the larger African American community, recognized a real and immediate need for this service. Ronald Starks rhetorically asked, "Just because a Brother or Sister commits a crime, is it correct for them to be cut off from their loved ones, friends and community with no communication?" Buses carried between 150 and 200 people every Sunday from the Party's office at 3287 North Green Bay Avenue, and later from 2470 North 3rd Street, to the relatively distant Wisconsin prisons in Waupun, Green Bay, and Fox Lake.[126]

The Panthers had a number of difficulties maintaining the busing service. First, P & R Bus Service ceased supporting the program when the name of the service was changed from "The People's Committee for Survival Free Busing to Prisons Program" to "The Milwaukee 3 Free Busing to Prisons Program," in honor of the Milwaukee Three.[127] Apparently P & R did not want to be associated with the Milwaukee Three's controversial court case, or the Black Panther Party, for fear of economic reprisals.

The high cost of the busing program also caused many problems. Ronald Starks estimated that it cost the Panthers at least $600 a month to run three buses to prisons that were between sixty and one hundred miles away. According to Michael McGee, the busing program was the most expensive program the Panthers offered, costing them roughly $450 per trip to Green Bay, and $180 per trip to the other Wisconsin prisons. Contributions from various individuals and bookstores, such as Rhubarb's, a locally owned bookstore, helped finance the busing program, but the Panthers were constantly short of funds. The exorbitant cost of the program forced the Panthers eventually to downsize it from a weekly service to a biweekly service by 1974.[128]

The Panthers initially received roughly $2,000 in funding for the program from Milwaukee Hunger Hike, a local nonprofit organization, but Hunger Hike stopped funding the program as soon as they realized that the People's Committee had become the Black Panther Party. Hunger Hike informed the Panthers that they could not give additional funds to the Party because "[t]he Milwaukee Hunger Hike, a charitable, non-profit organization, cannot by law fund a political party of any type."[129] Even though the People's Committee and the Black Panther Party differed only in name, this was reason enough for Hunger Hike to cease funding the program.

The Busing to Prisons Program was an invaluable service to a number of African American families, enabling prison inmates, as Michael McGee noted, to stay tied to the community and to their families.[130] One prison inmate remarked that the sheer numbers of participants in the program showed that "the high price of travel is the reason that many people do not visit their relatives and friends."[131] The Busing to Prisons Program, like the Party's sustained efforts to decentralize the MPD, illustrates the Panthers' deep concern with providing social services to a large segment of the Milwaukee African American populace.

Another pressing problem facing the low-income Black community of Milwaukee in the 1960s and 1970s was the lack of adequate health care. The north side of Milwaukee, home to many of the city's African Americans, lost its emergency hospital facilities in May of 1970. Various stopgap solutions were implemented, but the north side had to wait until August of 1972 for substantial emergency facilities. Even after the facilities were built, many people could not afford to pay the estimated $13.75 per visit, and in addition to not being able to afford the health services, many still found health care on the north side to be atrocious.[132] In 1975, columnist Cal Patterson of the *Milwaukee Courier* remarked that helpful doctors in the African American community were viewed as a "luxury."[133]

It was in this context that ex-Panthers attempted to meet the medical needs of the lower-income people of Milwaukee. In late 1969, the Black Panthers claimed they were trying to set up a medical clinic in the Black community, but they were dissolved less than two months after making this statement.[134] Despite lacking ties to the official organization, ex-Panthers established the People's Free Health Center in late 1970, at 1348 N. 27th Street. The free health center proved to be a much-needed social service, serving by 1972 roughly two thousand people of all racial and ethnic lines. The people's center reported that 60 percent of its clients were white, 30 percent were African American, and the remaining 10 percent were Chicanos. Unfortunately, the building that housed the health center was heavily damaged by a fire in November of 1972, putting a temporary end to the free health center.[135]

Ex-Panthers and members of the People's Committee for Survival recognized that the community still needed affordable health care, so they started the new People's Free Health Center in early 1973, at 2636 North 3rd Street. The coordinator of the health center, Geneva McGee, stated that "all medical care at the Clinic will be provided to the patient free. We believe that good health care is the right of all people and not a privilege of the wealthy."[136] The health center was run by two paid staffers, McGee and Charlotte Nash, and roughly twenty volunteers. Most of the volunteers were white doctors and dentists who donated their time. A medical resident at Milwaukee Children's Hospital, for example, allotted his Monday evenings free of charge for children referred to him by the center.[137]

The Panthers did not expect the center to be a fully functional hospital; they merely hoped that the clinic would serve as an "entry point into the medical system." As the *Milwaukee Courier* reported, "Many of the people reached by the Center know little about doctors and hospitals and have used them only in emergencies." The center provided preventive health care, such as the high blood pressure screenings given every weekday except Tuesdays, from 1 to 6 P.M. High blood pressure, like sickle cell anemia, was a serious concern among African Americans; according to the Center, one out of ten Blacks suffered from high blood pressure.[138]

Much like the Busing to Prisons Program, the People's Health Center was continually in desperate need of funds. As of 1975, the only regular financial assistance for the health center came from Milwaukee's Social Development

Commission, and even that was minimal. Due to severe financial constraints, clinic services were suspended for several months in 1975 mainly because the center could not afford "skyrocketing" malpractice insurance rates.[139]

In 1975, the People's Health Center, in conjunction with representatives from nearby St. Mary's Hospital, applied for funds from the University of Wisconsin–Madison's Physician Residency Program to establish a more permanent People's Health Center with greater resources. The application for funding was denied because the health center only had a nurse practitioner as its primary administrator. Despite this temporary setback, "while the St. Mary's and People's Center proposal was never accepted, adopted, and put in place, elements of it continued to be discussed."[140]

The proposal by the People's Health Center served as the impetus for the creation of the Harambee Health Task Force, with Geneva McGee as a representative. The Harambee Task Force drafted a proposal that helped create the Isaac Coggs Community Health Center, which opened to the public in 1980. The Coggs Center gave complete checkups, as well as blood, urine, hearing, blood pressure, pregnancy, and glaucoma screenings, at no charge. It is important to note that "the origins of the Coggs Center extend back before the Harambee Health Committee coalesced, back to the turbulent 1960s when many people, particularly those who were black and of middle to low income, realized the necessity of controlling their own lives."[141] The origins of the Coggs Center, in fact, extend back to the creativity and vision of the Black Panther Party.

As of March of 1974, the community programs of the Milwaukee branch served roughly five hundred people a week, supporting these programs in a variety of ways. Obtaining financial backing for their programs was not an easy task, and a number of scholars have alleged that the Black Panther Party, including the Milwaukee branch, used strong-arm tactics to obtain money. The Milwaukee Panthers, like Panthers nationwide, claimed they did nothing of the sort.[142] In fact, the *Milwaukee Courier* noted that the Panthers "dig into their own pockets to . . . support the survival [community] programs."[143] Michael McGee also claimed that many employed Panther members contributed 40 to 50 percent of their salary to the Party so the community programs could function adequately.[144] Not only did individual Party members donate large sums of their salary to the Party, the Panthers also attempted to save money by renting poorly maintained, low-rent properties for their headquarters, which frequently doubled as their living quarters. For instance, the Panther's March 1974 headquarters, on 2470 North 3rd Street, was essentially a "collapsing" storefront.[145] Also, Panthers oftentimes lived eight or nine to a house so they could pool their resources and reduce the amount they each spent on rent.[146]

Michael McGee stated that as a Panther "[y]ou had to humble yourself a lot," because not only did Panthers have to go without basic comforts, many Milwaukee Panthers had to beg to raise money for their community programs. McGee estimated that some Panthers raised $300 a day begging, or "canning," as it was called. Canning was an essential element to the Party's survival, and five or six Panthers canned every day.[147]

In addition to canning in Milwaukee, the Milwaukee Panthers also went to Madison on occasion to solicit donations from the "radical" student body at UWM after the students had received their financial aid for the semester. The Party found the trips to Madison lucrative and reportedly raised as much as $2,000 per trip.[148]

The Milwaukee Panthers also picketed large merchants like Kohl's grocery stores for money and food donations for their programs. The Panthers participated in rallies, such as one sponsored by Students for a Democratic Society in September of 1969, to raise funds for their programs and bail money. The Party also held benefits, such as the showing of "The Cage," a play about oppressive prison life, in July of 1976.[149]

The multitude of programs and services provided by the Milwaukee Panthers clearly illustrate the Party's commitment to helping Milwaukee's lower-income and working-class African American community. Regardless of the need for and notoriety of these other community services, however, no program could match the impact and legacy of the Breakfast for Children Program.

Hunger was, and unfortunately still is, a very real threat for many citizens of Milwaukee, including thousands of children. So during the late 1960s and early 1970s, the Milwaukee Black Panthers attempted to meet the needs of the lower-income people of Milwaukee by establishing a Breakfast for Children Program. The Milwaukee Panthers stated, "None of our people . . . if we can help it, will have to beg for food to eat."[150] The Panther's breakfast program was a much-needed service not only because it combated childhood hunger in Milwaukee, but also because of the positive effects it had on a child's school attendance, alertness, and ability and desire to learn. For example, the Social Development Commission of Milwaukee noted that hungry children are twelve times as likely to suffer from dizziness, four times as likely to suffer from fatigue, and three times as likely to be irritable, making the learning process difficult for the child.[151]

Given widespread knowledge of the detrimental effects of hunger on a child's ability to function, the Panthers could not fathom why the Milwaukee Public School system did not have a breakfast program. The federal government had created a nationwide breakfast program in 1966 that offered substantial federal funding for local communities offering breakfast programs. As of 1969, however, the Milwaukee school system had "refused to take part in the federally financed free breakfast program"[152] and the Panthers were highly "critical of the Milwaukee School System for not providing" a breakfast program.[153] Dakin Gentry of the Milwaukee branch stated that "the schools and the board of education should have had this program instituted a long time ago. It is very difficult for our children to learn anything when they have empty stomachs."[154]

Nevertheless, the Milwaukee School Board seemed uninterested in the plight of inner-city, predominantly Black children and bristled at the thought of giving "handouts." Moreover, the Milwaukee School Board refused to implement a free breakfast program because the city of Milwaukee would have to fund a small portion of it.[155] Therefore, the Milwaukee Panthers believed they had to set the example for the Milwaukee School Board and the city of Milwaukee by establishing a breakfast program of their own.

In May of 1969, the Milwaukee Panthers began publicizing their proposed breakfast program to generate community awareness and to obtain funding. In a 1969 newsletter from the Milwaukee Black Panthers, the Party stated:

> The Black Panther Party is the People's Party. We will respond to the needs of the people. We are requesting churches, stores, businesses and individuals for space, food and money donations to feed some hungry children. We do not ask that you believe in our philosophy—just to help feed hungry children.[156]

Following the distribution of the newsletter, the Party held a rally at St. Boniface in May of 1969 as part of their efforts to draw attention to the breakfast program.[157] At the rally, the Panthers announced that their breakfast program would be a free program for schoolchildren, "both black and white."[158] The Panthers participated in a panel discussion on the Party at the UWM Student Union in May to draw further attention to the breakfast program and to the Party as a whole. At the UWM Student Union, the Party pleaded for community volunteers to help run the breakfast program, not only because the Party needed the extra help and resources, but also because the Party wanted the larger community to play an active role in providing for its citizens.[159]

The Panthers held one last rally on June 7th at Cross Lutheran Church's Youth Center, also known as the "Soul Hole," to further advertise their breakfast program. At the Soul Hole rally, Paul Crayton, lieutenant of religion of the Milwaukee Panthers and former intern pastor at Cross Lutheran, remarked, "It will be a free breakfast program for children, but if a few of you older people get hungry, just drop in too. We'll feed you too."[160]

Shortly after the fundraiser at the Soul Hole, the Panthers met with Reverend Joseph Ellwanger from Cross Lutheran, a church with four hundred members, roughly 40 percent of whom were Black, to ask permission to run the breakfast program out of the Soul Hole. Ellwanger tentatively approved the idea, but said he would have to consult with Cross Lutheran's church council. In the meantime, the Panthers presumptuously thought they had an agreement with Cross Lutheran, and they distributed flyers stating the program would be held at the church. But the church council of Cross Lutheran, an interracial body of the church's leaders, ruled that it would not allow this controversial Black militant group to use its facilities, regardless of their good intentions.[161] Ellwanger issued a press release stating that the church could not work "with an organization openly encouraging the violent overthrow of the government and thus violence against people."[162] Furthermore, Ellwanger claimed that the church did not want to give the impression that Cross Lutheran agreed with the militant teachings of the Party. Ellwanger also stated, however, that the church "recognized they [Panthers] were attempting to fill a need"[163] and that "the council did not feel the Panthers' breakfast program was bad but that the children's needs could be better met by the federally financed program."[164]

As a result of the untimely falling out with Cross Lutheran, the Panthers were forced to operate the breakfast program out of the Paul Craytons' home at 1728 North 16th Street. Crayton recognized that the situation was poor and even called the Panthers' facilities "inadequate," but despite the lack of physical space for the breakfast program, it was still well attended by the Black community, with about a hundred children attending on a daily basis. Initially, the children were served between 7:00 and 9:00 A.M. in rotating shifts of thirty. Mostly African American children ranging in age from infants to teenagers took advantage of the breakfast program,[165] and in it they found "plentiful helpings" of pancakes, sausages, oranges, and milk.[166] Unfortunately, the Panther's breakfast program, at least initially, appeared to adhere to prevailing gender norms of the era, as wives of three Panthers did the cooking and "several teenaged girls helped with the serving."[167]

The breakfast program functioned throughout the summer of 1969, but by mid-July, the Panthers reported feeding only fifty to seventy-five children daily, as opposed to the one hundred they had been serving only a month earlier, a decline that the Panthers reasoned was caused by the end of summer school. The breakfast program normally ran Monday through Friday from 7:00 to 9:00 A.M. during school and summer school sessions, but the Panthers changed the hours of operation to 9:00 to 11:00 A.M., and later to noon to 2:00 P.M. to try and accommodate the summertime schedules of children. The breakfast program, therefore, functioned more as a lunch program during the summer months. Many in the African American community applauded the Panthers' efforts. The *Milwaukee Courier* stated, for instance, that "the Black Panther Party is to be commended for taking the initiative in setting up such a program."[168]

The Panthers were able to sustain the breakfast program primarily through previously mentioned fundraising efforts, as well as through contributions from local grocers such as I & L Foods, a local grocery store, which donated $25 worth of food weekly to the breakfast program.[169] As stated earlier, however, the Panthers themselves donated their time and money to the breakfast program, which also accounted for its success.

The breakfast program of the Milwaukee Panthers, like all their programs, ceased operations when the Milwaukee branch was shut down in November of 1969. But because of the Panthers' initiative, the breakfast program lived on in other organizations.

Prior to the Panthers' breakfast program, many Milwaukee community organizations seemed to be dumbfounded that widespread hunger existed in Milwaukee. Immediately following the disagreement between the Panthers and Cross Lutheran, Reverend Joseph Ellwanger of Cross Lutheran called for a report from Cross Lutheran's church council to determine issues of childhood hunger in Milwaukee.[170] The church council deliberated and presented their findings to Ellwanger, who then promptly wrote a letter to countless Milwaukee organizations and churches. Ellwanger's letter stated, "The Church Council of Cross Lutheran Church, in their recent confrontation with the Black Panthers and their breakfast program proposal, were brought to a vivid awareness of several things. That there is a hunger need among Milwaukee children and youth."[171]

Following the report of the council, Ellwanger and others held a public meeting on July 21st at Cross Lutheran to discuss how to proceed with combating childhood hunger in Milwaukee. At the meeting, the Citizens for Central City School Breakfast Program (CCCSBP) was created. By the end of July, CCCSBP had issued a proposal to the Milwaukee School Board calling for a free breakfast program in Milwaukee's schools.[172]

In acknowledging the impetus for the creation of the CCCSBP and its proposed breakfast program, Reverend Ellwanger freely admits that the idea for his program came from the Black Panther Party.[173] Randy Marchese of the CCCSBP supports Ellwanger when he states, "We are fully willing to endorse the fact that the free breakfast program was initiated by the Panthers."[174]

The CCCSBP waged a long battle against the intransigent Milwaukee School Board, which was committed to not using any tax money for breakfast programs. Those against the breakfast program stated that "it's the parents' responsibility" to provide sustenance for their children, and other board members stated that the main problem was that "some of those welfare mothers are too lazy." Yet others stated, "The purpose of the Milwaukee public schools is primarily, one of education, not, as [school board] Representative Russell Darrow put it, 'charity.' "[175]

Constant pressure by the CCCSBP ultimately coerced the Milwaukee School Board to create experimental breakfast programs in three Milwaukee schools in 1970. Approval for the experimental breakfast programs was a positive step, although the CCCSBP had called for the program to be implemented in fourteen schools as of 1970.[176] Funding concerns continued to be the main impediment to a wide-scale breakfast program in Milwaukee, but Thomas Farley, food services director for the Milwaukee Public Schools, stated that financial concerns were "unsubstantiated." Breakfasts would not exceed 29.3 cents per meal, of which the federal government would pay 15 cents.[177]

In 1972, the CCCSBP convinced the school board to expand the breakfast program to twelve schools. In addition to the locally and federally funded twelve schools, the CCCSBP ran an additional eleven breakfast programs with additional federal funds they had received. All told, these breakfast programs fed more than two thousand children daily.[178]

Also in 1972, The People's Committee for Survival, the forerunner to the second wave of the Milwaukee Panthers, emerged as a community self-help organization in Milwaukee. As part of their community service efforts, the People's Committee launched their breakfast program on September 27, 1972, at Elite Church of God and Christ. Less than a year later, the People's Committee became the Black Panther Party of Milwaukee, and the Party formally took over supervision of the program, now located at a building on 2470 North 3rd Street. The Panthers had been forced to move out of Elite Church of God and Christ because the church raised the rent on the Panthers' use of their facilities. The church had mistakenly thought that the Panthers were making money on their breakfast program, and the church wanted its share.[179]

At the Panthers' breakfast program, breakfasts were served between 8:00 and 9:00 A.M. and consisted of eggs, toast, sausage or ham, and orange juice. Like the Panther breakfast program of 1969, children did not have to be signed in or registered in order to participate; they simply showed up and were fed.[180]

Like the 1969 program, the Panthers' breakfast program of the early 1970s was largely supported by donations from local businesses and individuals. As the *UWM Post* noted, however, "The Black Panthers receive moral support from the neighborhood but most of the people cannot afford to give financial support."[181] The breakfast program cost the Party roughly $300 a day to feed the children nutritious breakfasts, and Michael McGee stated, "We didn't feed those kids no junk."[182] Panther Roy Maxie, who helped oversee the breakfast program, also noted that "the Federal Government with its millions of dollars can't run a decent program," yet the Panthers could with very limited resources.[183] In addition to bearing the financial burden, some Panthers had to make real sacrifices, such as McGee, who had to wake up at 5:00 A.M. each day to get the breakfasts ready. Some Panthers also had to beg to raise money to fund the program, while in some instances, Panther members pleaded with clerks at grocery stores to sell them food for reduced prices or donate it to the Party for the good of the children.[184]

Despite the easy access of the program and the noble effort of the Panthers, the new breakfast program was not as successful as the 1969 program. In February of 1973, the People's Committee served fewer than fifty children a day, and by March of 1974, the Panthers were serving only twenty children daily.[185] The decrease in attendance could largely be explained by the creation of other breakfast programs run by less confrontational organizations and in the Milwaukee Public Schools during the Panthers' four-year absence.

The breakfast program, and the Party as a whole, lived on for three more years until the Milwaukee Party fragmented once again over how to best serve the community and its members went their separate ways. Even though the Panthers themselves no longer existed after 1976, their fight for a city-wide free breakfast program was carried on by the CCCSBP.

In 1974, the five-year-old CCCSBP was rewarded for its efforts with funding from the city of Milwaukee for a full-time staff person. Shortly after receiving the funds, the CCCSBP changed its name to the Hunger Task Force of Milwaukee (HTFM) to show that it was no longer an ad hoc organization and to recognize that it was receiving money from Milwaukee.[186]

In 1975, The Hunger Task Force continued the fight against the lethargic school board, which persisted in its lack of concern with childhood hunger. Illustrating this lack of concern was school board member Anthony Bussalachi, who stated that "the physical neglect of children is not our domain."[187] By 1975, the city of Milwaukee had once again reduced the breakfast programs to three inner-city schools. When proponents of a federally funded breakfast program proposed expanding the program to fourteen schools, the Milwaukee School Board went into an uproar. Reverend Ellwanger claimed that the breakfast program would be a reality "if the Board's priorities were less cost-oriented and more people-oriented, particularly poor-oriented." Supporters of the free breakfast program also asked, "If a free breakfast program cannot be worked into a total public school budget of some $245 million, . . . where are the Board's priorities?"[188]

In November of 1975, the school board voted 10–5 against expansion of the breakfast program. Opponents of breakfast expansion stated it would cost too much, that children waste much of the food, and that "parents should feed their own kids anyway."[189] Finally, in 1976, the Milwaukee Public Schools cut free breakfast programs altogether, and Milwaukee would not see another free school breakfast program until 1980.[190]

As of 1979, Milwaukee remained the only city of the nation's twenty-five largest cities that did not have a breakfast program. Regardless of the setbacks, the Hunger Task Force relentlessly pushed for a free school breakfast program, and in 1979 they were rewarded for their efforts with a federal grant designed to help them run an experimental breakfast program. As a result of this successful program and "enormous community pressure," the HTFM was able to convince the school board to implement a free breakfast program in sixteen elementary schools in the city of Milwaukee in 1980. In 1981, the breakfast program spread to forty-nine Milwaukee public schools, and by 1987, nine thousand children were being fed at free school breakfast programs.[191]

Besides the much-needed breakfast program, the Hunger Task Force of Milwaukee provided many other services to the city. For instance, in 1982 the HTFM began operating the Emergency Food Pantry Network in Milwaukee, which by 1987 was reaching 30,000 people every month, and 19,000 children every month by 1990. In 1993, HTFM provided the 125 food pantries in Milwaukee with seventy tons of food, enough to feed 38,000 people a month, 25,000 of whom were children. By 1997, the Hunger Task Force fed 44,000 people monthly, roughly half of them children.[192] As of 2003, the Task Force fed 45,000 people monthly at its various pantries and another 60,000 at its homeless shelters.[193] The Milwaukee Black Panthers never worked directly with the Hunger Task Force, but the history of HTFM, especially its origins, cannot be separated from the history of the Panthers.

In conclusion, the Panthers' breakfast program was a success because the Party galvanized the larger Milwaukee community into action on the issue of childhood hunger, which was the main goal of the breakfast program. As Panther Walter Chesser stated in May of 1969, the "community will hopefully take it [the Program] over." In June of 1969, the Panthers noted that they "hoped to turn the program over to private groups after first showing how it could be done."[194] The Party knew they did not have the widespread appeal or the resources to adequately serve the Milwaukee community on a prolonged basis, and this was not their purpose. In addition, the Panthers knew there were other pressing issues besides hunger, such as police brutality and lack of accessible health care for the poor, that they had to address.[195] In providing the spark, the Panthers hoped to instigate social change that would outlive their organizational existence, and that is what they accomplished with their breakfast program.

The community programs defined the Black Panther Party as an organiza-tion. Any examination of the Black Panthers that does not adequately address the community programs is neglecting one of the most tangible and enduring legacies of this often misunderstood Black Power organization.

Notes

1. Michael McGee, interview on WNOV with author, Milwaukee, Wisconsin, April 15, 2003, tape in possession of author.

2. Arwin D. Smallwood, *The Atlas of African-American History and Politics: From the Slave Trade to Modern Times* (Boston: McGraw-Hill, 1998), 152.

3. "Power!" vol. 9, *Eyes on the Prize*, prod. and dir. Louis J. Massiah and Terry K. Rockefeller, 60 min., 1990, videocassette, 33:00.

4. Cleveland Sellers with Robert Terrell, *The River of No Return: The Autobiography of a Black Militant and the Life and Death of SNCC* (New York: William Morrow & Company, 1973 [rpt., Jackson: University Press of Mississippi, 1990]), 263 (page citations are to the reprint edition).

5. Martin Luther King Jr., *Why We Can't Wait* (1964 [rpt., Penguin Books, n.d.]), 37.

6. "A Nation of Law?" vol. 12, *Eyes on the Prize*, prod. and dir. Terry K. Rockefeller, Thomas Orr, and Louis J. Massiah, 60 min., 1990, videocassette, 6:00.

7. *UWM Post*, April 9, 1968, 5.

8. Roy E. Finkenbine, *Sources of the African-American Past: Primary Sources in American History* (New York: Longman Publishers, 1997), 185.

9. Peter M. Bergman, *The Chronological History of the Negro in America* (New York: Mentor Books, 1969), 595.

10. William Van Deburg, *New Day in Babylon: The Black Power Movement and American Culture, 1965–1975* (Chicago: University of Chicago Press, 1992), 19–28.

11. Huey Newton, *Revolutionary Suicide* (New York: Harcourt Brace Jovanovich, Inc., 1973 [rpt., Writers and Readers Publishing, Inc., 1995]), 5, 116 (page citations are to the reprint edition).

12. "Power!" 36:35–36:44; *The Black Panther*, June 20, 1970, 22; David Hilliard and Lewis Cole, *This Side of Glory: The Autobiography of David Hilliard and the Story of the Black Panther Party* (Boston: Little, Brown and Co., 1993), 3; *Los Angeles Times*, January 31, 1972, part 1, 19; Van Deburg, *New Day in Babylon*, 155.

13. Newton, *Revolutionary Suicide*, 330.

14. Paul Chevigny, *Cops and Rebels: A Study of Provocation* (New York: Pantheon Books, 1972), 87; Newton, *Revolutionary Suicide*, 330; *Milwaukee Sentinel*, May 14, 1971, 1; Van Deburg, *New Day in Babylon*, 159.

15. Judson L. Jeffries, "Local News Coverage of the Black Panther Party: An Analysis of the Baltimore, Cleveland and New Orleans Press," *Journal of African American Studies* 7 (Spring 2004): 21–38.

16. Former FBI agent Curtis R. Jimerson, phone interview by author, November 23, 1997, transcript in possession of author.

17. *Los Angeles Times*, April 4, 1972, part 1, 8; *Los Angeles Times*, March 17, 1972, part 1, 24; Citizens Research and Investigation Committee and Louis E. Tackwood, *The Glass House Tapes* (New York: Avon Books, 1973), 25, 30; Kenneth O'Reilly, *Black Americans: The FBI Files* (New York: Carroll & Graf Publishers, 1994), 49–50; Steve

Weissman, ed., *Big Brother and the Holding Company* (Palo Alto, Calif.: Ramparts Press, 1974), 318.

18. Charles E. Jones, ed., *The Black Panther Party Reconsidered* (Baltimore: Black Classic Press, 1998), 1.

19. Chevigny, *Cops and Rebels*, 87. Chris Booker also speaks to this issue in his article "Lumpenization: A Critical Error of the Black Panther Party," in Jones, *The Black Panther Party Reconsidered*, 337–358.

20. *The Black Panther*, January 25, 1969, 17; July 12, 1969, 13; June 21, 1969, 11; *Los Angeles Times*, January 14, 1972, part two, 8; January 19, 1972, part one, 19.

21. Ollie A. Johnson, "Explaining the Demise of the Black Panther Party: The Role of Internal Factors," in Jones, *The Black Panther Party Reconsidered*, 400–402.

22. *Milwaukee Courier*, January 18, 1969, 2.

23. Van Deburg, *New Day in Babylon*, 3; Richard T. Shaefer, *Racial and Ethnic Groups*, 4th ed. (Harper Collins Publishers, 1990), 231; *UWM Post*, September 10, 1974, 5.

24. "Power!" 22:00.

25. William Lee Brent, *Long Time Gone* (New York: Times Books, 1996), 91, 124; *The Black Panther*, February 7, 1970, 3; U.S. House of Representatives, Committee on Internal Security, *Black Panther Party, part one, Investigation of Kansas City Chapter; National Organization Data: Hearings before the Committee on Internal Security*, 91st Cong., 2nd sess., 4, 5, 6, 10 Mar 1970, 2683.

26. *The Black Panther*, October 16, 1976, G.

27. Citizens Board of Inquiry into Hunger and Malnutrition in the United States, *Hunger U.S.A Revisited* (Washington, D.C., n.d.), 10–12.

28. *The Black Panther*, September 6, 1969; January 4, 1969, 16; April 27, 1969, 3; December 14, 1968, 15; G. Louis Heath, *Off the Pigs! The History and Literature of the Black Panther Party* (Metuchen, N.J.: Scarecrow Press, 1976), 86.

29. Johnson, "Explaining the Demise of the Black Panther Party," 401; *The Black Panther*, July 5, 1969, 15; September 13, 1969, 6, 19; House Committee on Internal Security, *Black Panther Party, part one*, 2693; Bobby Seale, *Seize the Time: The Story of the Black Panther Party and Huey P. Newton* (New York: Random House, 1970), 413; Akua Njeri, *My Life with The Black Panther Party* (Oakland, Calif.: Burning Spear, 1991), 11; Jimerson, interview; Heath, *Off the Pigs!* 99; G. Louis Heath, *The Black Panther Leaders Speak* (Metuchen, N.J.: Scarecrow Press, 1976), 125; *UWM Post*, April 14, 1972, 2.

30. Terry Cannon, *All Power to the People: The Story of the Black Panther Party* (San Francisco: Peoples Free Press, 1970), 35.

31. Pierre de Vise, *Misused and Misplaced Hospitals and Doctors: A Locational Analysis of the Urban Health Crisis* (Washington, D.C.: Association of American Geographers, 1973), 1.

32. Heath, *The Black Panther Leaders Speak*, 125; Heath, *Off the Pigs!* 98; *The Black Panther*, August 30, 1969, 16; House Committee on Internal Security, *Black Panther Party, part one*, 2638; Huey Newton, "War Against the Panthers: A Study of Repression in America" (Ph.D. diss., University of California, Santa Cruz, 1980), 93.

33. Leo Carroll, *Hacks, Blacks and Cons: Race Relations in a Maximum Security Prison* (Lexington, Ky.: Lexington Books, 1974), xi.

34. Erik Erikson and Huey Newton, *In Search of Common Ground* (New York: W. W. Norton & Company, Inc., 1973), 87; Newton, *Revolutionary Suicide*, 116–118; Former Black Panther Michael Fultz, interview by author, November 16, 1998, transcript in possession of author.

208   Picking Up the Hammer

35. *The Thirteenth Census of the United States*, 1910, vol. 3 (Washington, D.C.: Government Printing Office, 1913), 1090.

36. Neil McMillen, *Dark Journey: Black Mississippians in the Age of Jim Crow* (Urbana: University of Illinois Press, 1989), 262–263; Smallwood, *The Atlas of African-American History*, 111, 124; Joe Trotter, *Black Milwaukee: The Making of an Industrial Proletariat, 1915–1945* (Urbana: University of Illinois Press, 1985), 39. The Great Migration occurred primarily between 1914 and 1929, as hundreds of thousands of African Americans left the rural South mainly for the urban North.

37. *The Sixteenth Census of the United States*, 1940, vol. 2, part 7 (Washington, D.C.: Government Printing Office, 1943), 640.

38. Frank Aukofer, *City with a Chance* (Milwaukee: The Bruce Publishing Company, 1968), 34–35.

39. *The Seventeenth Census of the United States*, 1950, vol. 2, part 49 (Washington, D.C.: Government Printing Office, 1952), 49, 9, 49–57; *The Eighteenth Census of the United States*, 1960, vol. 1, part 51 (Washington, D.C.: Government Printing Office, 1962), 51, 26; *The Nineteenth Census of the United States*, 1970 (Washington, D.C.: Government Printing Office, 1973), 51, 15, 51–72.

40. Joe McClain, former president of the NAACP Youth Commandos, interview by author, May 6, 2005, tape in possession of author.

41. Peter K. Eisinger, *Patterns of Interracial Politics: Conflict and Cooperation in the City* (New York: Academic Press, 1976), 34; School of Social Work, University of Wisconsin–Madison, *Social Problem Indicators and Related Demographic Characteristics, Milwaukee* (Madison: University of Wisconsin–Madison, 1966), 2.

42. Aukofer, *City with a Chance*, 37.

43. Ibid., 35.

44. Martin Gruberg, *A Case Study in US Urban Leadership: The Incumbency of Milwaukee Mayor Henry Maier* (Aldershot, England: Avebury, 1996), 161; Henry Maier, *The Mayor Who Made Milwaukee Famous* (Lanham, Md.: Madison Books, 1993), 94–95.

45. McClain, interview.

46. Ronald Snyder, "Chief for Life: Harold Breier and His Era" (Ph.D. diss., University of Wisconsin–Milwaukee, 2002), 25, 37, 48–50.

47. Mark Braun, "Social Change and the Empowerment of the Poor: Poverty Representation" (Ph.D. diss., University of Wisconsin–Milwaukee, 1999), 63.

48. Ad Hoc Committee on Police Administration in Milwaukee (1968), Milwaukee Small Collection 177, University of Wisconsin–Milwaukee Archives, Milwaukee, Wis.

49. *Greater Milwaukee Star*, April 15, 1967, 1; April 22, 1967, 1, 5; May 6, 1967, 1; July 1, 1967, 1.

50. Henry J. Schmandt, John G. Goldback, and Donald B. Vogel, *Milwaukee: A Contemporary Urban Profile* (New York: Praeger Publishers, 1971), 155.

51. Braun, "Social Change and the Empowerment of the Poor," 53; Henry J. Schmandt and Harold M. Rose, *Citizen Attitudes in Milwaukee: A Further Look* (Milwaukee: Milwaukee Urban Observatory, 1972), 170. The year 1967 witnessed more than 125 civil disorders throughout the nation.

52. Aukofer, *City with a Chance*, 12–13.

53. Karl H. Flaming, *Who 'Riots' and Why?* (Milwaukee: Milwaukee Urban League, 1968), vii, xi, 2, 46.

54. Braun, "Social Change and the Empowerment of the Poor," 24; Schmandt and Rose, *Citizen Attitudes in Milwaukee*, 1, 18, 39, 50.

55. *Milwaukee Courier*, October 4, 1969, 1; January 31, 1970, 1; January 8, 1977, 1; *Milwaukee Star*, January 3, 1970, 5; October 9, 1971, 1; October 23, 1971, 1; *Milwaukee Star-Times*, February 4, 1973, 1; *UWM Post*, February 14, 1973, 4.

56. *Milwaukee Courier*, September 22, 1973, 3; August 30, 1975, 1.

57. Snyder, "Chief for Life," 80–81. In 1979, Louis Krause, a retired member of the Milwaukee police force, alleged that he and Officer Thomas Grady had placed a knife on Bell's person after Grady had shot and killed Bell. Both Mayor Maier and the Milwaukee Common Council demanded an investigation, but Breier ignored their pleas and no one could force him to conduct an investigation because a 1911 law gave lifetime tenure to the chief of police.

58. *Milwaukee Star*, January 13, 1968, 1; March 2, 1968, 4; February 17, 1968, 4; March 9, 1968, 4; *Milwaukee Sentinel*, June 12, 1969, 16; *Milwaukee Courier*, April 14, 1973, 8; *UWM Post*, April 30, 1971, 16; January 16, 1968, 9; *Milwaukee Courier*, July 10, 1971, 1.

59. Ad Hoc Committee on Police Administration in Milwaukee (1968), Milwaukee Small Collection 177, University of Wisconsin–Milwaukee Archives, Milwaukee, Wis.

60. National Association for the Advancement of Colored People (NAACP) Records, Milwaukee Manuscript Collection EP, Box 7, Folder 8, University of Wisconsin–Milwaukee Archives.

61. NAACP Records, Box 5, Folders 1 and 15.

62. Congress of Racial Equality (CORE) Records, Milwaukee Manuscript Collection 27, Box 1, Folder 6, University of Wisconsin–Milwaukee Archives.

63. Aukofer, *City with a Chance*, 39–40.

64. Ibid., 40.

65. CORE Records, Box 1, Folders 4 and 6.

66. Braun, "Social Change and the Empowerment of the Poor," 32.

67. Jay Wendelberger, "The Open Housing Movement in Milwaukee: Hidden Transcripts of the Urban Poor" (M.A. thesis, University of Wisconsin–Milwaukee, 1996), 16.

68. Lloyd Barbee, Milwaukee Manuscript Collection 16, Box 22, Folder 3, University of Wisconsin–Milwaukee Archives; Wendelberger, "The Open Housing Movement in Milwaukee," 26–27.

69. Wendelberger, "The Open Housing Movement in Milwaukee," 29–31.

70. McClain, interview; Wendelberger, "The Open Housing Movement in Milwaukee," 26.

71. NAACP Records, Box 5, folder 15; Wendelberger, "The Open Housing Movement in Milwaukee," 2, 26, 35–36. The Eagle's Club was a social club in Milwaukee that boasted a membership that included local judges and influential businesspeople.

72. McClain, interview.

73. Barbee, Box 22, Folder 10; Wendelberger, "The Open Housing Movement in Milwaukee," 48–49, 58; McClain, interview.

74. James Groppi, Box 16, Folder 1, Milwaukee Manuscript Collection, University of Wisconsin–Milwaukee Archives; Wendelberger, "The Open Housing Movement in Milwaukee," 84–87, 107.

75. Johnson, "Explaining the Demise of the Black Panther Party," in Jones, *The Black Panther Party Reconsidered*, 393. Johnson identifies 1968 through 1970 as the "peak years" of the Party. According to Johnson, Black Power organizations became much more appealing in the wake of the assassination of Martin Luther King Jr. in 1968, and the Panthers

also became more well known following the widely publicized imprisonment of Huey Newton in 1967 and the killing of Bobby Hutton, one of the first members of the Party.

76. *Milwaukee Sentinel*, June 12, 1969, 16; *Milwaukee Star*, July 18, 1970, 5; *Milwaukee Courier*, February 7, 1970, 3; September 27, 1969, 8; Miriam White, "The Black Panthers' Free Breakfast for Children Program" (M.A. thesis, University of Wisconsin–Madison, 1988), 84.

77. *Milwaukee Journal*, March 23, 1969, part 2, 1; *Milwaukee Courier*, March 30, 1974, 1; *Milwaukee Journal*, June 19, 1969, 1; *Milwaukee Sentinel*, June 12, 1969, 5, 16; October 23, 1969, 14.

78. *Milwaukee Journal*, March 23, 1969, part 2, 8; *Milwaukee Sentinel*, June 12, 1969, 16.

79. *Milwaukee Courier*, June 14, 1969, section 2, 8.

80. McClain, interview.

81. *Milwaukee Courier*, December 6, 1969, 4; March 1, 1969, 2; June 14, 1969, 1, sect. 2, 8; *Milwaukee Journal*, June 19, 1969, 1, 3; October 23, 1969, 3.

82. *Milwaukee Star*, September 29, 1969, 1, 4; *Milwaukee Courier*, September 27, 1969, 1.

83. *Milwaukee Journal*, September 22, 1969, 1, part 2; *Milwaukee Courier*, September 27, 1969, 6.

84. *Milwaukee Courier*, September 27, 1969, 1.

85. *Milwaukee Courier*, September 27, 1969, 8; *Greater Milwaukee Star*, August 14, 1971, 6; *Milwaukee Sentinel*, February 5, 1973, 5; Black Panther Party, Social Action Vertical File, MS-577, Box 6.

86. *Milwaukee Sentinel*, November 26, 1969, 8; The Party's Central Committee was the main decision-making body of the Party at the national level, consisting of ten to fifteen individuals, including Huey Newton and Bobby Seale.

87. *Milwaukee Courier*, January 24, 1970, 3; January 17, 1970, 1.

88. *Milwaukee Courier*, December 20, 1969, 1.

89. *Milwaukee Courier*, April 13, 1974, 3; *Milwaukee Journal*, November 26, 1969, 1.

90. *Milwaukee Sentinel*, November 26, 1969, 1.

91. McClain, interview.

92. *Milwaukee Courier*, December 20, 1969, 1; January 24, 1970, 3.

93. *Milwaukee Courier*, December 20, 1969, 1.

94. *Milwaukee Courier*, January 17, 1970, 1, 8.

95. *Milwaukee Courier*, January 24, 1970, 3.

96. McClain, interview.

97. *Milwaukee Sentinel*, November 26, 1969, 8.

98. *Milwaukee Courier*, January 17, 1970, 1.

99. *Milwaukee Sentinel*, November 26, 1969, 8.

100. *Milwaukee Courier*, March 30, 1974, 18.

101. *Greater Milwaukee Star*, April 27, 1972, 1.

102. *Milwaukee Courier*, March 30, 1974, 18; *Milwaukee Star-Times*, June 29, 1972, 4.

103. Black Panther Party Clippings File, Milwaukee Public Library.

104. *Milwaukee Courier*, March 30, 1974, 1, 18.

105. Charles E. Jones and Judson L. Jeffries, "'Don't Believe the Hype': Debunking the Panther Mythology," in Jones, *The Black Panther Party Reconsidered*, 34–35, point out that women made up a significant percentage of Party members; McGee, interview.

106. McGee, interview.

107. Ibid.

108. Ibid.

109. *Milwaukee Courier,* June 7, 1975, 4; February 21, 1976, 3.

110. McGee, interview.

111. Ibid.

112. Henry Maier, University of Wisconsin Manuscript Collection, Box 9, Folder 24, University of Wisconsin–Milwaukee Archives.

113. Barbee, Box 55, Folder 4; *Milwaukee Courier,* July 24, 1974, 1.

114. *Milwaukee Journal,* October 13, 1969, part 2, 9.

115. *Milwaukee Courier,* August 2, 1969, 1, 10; *Milwaukee Journal,* October 13, 1969, 9; *Milwaukee Courier,* August 2, 1969, 10; *Milwaukee Journal,* October 13, 1969, 9; *Milwaukee Courier,* August 2, 1969, 1, 10.

116. *Milwaukee Courier,* August 2, 1969, 1, 10.

117. Floyd W. Hayes III and Francis Kiene III, "'All Power to the People': The Political Thought of Huey P. Newton and the Black Panther Party," in Jones, *The Black Panther Party Reconsidered,* 167; *Milwaukee Courier,* January 17, 1970, 8; *Greater Milwaukee Star,* July 26, 1969, 2.

118. Social Action Vertical File, MSS 577, Box 56, Wisconsin Committee to Combat Fascism Folder.

119. Ibid.

120. Ibid.

121. *Milwaukee Courier,* July 20, 1974, 4.

122. Black Panther Party Clippings File.

123. *Milwaukee Courier,* May 11, 1974, 3; July 20, 1974, 4; April 16, 1977, 1, 11; Wisconsin State Legislative Reference Bureau, 608-266-0341. Governor Pat Lucey was in China at this time, so Martin Schreiber was the acting governor.

124. Snyder, "Chief for Life," 8. The Milwaukee Common Council finally stripped Breier of much of his power in 1984, including his lifetime tenure, after the heavily publicized killing of Ernest Lacy in 1981. Milwaukee police had beaten the twenty-two-year-old Lacy, an African American, in the back of a police van. Public outcry was so severe that the Common Council felt compelled to act, and they divvied up Breier's power among the Common Council, the mayor, and the Fire and Police Commissions. In typical Breier style, he retired rather than serve with diminished authority. Lacy's family was given a paltry $600,000 by the city of Milwaukee for this wrongful death.

125. *Milwaukee Courier,* September 2, 1972, 1.

126. Social Action Vertical File, MSS 577, Box 40, People's Committee for Survival folder; *Milwaukee Courier,* September 2, 1972, 1.

127. *Milwaukee Courier,* September 2, 1972, 1, 7.

128. *Milwaukee Courier,* July 15, 1972, 1; *The Black Panther,* March 23, 1974, 3; *Milwaukee Courier,* September 2, 1972, 1, 7; March 30, 1974, 1, 18; July 10, 1976, 14; McGee, interview.

129. Barbee, Box 56, Folder 22.

130. McGee, interview.

131. *Milwaukee Courier,* July 10, 1976, 14.

132. *Milwaukee Courier,* August 14, 1971, 1; August 28, 1971, 1; August 12, 1972, 1; September 2, 1972, 1; August 28, 1972, 1; January 4, 1975, 4.

133. *Milwaukee Courier,* January 4, 1975, 4.

134. *Greater Milwaukee Star,* September 13, 1969, 21.

135. *Milwaukee Star-Times*, November 23, 1972, 1. The cause of this fire was unknown.

136. *The Black Panther*, June 16, 1975, 2.

137. *Milwaukee Courier*, November 29, 1975, 1, 14; McGee, interview.

138. *Milwaukee Courier*, November 29, 1975, 14; January 17, 1976, 3.

139. *Milwaukee Courier*, November 29, 1975, 14.

140. Edwin Clarke and Steve Paulson, introduction by Belden Paulson, *The Harambee Health Experiment* (University of Wisconsin Extension: Center for Urban Community Development, 1983), 8, 9.

141. Clarke and Paulson, *The Harambee Health Experiment*, 12, 19, 38; McGee, interview. The name "Harambee" was chosen because it is the name of the neighborhood where the People's Free Health Center was located.

142. *Milwaukee Courier*, March 30, 1974, 1, 18; June 14, 1969, 1; August 16, 1969, 1; July 10, 1976, 1, 14; March 30, 1974, 18; *Milwaukee Sentinel*, April 7, 1973, part 2, 15; White, "The Black Panthers' Free Breakfast for Children Program," 86–87.

143. *Milwaukee Courier*, March 30, 1974, 18.

144. McGee, interview.

145. *Milwaukee Courier*, March 30, 1974, 1, 18.

146. McGee, interview.

147. Ibid. It was called "canning" because Panther members held out a can for people to deposit money into.

148. Ibid.

149. *Milwaukee Courier*, March 30, 1974, 18; *UWM Post*, September 26, 1969, 7; *Milwaukee Courier*, July 10, 1976, 1, 14.

150. *Greater Milwaukee Star*, June 21, 1969, 1.

151. Social Development Commission, *Children in Poverty: The State of Milwaukee's Children* (Milwaukee, n.d.), 12.

152. *Milwaukee Journal*, July 30, 1969, 2.

153. *Greater Milwaukee Star*, June 7, 1969, 5.

154. *Milwaukee Sentinel*, May 23, 1969, 20.

155. *Milwaukee Sentinel*, July 30, 1969, 8.

156. Social Action Vertical File, MSS 577, Box 6, Black Panther Party Folder.

157. *Milwaukee Courier*, May 17, 1969, 1.

158. *Milwaukee Sentinel*, May 23, 1969, 20.

159. Ibid.; *Greater Milwaukee Star*, June 7, 1969, 5.

160. *Milwaukee Courier*, June 14, 1969, section 2, 8. Crayton resigned from his role at the church for what he called "personal reasons."

161. Reverend Joseph Ellwanger, telephone interview with author, June 23, 1999; Social Action Vertical File, MSS 577, Box 6, Black Panther Party Folder; *Milwaukee Star*, September 27, 1969, 4; *The Black Panther*, July 5, 1969, 15; *Milwaukee Courier*, June 21, 1969, 1.

162. *Milwaukee Journal*, June 18, 1969, 1.

163. Ellwanger, interview.

164. *Milwaukee Journal*, July 30, 1969, 2.

165. *Milwaukee Courier*, June 21, 1969, 1, 6; *The Black Panther*, July 5, 1969, 15; *Milwaukee Courier*, June 21, 1969, 1.

166. *Milwaukee Journal*, June 18, 1969, 1, 22; *Milwaukee Courier*, June 21, 1969, 1.

167. *Milwaukee Journal*, June 18, 1969, 1.

168. *Milwaukee Courier*, July 12, 1969, 1;*Milwaukee Journal*, June 18, 1969, 1, 22; *Milwaukee Courier*, June 21, 1969, 4, 6.

169. *Milwaukee Journal*, June 18, 1969, 22; *Milwaukee Courier*, July 12, 1969, 1.

170. *Milwaukee Journal*, June 18, 1969, 22.

171. Henry Maier, Box 9, Folder 24.

172. *Milwaukee Journal*, July 30, 1969, 2.

173. Ellwanger, interview.

174. *Milwaukee Sentinel*, July 30, 1969, 8.

175. *Milwaukee Courier*, July 4, 1970, 1.

176. White, "The Black Panthers' Free Breakfast for Children Program," 96; Hunger Task Force of Milwaukee, University of Wisconsin–Milwaukee Collection, Box 1, Folder 17, University of Wisconsin–Milwaukee Archives; Ellwanger, interview.

177. *Milwaukee Courier*, July 4, 1970, 1, 6.

178. Hunger Task Force, Box 1, Folder 3; *Milwaukee Courier*, September 30, 1972, 3.

179. Social Action Vertical File, MSS 577, Box 40, People's Committee for Survival Folder; *UWM Post*, November 1973, 1; White, "The Black Panthers' Free Breakfast for Children Program," 85; *Milwaukee Sentinel*, February 5, 1973, 5; *Milwaukee Courier*, March 30, 1974, 18; McGee, interview.

180. People's Committee for Survival, Social Action Vertical File, MSS 577, box 40; *UWM Post*, November 1973, 1; *Milwaukee Sentinel*, February 5, 1973, 5; *Milwaukee Courier*, March 30, 1974, 18; McGee, interview.

181. *UWM Post*, November 1973, 1.

182. McGee, interview.

183. *UWM Post*, November 1973, 1.

184. McGee, interview.

185. Social Action Vertical File, MSS 577, Box 40, People's Committee for Survival Folder; *UWM Post*, November 1973, 1; White, "The Black Panthers' Free Breakfast for Children Program," 85; *Milwaukee Sentinel*, February 5, 1973, 5; *Milwaukee Courier*, March 30, 1974, 18.

186. White, "The Black Panthers' Free Breakfast for Children Program," 96; Hunger Task Force, Box 1, Folder 3; Ellwanger, interview.

187. *Milwaukee Courier*, December 6, 1975, 13.

188. *Milwaukee Courier*, November 1, 1975, 4.

189. *Milwaukee Courier*, November 1, 1975, 1, 4; November 29, 1975, 1, 14; December 6, 1975, 1, 13; November 8, 1975, 1, 6.

190. Hunger Task Force, Box 1, Folder 2.

191. Ibid.

192. Hunger Task Force, Box 2, Folder 63; www.hungertaskforce.org/all_about.htm.

193. http://www.hungertaskforce.org/Bringing_Food/index.html

194. *Milwaukee Journal*, May 23, 1969, 25, June 18, 1969, 22.

195. *Milwaukee Courier*, June 21, 1969, 6.

6

"Brotherly Love Can Kill You": The Philadelphia Branch of the Black Panther Party

Omari L. Dyson, Kevin L. Brooks, and Judson L. Jeffries

> Misery is when you heard on the radio that the
> neighborhood you live in is a slum but you always
> thought it was home.
>
> —LANGSTON HUGHES, *BLACK MISERY*

Few would have predicted that nearly two centuries after the signing of the Declaration of Independence, a multicultural gathering of hippies, white leftists, Black militants, and other activists of color from around the country would converge on the city of Philadelphia over Labor Day weekend in 1970 to rewrite what had been written in 1787 by this country's founding fathers in the City of Brotherly Love—"to draft a new constitution providing authentic liberty and justice for all."[1]

When the Party decided on Philadelphia as the host city, it recognized it would need the assistance of all who had any sympathy for its objectives. Finding a venue was the first order of business, and the Panthers wasted no time in asking the well-known and highly respected Father Paul M. Washington of the Church of the Advocate for the use of his church, to which he agreed. However, the church alone would not suffice. A much larger public space was needed as well, and the Panthers decided to approach Temple University and ask to make its large new gymnasium available. Father Washington joined a group of citizens that included Philadelphia Bar Association president Robert Landis to meet with Temple officials to win their cooperation. Temple agreed, and the site was set.[2]

The Black Panther newspaper reported that the conference was "the first step towards guaranteeing us the right to life, liberty and the pursuit of happiness . . . a Constitution that has the respect for the people; a Constitution that serves the people instead of the ruling class."[3] A variety of constituencies were represented as attendees assembled to discuss issues such as gender equality, universal health care, the right to bear arms, the purpose of a standing army, freedom to pursue one's own sexual orientation, and community control of the police. Others came to the conference for less substantive reasons, such as to get a glimpse of Huey Newton, who had recently been released from prison after serving nearly three years for voluntary manslaughter.

Reports on the number of people who attended the Revolutionary People's Constitutional Convention vary widely. Nearly ten thousand people reported for the opening of the convention at Temple University. Another source claimed that more than fourteen thousand people attended the three-day affair, while still another suggested that participation barely reached five thousand.[4] Still, the atmosphere was electric and the people were invigorated. Fiery speeches marked the first day of the much-anticipated conclave. New York Panther Michael "Cetawayo" Tabor (a member of the NY 21) proved to be a crowd favorite. Flanked by menacing guards at each side of the podium in McGonigle Hall, Tabor spoke for two hours; he submitted that the present constitution was inadequate and had historically functioned to exclude and oppress "240,000 indentured servants, 800,000 Black slaves, 300,000 Indians, and all women, to say nothing of sexual minorities."[5] Toward the end of his speech Tabor called on all minorities to become revolutionaries. All minorities—Blacks, Puerto Ricans, Mexicans, Orientals—"who live within the belly of the beast must take a revolutionary stand," Tabor exhorted as the audience chanted "power to the people."[6] Following Tabor, speakers included Audrea Jones, leader of the Boston branch of the BPP, and Panther attorney Charles Garry.

The day climaxed with a keynote speech by Newton, whose appearance was greeted with a response not unlike that reserved for movie stars or musicians. Euphoria broke out as he took the stage and told a wildly cheering audience that a new day was dawning for Black Americans and other minority groups. "We gather to proclaim to the world that for 200 years we have suffered this long train of abuses and usurpations," he said, referring to the Declaration of Independence, "while holding to the hope that this would pass. We recognize, however, that it has not passed and we are a people who enjoy no equal protection (under) the law, and our future action must be guided by our sufferance, not by our prudence."[7] The Black Panther Party "calls for a Constitution that will bring about a . . . government in which all groups will be adequately represented." It is a fact that we will change society, Newton said, as throngs cheered and applauded. "It will be up to the oppressors if this is going to be a peaceful change."[8] Newton astutely noted that the United States had changed since the writing of the Constitution, evolving from a small and fairly racially and culturally homogeneous country to an empire with a large and diverse population. The city of Philadelphia was a perfect example of the country's transformation. In 1970, Blacks made up approximately 34 percent of the city's nearly two million inhabitants, significantly higher than the 4 percent of nearly a hundred years earlier. As far as Newton was concerned, a constitution that reflected these developments was long overdue.

As hundreds of people waved flags and beat drums outside McGonigle Hall, inside the hall Newton lectured the audience on the growth of capitalism. "The democratic capitalism of our early days," he said, "became a relentless drive to obtain profits . . . until the selfish motivation for profit eclipsed the unselfish principles of democracy." The history of the United States, he said, "leads us to the conclusion that our sufferance is basic to the function of the government."[9] Unable to resist taking a shot at the city's administration, Newton lashed out at police commissioner Frank Rizzo, calling him "Bozo" and an oppressor, to the delight of the crowd. News reports indicate that Newton's remarks were followed by deafening shouts, screams, and applause that left the 4,500-seat auditorium abuzz. Despite the applause, some did not find Newton's speech especially impressive. Mumia Abu-Jamal believed that the audience's reaction was the result of "Newton's presence rather than his ideas and words."[10]

The convention adopted scores of resolutions explaining the principles of the new society for which its participants were struggling, but it did not formulate any unified political strategy for carrying out the struggle. Despite the lofty expectations that surrounded the three-day conclave, reviews were mixed. Milton McGriff opined that the Panthers missed a great opportunity to publicly demonstrate their influence in the city.[11] But Elbert "Big Man" Howard, deputy minister of information of the BPP, stated, "We know that the sessions were a success, despite the police raids ... to keep us from holding the sessions in a public building."[12] Substantively, the convention may have fallen short, but symbolically it was a rousing success. Returning to the city that was once the nation's capital, highlighting the contradictions between the ideals of democracy articulated in the country's most sacrosanct documents[13] and America's failure to live up to those ideals, was ingenious street theater. That Philadelphia, once considered the cradle of liberty and constitutional government, was the site of the Revolutionary People's Constitutional Convention was not lost on its attendees or on Philadelphia's city fathers. Moreover, the economic and social decline from which the city was suffering added to the site's significance. Philadelphia had always been one of the country's more prominent urban centers, but by the 1960s the city was in disrepair, especially in predominantly African American areas.

One could argue that Philadelphia's Black community was less well-off during the 1960s and early 1970s than it was in the late 1800s when W. E. B. DuBois published his landmark study *The Philadelphia Negro*. Although crime, poverty, and social isolation were featured prominently in DuBois's work, they were no less pervasive seventy years later. In addition to those challenges, Blacks in the 1960s were faced with rampant police brutality and the proliferation of gangs and gang activity, two issues that were conspicuously absent from the Philadelphia presented in DuBois's text.

To comprehend the state of Black Philadelphia during this period, one need only read the *Philadelphia Tribune* (the city's Black news daily) to grasp the degree to which the city's administration neglected its Black constituents. A cursory look at the paper reveals that crime, gang violence, police brutality, and dilapidated housing and other eyesores were given more coverage than any other set of issues. About crime, the title of one article said it all: "Low Crime Image Shot Up Here As Murders Increase 40%."[14] Gang violence, a problem that had historically been associated with Chicago, New York, and Los Angeles, was pervasive throughout Philadelphia, causing many of its Black residents to adjust their lifestyles accordingly. Comments littered throughout the paper indicated that some residents were unwilling to venture out after dark for fear of being robbed or being the victim of a stray bullet.

Blacks not only feared gangs, but they feared the police as well, sometimes more than they feared the gangs. The Philadelphia Police Department was as oppressive as any department on the East Coast, if not more so. Relations between the police department and the Black community had become so volatile that in February 1970 a suit was filed in U.S. District Court on behalf of all Black residents of Philadelphia accusing the mayor and police commissioner Frank Rizzo of violating the constitutional rights of persons by permitting police brutality to persist.[15] Three months later the NAACP filed a similar suit charging that the mayor, police commissioner, and district attorney's office were complicit in nonprosecutorial cases involving police brutality against Blacks. Said NAACP director Phillip Savage:

> A policeman knows he'll be protected and supported by those at the top if he commits a brutal act, so he's encouraged to do just that.... In fact, I cannot recall a single case when there has been a conviction in our courts of a policeman accused of brutality.[16]

To add insult to injury, some Blacks were forced to live in conditions that were unfit for livestock, let alone humans. These deplorable conditions were showcased in a special section of the *Philadelphia Tribune* called "Shame of the City," which depicted overstuffed trash cans, condemned houses, and rat-infested apartment buildings. The editor's note read, "dirt, filth, diseases, abandoned automobiles and houses unfit for human habitation may be found in 80 percent of the area known as the 'Philadelphia Ghetto.' Thousands of thousands of Negroes live in these sections which have become 'The Shame of the City' because police, politicians and disinterested private citizens have permitted them to become stamping grounds of killers, hoodlums, dope peddlers and gamblers who wouldn't dare try to operate in Germantown, Mount Airy, West Oak Lane and the Greater Northeast." "Shame of the City" had the double purpose of alerting the mayor and other city officials of areas that needed attending to, and of embarrassing the city nationally, hoping such humiliation would prompt those in power to act. Whether this tactic proved effective is debatable since these trends persisted throughout the early to mid-1970s.

From Wanna-bes to Black Panthers

The 1960s was obviously a time of turmoil and change. Like many other major cities, Philadelphia witnessed events that gave people both a sense of hope and a reason for despair and helped to politicize a generation of young Blacks: (1) indifference on the part of city government; (2) the assassination of Dr. Martin Luther King Jr.; (3) Black-on-Black gang violence; (4) rampant police brutality; and (5) the Black Power Conference in the summer of 1968 that had the theme of "Black Self-Determination and Black Unity Through Direct Action." But what may have impacted Blacks more than anything else was the revolt of 1964, an uprising that took place in the predominantly Black neighborhoods of North Philadelphia in August of that year. Tensions between Blacks and the police had been escalating for months over allegations of police use of excessive force. The unrest began on the evening of August 28th after Odessa Bradford, an African American woman, got into an argument with two police officers (one white, one Black) when her car stalled at an intersection at 23rd Street and Columbia. After Bradford refused to follow the officers' order to move her car, a ruckus ensued. The officers attempted to physically remove Bradford from the car. She resisted and a crowd assembled. A man from the crowd came to Bradford's aid and was quickly arrested along with Bradford. Rumors then spread throughout the city that a pregnant woman had been beaten to death by officers. Later that evening and throughout the next few days, angry mobs looted and burned mostly white-owned businesses in North Philadelphia. While no one was killed, 341 people were injured, 774 people were arrested, and more than two hundred stores were destroyed in three days of disorder, resulting in more than $3 million in damages.

Until the late 1960s many Blacks had accepted police repression of them. Indeed many of them had been socialized to do so by Philadelphia's educational system, which taught its students to obey law enforcement and not to question the actions of police officers. Eventually Blacks realized that the city's public school system cultivated Black inadequacy and a sense of inferiority. On November 17, 1967, more than four thousand Blacks voiced their dissatisfaction by holding a demonstration at the Board of Education, in search of "a better and Blacker education." Law enforcement's response was predictable. When the police were called to the scene they were led by George Fencl and the Civil Disobedience Unit, at which time police commissioner Frank Rizzo gave the order to "get their black asses."[17]

Some of the men especially moved by these developments were Mumia Abu-Jamal, Reggie Schell, Terry McHarris, Clarence "Stretch" Peterson, Jon Pinkett, and Craig Williams. Robbins, a local bookstore that sold left-wing literature and books by Black authors, attracted some of the city's budding militants, and it was there that a few of the young men happened upon one another. At these initial chance meetings, discussions would revolve around the plight of Black America, and more specifically Philadelphia. Before long, word got out that there was a group of guys meeting at Robbins who were talking about starting a local branch of the Black Panther Party. It was at the Black Power Conference in 1968 that most Black Philadelphians got their first opportunity to see a real-life Black Panther. The Panthers, most of whom were from the West Coast, handled security for the conference. They were unarmed but had a military presence about them that impressed some of the young Black males in attendance. Peterson remembers this period: "I was running around with the Black Coalition in West Philly when someone told me that there was a guy who was interested in starting a Panther chapter. I got his number and called him. I told him I wanted to join up with him."[18] As word of the group continued to spread, more people began hanging out at the bookstore, and the group swelled in number. The discourse that took place at the bookstore was often lively, giving the young men a venue to vent their frustrations; it also gave them an opportunity to be exposed to other dynamic points of view.

As young adults, they were well aware of the harsh conditions that Blacks endured but were unsure as to what course of action needed to be taken. By 1968, organizations such as the Revolutionary Action Movement (RAM), the Nation of Islam, and a host of other less conventional Black-oriented groups were working tirelessly to alleviate pain and suffering in Philadelphia. Their efforts, however, impacted small pockets of the population and their style did not resonate with the masses. For those looking for a more assertive freedom-fighting organization, the Panthers seemed like a good fit. Impressed with what the Black Panthers were doing in other cities, Abu-Jamal, Schell, McHarris, Peterson, Pinkett, and Williams set out to learn more about the Party in late 1968. Mumia Abu-Jamal stated, "I read an article in *Ramparts* magazine about the BPP and fell in love with them. The more I read about them, the more I wanted to be a part of them. I couldn't believe they existed!"[19] Excited about the prospect of joining the organization, Abu-Jamal and the others contacted national headquarters and spoke with June Hilliard (assistant chief of staff) about starting a branch in Philadelphia. Skeptical, Hilliard tried to gauge their sincerity. He was neither supportive nor discouraging, and after much discussion and several heated exchanges, Hilliard pronounced, "Look, you don't got to be no goddamn Panther to struggle."[20] Although his comments may have come across as harsh, Hilliard's message was clear—if they were not given a charter, they should not let that stop them from helping Black people.[21]

Undeterred, the group continued to push on, although a few of them wondered why Hilliard appeared so indifferent. Were requests like theirs one of many that national headquarters received on a daily basis? Were Hilliard and others testing them to see how serious they were about opening a branch? The men figured that members of the Central Committee were probably thinking that if these Philadelphia cats were serious about establishing a branch, Hilliard's response would not discourage them from doing so. On the other hand, if the group abandoned the idea then that would suggest they were not committed to the struggle in the first place. With this mindset the energetic group remained steadfast. They continued to meet amongst themselves and debate issues germane to the Black community.

Although most in the group did not fully understand what Panther work entailed, they began to carry out the type of work they envisioned the Panthers doing, such as selling the Black Panther newspaper,[22] organizing the community around the pressing social issues of the day, feeding children, and confronting police brutality.[23] Reggie Schell set out to find an office for the group and before long he secured a building at 1928 W. Columbia Ave. in North Philadelphia. The building was in serious disrepair, and the group spent a considerable amount of time renovating it. After weeks of cleaning and painting, the group had a place they could proudly call their base of operations, and the group was now ready to serve the people.[24] Commenting on the group's efforts, the *Philadelphia Tribune* reported that the "Black Panthers" were "setting up shop" in the city under spokesperson

Terry McHarris, who stated that the Panthers were dedicated to defending the needs of Black people. While his warning was primarily aimed at whites, McHarris took special care to single out conservative Blacks, saying "Negroes" in the Black community would be confronted and "eliminated" if they did not change their ways.[25] Although there was no official Panther branch in Philadelphia, McHarris and his comrades operated as if they were full-fledged Panthers with McHarris as the group's leader. Loose journalistic practices on the part of the *Philadelphia Tribune* resulted in reporters taking McHarris's story at face value. Had the paper contacted the national headquarters in Oakland they would have learned that the announcement of a Panther branch in Philly was a bit premature.

Despite McHarris's strengths as a spokesperson, his laid-back approach and his bout with alcohol and drugs caused him to be stripped of his leadership position and ultimately jeopardized his membership in the Party,[26] and in stepped Reggie Schell, an intense South Philly native six years removed from the military. In late 1968, Donald Cox, the strong, silent field marshal from national headquarters, Henry Mitchell (aka "Mitch"), and Sharon Williams, both from the Harlem office, were dispatched to Philadelphia at various times where they met with the group, inspected their facility, and put them through a rigorous orientation. Peterson recalls that Cox gave them "a list of required readings and instructed them on how to put together a free breakfast program." Impressed with the young men's enthusiasm and apparent dedication, Cox authorized a local branch. The group's timing was perfect, for a few short months later the Central Committee instituted a moratorium on new members as well as new chapters.[27] Of the original thirteen activists who gathered at Robbins and/or showed initial interest, only seven joined the branch. Reggie Schell was appointed defense captain; Craig Williams assumed the role of field marshal; Mumia Abu-Jamal took on the responsibility of communications secretary (formerly lieutenant of information); Clarence Peterson was designated as lieutenant of finance; Jon Pinkett was assigned the position of financial officer; Barbara McGriff (aka "Sista Love") took the position of deputy field marshal; and Gladys Hearns was the group's breakfast coordinator.[28]

Having been officially sanctioned by the national office, the branch was faced with making people aware of its existence. Acquiring an office and getting the blessing of the Central Committee was not enough; what the branch needed more than anything at that time was publicity. After a few brainstorming sessions and a request from the national office to organize a Free Huey rally, Schell decided they would stage the rally at the State Building at Broad and Spring Garden Streets near the hub of downtown. On May 1, 1969, fifteen to twenty Panthers assembled at the State Building in full Panther regalia. During the excitement some of the members passed out leaflets while others spoke to interested passersby over the chorus of "Free Huey." Cameras flickered like lightning during a summer evening storm. Some of Huey's articles were read over a loudspeaker and within an hour the small gathering had become an event. Over the ensuing months branch membership would increase eightfold.

As interest in the branch increased, aspiring members were instructed by national headquarters to establish Black Community Information Centers until the moratorium was lifted. Although these centers were not officially connected to the Party, they were to offer many of the same kinds of survival programs that the BPP provided.[29]

In the beginning, the branch was in constant contact with the national headquarters in Oakland. Schell made numerous trips to the Bay Area, where he met with members of the Central Committee, and he also attended regional meetings every Sunday in New York. At these meetings attendees gave reports on newspaper sales, discussed the status of their community programs, and informed comrades of the scheduled events and general goings-on in their respective communities.[30] These meetings were also an opportunity for members of one branch to interact and collaborate with branches in other states.

Survival Programs

Nationwide, the Panthers implemented a plethora of services designed to enhance the lives of poor people throughout the country. As Barbara Easley-Cox pointed out, some locales were limited in resources but provided programs and activities they could manage.[31] Philadelphia sponsored many of the types of endeavors that the national office boasted, including political education classes, which all chapters and branches were required to conduct for their members as well as for members of the community. Every Tuesday the community was invited to partake in political discourse about issues affecting their communities specifically and the city in general. Political education classes afforded the Panthers as well as members of the community an opportunity to get better acquainted.

The Panthers' message was that life's basic necessities are the right of every human being. Two such rights are the right to eat and survive and the right to learn, and the Panthers maintained that knowledge and freedom are inextricably linked. "The question becomes how and where to get information that will shed some light on our situation, so that we can change things for the better."[32] According to the Panthers, access to information was difficult because the better-equipped libraries were not close to the Black community.

Consequently, "to get as much written information as possible concerning our present-day situation," the Philadelphia Panthers initiated a People's Free Library, a feature unique to Philadelphia, mostly containing books written by Black authors.

About educating the Black community, Herbert Hawkins maintained,

> I think that at our height, people said that "you people are telling the truth."
> I think at an early point, people thought we were troublemakers. But, like I said,
> when you feed people the right information, they will go in the right direction.
> To me, that is what everything is about. We educated by example and the big
> thing is … we distributed information some people would call propaganda.[33]

In addition to their political education classes, the Panthers endeared themselves to the community by providing protective services to local welfare recipients. In 1969, three welfare mothers moved into an all-white neighborhood at 25th Street and Fairmount. Shortly after arriving, one of the women was greeted with a bullet through the front window of her house. After being contacted by the Welfare Rights Organization, the Panthers stood guard at the homes of the three women to deter further acts of violence.[34] After three days the Panthers withdrew without incident.

Shielding Philadelphia's Black residents from unnecessary acts of violence was something that the Panthers took seriously. Another example of this was their willingness to address head-on the issue of police brutality. While the Panthers did not patrol the police as Panthers did on the West Coast, they were vocal critics of the police department. In late 1969, several instances of excessive force prompted the Panthers to organize a campaign around the murder of Harold Brown, a seventeen-year-old high school student, by members of the Philadelphia Police Department. Testimony from residents in the neighborhood in which Brown was killed suggested that Brown may have pled for his life seconds before officers shot him. In response to this unsettling account, the Panthers launched their own investigation. After speaking with people who heard Brown beg for his life as well as those who claimed to have witnessed the shooting, the Panthers wrote a sixteen-page booklet on police brutality that detailed incidents of police use of excessive force and instructed citizens on what to do when stopped by a police officer. In a move considered audacious by many, the Panthers put up "Wanted" posters for the four patrolmen. Not surprisingly, the police department was outraged by this seemingly outlandish gesture. Needless to say, the accused officers were not prosecuted despite the uproar.

Not long after the Philadelphia Panthers put their initial survival programs in place in North Philadelphia, both community support and membership increased. Hoping to take advantage of their newfound popularity, the Panthers opened a second office at 2935 Columbia Avenue and helped set up Black Community Information Centers throughout the city in Germantown (on 428 W. Queen Lane), West Philadelphia (originally on 47th and Walnut Street and transferred to 3625 Wallace Street after a bombing), and South Philadelphia (initially on 15th and Rodman Streets).[35] Business hours were roughly from 7:00 A.M. to 7:00 P.M. In addition to providing community services, the centers gave people a place where they could get various other types of assistance. Traffic in and out of the center was so heavy that the Panthers decided to initiate opening up additional centers in Reading, Harrisburg, and Pittsburgh.[36] The Philadelphia Panthers' objectives were straightforward: to focus on programs and activities that could improve the general welfare of the community, such as free breakfast programs, free clothing drives, and health care initiatives.

Free Breakfast for Children Program

On Monday, July 7, 1969, the Panthers launched their first Free Breakfast for Children Program, a much-needed program that served approximately sixty-five children on that day. Mattie Gray, a volunteer, stated, "Hundreds of Black children begin their day with little or no breakfast at all." It is possible that Gray's estimates were on the conservative side given the number of poor Black families in North Philadelphia alone. The program focused attention on a historically oppressed group that the government—local, state, and federal—had failed to institute programs for: children. With limited resources, the Panthers successfully generated a program that some of the city's poorest communities took advantage of.[37] As word of the program got out, people from other parts of town started bringing their kids by to get breakfast. Demand was so high that additional breakfast programs had to be set up in North Philadelphia, West Philadelphia, Germantown, and South Philadelphia.[38]

Barbara Easley-Cox and Mumia Abu-Jamal have fond memories of the breakfast program: "during breakfast, we led the children in songs while feeding them 'food, thought, and love.'"[39] On a typical weekday, Panthers prepared breakfast at approximately 6:00 A.M. and served anywhere from twenty to seventy children daily, and upwards of five hundred children per month.[40] The program was financially supported by donations from local businesses and small contributions from private parties. Ethel Parish recommended that the branch get long-term commitments from businesses to help subsidize the breakfast programs. Establishing good relations with food chains as well as with mom-and-pop businesses was essential to maintaining well-stocked cupboards.[41]

In spite of the program's success, not everyone embraced the idea of giving school kids a free breakfast. City councilman Thomas Foglietta declared that Panthers "took over" a United Fund Settlement House (UFSH) on 8th Street and Snyder Ave. At a press conference in January 1970, the councilman stated that the Panthers preached hatred at the facility, that neighborhood residents—both Black and white—were up in arms, and that the United Fund Settlement House should cut off all funds to the Panthers. By the start of the new year, the Panthers had already approached officials at the UFSH where it was agreed that the Panthers would use their facility for a free breakfast program, but Foglietta failed to acknowledge this. Furthermore, testimony from area residents indicated that they were not opposed to the Panthers,[42] thus casting doubt on Foglietta's claim that the neighborhood was up in arms over Panthers' instilling hatred in children. It is doubtful that parents would have allowed the Panthers to indoctrinate their children with such venom in return for a free breakfast. The same bogus claim was made by Frank Rizzo, who tried to undercut the Panthers' influence in the community by offering breakfast and lunch programs through the police department.

As support for the breakfast program increased, so did the Panthers' popularity, and as the Panthers' reputation grew, merchants and shop owners were more willing to donate supplies to the group because they knew their contributions would be put to good use. Instead of seeking assistance from the city's social service agencies, some area residents began calling on the Panthers for various kinds of assistance. On July 23, 1972, the Panthers distributed two hundred bags of groceries and three hundred pairs of shoes to needy families throughout North Philadelphia. The coordinator of the program, William E. Broadwater, stated that the items were collected from merchants throughout the city. Recognizing that a free grocery giveaway would be highly popular, the Panthers thought it best to set one stipulation—only those families that arrived at the facility at 4:00 P.M. would be eligible to receive a bag of groceries. On the day of the giveaway, turnout was huge and two hundred families had to be turned away. As a concession, the Panthers promised that a bag of supplies would be delivered to their homes the following week.[43]

As a way of supplementing their breakfast program, the Panthers partnered with the city's "Free Lunch Program" in July 1971. The Free Lunch Program, administered by the city's Recreation Department and funded by the U.S. Department of Agriculture, provided 41,000 lunches daily to city agencies, community centers, schools, and churches for low-income children. This program was an ideal complement to the Panthers' breakfast program, but unfortunately, one year later, Panthers received disappointing news. Their center—one of nine community recreational centers—was dropped from the city's free lunch program because, according to William Harris, coordinator of special programs for the department, the lunch program exceeded the department's budget by a thousand lunches. Broadwater met with Harris and others at the department to determine if the reason for dropping the center from the program was because Panthers managed it,[44] but clearly the Panthers were not being singled out since there were eight other centers affected. More importantly, the removal of nine community centers from the city's lunch program was yet another example of the state's inability to meet the needs of its poorest residents. This development demonstrated to Blacks in bold relief the importance of being self-reliant rather than relying on the government for basic sustenance.

Free Clothing Drive

Like other Panther chapters and branches throughout the United States, Panthers in Philly not only provided food subsidies, but clothing as well. In October 1969, with the winter fast approaching, Panthers initiated a free clothing project at the Wharton Centre on 22nd and Columbia Avenue. On a national level, this program complemented the free health clinics, liberation schools, and free breakfast programs.[45] An article titled *Free Clothes in Philly* put the program in perspective:

> Instead of sitting around and talking about the fact that kids need clothes, we're going out and clothing them. While the pigs are shooting billions of our dollars up to the moon … we are dealing with the real situation. We hope to see the program implemented around the country, everywhere there is a need for it.[46]

The Panthers realized that some families simply did not have the money to buy their children adequate winter clothing. It was not unusual to see kids walking to school wearing windbreakers with several layers underneath in an effort to protect themselves from the city's brutal winters. As Reggie Schell recalled, they diligently sought donations from dry cleaners, local merchants, and members of the community who would have ordinarily given their clothes to Goodwill. He continued:

> After the program expanded, we began to give clothes and donated food to those in need. The doors to the drive would open after we had enough to give people what they needed. Sometimes we were overwhelmed by the amount of people and at times barely had enough.[47]

One reason the Panthers barely had enough items to go around was because of their inability to ingratiate themselves with the city's large department stores. The response from stores like John Wannamakers and Gimbles was indifferent at best and hostile at worst. The usual reply was "we already donate to charities and you (the Black Panther Party) are not a recognized charity."[48] Still the Panthers were resourceful enough to collect clothing for hundreds of families. In fact, on Saturday, December 6, 1969, Panthers distributed coats, gloves, hats, and scarves to 125 youths at the Church of the New Life on 3604 W. Fairmount Avenue.[49] In October 1970, the Panthers expanded the program, sponsoring a citywide free clothing program at four different locations. Of all the services the Panthers offered, the free clothing program had the longest tenure, lasting until the mid-1970s.[50]

Free Health Clinic

Months after expanding the free clothing project, local Quakers and doctors donated a facility and medical equipment to establish the Mark Clark Memorial Clinic (aka Mark Clark People's Free Medical Clinic).[51] By opening a clinic, the Panthers were able to address one of the most pressing needs among communities of color—the lack of adequate health care. Health professionals, volunteer doctors, and nurses from the Medical Committee for Human Rights (MCHR) organized and managed the clinic. Panthers invited members of the community to assist with the day-to-day running of the clinic, which was open from 5:30 to 9:00 P.M. every day except Tuesday and Wednesday. Located at 1609 Susquehanna Street in North Philly, the clinic's primary purpose was to treat basic ailments, and it also served as an emergency first aid center and emphasized a personal approach where a good "bedside manner" was the norm rather than the exception. Additional services included diagnostic testing; tuberculosis, measles, polio, smallpox, and diphtheria vaccines; blood tests; and free infant formula.[52]

In addition to these offerings, the clinic provided courses in parenthood for expectant couples, assessed patients' medical histories, conducted simple urine tests, and recorded blood pressures, temperatures, and pulse rates.[53] The childbirth course was especially popular because among other things it strongly encouraged the participation of the baby's father. Parents were taught breathing and delivery relaxation techniques; the course eliminated the need for anesthesia and painkillers. The Panthers were of the opinion that a natural childbirth was medically safer. They maintained that "everyone who has been through the course at the clinic ... experienced less discomfort during labor."[54]

In addition to the services mentioned above, the clinic also screened patients for sickle cell anemia. By May 1971, 3,500 people had been screened and 215 of them were diagnosed with having either the trait or the disease. Those who were found to have the disease were taken to Mercy-Douglas Hospital for further tests. Since the costs associated with that hospital were often out of reach for many of those the Panthers transported there, the branch sometimes subsidized their treatment.[55]

Aware that many Blacks could not afford health care, the Panthers also understood that most Blacks avoided seeing a doctor or going to a hospital unless it was absolutely necessary. Unfortunately, when the patient finally decided to seek medical treatment it was after his or her condition had gotten progressively worse. As a way of dealing with this reality, the Panthers instituted an outreach program that took the doctor to the patient. Among the features this outreach program provided were free speech and hearing evaluations. By the end of June 1971 more than 150 people had been evaluated.[56]

Making the City Safe

The Panthers understood early on that in order to make Philadelphia a place where Blacks could live peacefully and children could play, Blacks needed to feel safe in their communities. But because of pervasive gang activity, many Blacks were uncomfortable walking the streets of their own neighborhoods. While Chicago, Los Angeles, and New York have historically received the lion's share of scholarly attention where gangs are concerned, Philadelphia's gang problem was not a new phenomenon. In 1970, there were reportedly ninety-three gangs in the city, consisting of 5,300 members. Of those gangs, seventy-two were Black.[57]

Determined to keep Philadelphia from becoming another Chicago or New York, the Panthers set out to address the problem. The first order of business was to get the various gangs to come together in one place where they could hash out their differences. The Panthers not only wanted to quell gang activity, but, recognizing the revolutionary potential of many of those involved in gangs, they also wanted to heighten gang members' consciousness. In an article titled *Philadelphia's Gangs Organizing to Serve the Community*, the Panthers wrote, "these brothers are very important in our struggle for survival, we know that we must help preserve many of our future leaders, our beautiful young manhood."[58] Therefore, on November 7–9, 1969, the Panthers held a conference at the Central Branch of the YMCA. The meeting was prompted by the death of a young Black girl who was struck by a gang member's stray bullet while sitting on her front steps.[59] This tragedy may have served as the catalyst for such a conference, but community residents had long been fed up with gang killings. Police statistics reveal that from 1967 to 1970, one hundred people were killed by area gangs.

Clay Dillon reported that the Panthers' sessions focused on putting an end to gang violence. The Panthers pointed out to the two hundred or so gang members who attended the conference that they had a responsibility to create safe conditions for people in the community. "Women are afraid to walk the streets, day and night. Children are terrorized and brutalized on their way to and from school. This activity is ending as of this conference," said one Panther spokesman."[60]

Panthers blamed gang members for creating a climate of fear among their own people rather than promoting an atmosphere of brotherly love. Panthers chided young Blacks for joining gangs to get respect. They pointed out that the respect that they commanded was superficial because the community did not genuinely respect them. One Panther in particular scolded gang members, saying that "whenever the pigs want, they will cut off your electricity, gas and water . . . the more you keep on killing each other the better the pigs' chances are to justify their actions to the public." He tried to point out to the gangs that if they had respect within their communities the pigs would not be able to manipulate them or move on them as they had done in the past because the people would not have allowed it. But since the community does not support gangs, the police do with gang members what they please. One Panther submitted that "you won't have their [the community's] support or respect until you have done something for the people."[61]

Since some Party members had formerly been associated with gangs, they were able to relate to many of them, which enabled the Panthers to form alliances with several of the gangs. More importantly, because of the respect the gangs had for the Party, Panthers were able to encourage some gang members to redirect their energies in a positive direction. Some gang members were drafted by the Panthers to assist with the Panthers' breakfast program,[62] challenging the notion that gangs were a homogeneous group of incorrigible hoodlums. In all, what separated Panthers from many other organizations was that they were not armchair revolutionaries, but rather activists willing to put theory into practice. Unlike some groups that condescendingly lectured to the people about what was good for them, the Panthers were constantly on the streets interacting with residents, asking questions, conducting surveys, and seeking feedback from the community. The Party had its finger on the pulse of Black public opinion.

As a follow-up to the 1969 conference on August 11, 1970, a two-week workshop called "Gang Structure and its Influence in the Educational Process" was held at Temple University for teachers, counselors, and administrators. Led by the 12th and Oxford Street Gangs and keynoted by Dr. Bernard Watson, the event explored the factors that motivated youths to join gangs. To no one's surprise, high unemployment, poverty, and lack of economic opportunity were linked to the rise of gangs.[63] The following day, gang members

Jimmy Robinson, David Leach, and David Williams criticized the police force and the press for indirectly promoting gang warfare. Robinson said, "[Y]ou tell me to respect the police. They only use gang members to keep up the arrest figures." Regarding the press, he commented, "By calling each killing or beating in the ghetto a gang incident, and labeling gangs as 'notorious,' every other gang in the city wants that. But if a killing happens in the suburbs, it was a 'group of youths at a party.'"[64] With this statement, Robinson exposed three overlooked areas of gang violence: (1) how police perpetuated gang conflict; (2) how the press fueled gangs' desire for street credibility (i.e., respect); and (3) how the press framed violence in Black communities in comparison to violence committed in white neighborhoods.

Later in the day, Dr. Watson logically noted that when a young man has available to him a number of appealing and viable alternatives to joining a gang, delinquency decreases. As an example, he referred to the seven-month protest by Cecil B. Moore in 1965. That year, Moore, a prominent civil rights attorney, organized the community to force the desegregation of Girard College, an all-male institution in North Philly that catered to orphans interested in attending college.[65] Some of those who participated in the 1965 protest were members of the city's various gangs. Clarence Peterson remembers that Moore challenged him and other youths to mobilize against the real enemy rather than engaging in gang wars.[66] Although the workshop addressed critical issues associated with gangs, oddly, the *Philadelphia Inquirer* did not mention the Panthers' ongoing work with many of the city's gangs.

About a week later, Panthers held another meeting on gang activity. "Victims of gang violence" was the topic of the sparsely attended meeting at the Church of the Advocate on 18th and Diamond Streets.[67] It was revealed that since the beginning of 1969, sixty-five deaths had been related to gang warfare. The Panthers called upon North Philadelphia residents to "construct a community which is free of the bloody streets of the past." The Panthers charged police with instigating violence between rival gangs and claimed that "the Police Department and its countless undercover branches feed more fuel to the fire." Panthers cited instances where police officers picked up gang members, drove them to enemy territory, and dropped them off to be beaten, stabbed, or murdered.[68] According to one North Philadelphia resident, the Panthers' influence in the community was such that after the Panthers vacated their office on Columbia Avenue in early 1971, gang violence supposedly increased, especially among the Valley Gang, Norris Street Gang, and the Oxford Street Gang.[69] Although this was only one person's perspective, it suggests that the Panthers' role in helping to quell gang activity may not have been inconsequential.

The History of Black Political Influence
(or Lack thereof) and the City Council
Campaigns of McGriff and Williams

The Panthers' commitment to uplifting Black Philadelphians went far beyond community survival programs and working with gangs; they were open to a wide range of possibilities for effecting change, including using electoral politics as a means of improving Black lives.

Before 1950, Blacks' influence in city politics was nonexistent, and from 1950 to 1960 Blacks were bit players in a high-stakes political poker game. From 1850 to 1950 the Republican Party had a stranglehold on the city, and although Blacks were firmly in the Republican camp, they did not reap the benefits of the Republican machine. According to Carolyn Adams et al., two reasons account for this monopoly. The first suggests that the Quakers, who avoided mixing politics with business, held sway with the upper echelon of the business community with whom Blacks had little leverage. The second reason is that the Republican machine endorsed protective tariffs and safe-guarded U.S. manufacturing companies from foreign competitors. Hence, civic responsibility and community prosperity took a back seat to the city's business interests. Business elites were unwilling to "bite the hands" that fed them huge profits and provided them with unlimited amounts of patron-age. Consequently, "Philadelphia industrialists were not moved to throw the Republican rascals out, for doing so would have meant losing powerful allies in Congress."[70] With such an emphasis on commerce, those in power practi-cally ignored things such as affordable low-income housing, well-paying jobs, and well-equipped schools for those trapped in the inner city. Blacks felt this neglect more than any other group.

In 1951, city reform brought down the machine and ousted the self-absorbed Republicans, and in the process the deplorable conditions of the inner city became the focus. Industry and community leaders proposed a plan to usher in the municipality of the future. That year the Home Rule Charter was adopted, which called for a "strong mayor" form of govern-ment, retained the City Council while reducing its size, fortified the civil service system based on merit, and gave the city planning commission more responsibility while reducing the number of departments and boards.[71] The importance of the charter was that it shifted political power from the state to the city. But Peter McGrath argued that the mayoral powers, the smaller city council, and the downsizing of departments inadvertently presented problems. McGrath maintained that communication between city officials and their constituents was impaired because there were fewer councilmen to address citizens' needs.[72] Moreover, cutting departments and boards made tackling the city's problems more difficult, not less.

By 1951, Blacks had deserted the Republican Party and had chosen to support Democrats Joseph Clark and later Richardson Dilworth. Under the leadership of Mayor Clark and City Controller Dilworth, the government took a more active role in the economic and social life of the city with a special interest in the downtown area.[73] Conrad Weiler contends that the civil service reforms implemented by the Clark administration as well as the appointment of a Black to the Civil Service Commission earned the Black community's loyalty.[74] Clark's administration laid the groundwork for the election of Dilworth, who was responsible for the development of high-rise public housing.

The Clark and Dilworth administrations produced dividends for a sector of the Black community. Rev. Marshall L. Shepard was elected recorder of deeds, becoming the first Black to hold a major elective office in Philadelphia, and Rev. William Gray, a Black minister from North Philly, was appointed to the Board of the Redevelopment Authority. These breakthroughs opened the door for Blacks to hold elected, bureaucratic, and appointed positions in Philadelphia.[75] By the 1960s, Black political participation was no longer relegated to simply helping vote a politician into or out of office. Blacks alone were now able to influence the outcomes of elections. Although electoral politics provided vast opportunities for some Blacks, on the whole most Blacks were unaffected. Still, the election of Black politicians by Black voters instilled a sense of political efficacy that had previously been absent.

Consequently, in May 1969, the Panthers, after much deliberation, decided to pursue political office. Schell, in concert with others, agreed that the Panthers would run for city council, and he urged Milton McGriff and Craig Williams to run in the 7th and 1st Districts, two seats that had become vacant due to the untimely deaths of the incumbents. Of the two, the 1st District was considered the most wide-open contest. The Democrats threw their support behind Nate F. Carabello, a short, stocky, mustachioed thirty-two-year-old attorney and political novice. The Republicans countered with William J. Cottrell, a forty-nine-year-old "self-made man" who had worked his way through law school. He too was a relative newcomer to politics. Williams, twenty-seven, an articulate veteran of the Air Force, was among three candidates running as independents; the others were Leonard Galloway, a twenty-eight-year-old African American in the women's clothing business who ran on the Consumer Party ticket, and Thomas K. Gilhool, thirty-one, an attorney and an independent Democrat who represented the Urban Action Party. Gilhool was in the unique position of having won the endorsement of Mayor James Tate while bucking his own party.[76] None of the three independents was given much of a chance.

The 7th District race was considered less of a toss-up than the 1st District election. Harry P. Jannotti, a forty-five-year-old Democrat and former deputy chief clerk of the City Council, was regarded by most as the overwhelming favorite, primarily because the 7th was one of the strongest Democratic strongholds in the city. William H. Wright, the Republican, was a sixty-three-year-old schoolteacher with nearly forty years in the public school system. McGriff, twenty-eight, and Fred C. Barnes, a forty-six-year-old bartender running on the Consumer Party ticket, were the two independents. According to the *Philadelphia Daily News*, McGriff, the salesman who had been particularly impressive "while cutting through traditional campaign dialogue to emphasize the needs of the district," was a long shot.[77]

When asked why he chose to run McGriff and Williams, Schell explained that they were "more mature and more sophisticated than some of the younger guys. They came across very professional and were ideal in terms of allaying voters' fears that the Panthers were violent and only interested in guns."[78] The Panthers' decision to run raised more than a few eyebrows among those in power. When reporters from the *Philadelphia Tribune* contacted the office of City Council president Paul D'Ortona for comment, a spokesman for D'Ortona responded, "[I]ts their prerogative. If they [the Panthers] can qualify for the seats, nobody can stop them from running."[79] In order to run, the Panthers had to petition the secretary of state to get on the ballot as a third party. After the Panthers collected the required number of signatures and were given a place on the ballot, they were then faced with the formidable task of putting together an effective campaign.

A few weeks before the election, in an open letter to Mayor Tate, McGriff sarcastically called on the mayor to attend to some of the district's most glaring needs; among them was an adequate medical facility for the residents of North Philadelphia. Said McGriff, "[A]re you in favor of Free Clinics and Hospitals, Jim? I mean, do poor people have a right to be healthy?" McGriff promised to "propose a bill that will provide a hot breakfast and a wholesome lunch, free, for every child that wants them."[80]

The primary impetus for the Panthers' foray into electoral politics was dissatisfaction with those who had held those seats in the past. For years, the Democrats had taken the Black vote for granted, making special entreaties to the African American community during the campaign, but once elected conveniently forgetting that the Black vote had helped get them elected. Consequently, the Panthers felt there was a disconnect between the politicians who occupied those seats and the people who lived in those districts. Indeed, most of those who occupied those seats in the past felt no particular attachment to the Black community.

Early in the campaign, Schell stated that "councilmen who don't even reside in the district call themselves representing the people." Schell and others canvassed both districts imploring residents to register and vote for McGriff and Williams. The Panthers believed that the election of McGriff and Williams would be an important step toward gaining "community control of the police." Schell envisioned a community whose police officers lived in the neighborhoods in which they worked.[81]

The Panthers put together a commendable get-out-the-vote drive. They leafleted parks, posted signs in stores and bars, and handed out flyers in front of churches. Dozens of people signed on as campaign volunteers. Buoyed by the excitement that surrounded both elections, many volunteers continued their connection to the Party, staying on as community workers for the branch even after the elections were over. As part of their campaigns, both McGriff and Williams held "coffee klatches" where district residents visited with them and asked questions about their platform. On Election Day, however, both McGriff and Williams lost by huge margins. Williams's race was especially tough as he faced a Black incumbent who was relatively popular among the Black electorate.

The Panthers' effort was a valiant one, but they simply did not have the type of political organization in place to make a serious run for elected office. Most of all, the Panthers lacked the financial resources to promote the campaigns of William and McGriff; consequently they were reduced to knocking on doors and passing out flyers.[82] Media advertising, which is essential to most viable political campaigns and accounts for a disproportionate amount of the money spent by politicians, was not an option for the Panthers, whose operating budget had always been meager.

Although McGriff and Williams lost by landslides, their campaigns served notice to the political establishment that the Black community would no longer stand by and allow whites to do all the political wrangling. Win or lose, the progressive Black voice would be heard. Moreover, the Panthers' actions demonstrated to Blacks that there was more to party politics than just the Democrats and Republicans. "Blacks did not have to be prisoners of the Democratic Party, they could run as Independents."[83] More than anything the campaigns of McGriff and Williams made people aware of the Black Panther Party's desire to shift the balance of power in the city of Philadelphia. By 1970 the chapter had solidified itself as a vehicle for progressive change. No one was more aware of this than police commissioner Frank Rizzo.

Rizzo's Response to the Revolutionary People's Constitutional Convention

As the summer of 1970 came to a close, Rizzo became increasingly concerned about the impending Revolutionary People's Constitutional Convention, scheduled to begin on September 4th at Temple University. "We don't want it here," Rizzo declared. "But if it's peaceful, we're not going to stop it."[84] The events that unfolded the week before the conference suggest that Rizzo's remarks may have been a bit disingenuous. The constant arresting of Panthers as well as the raiding of their offices the night of August 31, 1970, may have been undertaken by the police department to undermine the Panthers' ability to host the Revolutionary People's Constitutional Convention. At the very least, local authorities may have surmised that an onslaught of that magnitude would have put tremendous strain on the branch, making it nearly impossible for the Panthers to provide the kind of accommodations one would expect from the hosting delegation. Fortunately, community support for the conference was strong. Two of the Panthers' biggest challenges were providing housing and transportation for the delegates. Peterson notes,

> We had people coming in from all over the country, so we had people donating houses, apartments. People could go anywhere in the city and get rides. People in the community would give rides. We did not have people going to hotels, we were using people's houses. We put out a call for donations with leaflets, radio, posters, and word of mouth. We made charts to organize where people would stay and how they would be transported. We asked, if you are willing to volunteer, contact us.[85]

The police department's actions leading up to the convention were not surprising given the opposition from some sectors of the political establishment. Many people, including several state representatives, opposed the event. Specifically, Democrat Francis E. Gleeson Jr. and Republican Richard A. McClatchy Jr. were against Temple University's hosting the event.[86] According to Father Washington's autobiography, once Washington and his group won the cooperation of Temple University officials, the FBI passed word to "the White House, Vice President, Attorney General, the military and the Secret Service" that Temple had agreed to make its facilities available to the Panthers. "The FBI readied its secret agents and informants to attend the events at the university and the church."[87]

It is important to note that the event came on the heels of a bloody weekend in which one officer was murdered and three wounded. Rizzo was understandably outraged. He blamed the Panthers even though there was no evidence linking them to the crimes. "Yellow dogs," he screamed at them through the television, daring them into the streets for a shootout. "We'll give them ten to our three."[88] With Rizzo in this state of mind, it was little wonder that many feared the convention would touch off a bloodbath.

To head off any potential trouble, an emergency meeting was called by community leaders at the Episcopal Church House on Rittenhouse Square. Muhammad Kenyatta, Sister Falaka Fattah, and the Rev. David Gracie, among others, held a press conference to announce that a federal injunction would be sought to halt police raids of Panther offices. Federal judge John Fullam promptly answered the call, issuing an injunction against the Philadelphia Police Department, which had the effect of dramatically reducing their activities and even their physical presence in the area in which the convention was held.[89]

The convention went ahead as planned, lasting three days, most importantly without incident. Prior to the convention, several local organizations pledged their support to the event and asked Philadelphians to refrain from engaging in civil rights demonstrations. On September 2nd, the Greater Philadelphia Movement sent a telegram to Governor Raymond Shafer saying that although they did not necessarily endorse the conference, they believed that "the participants should be guaranteed their constitutional rights of peaceful assembly." A day later, the Urban Coalition sent out a public plea asking Philadelphians to avoid irrational action that could lead to unnecessary division. At the conclusion of the convention, both the Greater Philadelphia Movement and Philadelphia Urban Coalition sent telegrams to police commissioner Rizzo commending him and his department for maintaining peace and order during the convention.[90] Even organizations like the American Civil Liberties Union (ACLU), the Religious Society of Friends, and Citizens for Progress—all long-standing critics of the police— congratulated the department on its handling of the conference. In response, Rizzo stated, "I am extremely pleased that the Black Panther conference was completed here without incident." He continued, "[T]he conference proved once again that if people come to Philadelphia and obey the law, they will have no interference from the police."[91] Rizzo's statement was clearly not a reflection of his true feelings about the Panthers nor did his remark mirror the way his police department had dealt with the Panthers in the past.

Political Repression through a Psychoanalytic Lens

Oftentimes, explanations concerning the demise of the Black Panther Party center on overt acts of repression such as raids and arrests. While this is useful in putting such state opposition into context, what has been missing is an analysis of the subliminal undercurrent under which certain governmental actors operated. The term "repression" is commonly linked to Sigmund Freud and his development of psychoanalytic theory. Freud argued that individuals develop a fixation (or an excessive attachment) to a person or object due to frustration or overindulgence, which will hinder or cause them to overexert expressions of sexual or aggressive energy to a person or object.[92] On an unconscious level, a fixation develops into defense mechanisms that prevent movement beyond a fixated state.

Defense mechanisms help protect an individual's ego and reduce anxiety/discomfort by distorting perceptions of reality. Repression is an example of a defense mechanism in which anxiety-provoking thoughts and feelings and/or traumatic events are involuntarily transferred to the unconscious.[93] An example of repression occurs in *passing* whereby individuals from a subjugated race seek membership into a privileged race. This is evident with J. Edgar Hoover, who many thought was not only a homosexual and sexist, but someone who was conflicted about his racial identity.[94] Therefore, as a way of concealing his sexual orientation and his racial identity, he overcompensated by acting viciously toward homosexuals and Blacks.[95] Repression is maintained by other defense mechanisms, but projection, reaction formation, and omnipotence are the focus of this discussion.

Through projection, individuals attribute their own undesirable traits to others.[96] In the case of the Panthers, they worked to defend themselves and their community from the brutal acts of white rogues, yet were depicted by the media as well as by law enforcement as "violent" criminals. In Philadelphia, Panthers faced opposition from police officers who circulated rumors that they were criminals who blackmailed store owners, and were communists as well as racists.[97] These statements reflected attributes that some police officers may have possessed themselves.

Reaction formation occurs when individuals adopt behaviors that belie their true feelings.[98] For example, individuals of a particular race may consign persons within another racial group to an inferior position. Unconsciously they believe themselves to be inferior, but they will behave in ways that suggest otherwise. In the process of liberation, a thorough analysis of oppression will reveal that the oppressor is as much in need of liberation as the oppressed. While the oppressed seeks liberation from being dehumanized, the oppressor profits from dehumanizing.[99] Consequently, any perceived struggle for freedom by those in the majority will be met with fierce resistance via ideological and repressive state apparatuses. Thus, the government responded to the Panthers' quest for freedom with measures typically reserved for an enemy of war.

Finally, the notion of omnipotence manifests when individuals handle stressors by presenting themselves as superior to *Others*.[100] Historically, white elites have devised ways to keep Blacks subjugated and have reinforced their superiority through practices, beliefs, and ideas (i.e., ideology). Panther practices such as "defending themselves against a gun with a gun" and "pig-baiting" challenged the white supremacist ideology and in the process altered the mentality of many Blacks who feared white reprisal or who truly saw whites as superior.[101]

Such defense mechanisms—from a macro level—used against Panthers served as an effective way for the government to justify its actions and maintain social order via repression. On a deeper level, white backlash against the Panthers reflected how unconscious desires were transformed into a political weapon to destroy and dehumanize a portion of the Black population. This will be evidenced in an examination of repression and its effects on the Philadelphia branch of the Black Panther Party.

Panthers in a State(s) of Siege

The first raid of Panther offices occurred in summer 1969. Police ransacked the office and confiscated a shotgun, a typewriter, a mimeograph machine, and files, and they arrested Reggie Schell for allegedly stealing an M-14 rifle. Schell posted bail and was released within seventy-two hours.[102] Mumia Abu-Jamal and Clarence Peterson talked candidly about the day their central office was raided in 1969. Abu-Jamal stated,

> I will tell a story about the night our central office on Columbia Ave. got raided, and we got busted at the bar across the street. The people, on their own, started throwing bricks and bottles at the cops, telling 'em to "leave them alone!" "Them boys ain't did nothin'!" It was probably my most beautiful memory of those days. They felt we were a part of them and their lives. We fed their babies; we showed we cared; and when the chips were down . . . so did they.[103]

Peterson's account was vivid:

> We had our first raid in summer, 1969 on 1928 W. Columbia Ave. We were across the street at the bar . . . we looked across the street and noticed a lot of bright lights and a whole lot of cars. We approached the office and the cops jumped out and put us against the walls. We were taken to the station and our lawyers got us out. There was no reason for the arrest.[104]

The reaction on the part of members of the community shows the deep-rooted frustration and anger that some Blacks harbored toward the police department.

In spite of the repressive maneuvers directed against them, the Panthers understood that as they educated and raised the social consciousness of the community, the community, in turn, would gain a better understanding of the Panthers' goals and objectives and thus would come to a deeper understanding of Black people's struggle in the United States and abroad. An example of the Panthers' efforts to educate the community occurred shortly before Thanksgiving in 1969, when Panthers met with representatives from the West Oak Lane–East Mt. Airy Taskforce on Black-White Relations. Made up of middle-class Blacks and whites, the task force was intrigued by the Panthers' call for Blacks to control their communities.[105] This meeting challenged participants to examine how media representations shaped their image of the Panthers and to reflect on what they accepted as truth.

Less than a month after the meeting, the Panther organization suffered a crushing blow: two of its most promising comrades were killed. On December 4, 1969, the city of Chicago became the scene of one of the most violent acts of repression taken against a dissent group in the twentieth century when members of the police department raided the Panthers' headquarters there and murdered Mark Clark and Fred Hampton. The office was riddled with bullets from police gunfire. A coroner's report revealed that Hampton had been shot at point-blank range while he slept. Doc Satchel, Blair Anderson, Verlina Brewer, Brenda Harris, Deborah Johnson, Louis Truelock, and Harold Bell were lined up against a wall and taunted while police shot at them.[106]

Days after the slaying, Father Paul Washington opened his church to the Panthers, where a memorial service was held for Hampton and Clark.[107] Abu-Jamal remembered that "Fred Hampton's assassination had a dramatic effect on Philadelphia, for it taught us all what was possible."[108] Images and headlines were circulated nationwide as people cringed and questioned the rationale for such force. Days later, on the West Coast, police raided Panther offices in Los Angeles. One of the planned raids was met with resistance, which led to a four-hour shootout, leaving six Panthers wounded.[109]

On December 10th, days after the events in Los Angeles, twenty-three organizations in Philadelphia pledged to prevent further attacks against the Panthers in their city. Representatives from organizations such as the Spring Garden Community Services Center, the Black Economic Development Conference, and the National Lawyers Guild, convinced there was a national conspiracy against the Panthers, called for an indictment and prosecution of those responsible.[110] Speaking on behalf of the National Lawyers Guild, attorney Harry Lore said:

> The systematic homicide of members of the Black Panther Party is every bit as calculated as the massacre at My Lai. . . . The administration appears ready to investigate murder in Vietnam, but not here in our own country. On behalf of

the National Lawyers Guild, we denounce, in the strongest terms, the political murders of members of the Black Panther Party, and call for the immediate indictment and prosecution of those responsible.[111]

On December 16, 1969, Rev. Donald R. Gebert, Rev. Roger Zepernick, Peter Z. Weimer, and Emily Clippinger wrote an open letter (published in the *Philadelphia Tribune*) to Mayor James H. J. Tate that focused on the treatment and abuses that the Panthers were subjected to on a national scale. The authors implied that there was a possible conspiracy to oust an influential *voice* from the Black community. Given the horror that transpired in Chicago and Los Angeles, the letter expressed concern about race relations in Philadelphia, especially if police officers continued to engage in the type of Gestapo tactics for which Hitler's Germany was famous. The group sought reassurance from the mayor's office that police officers would be sensitive to the social climate and would consider it in future interactions with Panthers and other minority groups.[112]

Four days later, on December 20, 1969, a group of twenty-six people of varying backgrounds and from different parts of the country assembled to address the violent attacks against the Party nationwide that had resulted in the deaths of several members over the previous two years. The committee was led by Roy Wilkins, executive director of the NAACP, and Arthur Goldberg, a former U.S. Supreme Court justice. The group also included William T. Coleman, a well-known Philadelphia attorney, and Mayor Richard Hatcher of Gary, Indiana. The committee drew up a four-point program with the objective of investigating the actions of the various law enforcement agencies involved in raids of Panther offices and to recommend criminal sanctions if the committee found that the Panthers' civil rights were violated.[113] Although physically removed from the events of Chicago and Los Angeles, key leaders in Philadelphia as well as from around the country felt compelled to launch their own investigation. Despite Coleman's presence on this committee, a similar fate awaited the Philadelphia Panthers.

The committee's findings as well as the public outcry over law enforcement's handling of the Panthers nationwide did not seem to deter the Philadelphia Police Department. On the morning of March 8, 1970, the Panther office on Walnut Street, which was across the street from West Philadelphia High School, was firebombed. As Clarence Peterson recalled, "William Brown's West Philly office was just put together and was an ideal spot for organizing." Whether the firebombing of this particular office was related to the Panthers' frequent after-school meetings with students, or was in response to Brown's refusal to become an informant for the police, is debatable.[114] Luckily, no one was injured. And soon thereafter, William Julye, a local beer distributor, was kind enough to provide the Panthers with a new office on 36th and Wallace Streets. Soon after the Panthers moved into their new digs, police harassment increased.

As animosity between Panthers and police escalated, the disdain that police commissioner Frank Rizzo had for the Panthers would come to the fore. There had been two recent acts of violence in Philadelphia. First, on Saturday, August 29th, in a failed attempt to blow up a police guardhouse in Fairmont Park, Sgt. Frank VonColin was killed and another officer was injured.[116] There were seven suspects; five were apprehended and the remaining two eluded capture and were identified as "militants." Second, in an unrelated incident, two patrolmen were shot and wounded on the night of Sunday, August 30th. The gunmen were not identified as "militants," but one suspect was taken into custody and the other remained at large. Earlier that day, Commissioner Rizzo—rumored to be the eventual successor to FBI director J. Edgar Hoover[117]—announced on a local radio station that "every Black revolutionary would be locked up by sunup."[118]

Even though there was no evidence linking the Panthers to any of the shootings, police had reason to believe that one of the seven suspects alleged to have murdered Sgt. VonColin had Panther connections.[119] Rizzo said that an informant notified police that he had seen grenades and other weapons in the 3625 Wallace Street office when he met with Alvin Joyner (one of the five suspects charged with the murder) three weeks prior to the shooting. On August 31st Rizzo contacted a local TV station as well as two of the city's newspapers (the *Philadelphia Daily News* and *Philadelphia Inquirer*) and instructed reporters to meet him at the Panther office at 3625 Wallace Street. In the wee hours of the morning, Rizzo obtained warrants for the arrest of Panthers at 428 W. Queen Lane, 2935 Columbia Avenue, and 3625 Wallace Street.[120] The raiding party consisted of three teams of forty-five police officers, and eight to ten detectives. In tow were reporters from the *Daily News* as well as the *Inquirer*.[121]

At the Queen Lane location, officers kicked in the door and ransacked the dwelling. Clarence Peterson recalled,

> the order was for no one to be present at the Queen Lane office. Despite orders, one person was staying there who was not supposed to be there and cops came in and arrested him, but he was let go.[122]

At the Columbia Ave. office, Schell was awakened by a Panther on guard duty who shouted, "Cap, they're here." Groggy and struggling to focus, Schell peered out the window to see police officers positioned across the street.[123] Tear gas was tossed into the office from three different locations—the entrance, roof, and rear of the house. Schell remembers that night (August 30) as being especially muggy, and since their offices were not equipped with air-conditioning most of the Panthers were dressed in loose-fitting clothing while others were in their underwear. After the tear gas was launched, a shootout ensued between Panthers and the police. The gunfire lasted only a few minutes, after which the Panthers were led out of the building in single file. With guns pointed at the back of their heads, they were told that "if you stumble or fall we're gonna kill you."[124] They were led to the front of the building, forced against the wall with their backs facing police, and strip-searched by officers. Then without warning one officer fired a .45 caliber sub machine gun just above them as pieces of brick fell on their heads. Schell recalled, "I did not know whether we were going to live or die."[125] Satisfied that the Panthers had been thoroughly humiliated and terrorized, officers took them into custody.

Later that morning at around 6:00 A.M., police raided the West Side office. As a light drizzle fell, officers assumed their positions and Inspector Robert Kopsitz attempted to enter the premises by slamming an ax into the front door. After Kopsitz struck the door repeatedly, another officer shouted, "Police. We have a warrant. Throw your weapons out now." William Brown recalled this ghastly morning: "They kicked in the door and were able to get tear gas in the building; it was the same kind that was used in Vietnam."[126] Gunfire was exchanged, but within minutes of the incursion, seven people (six men and one woman) exited the building as two Panther members threw down their weapons. Ordered to stand against the wall, the men were ordered to strip naked.[127] A photo of six Panthers and their bare bottoms appeared on the front page of the New York Daily News and was then placed in Associated Press and distributed nationwide. Rev. Richard Womack, a native of Philadelphia, remembered, "all of us that saw it thought it was humiliating. I thought it was extremely degrading and emasculating and the News Media published it. . . ."[128]

The group's headquarters was destroyed as police ripped out plumbing fixtures and wrecked furniture.[129] After the raid, the police cleared the office, boarded up the front door, and stapled a sign to the door that read, "Unfit for human habitation."[130] Photos taken of the Wallace Street office were circulated around the country;[131] they not only captured the degradation of the Panthers but sent the implied message that Black militants would not be coddled in Philadelphia as they were in some other cities. After the arrest, Brown says the abuse continued at the station: "They took us to the station with chains on our hands and put us through a gauntlet back into the cells. Police officers were lined up along the wall and they whacked us with their clubs. And then, they proceeded to take us to the cells where the air conditioner was turned up. They would harass us by telling us 'you're not Panthers, you're pussies.' They called us 'niggers.' It was psychological torture. We were held for about a week. We got out right before the plenary session."[132]

When the smoke cleared, three police officers were wounded in North Philadelphia. A total of fourteen people were arrested, and Judge Leo Weinrott set bail for each person at $100,000. Panthers ranged in age from seventeen to twenty-nine, and charges ranged from assault with intent to kill to violation of firearms regulations. Posting bail proved especially difficult since according to Frank Donner, Philadelphia police made off with an estimated $1,500 to $1,700 of the Panthers' money during the raid.[133]

Responding to critics who maintained that he was heavy-handed in dealing with the Panthers, Rizzo exclaimed, "I'll never apologize for those raids. I'm not going to quarterback my commanders . . . I support them. They acted lawfully and with restraint."[134] Rizzo reveled in the department's triumph, saying, "Imagine the big Black Panthers with their pants down!"[135] One witness stated that it was a disgrace to see the Panthers unclothed and hauled away like dogs. Community respondents commended the Panthers for providing free breakfasts, clothing, and barbecues and for their efforts to curtail gang activity. One witness commented that the Panthers' efforts resulted in a decrease in crime.[136]

On September 2nd, as an illustration of the rapport the Panthers had developed with members of the community, people in the community—despite police orders—entered the premises, replaced furniture, and cleaned up the office.[137] Clarence Peterson recalled that day:

> It was the most beautiful experience I've ever had in my whole life. I really cried because the people opened up our offices again. Even after the cops had took out the copper and took out all the furniture, they had a truck that took all the furniture out [of] our offices. We did not think our office would open again. The people in the community put everything back in the office. They put furniture back . . . they fed us for about a week . . . they kept our kids. It was something that I have never seen or heard of before. It was really something . . . it was out of sight . . . they told the cops that "these are our Panthers, so leave them alone."[138]

In light of the shambles the police left the Panthers' office in, the people had to make do with what was left. Some of the Panthers' belongings were confiscated, while other items were damaged during the raid. Later that day, after members from the community reopened the office, Rizzo ordered the confiscated belongings (e.g., furniture, etc.) returned to the North Philadelphia office; it was standard operating procedure for the police department to repair items that were damaged in the course of a raid. As men from the police garage (who were accompanied by two members of the Civil Disobedience Squad) unloaded the damaged goods, Panthers refused to accept the items, demanding they be returned in their original state.[139]

In response to the raids, William Kunstler, an attorney famous for defending left-wing radicals, came to Philadelphia from New York to raise bail for the fourteen arrested Panthers and help local attorneys file a federal injunction to halt future raids on Panther offices in Philadelphia.[140] Kunstler accused the government of scapegoating the Panthers.[141] Community leaders across racial lines appeared in court on September 3rd to hear arguments to lower Schell's bail. The Religious Society of Friends (Quakers) posted bail for Schell after it was reduced by common pleas judge Thomas M. Reed from $100,000 to $2,500. To do so they had to put up the deed to the building that housed the Mark Clark Memorial Clinic. In addition to getting Schell's bail lowered another common pleas judge, Herbert S. Levin, reduced the bail for the remaining Panthers in amounts ranging from $100 to $5,000. After Schell's release, the other Panthers posted bail through Southern General Insurance, a local bail bonding company.[142] Those arrested were released by Friday, September 5, 1970, four days after the raid.

Not everyone blamed the police department for the Panthers' woes. Monroe C. Beardsley, president of the ACLU, chastised both the Panthers and the police, especially Rizzo, for their role in agitating this confrontation. He upbraided the Panthers for their inflammatory posters, writing, and speeches and expressed disappointment with Rizzo for taunting Panthers and forcing them into compromising situations. Specifically Beardsley stated:

> We condemn the dehumanization implied in their systematic use of the word "pig" to describe all policemen, but such provocations, however severe, cannot excuse differential and especially harsh treatment by the police department.... Nor can they excuse attempts by the commissioner—a public servant charged with keeping the peace—to force the Panthers into violent actions and reactions.[143]

Within a week of the Panthers' arrests, the Panthers, along with members of the Young Lords and the Southern Christian Leadership Conference (SCLC), filed a suit requesting that the Philadelphia Police Department be put into federal receivership. The defendants were Mayor Tate, Commissioner Rizzo, managing director Fred Corleto, and district attorney Arlen Specter. The plaintiffs charged that Rizzo persistently harassed Black citizens and that the recent treatment of Panthers marked the apex of a series of offenses against Blacks. The suit was postponed by U.S. district judge John P. Fullam until November 2nd.[144]

On November 2nd, more than twenty-two community groups—calling themselves the Coalition of Organizations for Philadelphia Police

Accountability and Responsibility (COPPAR)—met to put a permanent restraining order on the Philadelphia Police Department. At the hearings, twenty-three witnesses testified and thirty-five more were prepared to testify on alleged police misconduct and brutality. Judge Fullam recessed the hearings to December 1st to give the city solicitor's office time to build a defense.[145] At the following hearing, more than seventy Black witnesses testified to cases of police harassment and abuse.[146]

Defenses Reinforced for Revolution's Sake

Historically, the U.S. government has been adept at utilizing strategies that lead people to believe that harassment experienced by dissidents is of their own doing. This conditioned mentality is to blame the victim rather than to blame the system that produced the victim. With the power to influence and the means to produce and reproduce "reality," a repressive government can easily manipulate the minds of its citizens.

In late 1970, Beatrice Camp and Jennifer Siebens from Oberlin College conducted a study for the Lawyers Committee for Civil Rights under the Law. They discovered that the city's two major daily newspapers (*Philadelphia Inquirer* and *Philadelphia Bulletin*) conspired with the Philadelphia Police Department to conceal information about police brutality and misconduct.[147] Furthermore, Camp and Siebens found that the papers methodically ignored objective journalism standards by privileging stories from police officers' points of view and ignoring eyewitness accounts.

Camp and Siebens's work revealed how the press and the police department colluded to regulate the kind of stories that would be covered and how they would be presented to the public. In the case of the Panthers, the public was often fed misinformation that had a far-reaching effect on public opinion. This is especially true when there are two newspapers published in the same city. When a person reads two major papers that corroborate one other, "reality" is confirmed. This is an effective way to undermine a dissident group's influence, because there is a high probability the larger population will (1) fail to identify with many of the grievances identified by the group, (2) view the dissidents, not the system, as the problem, (3) perceive the need for police to carry out *certain* practices, and (4) leave individuals susceptible to becoming the *Other* (i.e., objectified), wherein the problem is *theirs* rather than *ours*.

There is no doubt that COINTELPRO was a complex and callous measure of social control. With little remorse and little or no impunity, the FBI exacted its cruelest punishment on Black radicals. Despite the assistance of support committees for social justice, locally as well as nationally, government harassment continued.

Panthers in Philly were aware that the government was out to neutralize them, but they did not realize how calculated the state's efforts were. The government's most effective tactic was arrest. Huge sums of money spent to bail Panthers out of jail crippled the branch economically. For example, Milton McGriff described an arrest and roust in Atlantic City, New Jersey:

> I got arrested in Atlantic City on the 4th of July weekend [1969]. We went down to sell papers and no sooner than we got out of the car, the police stopped us and asked us what we were doing. We told them that we were selling the papers. They took us to the station and arrested us because we did not give them any more information than our names and that we were Panthers. We paid $50 in bail and were released within twenty-four hours.[148]

Fifty dollars was a considerable amount in the late 1960s, especially to a militant group for whom money was always in short supply. Furthermore, Panthers claimed that police officers would steal cash from Panther offices during raids. Constant rebuilding efforts also had an adverse impact on the branch. After most raids much time was spent putting things back in place, making repairs, replacing equipment, and the like.

Internally, Huey Newton's leadership was questioned when he ordered the organization to deemphasize the gun and focus on the community survival programs.[149] This led to a rift between Newton and Eldridge Cleaver that eventually took its toll on the organization as well as on individual chapters and branches. To compound matters, many key Panther leaders were either exiled (e.g., Donald Cox, Eldridge Cleaver) or jailed (e.g., Bobby Seale, David Hilliard). By 1970, a number of Philadelphia Panthers left the branch. Several resigned after witnessing internal strife at the national level, which challenged their notion of communalism and the meaning of Pantherhood. Others were simply exhausted from years of hard work and long hours of Panther activity. Many of them were doing Panther work while simultaneously trying to fulfill their responsibilities as parents and spouses. Some of the Panthers devoted their entire lives to the organi-zation and as a result never had enough money to sufficiently provide for themselves or their families because they were full-time revolutionaries.[150]

Attrition also helped undermine the branch. Several members were summoned to Oakland to work on the mayoral and city council campaigns of Bobby Seale and Elaine Brown in 1972–73. Others were transferred to other branches, like Schell, who was ordered to transfer to the New Haven branch. Already under intense scrutiny, Schell resigned rather than accept a transfer.

His departure was a major loss for the branch. About Schell, Herbert Hawkins said,

> Reggie was the baddest leader I knew personally.... I knew what the man
> represented. This man really had a love for the people. I could remember
> when I would sit on task and come back drunk and he would be on my ass like
> white on rice. He was like a big brother to me. And you could tell that he was
> trying to do the job right and it was no opportunist or get rich thing.[151]

Although the branch continued to function under Herbert Smith and later William Brown and Paula Robinson, a number of Panthers went with Schell to establish the Black United Liberation Front (BULF). The branch underwent some restructuring after Schell left. Brown recalls:

> The Breakfast program ended. We were able to hold on to the clinic though
> until 1973. Also several new programs were put in place that included an
> Early Childhood Development Program, an after-school program, and a
> project that catered to senior citizens called SAFE (Seniors Against a Fearful
> Environment). SAFE was designed to provide the elderly with protection
> when they would go grocery shopping, visit the doctor, or travel to and from
> their place of work.[152]

Two years after Schell's departure, Smith left for Oakland, where he served as the campaign manager for Bobby Seale's and Elaine Brown's mayoral and city council campaigns, respectively. Despite the exodus, Karim Amin—who was reported to be a Panther—stated that the group was still active in the community. Although their membership was reduced, they continued to sponsor clothing drives, acted as legal aids in prisons, and worked with gang members. The branch remained open until 1973.[153]

Conclusion

Steve McCutchen, a Panther who served in both the Baltimore and Oakland offices of the Black Panther Party, claimed that of all the cities in which he worked as a Panther, Philadelphia had the most vicious police department he had encountered.[154] In a city where the police commissioner was nicknamed the "Cisco Kid," it is a wonder the Panthers were able to gain a foothold in the community, but they did. And the Panthers remained steadfast and dedicated despite opposition from the state. The community survival programs offered by them were as extensive and effective as those of any chapter or branch on the East Coast. Panthers not only provided food, clothing, and medical assistance to the needy, but they also immersed themselves in the community's problems, mediating gang truces and offering mentorship to wayward youth.

It may be difficult to detect today, but the Panthers made a difference in the City of Brotherly Love at a time when many of its poor Black citizens were most in need of help. In doing so they were able to win the hearts and minds of the people. This is not to say that the Black community was 100 percent in support of the Panthers. There were those in the Black community who were leery of the Panthers because of their rhetoric and media reports that depicted the Panther organization as a violence-prone fringe group. For the most part, though, the Black community stood behind the Panthers when they needed it most. A clear indication of this was when, after police had raided and condemned a Panther office, neighborhood residents tore down boards and placards and put things back in place by the time Panthers had been released from jail. Clearly the Panthers could not have been as effective without the support of the community. The relationship between the Philadelphia branch and the community was not an asymmetrical one where the Panthers were the leaders and the people were the followers. Instead the Panthers' relationship to the community resembled an adage uttered many times by Huey Newton: "The People Are My Strength."

Notes

1. George Katsiaficas, "Organization and Movement: The Case of the Black Panther Party and the Revolutionary People's Constitutional Convention of 1970," in *Liberation, Imagination, and the Black Panther Party*, ed. Kathleen Cleaver and George Katsiaficas, 142 (New York: Routledge, 2001).

2. Paul M. Washington and David McI. Gracie, *"Other Sheep I Have": The Autobiography of Father Paul M. Washington* (Philadelphia: Temple University Press, 1994), 131.

3. Ibid.

4. Dennis Kirkland, David Umansky, and Cliff Linedecker, "Words Hot, People Cool at Temple," *The Philadelphia Inquirer*, September 6, 1970, 1, 11; Pamala Haynes, "Panthers' Meeting Began, Closed on Peaceful Note," *The Philadelphia Tribune*, September 8, 1970, 1, 3; "Huey Newton to Speak at Black Panther Unit Conference at Temple," *The Philadelphia Tribune*, August 15, 1970, 2; Fred Hamilton, *Rizzo* (New York: The Viking Press, 1973), 85.

5. "Not to Believe in a New World after Philadelphia is a Dereliction of the Human Spirit," *The Black Panther*, September 26, 1970, 17.

6. Dennis Kirkland, David Umansky, and Cliff Linedecker, "Words Hot, People Cool at Temple," *The Philadelphia Inquirer*, September 6, 1970, 1, 11.

7. Ibid.

8. Thomas J. Madden, "Newton Hails 'New Day Dawning,'" *The Philadelphia Tribune*, September 6, 1970, 1, 7.

9. Ibid., 7.

10. Mumia Abu-Jamal, personal communication, October 13, 2005.

11. Milton McGriff, personal communication, November 1, 2005.

12. Acel Moore and John Clancy, "Revolutionaries Reassert Goals as Parley Ends," *The Philadelphia Inquirer*, September 8, 1970, 1.

13. America's most sacrosanct documents are the U.S. Constitution, the Declaration of Independence, and the Bill of Rights.

14. "Low Crime Image Shot Up Here as Murders Increase," *The Philadelphia Tribune*, December 26, 1970, 2.

15. "Suit Charges City Ignores Repeated Brutality of Police," *The Philadelphia Tribune*, February 21, 1970, 1.

16. "NAACP to File Brutality Suit Against Rizzo," *The Philadelphia Tribune*, May 5, 1970, 5.

17. Mumia Abu-Jamal, *We Want Freedom: A Life in the Black Panther Party* (Cambridge, Mass.: South End Press, 2004).

18. Clarence Peterson, personal communication, April 16, 2006.

19. Abu-Jamal, personal communication.

20. Dick Cluster, ed., *They Should Have Served That Cup of Coffee* (Cambridge, Mass.: South End Press, 1979).

21. Reggie Schell, personal communication, January 27, 2006.

22. Of the 150,000 papers sold nationally per week, the Philadelphia branch approximated 6.7 percent of sales. See Abu-Jamal, *We Want Freedom*.

23. Abu-Jamal, *We Want Freedom*.

24. Abu-Jamal, personal communication; Abu-Jamal, *We Want Freedom*.

25. "Black Panthers Unit Brands Branche and Jeremiah X 'Fronts,'" *The Philadelphia Tribune*, October 12, 1968, 1, 26.

26. Abu-Jamal, *We Want Freedom*; Reggie Schell, personal communication, September 30, 2005.

27. Cluster, *They Should Have Served That Cup of Coffee*; Peterson, personal communication. The national headquarters instituted a moratorium to minimize infiltration of government informants.

28. Abu-Jamal, personal communication; Schell, personal communication, January 27, 2006.

29. Schell, personal communication, September 30, 2005.

30. Schell, personal communication, September 30, 2005; January 27, 2006.

31. Barbara Easley-Cox, personal communication, January 22, 2006.

32. "No Knowledge, No Freedom," *The Black Panther*, November 11, 1971, 19.

33. Herbert Hawkins, personal communication, November 16, 2005.

34. Reggie Schell, personal communication, May 3, 2006.

35. Schell, personal communication, September 30, 2005; "Panther Leader Calls Bombing 'Sneak Attack,'" *The Philadelphia Tribune*, March 17, 1970, 4.

36. "Panther Leader Calls Bombing 'Sneak Attack,'" *The Philadelphia Tribune*, March 17, 1970, 4; Abu-Jamal, personal communication.

37. "City's Poor Children Fed by Black Panthers," *The Philadelphia Tribune*, July 8, 1969, 1, 2.

38. Schell, personal communication, September 30, 2005; Abu-Jamal, personal communication.

39. Barbara Easley-Cox, personal communication, October 15, 2005; Abu-Jamal, personal communication.

40. Easley-Cox, personal communication, October 15, 2005; Schell, personal communication, September 30, 2005.

41. Ethel Parish, personal communication, October 26, 2005.

42. Len Lear, "Panthers Don't Teach Racism, Leader Says," *The Philadelphia Tribune*, January 27, 1970, 8.

43. "Needy Given Food by Black Panthers," *Urban Archives*, July 23, 1972.

44. "City Removes 9 Centers from Free Lunch List," *The Philadelphia Inquirer*, July 29, 1972.

45. "Panthers to Begin Giving Free Clothing to Children Sunday," *The Philadelphia Tribune*, October 21, 1969, 7; Easley-Cox, personal communication, January 22, 2006.

46. "Free Clothes in Philly," *The Black Panther*, October 18, 1969, 8.

47. Schell, personal communication, September 30, 2005.

48. "Free Clothes in Philly," *The Black Panther*, October 18, 1969, 8.

49. Clay Dillon, "125 Youngsters Given Free Clothing by Black Panthers," *The Philadelphia Tribune*, December 9, 1969, 3.

50. "Panthers to Hold Clothing Program Sun.," *The Philadelphia Tribune*, October 10, 1970, 3; "Black Panthers: Little Left," *The Philadelphia Daily News*, March 24, 1975.

51. Pamala Haynes, "Panthers' Meeting Began, Closed on Peaceful Note," *The Philadelphia Tribune*, September 8, 1970, 3; Laurence H. Geller, "Panthers' New Medical Clinic Attracts 'Active' Idealists," *The Philadelphia Tribune*, March 24, 1970, 5.

52. L. H. Geller, "Panthers' New Medical Clinic Attracts 'Active' Idealists," *The Philadelphia Tribune*, March 24, 1970, 5.

53. "'Brotherly Love' Can Kill You," *The Black Panther*, December 11, 1971, 9.

54. Ibid.

55. Ibid.

56. Ibid.

57. Pamala Haynes, "100 Slain by Gangs Here Since 1967, U.S. Congress Crime Probers Are Told," *The Philadelphia Tribune*, July 18, 1970, 1.

58. "Philadelphia's Gangs Organizing to Serve the Community," *The Black Panther*, June 12, 1971, 4.

59. Clay Dillon, "Gang Members Told to Stop Killings Here," *The Philadelphia Tribune*, November 11, 1969, 1.

60. Ibid., 2.

61. Ibid.

62. Schell, personal communication, September 30, 2005.

63. Elliot Brown, "Gang Problems Linked to Poverty," *The Philadelphia Inquirer*, August 11, 1970, 25.

64. Barbara Reiim, "Teen Gang Members Say Police, Schools, Press Incite 'Wars,'" *The Philadelphia Inquirer*, August 12, 1970, 33.

65. Girard College was desegregated after a U.S. Supreme Court decision in 1968.

66. Clarence Peterson, personal communication, April 14, 2006.

67. Ibid.

68. T. Cross, "Local Panthers Assail Gangs; Call for 'Bloodless Community,'" *The Philadelphia Tribune*, September 1, 1970, 14.

69. "Panthers Kept the Peace, Says Heroine of Gang Attack," *The Philadelphia Tribune*, March 20, 1971, 27.

70. Carolyn Adams et al., *Philadelphia: Neighborhoods, Division, and Conflict in a Postindustrial City* (Philadelphia: Temple University Press, 1991), 13.

71. See Adams et al., *Philadelphia: Neighborhoods, Division, and Conflict*; Conrad Weiler, *Philadelphia: Neighborhood, Authority, and the Urban Crisis* (New York: Praeger, 1974); Peter McGrath, "Bicentennial Philadelphia: A Quaking City," in *Philadelphia, 1776–2076: A Three Hundred Year View*, ed. Dennis J. Clark (Port Washington, N.Y.: Kennikat Press, 1975).

72. McGrath, "Bicentennial Philadelphia."

73. William W. Cutler, "The Persistent Dualism: Centralization and Decentralization in Philadelphia, 1854–1975," in *The Divided Metropolis: Social and Spatial Dimensions of Philadelphia, 1800–1975*, ed. William W. Cutler III & Howard Gillette Jr. (Westport, Conn.: Greenwood Press, 1980).

74. Weiler, *Philadelphia: Neighborhood, Authority, and the Urban Crisis*.

75. Ibid.

76. Bill Fidati, "Special Council Races Almost Unpredictable, Even Without Women," *Philadelphia Daily News*, November 1, 1969, 4, 13.

77. Ibid., 4, 13.

78. Reggie Schell, personal communication with Judson L. Jeffries, April 2006.

79. Clay Dillon, "Panthers Run for Council," *The Philadelphia Tribune*, September 6, 1969, 1, 3.

80. "Panther Candidate Bares Claws in Letter to Tate," *The Philadelphia Tribune*, October 18, 1969, 9.

81. Clay Dillon, "Panthers Run for Council," *The Philadelphia Tribune*, September 6, 1969, 1, 3.

82. McGriff, personal communication.

83. Schell, personal communication, January 27, 2006; April 2006.

84. Joseph R. Daughen and Peter Binzen, *The Cop Who Would Be King: Mayor Frank Rizzo* (Boston: Little Brown Company, 1977), 149.

85. Peterson, personal communication, April 16, 2006.

86. Dennis Kirkland and William Thompson, "Hundreds Gather in Phila. For Panthers' Convention," *The Philadelphia Inquirer*, September 5, 1970, 1.

87. Washington and Gracie, *"Other Sheep I Have,"* 131.

88. Hamilton, *Rizzo*, 85.

89. Washington and Gracie, *"Other Sheep I Have,"* 133.

90. "GPM Urban Group Praise Rizzo's 'Restraint' During Panther Parley," *The Evening Bulletin*, September 11, 1970. The Greater Philadelphia Movement was an organization composed of civic leaders that conducted research on some of the city's most pressing problems. The Urban Coalition was a group that included leaders committed to programs that enabled the disadvantaged to share in the city's bounty.

91. Gerald McKelvey, "Rizzo's Critics Hum Different Melody, Praise Police Handling of Convention," *The Philadelphia Inquirer*, September 9, 1970, 1.

92. Lester A. Lefton, *Psychology*, 6th ed. (Needham Heights, Mass.: Allyn & Bacon, 1997).

93. The ego is one of the three main divisions of the mind and is involved with control, planning, and conforming to reality.

94. Cartha DeLoach, *Hoover's FBI: The Inside Story by Hoover's Trusted Lieutenant* (Washington, D.C.: Regnery Publishing, Inc., 1995); Millie McGhee, *Secrets Uncovered: J. Edgar Hoover—Passing for White?* (Rancho Cucamonga, Calif.: Mildred McGhee Morris, 2000); Richard G. Powers, *Secrecy and Power: The Life of J. Edgar Hoover* (New York: The Free Press, 1987); Anthony Summers, *Official and Confidential: The Secret*

Life of J. Edgar Hoover (New York: G. P. Putnam's Sons Publishers, 1993); <http://en.wikipedia.org/wiki/J._Edgar_Hoover>, accessed February 3, 2006.

95. *FBI's War on Black America* (film), prod. Denis Mueller (2000); DeLoach, *Hoover's FBI.*

96. Lefton, *Psychology;* Francis C. Welsing, *The Isis Papers: The Keys to the Colors* (Chicago: Third World Press, 1991).

97. Schell, personal communication, September 30, 2005.

98. Lefton, *Psychology.*

99. Paulo Freire, *Pedagogy of the Oppressed* (New York: Continuum International Publishing Group, 2000).

100. Defense mechanisms. <http://www.coldbacon.com/defenses.html>, accessed January 29, 2006.

101. Judson L. Jeffries, *Huey P. Newton, the Radical Theorist* (Jackson: University Press of Mississippi, 2002).

102. Schell, personal communication, September 30, 2005; February 4, 2006. This arrest was connected to a raid at Schell's sister's house in Fort Bragg, North Carolina, in which officers searched for her boyfriend, who was alleged to be linked to a bank robbery. During the raid, officers found information on Reggie Schell (e.g., identification, Panther/class notes) and an M-14 rifle—claimed to be stolen—from the Fort Bragg army base.

103. Abu-Jamal, personal communication.

104. Peterson, personal communication, April 14, 2006.

105. "Northwest Group Hosts Panthers; Are 'Impressed,'" *The Philadelphia Tribune,* November 1, 1969, 32.

106. Ward Churchill and Jim Vanderwall, *Agents of Repression: The FBI's Secret Wars against the Black Panther Party and the American Indian Movement* (Cambridge, Mass.: South End Press, 1990).

107. Schell, personal communication, May 3, 2006.

108. Abu-Jamal, personal communication.

109. Jack Olsen, *Last Man Standing: The Tragedy and Triumph of Geronimo Pratt* (New York: Doubleday, 2000); Churchill and Vanderwall, *Agents of Repression.*

110. "23 Groups Here Pledge Panthers Their Support," *The Philadelphia Tribune,* December 13, 1969, 3.

111. Ibid.

112. "More Support for Panthers," *The Philadelphia Tribune,* December 16, 1969, 9.

113. Laurence H. Geller, "Coleman on Committee Probing Slaying of Two Black Panther Members," *The Philadelphia Tribune,* December 20, 1969, 2.

114. Clarence Peterson, personal communication, April 14, 2006.

115. "Panther Leader Calls Bombing 'Sneak Attack,'" *The Philadelphia Tribune,* March 17, 1970, 4; Pamala Haynes, "Bail Money for Panthers Put Up by Quakers Group," *The Philadelphia Tribune,* September 8, 1970, 2.

116. William J. Speers, "A Week of Violence: The Facts and the Meaning," *The Philadelphia Inquirer,* September 6, 1970, 1, 10; James Higgins, "Panic Over Panthers: Philadelphia Boomerang," *The Nation,* October 12, 1970, 332–336.

117. James Higgins, "Panic Over Panthers: Philadelphia Boomerang," *The Nation,* October 12, 1970, 332–336.

118. Reggie Schell, personal communication, January 18, 2005; Abu-Jamal, *We Want Freedom.*

119. William J. Speers, "A Week of Violence: The Facts and the Meaning," *The Philadelphia Inquirer*, September 6, 1970, 1, 10.

120. "Report of Panther Weapons Led to Raids, Rizzo Says," *The Philadelphia Inquirer*, September 4, 1970, 3.

121. James Higgins, "Panic Over Panthers: Philadelphia Boomerang," *The Nation*, October 12, 1970, 332–336.

122. Peterson, personal communication, April 14, 2006.

123. Ibid.; Schell, personal communication, February 4, 2006.

124. Schell, personal communication, February 4, 2006; Cluster, *They Should Have Served That Cup of Coffee.*

125. Schell, personal communication, February 4, 2006.

126. William Brown, personal communication, February 10, 2007.

127. J. Higgins, "Panic Over Panthers: Philadelphia Boomerang," *The Nation*, October 12, 1970, 332–336.

128. Richard Womack, personal communication, February 10, 2007.

129. Higgins, "Panic Over Panthers."

130. Cluster, *They Should Have Served That Cup of Coffee.*

131. "Nightstick Control," *New Republic*, August 25, 1979, 3.

132. William Brown, personal communication, February 10, 2007.

133. Anthony Lame and Ken Shuttleworth, "Panther Captain Released After Bail Is Cut to $2500," *The Philadelphia Inquirer*, September 25, 1970, 9; Robert Terry and Charles Gilbert, "3 Policemen are Wounded in N. Philadelphia," *The Philadelphia Inquirer*, September 1, 1970, 1; James Higgins, "Panic Over Panthers: Philadelphia Boomerang," *The Nation*, October 12, 1970, 332–336; Pamala Haynes, "Bail Money for Panthers Put Up by Quakers Group," *The Philadelphia Tribune*, September 8, 1970, 2; Schell, personal communication, February 4, 2006; Frank Donner, *Protectors of Privilege: Red Squads and Police Repression in Urban America* (Berkeley: University of California Press, 1990), 216. Panthers arrested included Donna Marie Howell, Joseph T. Saunders, Linda Harper, Reggie Schell, Barbara McGriff, Robinetta Gladden, James Scott, R. J. Thomas, Anthony Jones, Herbert Hawkins, William Brown, and Walter Williams. Robert Jones and Pat Lucas (who were engaged and expecting a child) were not members of the Party; they made their home on the third floor of the West Philadelphia office.

134. Dennis Kirkland and John P. Clancy, "Panthers Refuse Goods Returned by City Policemen," *Philadelphia Inquirer*, September 1, 1970, 1.

135. "Nightstick Control," *New Republic*, August 25, 1979, 3.

136. Laurence H. Geller, "Many Criticize Police Raid on Black Panthers' Center," *The Philadelphia Tribune*, September 1, 1970, 1, 2.

137. Ibid.

138. Peterson, personal communication, April 14, 2006.

139. Dennis Kirkland and John P. Clancy, "Panthers Refuse Goods Returned by City Policemen," *Philadelphia Inquirer*, September 1, 1970, 1.

140. "Group to File Suit to Halt Police Raids on Panthers," *The Philadelphia Inquirer*, September 1, 1970, 3.

141. Len Lear, "Gov't Attacks on Panthers Called A Cover Up for its Own Racism," *The Philadelphia Tribune*, September 26, 1970, 8.

142. Anthony Lame and Ken Shuttleworth, "Panther Captain Released After Bail Is Cut to $2500," *The Philadelphia Inquirer*, September 25, 1970, 9; Pamala Haynes, "Bail Money for Panthers Put Up by Quakers Group," *The Philadelphia Tribune*,

September 8, 1970, 2; Pamala Haynes, "Panthers' Captain Gets Community: Schell's Bail Case is Continued; Convention Slated to Open Today," *The Philadelphia Tribune*, September 5, 1970, 1, 2.

143. Len Lear, "Fanatical Panthers, Police Trying to Provoke Each Other to Bloodshed, ACLU Insists," *The Philadelphia Tribune*, September 8, 1970, 24.

144. Len Lear, "Police Brutality Suit Is Postponed," *The Philadelphia Tribune*, October 3, 1970, 4.

145. Laurence H. Geller, "22 Community Groups Seek Order to Restrain Police," *The Philadelphia Tribune*, November 10, 1970, 1, 2.

146. Laurence H. Geller, "Police Restraining Case Here Rested by Complainants," *The Philadelphia Tribune*, December 8, 1970, 1, 3.

147. Len Lear, "Daily Papers and Police Conspire to Hide Truth, Researchers Find," *The Philadelphia Tribune*, December 5, 1970, 5.

148. McGriff, personal communication.

149. Jeffries, *Huey P. Newton, the Radical Theorist*.

150. Abu-Jamal, personal communication, October 13, 2005; Parish, personal communication; McGriff, personal communication; Schell, personal communication, September 30, 2005; Hawkins, personal communication.

151. Herbert Hawkins, personal communication, October 13, 2005.

152. William Brown, personal communication, February 10, 2007.

153. "Black Panthers: Little Left," *The Philadelphia Daily News*, March 24, 1975; Abu-Jamal, personal communication.

154. Steve McCutchen, personal communication, April 27, 2006.

7

To Live and Die in L.A.

Judson L. Jeffries and Malcolm Foley

Black Life in Modern Los Angeles

For ten years (from 1955 to 1965), Watts was the main port of entry for most Blacks migrating from Louisiana and Texas. No city experienced more of a Black population boom than did Los Angeles after World War II, where the Black population increased eightfold, from 75,000 in 1940 to 600,000 by 1965. This influx was mainly attributed to the employment prospects that existed in Los Angeles's shipyards, manufacturing economy, and aerospace industry.

The aircraft buildup played an especially prominent role in luring southern migrants to the city, as the warm weather and abundance of sprawling, open land attracted the earliest makers of aircraft, and Greater Los Angeles became the most important aircraft production center in the nation. Until the 1930s, most aircraft were built manually. Donald Douglas, the founder of the Douglas Aircraft Company, established his factory on an airfield in Santa Monica. The Lockheed Aircraft Company was established in Hollywood, and North American Aviation was established in Inglewood. After Congress authorized a massive defense buildup in 1940 and the Japanese attacked Pearl Harbor in 1941, these factories expanded enormously, creating thousands of jobs. However, by the late 1950s, these opportunities had dried up for Blacks, as employers replaced them with Mexicans, Salvadorans, Guatemalans, Armenians, Chinese, Koreans, Vietnamese, and Filipinos. Illegal immigrants were especially sought-after because they could be paid less and were offered few if any benefits.

From 1959 to 1965, a period Mike Davis calls the winter of discontent, one begins to see the absolute income gap between Blacks and whites widened significantly.[1] In South Los Angeles, median incomes declined by almost a tenth, and Black unemployment skyrocketed from 12 percent to 20 percent (30 percent in Watts). Twenty percent of Watts residents were on the dole, compared to 5 percent for the rest of the country. Moreover, the poverty rate in Watts was an astonishing 41 percent, while it was "only" 20 percent in nearby Willowbrook. Despite picturesque, palm tree–lined streets, and quaint bungalows with manicured forest-green lawns, South Los Angeles's housing stock was dilapidated, the "largest blighted area of any U.S. city" according to the Regional Planning Commission.[2] What's more, there appeared to be few in the African American community with the political clout to help ameliorate these conditions.

By contrast, in places like New York and Chicago, Black politicians had some clout, even as early as the 1940s. In New York, Blacks could count on the fiery Adam Clayton Powell Jr., and Oscar DePriest and William L. Dawson were two of the first Black northern big-city congressmen elected in Chicago. If Blacks in those cities needed an advocate, it had three in Powell, DePriest, and Dawson.

Until 1962, no African American had ever been elected to anything in Los Angeles, and Black Angelenos had no representation to speak of. That year Black Angelenos sent Mervyn Dymally and Douglas Ferrell to the state legislature and elected Gus Hawkins to Congress. The following year, three African Americans, including former LAPD veteran Tom Bradley, were elected to the City Council. Ironically, some of the backwater towns and hamlets from which many of the Black migrants fled had less dismal records in this area.

Suffice to say that when Black migrants arrived in Los Angeles, they quickly learned that while they may have escaped the scorching burn of water hoses and cattle prods, they had not entered the land of milk and honey they had envisioned on their long trek from the South. Many whites, on the other hand, saw Los Angeles as the picture of paradise, the representation of the American dream, one that featured a palatial yet affordable home with an in-ground swimming pool and a glamorous job, possibly as an exec for a major Hollywood studio. Los Angeles always had the film industry and was fast becoming the center of the recording and television business as well.

For many Blacks, Los Angeles turned out to be a nightmare as whites made plain their feelings toward them. Almost every attempt by civil rights groups to expand job and housing opportunities was met with white hostility. One example of this contempt surfaced in November of 1964, when California voters repealed the Rumford Fair Housing Act, an act designed to challenge entrenched patterns of social bias in the housing market, in a constitutional referendum by a two-to-one margin. Support for repeal was extraordinarily high in southern California and was in the 80 to 90 percent range among the white population surrounding the African American community in Los Angeles County.[3] The vote was widely viewed as a hardening of white sentiment with respect to integrated housing. James N. Upton says that African Americans viewed Proposition 14 (the repeal of the Rumford Act) as Los Angeles's version of the "Berlin Wall," bolstering residential segregation.[4] To some Blacks, such resentment was not surprising. In his book *Burn, Baby! Burn: The Autobiography of Magnificent Montague*, a popular Los Angeles deejay implies that "1965 Los Angeles was no different than the Los Angeles of 1955."[5]

The contempt white voters displayed in 1964 was not a new phenomenon or an isolated occurrence. Indeed, this resentment fomented a Black rage that would manifest itself in violent protest throughout the 1960s. Case in point: On Memorial Day of 1961, youngsters calling themselves Freedom Riders battled police in Griffith Park over an incident involving a merry-go-round. When a teenage boy was arrested for riding the merry-go-round without a ticket, more than two hundred young Blacks surrounded the police. When the police refused to release the youth, the crowd grew agitated and seventy-five police officers were called in. A fracas ensued in which Blacks pelted officers with bottles and rocks, sending five of them to the hospital.

By the summers of 1963 and 1964, when disturbances were sprouting up in various places around the country, Los Angeles Blacks, or at least those whom whites considered respectable, churchgoing, middle-class Blacks, called for a meeting with the city's white leaders to voice a number of concerns. Dr. Christopher L. Taylor, a dentist and chairman of the Los Angeles chapter of the National Association for the Advancement of Colored People (NAACP), was among the speakers who issued a warning to those assembled at the Statler Hotel. Taylor said,

> We are already suspect with many elements in our community because we are taking the course of conference first instead of action now. If we cannot together work out our immediate achievable goals, the techniques of direct action will prevail out of sheer frustration and desperation. Direct action based on frustration and desperation, and the fear that is the inevitable reaction, are not the kind of emotions easily controlled.[6]

That afternoon, Norman B. Houston, an insurance company executive, implored management, organized labor, and government to work together for merit employment in the recruitment, selection, training, promotion, and job assignment of Blacks and Mexican Americans.[7] Houston was undoubtedly buoyed by Dr. Martin Luther King Jr.'s visit to L.A. that spring when he spoke at a rally at Wrigley Field at the invitation of some of the city's most well-respected civil rights leaders. More than fifty thousand people reportedly turned out as King, reviewing the struggle for fair treatment and equal opportunity in the South, pled eloquently for a similar commitment in the City of Angels. When asked what could be done to help Birmingham, he answered, "The best thing you can do is make Los Angeles free."[8] What King may have underestimated, but the natives understood all too well, was that while Los Angeles was not in the South, racism was nevertheless firmly entrenched there. Blacks had been trying to make Los Angeles free for years, with efforts dating back to as early as the late 1880s.

Because Los Angeles has not received nearly the amount of scholarly attention that other major cities such as New York, Chicago, Philadelphia, or Detroit have received, some have been under the impression that Black dissent in Los Angeles is a relatively new phenomenon. In fact, Los Angeles has a rich and storied legacy of Black protest that compares favorably with other major American cities. Many Blacks, via organizations like the NAACP, Congress of Racial Equality (CORE), the Urban League, and others, worked tirelessly on behalf of Blacks and poor whites long before the dissident movements that emerged during and after the Watts uprising.

A Tradition of Activism

The first civil rights organization in Los Angeles to establish long-standing ties to the community was the Afro-American Council (AAC). At one time known as the Afro-American League, the AAC was a national federation of state and local branches that existed from the late 1880s into the early twentieth century. Newspaper editor T. Thomas Fortune of New York jump-started the formation of the national organization in 1887. Increasingly alarmed by the denigration of the Fourteenth and Fifteenth Amendments, he issued a call to Black leaders across the country, insisting that a nationwide organization was needed to oppose the rise of Jim Crow in the South.[9] The result was the short-lived Afro-American League. Black leaders in Los Angeles first formed a local branch of the league in the late 1880s.

In 1906, James Alexander, president of the AAC, published a statement of principles, "Appeal to Reason," which was penned as an open letter to Black

Californians. "Appeal" urged civil rights activism and electoral pragmatism, especially at the local level: "What President Roosevelt may say in praise of us at the nation's capital, or what [Senator] Ben Tillman of South Carolina, or Gov. [James] Vardaman of Mississippi may say in abuse of us does not [affect] like conditions." Municipal officials "are of the greatest importance to us," for they are "the main artery for the building up of a city of contented, happy homes, the establishment of water, sanitary, fire and police departments, the enforcement of law and order without prejudice." Equally important, the wise "use of our ballot" would result in elected officials who would "[give] us a chance to earn a livelihood by giving us positions."[10]

Some of the other early prominent Black organizations included the Sojourner Truth Club and the California Association of Colored Women's Clubs. Marcus Garvey's Universal Negro Improvement Association also had a strong following in Los Angeles during the early 1900s.

One of Los Angeles's most influential Black organizations was the Forum. Formed in 1903 at the First A.M.E Church, it was created with the express purpose of establishing a Black united front to aid in advancing and strengthening the race along moral, social, intellectual, and financial lines, as well as imparting Christian values. Established by some of the city's most prominent Blacks including J. L. Edmonds, Frederick Roberts, and Rev. J. E. Edwards, the Forum urged African Americans to develop a sense of pride in race and self, championed the need for Black laborers to purchase land, and encouraged businesses to hire Blacks in nonmenial positions.

Perhaps the Forum's greatest contribution was promoting a burgeoning sense of community by providing an arena for public discourse, lively exchange, and political dialogue. Even the humblest citizen had access to these meetings and could voice his or her grievance before the entire body. In his book *Bound for Freedom*, Douglas Flamming says that the Forum was a kind of town hall meeting for the city's African American community, an open space for spirited debate, indignation, and an important venue for Black activism.[11] One of the Forum's unique offerings was the "committee on strangers" which helped new migrants adjust to the pace and tenor of Los Angeles. Before long the Forum became the foremost "colored institution" assisting newly arrived Blacks from the South.[12]

By the 1920s, the Forum was at its apex. Politicians—Black and white—sought the support and votes that the Forum could provide. Even former governor Hiram Johnson came to a meeting to garner support for his 1922 U.S. Senate bid. The rapid growth of the Black community worked against the continued effectiveness of the organization, and, as Blacks started to reach out to other institutions, attendance dwindled significantly. The group held its last meeting in 1942.

Historic Central Avenue

When Blacks were not scraping to make ends meet or agitating for social change, they sought relief from Los Angeles's harsh daily grind in the refuge of the city's nightlife. One had to laugh to keep from crying, as the old saying goes, and Los Angeles's nightlife kept many a Black person sane. Central Avenue was the site of this nightlife; it was where Black folk went to let off steam and regroup for the challenges that awaited them the next day.

The "Avenue," as it came to be known, was the musical and literary scene that appeared to be partly modeled after the Harlem Renaissance. In fact, while on a tour of Los Angeles, the renowned Chandler Owen, editor of the *Messenger*, was overwhelmed by the sense of Black community he discovered on Central Avenue. The homes, churches, nightclubs, and businesses reminded him of his own neighborhood in New York City. Here on Central Avenue, he told his *Messenger* readers, he had found "a veritable little Harlem in Los Angeles." It wasn't Harlem though, not even close. By the 1920s Harlem was overwhelmingly Black. By contrast, only 6 percent of Central Avenue's residents were African American. Still it was the place to be for anyone with an ear for music and an eye for pageantry. Groups like the Lafayette Players performed at the Lincoln Theater, bringing theatrical productions to the Black community. Literati from Langston Hughes to native son Arna Bontemps periodically spent time in this dynamic artistic colony. Poetry readings by local and nationally known writers became standard Sunday fare at the 28th Street all-Black YMCA.

While the literary output of Black Angelenos paled in comparison to that of New York, the plethora of poetry houses, writers' collectives, music establishments, and nightclubs in the area made Central Avenue the cultural Mecca of the city. It was the jazz clubs more than anything else that brought people to Central Avenue. The Kentucky Club at 25th Street and Central with its racing décor, the Club Alabama, the Savoy at 55th Street and Central, the Apex Night Club at 4015 Central Avenue, "where mirth, pleasure and happiness reigns supreme," and many other establishments all provided an opportunity for Black musicians to develop a following and for patrons to have good, clean fun. For example, the Lincoln Theatre, a large, Black-owned theater that opened at 23rd and Central in 1926, offered stunning stage shows and packed in audiences on weekends.

Some of the biggest acts in Black music cemented their legend on Central Avenue. Jelly Roll Morton perfected his "New Orleans" style at the Cadillac Café (at 5th Street and Central Avenue). The Black and Tan Orchestra from Texas also lit up Central Avenue, along with Kid Orgy's Original Creole Jazz Bands. When he left Fort Worth and relocated to Los Angeles, Ornette

Coleman was so far ahead of his time that musicians told him he could not play, and rumor had it that a bandleader who hired him at one point paid him not to play. Ignoring the critics, Coleman continued to push the envelope. He felt fortunate to encounter other musicians who felt the same way.

By the late 1950s Coleman had become a cultural icon in Los Angeles. Praised a generation later by some as "the most influential single figure to emerge in Jazz since Charles 'Bird' Parker," Coleman and a small circle of musicians (Eric Dolphy, Don Cherry, Ed Blackwell, Scott Lafaro, Red Mitchell, Billy Higgins, and Charlie Haden) spent the Eisenhower years trying to foment a musical revolution called free jazz—an almost cataclysmic widening of the improvisational freedom that Bird and Dizzy Gillespie had pioneered in the 1940s.[13]

Central Avenue was the home to many dreams—a fact that helps explain the historical significance of this community. The Avenue was the center of the Black existence: "if you wanted to meet any of the people you . . . went to school with or had ever known, you could walk up and down Central Avenue and you would run into them. It was the hub of Black life." One longtime resident of the area expressed the importance of the street this way: "you didn't want to hit the Avenue with dirty shoes."[14]

Given the Avenue's illustrious history and its place in Black Los Angeles lore, it was only fitting that the Panthers opened their first official and independent office there—a storefront at 4115 S. Central. By late 1969, additional offices were established—one at 334 W. 55th Street, the others at 1100½ W. Exposition Boulevard and 84th Street and Broadway.

Bunchy Carter and How the Panthers Got Started in Los Angeles

The legend surrounding the arrival of the Black Panthers in Los Angeles reads like a made-for-TV Hollywood story. The formal announcement was reportedly made one vibrant Sunday afternoon in February 1968 at a community poetry reading sponsored by the Black Student Alliance under the guidance of Harry Truly, a professor at Cal State L.A., who believed that the Black Student Alliance had a responsibility to promote revolutionary art. Among the participants that day were C.R.D. Halisi of Us, a young Stanley Crouch, a well-known Watts poet named Ojenke, and the renowned Quincy Troupe. Several members of the already established Black Panther Political Party also read poems.

According to Elaine Brown, a few hours into the festivities the double doors to the hall flung open and in walked Alprentice "Bunchy" Carter. Bunchy was said to be a dangerous man, one who commanded the respect of

Los Angeles's toughest cats. Bunchy was always dressed in a sharp suit with pimp socks and shined knobs,[15] and women supposedly swooned in his presence. In her book A *Taste of Power*, Brown describes Bunchy:

> His face was black alabaster; his eyes, Black diamonds, set off by carved eyebrows and distinct black eyelashes. His skin was as smooth as melted chocolate, unflawed, with a reddish gloss. He was a vision of Revelations, a head of soft black wool refined to an African Crown.[16]

Bunchy was also an ex-con; he did four years in Soledad State Prison for armed robbery. Some say he attempted to rob a bank. Bunchy became a Muslim minister in prison after meeting and being influenced by Eldridge Cleaver. Bunchy earned his reputation as a teenager as leader of the Slauson Renegades, an offshoot of the Slauson gang's hardcore inner circle. But the image of Bunchy as a hardcore street thug is not a well-rounded one; there was another side to him that is seldom discussed. While he was deputy minister of defense he was also a student at UCLA. As a kid his mother enrolled him in dance class, and some claim that he even appeared in a Little Rascals episode once.

Apparently Bunchy met Huey in 1967 shortly before the Donald Frey incident, and the meeting reaffirmed what he had been mulling over since he had heard how a phalanx of armed Panthers marched into the San Francisco airport and escorted an arriving Betty Shabazz to a speaking engagement.

Bunchy, known for his sense of style, apparently had a flair for the dramatic. Upon making his grand entrance into the Black Congress that day in February 1968 flanked by twenty of his most trusted street cronies, Bunchy immediately declared that "no one invited us, but we thought we'd come anyway." His opening statement must have struck some as a bit odd since the festivities were open to the public. Nevertheless, everyone appeared momentarily stunned. "I've got a few poems of my own," Bunchy continued. "Right on," someone yelled out. Bunchy led off with the inflammatory *Niggertown* and concluded with the more sensitive *Black Mother*, the final stanza of which read:

> For a slave, a natural death who dies, can't balance out two dead flies. I'd rather be without the shame, a bullet lodged within my brain, if I were not to reach our goal let bleeding cancer torment my soul.

Upon finishing, Bunchy thanked the audience and quickly got down to business. "I came here to make an announcement," he said triumphantly. "We have just officially formed the Southern California chapter of the Black Panther Party for Self-Defense." "Right on," yelled some of those in attendance. "I am here today to make it blatantly clear that we are the Black Panther Party, that there is but one Black Panther Party and that is the Party headed by minister of defense Huey P. Newton—ain't that right John Floyd." (Floyd was the head of the Black Panther Political Party, a different group.) "I said, ain't that right John Floyd!" repeated Bunchy as Floyd sat silently. "And we don't want to hear about another soul trying to use our name again unless authorized by the Central Committee of the Black Panther Party. Is that clear, John Floyd!" Those in attendance interpreted Floyd's silence in different ways. Some thought Floyd was intimidated by Bunchy, while others viewed his refusal to answer as an act of defiance. Whatever the case, in the midst of provoking Floyd, Bunchy snapped his fingers and one of his comrades came over and handed him a banner. Bunchy unwrapped it to reveal the famous poster of Huey, the one where he is seated in a high-back rattan chair with a shotgun in one hand and a spear in the other. "This is Huey P. Newton," Bunchy lectured. "Huey has done what you niggers are talking about, thinking about doing. He has dealt with the pig! He has set the example and showed us that we, too, must deal with the pig if we are to call ourselves men. From this point forward, Brothers and Sisters, if the pig moves on the community, the Black Panther Party will deal with him. . . . What will we do, Brothers?" he shouted. One brother stepped forward, sawed-off shotgun in hand, and pronounced, "We'll put his dick in the dirt, Bunchy." "That's right," Bunchy responded. "We're here to say that the vanguard party will deal with the pig. We'll kill the pig! Off the motherfucker! We will destroy him absolutely and completely or, in the process, destroy the gravitational pull between the earth and the moon!"[17]

Other Panthers admit that there was an excitement in the air that day, but they recall a less flamboyant beginning. Roland Freeman, a section leader, remembers that a small cadre was invited to a meeting and from that a committed nucleus was formed. This initial group took the oath of the Mau Mau, a tribe of dedicated Kenyans under the leadership of Jomo Kenyatta that resisted colonial power. The Mau Mau pledged that they would never give in nor give up. The initial core of Panthers pledged a similar oath.[18]

Los Angeles's Militant Community

By the time the Panthers got under way, there was a community of militant organizations already established in Los Angeles, all of which were founded in the years following the Watts revolt. Among them were the small and close-knit Black Panther Political Party, the Community Alert Patrol (CAP), the Sons of Watts, SNCC, the Self Leadership for All Nationalities Today (SLANT), the Malcolm X Foundation, the Marxist Leninist Maoist and, of course, Maulana Karenga's Us, which stood for "wherever we are Us is" and "Us against Them." By 1968 Us, which had been on the scene for three years and had developed a reputation for being ultra pro-Black, was the premier Black militant organization in Los Angeles. The group held tremendous sway among radical-thinking Blacks. Even one high-ranking Panther admitted that Us was "the best organized and disciplined group in L.A., and the only organization with a uniform ideology, and most important, with an army."[19] Indeed, it was Maulana Karenga who promoted what he called "operational unity" under the auspices of TALO (Temporary Alliance of Local Organizations), militant activists partnered on a variety of local community efforts.

This community of militants was mostly made up of young Black males. If arrest records are representative of the people who were involved in the Watts rebellion, then 41 percent of those involved were between the ages of twenty-five and thirty-nine. This age bracket matches the ages of those who either founded the organizations mentioned earlier or held high-ranking positions within them. Furthermore, 42 percent of those arrested ranged in age from fifteen to twenty-nine,[20] which mirrors the age demographic of those most likely to be among the Black Panther Party's rank and file.

It is interesting to note that gangs and gang violence began to dissipate after the Watts uprising. Many gangs called for a truce, and by the end of 1965 some of the more high-profile Black gangs, including the Businessmen, Farmers, Gladiators, Revel Rousers, and the Slausons, began to wither away. According to Sergeant Warren Johnson, "during the mid and late 1960s, juvenile gang activity in Black neighborhoods was scarcely visible to the public at large and of minimal concern to South L.A. residents."[21] Instead of joining gangs, young men began to organize and become politically active. The Watts disorder may have played some part in raising the consciousness of some of these young men, as well as served as the impetus for the birth and development of some of these militant groups. The formation of these organizations offered young Blacks a vehicle for Black solidarity and self-actualization that occupied the time and redirected the energies of young men that might have been spent in gang mischief. The emergence of these groups also implied that for some Blacks the nonviolent philosophy of civil disobedience was passé; Black Power was in.

An Informant Helps Launch the Chapter

Unfortunately for the Panthers, the Southern California chapter was compromised from the start as one of its organizers was an informant. Earl Anthony, a graduate of the University of Southern California, joined the Party while attending law school in San Francisco in 1967 and quickly became a captain.[22]

Anthony was raised in a middle-class household where education was highly valued, but he was not removed from the daily atrocities that many Black Angelenos faced on a daily basis. He was well versed in the history of

Black suffering and the various movements Blacks undertook to alleviate that oppression. Indeed, Anthony set out to become a champion for that struggle. Before joining the Party he engaged in political organizing and at one point joined the Nation of Islam, becoming what he called a renegade Muslim. Anthony was profoundly attracted to the Muslims' pro-Black doctrine and their "do for self" approach to problems within the Black community. Like many others, Anthony had difficulty adhering to the Nation of Islam's ultra-strict codes of behavior and the far-out theory about the evolution of the white race. He thought he found his calling in the BPP. But less than a year after joining the organization, something unexpected happened—he found himself in a quandary for a middle-class kid who had never had any trouble with the law, and he allowed himself to be manipulated by agents of the Federal Bureau of Investigation (FBI).

Anthony's role in undermining the Los Angeles branch as an informant is interesting if for no other reason than that it flies in the face of Karl Marx's argument regarding the role of both the lumpen proletariat and the proletariat in the revolution. In Marx's view the lumpen proletariat was the most unreliable sector of the population, not to mention the most susceptible to co-optation by those in power. He reasoned that because the lumpen's way of life was so precarious, he was vulnerable to bribery, which made him a likely candidate for the part of stool pigeon. Yet in a chapter that was overwhelmingly lumpen in composition, it was the proletariat Anthony who became the agent provocateur. At the time he was perhaps the organization's highest-ranking informant. Not long after Anthony held the rank of captain, Eldridge Cleaver made the unilateral decision to appoint him deputy minister of information.[23]

The FBI ordered Anthony to encourage Cleaver to set up a chapter in Los Angeles. The FBI's goal was to foment ill will between the Panthers and the Us organization so that they might neutralize one another, perhaps even kill each other off.[24] The idea of starting a chapter in Los Angeles was well received by Cleaver. Eager to expand the Panthers' base in the state, Cleaver did not need much coaxing, especially since he already had in Los Angeles a trusted contact in Bunchy, who was eager to join the Party. Moreover, Cleaver saw this as an opportunity to mobilize Los Angeles's leftist community around the Huey P. Newton Legal Defense Fund. Cleaver directed Anthony to enlist Bunchy's help in organizing the chapter, and they began by mustering support for a Free Huey birthday celebration. In November of 1967 Anthony relocated to his hometown of Los Angeles.

By early December he and Bunchy started laying the groundwork for the Southern California chapter of the BPP. Recognizing the difficulty of pulling off a Free Huey birthday celebration by themselves, especially given the time constraint, they sought the manpower and resources of the Black Congress, housed in a building located in the heart of the Black community at Florence and Broadway that included a confederation of many of Los Angeles's Black organizations. Governed by an executive committee of representatives of each member organization, the Black Congress fostered Black unity and promoted community control of Black neighborhoods and the creation of Black institutions. In doing so, the Black Congress encouraged its member organizations to move collectively. Included among the Black Congress's significant projects was the attempted secession and incorporation of Watts as a renamed and independent "Freedom City." Anthony and Bunchy approached the Black Congress about the idea, offering Stokely Carmichael as the keynote speaker. The proposal did not require much selling; after all, Newton was in jail at the time and considered a martyr by many in the movement. The motion to sponsor the celebration was put on the floor by Karenga and a consensus was reached. That the motion was put forward by Karenga is ironic, but of course he probably had no way of knowing that Anthony and Bunchy were in the preliminary stages of expanding the Party's base of operations.

The Chapter's Official Start

February 18, 1968, marked the official beginning of the chapter. In less than a month Bunchy had recruited twenty men, most of them from the Teen Post, an antipoverty program where Bunchy worked as a counselor. In fact, the Panthers initially operated out of the Teen Post's office. From the Teen Post the Panthers moved to an office in the Black Congress.

As a reward for his hard work in helping bring the chapter to fruition, the Central Committee made Bunchy deputy minister of defense. By July the chapter's ranks had swelled to more than four hundred, due mainly to the efforts of Bunchy, who appealed to Los Angeles's street thugs in a way only a former gang leader could. It is likely that no one else could have elicited the type of respect that Bunchy commanded. Long John Washington stated flatly that "many of the Slausons joined the BPP because Bunchy made us."[25] In general, Bunchy's recruits were a mixed bag of his former Slauson comrades, men with whom he served time in prison, and brothers from other gangs. Working alongside one another, "they were armed with Bunchy's politics combined with a history of violence and a street code of silence and loyalty."[26]

Not all the Los Angeles Panthers were former gang bangers or ex-cons. The majority of them were straitlaced young men and women from lower- and working-class families. Some of them held entry-level jobs in the retail and service sectors of the city. Many of them had completed high school, but some had not. Several had attended and graduated from college. Most of them had no history of activism before joining the BPP. Many who joined the Los Angeles office did so because the BPP was the first organization they saw that was willing to stand up to the police on behalf of the Black community. Roland Freeman said, "I liked the idea of self-defense."[27] Marvin Jackson, who joined the BPP approximately six months after being discharged from the army, echoed a similar sentiment, saying, "I joined the Panthers because they took a confrontational stance against the police."[28] Wayne Pharr, an ex-Slauson who eventually rose to the rank of captain, explained that he believed in self-defense and the "world wide uplift of Black people."[29]

It would not take long for the Panthers to become the largest Black militant group in Los Angeles. Aside from Carter and Anthony, others who helped build the chapter were Raymond "Masai" Hewitt, Gwen Goodloe, Elaine Brown, John and Erika Huggins, and Elmer "Geronimo" Pratt. Pratt, once a member of the U.S. Army's 82nd Airborne Division and a decorated Vietnam veteran, played a key role in training his comrades in combat readiness. John Huggins, a veteran of the navy who also served in Vietnam, was a tireless worker who would eventually become deputy chairman. Goodloe, Brown, and Erika Huggins were instrumental in putting many of the survival programs in place. Masai, the well-read street scholar, set up the chapter's weekly political education classes. About Hewitt, Pratt remembers that "he ends up being one of the best educators—and the more he teaches, the more I like him, because I'm learning. Because I've never had time to go deep into Das Kapital. . . . He's making sense of the economy, of fascism, of slavery, socialism—all this economic analyses [sic]."[30]

The Los Angeles office was one of the largest in the organization; exactly how large is difficult to discern. The office had three components: the social/political element, the military, and the underground. The social/political element worked closely with the community and was primarily responsible for putting the survival programs in place; they did the day-to-day grunt work necessary to meet the needs of the people. Much of the Panthers' community support was the result of this work, which enabled the chapter to ingratiate itself with the community and win the hearts and minds of the people. The military dimension consisted of the chapter's foot soldiers. They acquired weaponry and trained themselves and others in warfare in preparation for the revolution that was certain to come, and the underground, composed of small cell units, were hardened street types that would do whatever needed to be done for the organization, in the name of the revolution.

The underground consisted of only those men Bunchy could vouch for, men he had seen throw down in the streets of Los Angeles, men who had been tested—some by Bunchy himself. The underground had its own code of ethics. For instance, it reportedly did not rob individuals, it robbed institutions. Conversations with former Panthers show that Carter did not want aboveground Panthers interacting with the chapter's underground unless the interaction was initiated by him. The identities of the underground members were not known to the general body. Consequently, even today few aboveground Panthers can state the names of those who served underground. Having such a bifurcated setup was clearly advantageous if someone was interrogated by authorities. He or she could not reveal what he or she did not know.

The Party was popular, not only among gang members, but also among dropouts, ex-servicemen, runaways, men and women who lived on the street, and Black youth looking to get involved politically for the first time in their lives. Most joined for the right reasons, but some did not. One dedicated member of the chapter admits that she initially joined the Party for the wrong reasons. Said Talibah Shakir,

> I chose the BPP over the Us organization, SNCC, RAM and others because of all the wrong reasons. I joined because the brother that talked to me about the BPP was fine—I joined because of the visibility of the BPP; I joined because one day I ditched school to celebrate Malcolm X's Birthday, and at the Black Congress on Broadway in Los Angeles, I saw how powerful Bunchy Carter was when he made Karenga back the fuck up.[31]

There was the sense of bravado that was associated with being a Panther, but there was also the feeling of gratification one got from working to improve Black people's lot. Of course there was also the uniform—black leather jacket, the beret set off by the powder-blue shirt—not to mention the looks of admiration one got when dressed in full Panther regalia. And there were the guns, for better or for worse. Said Long John Washington, "[T]he BPP's persona of being a cop killer brought dishonorable people looking for glory."[32] On the other hand, the gun attracted those who believed that the time had come for Blacks to arm themselves against the wanton violence of psychopathic police officers.

The Panthers' Community Efforts

It would take the Party nearly two years to establish strong community ties, primarily because of an inability to set up its community survival programs. The Panthers were able to serve free dinners from time to time, but not with any regularity because they had no access to a proper facility and, more importantly, because the bulk of the funds raised were siphoned off for other purposes. Constant police harassment kept the Panthers hustling from one jail to another, bailing out their members, getting medical treatment for those beaten when arrested, and paying parking tickets and excessive fines to retrieve their vehicles from police impounds.

Although the Panthers were slow in setting up their survival programs, they were still active in the community. On a few occasions the Panthers hosted community cookouts. In late 1968, the chapter sponsored a barbecue in an area called South Park, and hundreds of people partook in the festivities.[33] One of the Panthers' more substantive efforts involved ridding the community of drugs. Indeed, the one thing that shop owners and other residents noticed shortly after the Party opened its office on Central Avenue was that drug activity declined. Before the Panthers arrived, drug pushers peddled their wares openly on the street. Determined to make the neighborhood safe for children as well as the elderly, the Panthers set out to run the pushers out of the community. Those who ignored the Panthers' appeals were either shaken down until they left of their own accord, or were driven out. Physical violence was of course the last resort as most pushers, after having been shaken down a few times, realized that Central Avenue had gotten bad for business and simply moved on.

Almost a year and a half after the chapter was founded, the Panthers were finally able to launch the first of three free breakfast programs. Garnering support for the program proved more difficult than many had expected. According to their records, 250 to 300 letters were sent to retail and wholesale stores in the community requesting supplies for the program. The response was dismal;[34] not a single merchant responded to their queries. Undeterred, the Panthers came up with a plan. For food they would convince officials at UCLA's dining halls to donate their leftover items rather than discarding them at the end of the day.

The initial breakfast program (called the John Huggins Breakfast Program for Children in honor of the slain deputy chairman) was established in early 1969 at the University Seventh-day Adventist Church, much to the chagrin of the congregation. Despite the parishioners' uneasiness about the Panthers, associate pastor Reverend Lorenzo Payte gave the Panthers permission to use the church's facilities with one stipulation: that no meat be served. Realizing that for many people breakfast is not a complete meal unless meat is included, the Panthers discovered veggie burgers and passed them off as sausages. Between forty and fifty children ages three to fourteen were served daily.[35]

Some of the church's members were adamantly opposed to having any association with the Panthers. The Panthers claimed that after seeing how successful the program was, support grew exponentially. Whether this is true or not is debatable. What is interesting, though, is that shortly after the breakfast program began, Reverend Payte was informed that he was being transferred to another church, casting doubt on the claim about the congregation's change of heart. If Payte's transfer was related to his work with the Panthers, it would not have been the first time a man of the cloth was reassigned after he appeared receptive to the Panthers' message. Weeks earlier, in October 1969, the bishop of the San Diego diocese abruptly transferred Frank Curran to New Mexico after it was discovered that he had allowed the Panthers to use the church to feed indigent children in the San Diego area.

At any rate, since the Panthers were planning to set up additional breakfast programs throughout Los Angeles, they realized that to be successful they needed to assuage concerns that other congregations might have about allowing them to use their churches. After much deliberation, a small group led by Gwen Goodloe went before the Los Angeles Conference of Baptist Ministers with a presentation of the goals and objectives of their community survival programs.[36] Impressed, the ministers voted unanimously to give the Panthers their endorsement and commendation.

Using churches to sponsor the breakfast program was encouraged by the national headquarters for several reasons: (1) it could accommodate large groups of people, (2) holding it in a house of God would make it less likely that the police would barge in and harass its occupants, or so the Panthers thought, (3) it gave the Panthers a degree of legitimacy among those who may have been leery about allowing their children to frequent a program put together by Black militants, (4) it allowed the Panthers to concentrate on serving the people without the worry of dealing with securing a location that met all the building codes and the like, and (5) the Panthers were not required to pay rent, which allowed them to expand existing survival programs or create new ones.

The breakfast program was not the only endeavor the Panthers offered community residents. Other services included free food and clothing giveaways and of course the police patrols made famous by the Bay Area Panthers. Police patrols in Los Angeles did not mirror those being carried out up north. By the time the Southern California chapter was founded, citizens were no longer allowed to carry guns openly because of a law passed in the spring of 1967. Consequently the police patrols were not as high-profile and perhaps did not lend themselves to the kind of combustible interactions that were present in northern California. Police patrols in Los Angeles were low-key. Also, since the Los Angeles Panthers did not carry weapons in full view, the patrols may not have been as effective since police officers might have been more likely to provoke an incident with someone they believed to be unarmed.

The same year the breakfast program got under way, the Panthers opened the Bunchy Carter Free Clinic, which was staffed with volunteer doctors and nurses.[37] The Panthers also put in place a Busing to Prisons Program that catered to Black families that either did not have the means or the transportation to visit their loved ones who were often incarcerated in facilities that were hundreds of miles outside of the city. Later a liberation school for elementary-age kids was established in nearby Compton, California.[38]

The Panthers' most impressive effort may have been the Walter "Toure" Pope Community Center. Named in honor of a fallen comrade, the center was established in October 1969. With donations from some of Hollywood's most popular celebrities, the Panthers were able to offer a number of services such as the chapter's second free breakfast program, political education classes, and an information center. According to members of the chapter, the community center was designed to bring them closer to the people and to more effectively meet the needs and desires of the Black community.[39]

Within a month of the center's opening, the Panthers were visited by a group of U.S. Marines from Camp Pendleton. Booker White, a Black folk singer, also stopped by that day because, he said, "I want to sing for the people and the children."[40] After breakfast the GIs pledged their support to the community center, donating $70 to the breakfast program and promising to return the next time they were in town. With small donations like these, the Panthers were able to open their third breakfast program in early 1970. With this program, located at the home of Mrs. Leona (Be-Be) Murphy at 1002½ 41st Place, the Panthers were fast expanding their survival offerings.[41]

The Panthers' community service programs were an important feature of the organization's Ten-Point Program. Putting these endeavors in place was a necessary step toward uplifting the masses of Black Angelenos politically. One cannot expect "the people" to move against the forces of oppression if they are in poor health, are intellectually impoverished, or have empty stomachs, the Panthers would say. Second, it was imperative that the Black community be provided with the essentials since the state had made it clear through its inaction and indifference that no such programs were forthcoming.

As Marcus Garvey had done before them, the Panthers assumed this responsibility. Taking up this mantle is crystallized eloquently in an article titled "L.A. Pigs Vamp on Free Breakfast Program." In this piece the Panthers maintain that

> these programs exist because the government has not provided them [the people] with even the basic necessities of life, food and shelter, as are the natural rights of human beings, and is the duty of the institutions by which they elect to be governed to provide. And so we, the Black Panther Party then have taken upon ourselves the struggle of not only preparing for the total liberation of all people, but the temporary alleviation of some of the ills which the great masses of people suffer.[42]

While the Panthers' offerings were clearly altruistic, they were also politically strategic. By serving the people, the Panthers highlighted the inherent contradictions of the state, which was instrumental to the politicization of the Black community. This was important, for the people would not follow the Panthers if they did not trust or have confidence in them. Without the support of the people, the Party would be crushed by the ruling elite (which possessed little fear of being held accountable) or would simply wither away due to lack of need.

Fortunately, because of the Panthers' strong community ties, they were able to expand throughout the state. Over the course of a few years, Panther operations in southern California grew to include outposts in Bakersfield, Riverside, Santa Barbara, Pomona, Pacoima, Pasadena, and San Diego. Still, the Los Angeles office remained the strongest unit in California outside of the Bay Area. It appears that as the Southern California Panthers grew, so did the attacks on them.

The LAPD and the Black Community It Is Not Sworn to Protect or Serve

If Blacks in Oakland thought the police force was hostile to African Americans there, it is perhaps because they had not spent much time in Los Angeles. No government agency attracted more attention from the news media after World War II than did the LAPD.[43] Several television series portrayed the Los Angeles Police Department as an impartial and professional guardian of law and order. In reality, the police force more closely resembled the movie L.A. Confidential than it did television's Adam-12 or Dragnet.

Some of the most well-publicized scandals in law enforcement occurred in Los Angeles. By the 1920s corruption was firmly entrenched within the police department, and bribery, shakedowns, and graft were commonplace. And by the late 1940s and early 1950s the force had developed a reputation for being insensitive to residents of color. For example, in the mid-1960s when a Black man was rushing his pregnant wife to the hospital, a police officer shot and killed him. When the police chief was asked what he intended to do about the killing, he responded, "I am going to do nothing. Police are not supposed to stand by and watch a car speeding down the street at eighty miles per hour."[44]

To some extent the philosophy of the LAPD seemed to reflect a disparaging view of human nature. As William H. Parker, former chief of the LAPD, once remarked, "I look back over almost . . . thirty-five years of dealing with the worst that humanity has to offer. I meet the failures of humanity daily, and I meet them in the worst possible context. . . . I think I have to conclude that this civilization will destroy itself, as others have before it."[45] Such pessimism regarding the nature of society and the progress of mankind may have been a natural product of numerous encounters with the criminal public; unfortunately it also may have had an unfavorable effect on the performance of many police duties. Conditioned by the belief that people are fundamentally immoral or depraved, some police officers may have found it difficult to grant civilians, especially minorities, the respect necessary to establish a relationship of mutual trust and cooperation.

Many of the problems that took center stage in Los Angeles during the middle to late 1960s, such as illegal surveillance of the department's critics, harassment of militants and hippies, and use of excessive force against people of color, have their roots in the administration of William H. Parker. Parker ushered in a new era of policing in Los Angeles. A well-educated man from the flatlands of South Dakota, Parker joined the department on the precipice of the Great Depression. After spending fifteen years on the force, he went off to war and earned several medals in World War II. He returned to the department a hero and rapidly climbed the ranks to chief of police in 1950, serving until his death in 1966.

Days after being sworn in, Parker promised "with all the fiber of [my being to] see to it that crooked rats who would change the City of Angels to the city of diablos will not do so" and that the LAPD would "work for the community, not rule it."[46] Only half of that promise would be kept. Parker transformed the ethos of the department in many ways. Taking bribes and accepting payoffs were no longer tolerated. He believed that officers should be of high moral character and vigorously trained. He recruited lean athletic types with military experience. The beer-bellied officer with a penchant for donuts was discouraged from applying, urged to retire, told to find other employment, or ordered to shape up or ship out. High physical fitness standards were put in place to separate the men from the slobs.

Parker embraced a paramilitary police model that would earn the force both fame and infamy. Professionalism became the department's ethos, earning it a reputation as "the finest [police department] in the world."[47] Parker also advocated proactive policing. In his book *To Protect and to Serve*, Joe Domanick implies that hassling people was a by-product of proactive policing. Unfortunately, people in areas like South Central received a disproportionate amount of that harassment. Just hanging out and swapping stories with the fellas on the corner got you checked out. Riding in a car with two or more other "Brothers" got you stopped.

Said one officer who went through the academy during Parker's regime, "the entire essence of an L.A. officer's training and development at the academy was that we were the people who had the responsibility for eliminating the lice from the community. It was a responsibility that was taken seriously." To carry out that responsibility, the city furnished Parker with the latest technology. Parker asked for and received a seventeen-helicopter, one-fixed-wing, seventy-five-officer LAPD Air Support Division, "the largest airborne municipal law enforcement system in the world," under the guise that the aircraft would be used for riot control only. In truth, the helicopters were used to fight everyday street crime. Said one LAPD pilot, "we [would] watch for people running who weren't dressed as joggers. We [would] try to figure out what they're running from, while keeping track of them. . . . We [would] watch for, maybe, a guy standing by the curb, with a lot of people driving up to talk to him. That could be drugs."[48]

Parker's commitment to keeping Los Angeles from becoming the cesspool he believed New York and Chicago had become was evident as he made his city inhospitable to East Coast gangsters who had ambitions of expanding westward. Gangsters would be met at the train station or the airport by Parker's men and taken to an undisclosed location, where they would be beaten to a pulp and sent home. Parker was determined to make Los Angeles the safest city in the world; under him the department adopted the motto "To Protect and To Serve."

Although Parker was able to reduce crime and improve the caliber of the department's recruits, the LAPD as a whole still suffered from the perception that it was notoriously corrupt, a perception that was not entirely unwarranted. The corruption was simply of a different nature than before. Sure, bribery and payoffs had all but disappeared. However, rumor had it that Parker employed the Organized Crime and Intelligence Division of the LAPD to keep tabs on politicians and celebrities for purposes of blackmail. Under Parker, the LAPD cemented its reputation for brutality, particularly within the minority community. A study of coroners' records from 1947 to 1966 revealed that of the 319 persons killed by members of the LAPD, more than half were people of color. Also, 313 of the deaths were ruled justifiable homicide; five were considered accidental, excusable, involuntary, or undetermined, and only one was classified as unjustifiable.[49]

Parker had been in office a little more than a year in 1951 when the public got a sense of how minorities would be treated under his administration. On Christmas Eve 1951, a fracas broke out between police officers and several Mexican American males in a downtown bar, after which the men were hauled to Central Station where officers took turns pummeling them. After the incident, known as "Bloody Christmas," two officers were forced to retire, eight others were indicted, and thirty-six more received official reprimands.

Although Parker had taken action, his feelings about Mexicans were far from egalitarian. Before the U.S. Civil Rights Commission in 1959, he said, "Some of these people have been here since before we were, but some of them aren't far removed from the wild tribes of Mexico."[50] Given Parker's remarks, one wonders if the disciplinary actions he meted out in 1951 were done because the beatings took place inside a police precinct, where members of the press happened to be that night. Had the incident occurred on the street and away from the cameras, would Parker have reprimanded the officers? The answer may lie in the events that unfolded in 1961 when members of the LAPD and the Nation of Islam clashed on the streets of Los Angeles. Officers stopped two Muslims who were employed at a local dry cleaner and thus had a suspicious amount of clothing in their possession. Witnesses say that the Muslims were being manhandled by the officers. Police say the Muslims resisted arrest. Shots were fired, by whom is unclear, but seventy-five officers would converge on the scene and spray the Muslim house of worship with bullets. When the melee ended, one Muslim was dead, four were seriously wounded, and one was permanently disabled. Three officers were also injured. No reprimands were issued.

No one except the mayor (who maintained that race relations in Los Angeles were among the best in the country) was surprised when Watts imploded four years later—the result of worsening conditions and police harassment of African Americans.

Parker was a complex figure. He preached professionalism, yet he had his men spy on those he considered enemies of the department. He demanded that his troops be of high moral character, yet he showed no desire to racially integrate police squad cars and other assignments. In fact, eight years after the U.S. Supreme Court ruled that segregation in public schools was unconstitutional, thirteen years after his predecessor had promised to integrate the department, and fourteen years after President Harry Truman ordered the integration of the armed forces, Parker finally begrudgingly integrated the department's patrol cars, but only because Sam Yorty pledged to do so if the voters elected him mayor. Not wanting to be upstaged, Parker relented.[51]

In the end, Parker created an insular and unaccountable bureaucratic power that he passed on to his successor. And because Parker always felt he was right, it was only natural that the hierarchy that developed under him would believe it was right, also. Parker showed the city that the chief of police was not just some run-of-the-mill goddamn civil service department head, but instead was one of the most important political players in the city. His message was clear: independence from "political interference" meant that "nobody fucked with his department, but he could pop anybody he wished."[52]

Parker's death preceded the Panthers' arrival by two years. It is safe to say that the Panthers would have ranked high on his list of those he considered among the city's riffraff and would have been treated accordingly.

Nevertheless Parker left a legacy that for all intents and purposes represented the crosshairs into which the Black Panthers would eventually step.

Chief Reddin and the Panthers

When the Panthers opened their Los Angeles office, Tom Reddin was the city's chief of police. Although Reddin was not a Parker clone, he was no Keystone Cop. He served until May 1969 before retiring suddenly to take a lucrative position at a local television station. Reddin was not as fanatical about law and order as Parker had been, but he was just as vigilant. Under him, the department's fearsome Metropolitan Division of fifty-five swelled to 220 members. These officers would go out and "roust anything strange that moved on the streets."[53]

Reddin believed that the Panthers represented a threat to the safety of his officers and their authority on the streets. He recognized, however, that to a certain extent the Panthers' views reflected the dissatisfaction of many inner-city Blacks with city government and thus deserved a hearing. Consequently, Reddin met with Panther officials and discussed with them different ways to improve police relations with the community. These meetings aroused resentment among rank-and-file officers. All Black militants, as far as they were concerned, were the enemies of the police department and had to be suppressed to the fullest extent. Reddin responded to these grumblings early on, declaring that "sitting down to talk with militants of whatever persuasion does not mean an automatic compromise of position or giving in to pressure." It means very simply "that conditions in society today demand that we communicate with all segments of the community."[54]

Despite Reddin's public appearance of cooperation, the police kept Panther leaders under close surveillance and looked for the least little opportunity to provoke a confrontation with them.[55] In fact, the Panthers became one of the Metro Division's pet projects as the unit often stopped known Panther vehicles on general principle. Officers would rip out side compartments, disassemble dashboards, and smash tail lights on the assumption that the vehicle would be stopped again before the driver could return home or make the necessary repair. Other times Panthers would be ordered out of the car at gunpoint, where they would be provoked into giving the officer an excuse to shoot them. Mostly though, these stops were designed to intimidate the Panthers and to make them aware that Los Angeles was not Oakland. Al Armour recalled that on one occasion he was forced out of the car and made to get on his knees, after which an officer fired several shots just above his head. Armour's experience may have been an extreme one, but it shows the level of enmity that members of the LAPD had for the Panthers.

Police harassment of the Panthers became so intense according to Wayne Pharr that many Panthers stopped driving, opting instead to walk or take the bus when they needed to go somewhere.[56] Driving made it easier for police to instigate trouble under the subterfuge of the routine traffic stop or some other type of moving violation.

When the police were not hassling and rousting the Panthers, they were ridiculing and taunting them. According to Geronimo Pratt, two Metro Squad members spent their evenings riding up and down Central Avenue "wearing foot-high Afro wigs and bright dashikis and yelling 'Power to the People!' through a high-powered bullhorn."[57]

Murder at Montclair

Six months after the Panthers announced their arrival, four of its members were involved in a deadly skirmish that came to be known as Murder at Montclair. On August 5, 1968, two police officers followed a car, which according to them was being driven erratically, to a gas station at West Adams Boulevard and Montclair Street. Inside the car sat four Panthers. In court, when the officers were asked why they followed the vehicle, they responded that the occupants appeared "suspicious."[58] The exact details of the incident are sketchy. The officers approached the vehicle and asked the driver, Steve Bartholomew, to produce his license. After Bartholomew admitted to not having a license, police claimed they were about to question passengers Tommy Lewis, eighteen, Robert Lawrence, twenty-two, and Little Tony, twenty-one, when suddenly they were hit by gunfire. The officers returned fire. When the fusillade ended, two young men lay dead, another died en route to the hospital, and a fourth Panther escaped. One officer was critically wounded in the abdomen, and the other was shot in both legs. Little Tony, the brother of Steve Bartholomew, somehow managed to elude the spray of gunfire and fled the scene.

Another report indicated that after the car pulled into the gas station, Bartholomew got out and opened the hood. According to an eyewitness, the driver of the squad car stepped out and walked toward Bartholomew, while the second officer walked over to the side and rear of the vehicle. At this point the eyewitness admitted that things happened so quickly that he could not be certain, but he thought the second officer opened fire on one of the occupants as he was getting out of the car.

Yet another report had one officer ordering Bartholomew to open the trunk while the second officer directed the others out of the car. Without warning, according to witnesses, the second officer opened fire on Robert Lawrence. Steve Bartholomew charged the first officer and was shot but not killed. Then Tommy Lewis emerged from the back seat and was shot. Panthers claimed that one of the officers walked up to Steve Bartholomew where he lay wounded and shouted, "Nigger, you should be dead . . . nigger," then shot him four or five times in the head."[59] Given the time of day and the location of the incident (a gas station located at a busy intersection), this seems unlikely.

As one might imagine, the deaths of Bartholomew, Lawrence, and Lewis caused quite a stir in the Black community. Hearing rumors of the possibility of another Watts uprising, Governor Ronald Reagan authorized Lieutenant Governor Robert Finch to look into the situation. Mayor Sam Yorty met with Finch and assured him that there was little to be concerned about.[60]

The outcry had barely fizzled out when two more Panthers were shot and one killed by police officers in October. Again the details vary. But Bruce Richards was wounded in the battle and charged with attempted murder, and Walter "Toure" Pope was killed.

No Panther branch or chapter experienced more harassment and suffered more casualties than the L.A. Panthers. The situation had gotten so bad that "safe houses" had to be established in order to stay out of the LAPD's line of fire. In April 1969, as members of the BPP were meeting at their Central Avenue location, one hundred officers surrounded the building. Recognizing the danger they were in, Elaine Brown and Joan Kelley astutely notified the media and briefed them on the situation, prompting the officers to withdraw. Weeks later the LAPD successfully carried out its first raid of Panther offices, arresting nine of the occupants. During the month of April, the LAPD made fifty-six arrests of forty-two Panthers.[61]

Los Angeles Panthers Get a Taste of Chicago

Months later, on September 8, 1969, police raided the Watts breakfast program, undoubtedly as part of an FBI directive to eradicate the Panthers' breakfast programs. On May 15, 1969, in an internal memo, FBI director J. Edgar Hoover wrote, "The Breakfast for Children Program represents the best and most influential activity going for the BPP and, as such, is potentially the greatest threat to efforts by authorities to neutralize the BPP and destroy what it stands for."

Perhaps the most dramatic and widely known raid occurred in early December of 1969. The LAPD deployed its highly lethal SWAT teams along with three hundred uniformed officers to raid three Panther facilities. Illegal weapons were the justification for the raids, which were eerily similar to those that occurred in Chicago four days earlier. More specifically, the government's plan called for the police to zero in on Geronimo Pratt's bedroom.

Fortunately for Pratt, the leader of the chapter at the time, he often slept on the floor, and did so that night. As in Chicago, a government informant (Melvin Cotton Smith) provided the LAPD and the FBI with the floor plan of the dwelling. Like William O'Neal in Chicago, Smith had been in charge of security in Los Angeles. Given what had transpired in Chicago days earlier, the Los Angeles Panthers were not entirely unprepared—the walls of the house had been fortified with sandbags and the windows with steel planks, and gas masks had been acquired to stave off tear gas.

After exchanging gunfire with the authorities and holding them off for nearly four hours, the Panthers surrendered. Apparently the Panthers posed more of a challenge than some had expected. According to news reports, midway through the firefight, at 6:50 A.M., Mayor Yorty contacted the secretary of the army requesting reinforcements. The request apparently fell on deaf ears. Finally, after three hours and ten minutes had gone by, the request was approved, but by then the battle had ended. Miraculously, no one was killed.

Livid at the army's foot-dragging, Yorty supposedly complained that "our officers were sitting ducks and were outgunned by the occupants of the building."[62] No one, including the army's upper echelon, believed that the LAPD was outgunned by the Panthers, which may explain why the secretary acted cautiously and shrewdly waited until the Panthers had surrendered before approving Yorty's request.

Local and National Responses to the Raids

The raid on Panther headquarters prompted a flurry of responses and reactions. On a national level, Representatives Louis Stokes (Ohio), Abner J. Mikva (New York), William C. Clay (Missouri), Shirley Chisholm (New York), John Conyers (Michigan), Don Edwards (California), Augustus F. Hawkins (California), and William F. Ryan (New York) asked President Nixon to have the National Commission on Violence investigate the raids of Panther offices in Los Angeles and Chicago. Locally, at a community meeting held at the Second Baptist Church the afternoon of the riot, people were furious. Franklin Alexander shouted from the audience that "the Police are Vamping on the Community."[63] Some of the notables at this gathering of nearly three hundred people were longtime civil rights activist Rev. Thomas Kilgore, John Mack of the Urban League, and California state senator Mervyn Dymally. Most agreed that an organization or coalition should be formed to unify the community. The difficulty of such an effort was evidenced by the ideological differences between the NAACP, CORE, the Urban League, and the Black Panther Party. In fact, during the LAPD's search for the Panther who fled the service station in the summer of 1968, Bobby Seale lashed out against leaders of CORE and the Urban League who were urging the Panthers to surrender Little Tony to the police. Said Seale, "they are bootlicking niggers. . . . the Black Panthers will never give up one of its own to the murdering racist pigs."[64]

The meeting was the first step toward bridging the schism that existed between the assimilationists and nationalists, the moderates and radicals, and the young and old. Most were willing to put aside their differences to unite against an institution that most Blacks believed was insensitive to their concerns at best, and hostile to them at worst.

Many white officials were surprised that the Black community rallied behind the Panthers. Even those Blacks who did not wholly believe in their tactics could not deny the Panthers' dedication to the community. For some Blacks the attack on the Panther headquarters was more than just an affront to the Panther organization itself; it was also an affront to the Black community and its right to self-determination. "This involves far more than just the attack on the Panther headquarters. This is an organized attempt to silence all strongholds of black dissent,"[65] one Black resident remarked.

Booker Griffin, a columnist for the Los Angeles Sentinel, covered the raids in great depth. Aware of the police raid on Panther offices in Illinois days earlier that left Mark Clark and Fred Hampton dead, Griffin pointed out that the raids were part of a greater plot. Said Griffin, "Raids on three Panther locations early Monday morning brought the full force of the authoritarians' national conspiracy against the Party to grotesque reality in our backyard."[66] In one particular news article, Griffin makes two very insightful points. He first contends that the ethical practices of local enforcement are what gave rise to the Panthers. Second, he maintained that one of the reasons the Panthers received so much support was because many in the African American community could identify with their struggles. The Panthers gave voice to a cross section of the community that organizations such as CORE, NAACP, and the Urban League were not able to reach.

While the Panthers' version of police provocation drew sympathy from many quarters, police officials tell a very different story. Former police chief Daryl Gates wrote in his autobiography that the precipitating event occurred on the evening of Friday, November 28, when a young woman complained to Captain Ted Morton about the noise blasting out of a loudspeaker at a nearby residence. Morton approached the dwelling and was permitted to step inside, whereupon he was met with a .45-caliber automatic pistol pointed at him. Morton quickly identified himself as a police officer. "I don't care who you are," said Black Panther George Smith. "I'm counting to three and you'd better be out of here by then." Morton turned and found himself looking down the barrel of a pump-shotgun held by Panther Paul Redd. Redd began to count. Morton left.

Morton went back to Newton Division and wrote out a crime report charging assault with a deadly weapon, and arrest warrants were issued for Smith and Redd. Given the Panthers' reputation, the police assumed that serving the warrants would not be easy. On the morning of December 8, a forty-man assault team, sixteen of them members of SWAT, were deployed to the address. At 5:30 A.M. the entry team banged on the door at 4115 South Central, announcing, "There's a warrant for your arrest. Open the door." Hearing movement but getting no response, they tried to force open the door, to no avail. A shootout ensued. Hours passed. High-powered rifles continued to fire steadily across the street at one another. Finally, according to Daryl Gates, a deputy chief at the time, it was decided that the police needed a grenade launcher, but the LAPD did not have one. Only the military had them. Gates called the U.S. Marines at Camp Pendleton to find out if the LAPD could borrow their grenade launcher. The commanding officer said, "You're probably going to have to get permission from the Department of Defense and probably the President of the United States." Just as he said that, Gates writes, the officer followed up with "we'll get the equipment together and put it on the road, so you'll have it if you get permission." Said Gates,

> I called Mayor Sam Yorty and asked if he would make the call to Washington. My words seemed unreal. Anytime you even talk about using military equipment in a civil action, it's very serious business. You're bridging an enormous gap. We are not like a military force, going in and blasting a building to smithereens, not caring who gets killed in the process. That's not what the police do. SWAT's objective—our objective—is always to save lives. But having reached this point, we could not see any alternative.

Within the hour "the Pentagon got back to us . . . we had permission to use the grenade launcher." Nobody, not even in the media, ever learned the whole truth: that in a nondescript military vehicle parked in a side street nearby sat one very frightening military grenade launcher.[67]

Raid Has Far-Reaching Consequences

The impact of the December 1969 raid was far-reaching. The raids affected many area businesses, forcing many shop owners to close their doors. One shop owner was quoted as saying, "I was afraid to get out on the street because a black man on the street . . . would be considered a Black Panther by police." Some businesses sustained heavy damage to their property. Neighbors had difficulty breathing due to the large amounts of tear gas in the air. Mrs. Jesse Mae Jones said, "The tear gas came in our windows and we were all choking not knowing what was happening. We rushed to the wash basin to splash water on our faces and gargle. We didn't know what to do or to think."[68] Some residents even complained that they felt terrorized by the police. Suffice to say, the heavy-handed manner in which the LAPD handled the situation was indicative of the department's indifference toward the Black community.

Whites Fear Black Takeover

That the LAPD would draw a bead on the Panthers was not unexpected. By 1965, Blacks had migrated into the city in significant numbers, much the same way they had moved into major cities throughout America. In fact, Chief Parker warned that by 1970 the city would be nearly half-Black. During a television interview in 1965, he proclaimed, "[I]f you want any protection for your home and family . . . you're going to have to get in and support a strong police department. If you don't do that, come 1970, God help you!"[69] The fact that Los Angeles's Black population never exceeded more than 17 percent of the city's total population was beside the point. Many whites believed Parker, and as a result turned a blind eye to the Gestapo tactics used against the Panthers by law enforcement. Furthermore, fear of a Black take-over enabled the mayor to masterfully play the race card and push back Tom Bradley's 1969 challenge to his incumbency.

Bradley had run a solid campaign and led comfortably heading into the last week of the race, and on election night he reportedly had a fifteen-point lead. However, as the night grew old absentee ballots began to trickle in. Historically, absentee ballots tend to go against Black candidates when their opponent is white, and this contest was no different. By the end of the night Bradley had lost a close race. How did a seemingly insurmountable lead dissipate in a matter of hours? Because Yorty played on the fears that many whites had of a Black-run city.

In predominantly white areas of the city, for example, bumper stickers with a Black fist proclaiming "Bradley Power" appeared on billboards, buildings, and street signs. Yorty campaign ads beneath a big picture of Bradley asked, "Will you be safe with this man?" And "make Los Angeles a black city" brochures—designed to look like Bradley campaign literature—were being left on the porches and doorsteps of white residences.

Perhaps the best illustration of the type of campaign Yorty waged, and a harbinger of what was to come, was a picture taken the night of the primary months earlier, as Tom Bradley was delivering his victory speech. With flashbulbs popping, there inadvertently turned out to be "only blacks on the platform" except for Stephen Reinhardt, a top Bradley aide. The image was precisely counter to the rainbow coalition the Bradley campaign was trying to project, and the next day when Reinhardt saw the picture in the papers, he winced but then forgot about it. "I thought," he would later say, "it was the last time I would see that picture. I was wrong. The picture appeared on a Yorty mailer the weekend before the general election—but there was one difference: my face was colored black, and the message underneath read, 'we need a mayor for our city.'"[70] The message was clear—if Bradley was elected he would fill all of his appointments with other African Americans.

Yorty's underhanded tactics were successful because whites heeded Parker's warning, erroneous as it was. In their minds, under a Bradley regime, Blacks (with the Panthers leading the charge) would have taken over the city and moved on its white residents by killing all the men and raping all the women. Voting against Bradley enabled whites to derail any plans Bradley or other subversive Blacks may have had along those lines.

Again, the idea of a Black takeover, as preposterous as it was, was for some whites very real. Even Charles Manson bought into the idea. Manson and his followers hoped to start a massive race war that would lead to the extermination of Blacks. Manson's plan involved killing several prominent whites and leaving behind clues that would lead the police to believe that the Black Panthers were responsible.[71] The fact that a schizophrenic like Manson believed that a Black takeover was in the works may provide some insight into the mind-set of other whites who were of the same opinion.

Friends, Supporters, and Allies Beware

Much has been made of the government's penchant for cultivating ill will between the Panthers and other Black groups such as Us[72] and the Blackstone Rangers. But insufficient attention has been given to the government's harassment of the Party's white supporters. Not content to harass the Panthers, the FBI also set out to make life miserable for their white friends and allies. In June 1969, sheriff's deputies along with FBI agents armed with rifles and shotguns forcibly entered the apartment of Joanne Gilbert, a young lady who had been assisting the Panthers with the John Huggins Breakfast Program, under the pretense that they received an anonymous tip that she was harboring two Panthers who were suspects in the murder of a Santa Ana police officer.[73]

The FBI made a series of attempts to destroy the confidence between the Panthers and Donald Freed, one of their major supporters. Freed, a writer and an award-winning playwright, headed an organization of BPP sympathizers called "Friends of the Panthers" that included Shirley Sutherland, Elliot Gould, and Elizabeth Taylor, among others. Sutherland, wife of Donald Sutherland, had long been active in humanitarian efforts. She was involved in establishing health care centers in Canada, where her father had been the premier of Saskatchewan. The committee's primary task was to raise money for bail and various others court costs.

In July 1969, the Los Angeles FBI field office sent the Panthers a memorandum bearing Freed's name and address. Written in a condescending tone and including a list of six precautions whites should keep in mind when dealing with the Panthers, the memo was calculated to cause a "rift between the Black Panther Party and their assisting organizations."[74] A few days later, the bureau posted leaflets in a park near a Panther-sponsored national conference in Oakland alleging that Freed was a police informant.[75]

When efforts to sully Freed's name proved unsuccessful, the FBI took great pains to pursue an intensive local investigation of Freed for "harboring" and "possession of illegal firearms." The contents of one particular memo read,

> It is felt that any prosecution or exposure of either Freed or [name deleted] will severely hurt the BPP. Any exposure will not only deny the Panthers money, but additionally, would cause other white supporters of the BPP to withdraw their support. It is felt that the Los Angeles chapter of the BPP could not operate without the financial support of white supporters.[76]

That same year Freed and Sutherland were arrested on charges of illegally possessing hand grenades. Charges were finally dropped when it was learned that the "radical" who delivered the explosives to the Sutherland home was in fact a government agent.[77] When that tactic failed, Phil Denny, an agent assigned to the COINTELPRO division of the Los Angeles field office, managed to get Freed fired from San Fernando Valley College and prevented his obtaining a new faculty position at Cal State Fullerton.[78]

The FBI attempted to get at another Panther supporter, Ed Pearl of the Peace and Freedom Party (PFP), by sending him a cautionary letter bearing a fictitious signature. A bureau memo describing the letter says:

> The writer states that although he is not a member of the BPP, he is a Mexican who is trusted by BPP members. The writer advises that he has learned from BPP members that certain whites in the PFP who get in the way of the Panthers will be dealt with in a violent manner. The object sought in his letter is to cause a breach between the PFP and the BPP. The former organization had been furnishing money and support to the latter.[79]

Hollywood celebrities who were supportive of Panther goals or who attended Panther functions were also targeted. Whites were especially despised by the FBI, and celebrities who lent their name to Panther causes earned Hoover's undying contempt. Movie producer Bert Schneider as well as actors Marlon Brando, Barbara Nash, and Candice Bergen were just a few of the celebrities who were pestered by the FBI.

In June of 1970, FBI headquarters approved an anonymous letter inform-ing *Variety* gossip columnist Army Archerd that Jane Fonda had appeared at a Panther fund-raising gala, noting, "It can be expected that Fonda's involve-ment with the BPP cause could detract from her status with the general pub-lic if reported in a Hollywood 'gossip column.'"[80]

The bureau's attempts to destroy the Panthers were far-reaching. In a study entitled "Local News Coverage of the Black Panther Party," the author dem-onstrated that the Panthers were usually depicted as gun-toting anti-white demagogues.[81] With the release of FBI documents, we now know that in some cases the bureau and the media were in collusion in this depiction. In 1970 the Los Angeles office identified two local news reporters it believed might be willing to help in the effort to discredit the BPP, and they received permission to

> Discreetly contact [name deleted] for the purpose of ascertaining his amenability to the preparation of a program which would present the true facts about the Black Panther Party as part of counterintelligence effort.[82]

Los Angeles headquarters also supplied information and materials to a Los Angeles newsroom that expressed an interest in airing a series of unflattering stories about the Panthers.[83] Specifically, in July 1970, the FBI passed along information to a Los Angeles TV news commentator who agreed to air several anti-Panther news segments, especially on the subject of white liberals contrib-uting to the BPP.[84] In October the Los Angeles division sent headquarters a copy of an FBI-assisted television editorial and reported that another newsman was preparing yet another editorial attack on the Panthers.[85]

The manner in which the Panthers were framed by the media may have paled in comparison to how their supporters were portrayed. One promising actress had her reputation smeared and her personal life turned topsy-turvy when a fabricated story made its way into the *Los Angeles Times*. In correspon-dence sent by the Los Angeles office to J. Edgar Hoover on April 27, 1970, one agent wrote,

> Bureau permission is requested to publicize the pregnancy of Jean Seberg, well-known movie actress, by_____ Black Panther Party (BPP)____ _____ by advising Hollywood gossip columnists in the Los Angeles area of the situation. It is felt that the possible publication of Seberg's plight could cause her embarrassment and serve to cheapen her image with the general public.[86]

It was proposed that the following letter from a fictitious person be sent to local columnists:

> I was just thinking about you and remembered I still owe you a favor. So ____ _____ I was in Paris last week and ran into Jean Seberg, who was heavy with

baby. I thought she and Romaine had gotten together again, but she confided the child belonged to _____ of the Black Panthers, one_____. The dear girl is getting around!

Any way, I thought you might get a scoop on the others. Be good and I'll see you soon.[87]

Love,
Sol!

In a memo written weeks later to Hoover, an agent wrote that the bureau felt it would be better to wait approximately two additional months until Seberg's pregnancy would be obvious to everyone.[88] Joyce Haber, a well-known Hollywood gossip columnist, eventually published a story in the *Los Angeles Times* that sullied the actress's image, referring to Seberg as Miss A. An excerpt of the letter is below. The article reads,

> the outgoing Miss A was pursuing a number of free-spirited causes, among them the black revolution. She lived what she believed which raised a few Establishment eyebrows: Not because her escorts were often blacks, but because they were black nationalists.
>
> And now, according to all these really "in" international sources, Topic A is the baby bliss A is expecting, and Papa's said to be a rather prominent Black Panther.[89]

To make matters worse, *Newsweek* picked up the story. Apparently upon seeing the exposé, Seberg went into premature labor at the beginning of her third trimester.

The concocted story put a tremendous strain on Seberg's marriage. She was verbally and physically abused by her husband, Romain Gary, who was convinced the story was true. The stress apparently proved too much for Seberg, and she gave birth to a stillborn child. Determined to show the story for what it was, Seberg insisted on an open casket so that everyone could see her white infant. The negative publicity and the death of her child caused her to have several nervous breakdowns over the years. Some say that Seberg never recovered from the ordeal, attempting to take her own life every year on the anniversary of the baby's death. Severe chronic depression eventually got the better of Seberg and she committed suicide in 1979. In December 1980 her husband shot and killed himself in Paris.

Conclusion

No chapter or branch suffered more casualties than did the Los Angeles Panthers. Being a Panther in Los Angeles meant putting one's life in peril on a daily basis. Given the assault launched against the Los Angeles office, it is amazing that more Panthers were not killed. Even more amazing was the Panthers' ability to focus on their objectives while in the throes of such intense commotion. Although in a state of siege, Panthers were able to put in place a set of programs designed to increase poor people's lot. While the chapter was obviously unable to uplift the entire Black community, many lives were touched by the Panthers' efforts. Not only were more than a few households impacted by the breakfast programs, the free grocery and free clothing giveaways, and the free tuberculosis testing, but the entire community was affected by the example set by the Panthers.

For years Black Angelenos had allowed themselves to be manhandled and treated with indifference by the state. The LAPD treated Blacks as subhuman and met little or no resistance from a fearful African American community. The Panthers demonstrated that it was important for Blacks to stand up to the police. Many Panthers resigned themselves to the fact that they were either going to make Los Angeles a place where Blacks could live peacefully and flourish, or they were going to die trying. There was honor in showing the police that their disregard for Black life would be met with unusual valor and resistance. The Panthers reversed the image of police omnipotence.

It was also equally important for the Panthers to exhibit a do-for-self approach, one that showed Blacks that they did not have to subject themselves to the humiliation of begging the city's social service agencies for assistance. Going to a welfare office, for example, could often be a degrading experience. The applicant would have to sit and reveal details of her personal life while the often white caseworker spoke condescendingly and belittled the applicant, all the while never bothering to make eye contact.

The Panthers' contributions were made at great risk to themselves, but so were those of their supporters. Several Hollywood celebrities risked being blacklisted by associating with the Panthers, and at least one suffered tremendously as result of her support of the Panthers. The role the FBI and the press played in the eventual suicide of Jean Seberg is indicative of the depths to which the government stooped to quell dissent. Destroying innocent lives in the process was simply an unfortunate by-product of maintaining a compliant populace.

Notes

1. Mike Davis, *City of Quartz: Excavating the Future in Los Angeles* (New York: Verso, 1990), 296.

2. *Los Angeles Times*, October 22, 1972.

3. Anthony Oberschall, "The Los Angeles Riot of August 1965," in *The Black Revolt*, ed. James A. Geschwender, 269 (Englewood Cliffs, N.J.: Prentice Hall, 1971).

4. James N. Upton, "Citizen Participation and Democratic Theory: The 1965 and 1992 L.A. Riots," in *Black and Latino/a Politics: Issues in Political Development in the United States*, ed. Jessica Lavariega Monforti and William E. Nelson Jr. (Miami: Barnhardt and Ash, 2006).

5. Magnificent Montague and Bob Baker, *Burn, Baby! Burn: The Autobiography of Magnificent Montague* (Urbana: University of Illinois Press, 2003), 125.

6. Elizabeth Poe, "Watts," *Frontier* (September 1965): 5–7.

7. Ibid.

8. John and LaRee Caughey, "A New Force—the Blacks," in *Los Angeles: Biography of a City*, ed. John and LaRee Caughey, 461 (Berkeley: University of California Press, 1976).

9. Douglas Flamming, *Bound for Freedom: Black Los Angeles in Jim Crow America* (Berkeley: University of California Press, 2005), 129.

10. James M. Alexander, "Appeal to Reason," attached to J. B. Wilson to Hon. Geo C. Pardee, June 25; James M. Alexander, "Official Call of the Afro-American State Congress, to Convene at Riverside, California, August 27–29, 1906," both in file.

11. Flamming, *Bound for Freedom*, 129.

12. Lonnie G. Bunch III, "A Past Not Necessarily Prologue: The Afro-American in Los Angeles," in *20th Century Los Angeles*, ed. Norman M. Klein and Martin J. Schiesl, 107 (Claremont, Calif.: Regina Books, 1990).

13. Davis, *City of Quartz*, 62–63.

14. *Flash*, December 31, 1929, 11; July 27, 1929, 12.

15. Bobby Seale, *Seize the Time* (New York: Random House, 1970), 269.

16. Elaine Brown, *A Taste of Power: A Black Woman's Story* (New York: Pantheon, 1992), 118.

17. Ibid., 125.

18. Roland Freeman, interview by Judson L. Jeffries, January 2006.

19. Earl Anthony, *Picking Up the Gun* (New York: Dial Press, 1970), 73.

20. Oberschall, "The Los Angeles Riot of August 1965," 269.

21. *Los Angeles Sentinel*, February 10, 1972.

22. A captain was the highest position within the rank and file; he or she was the direct link between the foot soldiers and the official ministries.

23. Earl Anthony, *Picking Up the Gun* (New York: Dial Press, 1970).

24. Citizen's Research and Investigation Committee and Louis E. Tackwood, *The Glass House Tapes: The Story of an Agent-Provocateur and the New Police-Intelligence Complex* (New York: Avon Books, 1973).

25. Long John Washington, interview by Malcolm Foley, August 28, 2005.

26. Brown, *A Taste of Power*, 141.

27. Roland Freeman, interview by Malcolm Foley, July 25, 2005.

28. Marvin Jackson, interview by Malcolm Foley, July 25, 2005.

29. Wayne Pharr, interview by Malcolm Foley, July 6, 2005.

30. David Hilliard and Lewis Cole, *This Side of Glory* (Boston: Little Brown, 1993), 213–214.

31. Talibah Shakir, interview by Judson L. Jeffries, March 2006.

32. Washington, interview.

33. "Panthers Get Permit to Use Park," *Los Angeles Times*, October 25, 1968, D6B.

34. "LA Panthers Begin Free Breakfast Program," *The Black Panther*, June 14, 1969, 3.

35. "LA Open First Community Center," *The Black Panther*, November 11, 1969, 2.

36. Ibid.

37. "L.A. Oppression," *The Black Panther*, November 11, 1969, 2.

38. Talibah Shakir, interview by Judson L. Jeffries, March 2006.

39. "LA Open First Community Center," *The Black Panther*, November 11, 1969, 2.

40. Ibid.

41. *The Black Panther*, February 28, 1970.

42. "L.A. Pigs Vamp on Free Breakfast Program," *The Black Panther*, September 13, 1969, 6.

43. Martin J. Schiesl, "Behind the Badge: The Police and Social Discontent in Los Angeles Since 1950," in Klein and Schiesl, *20th Century Los Angeles*, 153.

44. Joe Domanick, *To Protect and to Serve* (New York: Pocket Books, 1994), 194.

45. *The Police: An Interview by Donald McDonald with William H. Parker* (Santa Barbara, Calif.: Center for the Study of Democratic Institutions, 1962), 25.

46. Ibid., 103.

47. Ibid., 162.

48. Ibid., 112, 115.

49. Ed Cray, Testimony before the Assembly Interim Committee on the Judiciary, Los Angeles: State of California, October 16, 1967.

50. Quoted in Sophia Spalding, "The Constable Blunders: Police Abuse in Los Angeles's Black and Latino Communities, 1945–1965" (Thesis, UCLA, Department of Urban Planning, 1989), 11.

51. Domanick, *To Protect and to Serve*.

52. Ibid., 198, 199.

53. Daryl F. Gates with Diane Shah, *Chief: My Life in the LAPD* (New York: Bantam, 1992), 112–114.

54. Los Angeles Police Department, "The Chief's Message," April 24, 1968; Matthews, "Chief Reddin," p. 92.

55. Schiesl, "Behind the Badge," 169.

56. Pharr, interview.

57. Jack Olsen, *Last Man Standing* (New York: Random House, 2000), 51.

58. "Panther Threats Make Boy, 12, Cry in Court," *Los Angeles Sentinel*, D2.

59. Anthony, *Picking Up the Gun*, 137.

60. Phil Fradkin and Dial Torgerson, "Negro Leaders Urge Suspect in Police Shootout to Give Up," *Los Angeles Times*, August 7, 1968.

61. "Repression and Harassment of L.A. Panthers Stepped Up," *The Black Panther*, May 31, 1969, 20.

62. Jim Cleaver, "Area Residents Show Anger Over Shootouts," *Los Angeles Sentinel*, December 11, 1969, A1.

63. Ibid.

64. Dial Torgerson, "Police Seize Panther Fortress in 4-Hour Gunfight Arrest," *Los Angeles Times*, December 9, 1969, B27.

65. Jim Cleaver, "Area Residents Show Anger Over Shootouts," *Los Angeles Sentinel*, December 11, 1969, A1.

66. Booker Griffin, "Panther Genocide Plot Arrives in L.A.," *Los Angeles Sentinel*, December 11, 1969, A7.

67. Gates, *Chief: My Life in the LAPD*.

68. Charles Baireuther, "Panthers-Police Shootout Brings Mixed Reactions," *Los Angeles Sentinel*, December 11, 1969, A3, C12.

69. Domanick, *To Protect and to Serve*, 294.

70. J. Gregory Payne and Scott C. Ratzan, *Tom Bradley: The Impossible Dream* (Santa Monica, Calif.: Roundtable Publishing, 1986), 91, 106.

71. "Sharon Tate Campaigned for Bradley," *The Philadelphia Tribune*, December 9, 1969, 1.

72. Much has been written about the Us-Panther feud and it will not be discussed in this chapter. We contend that both the Panthers and Us have histories of their own and they should not be defined by this strained relationship. While many see the histories of the Los Angeles offices of the BPP and Us as inextricably linked, they are not.

73. "L.A. Friends of Panthers," *The Black Panther*, July 5, 1969, 17.

74. Memorandum from FBI headquarters to Los Angeles field office, July 25, 1969.

75. Memorandum from San Francisco field office to FBI headquarters, July 28, 1969.

76. Memorandum from Los Angeles field office to FBI headquarters, September 24, 1969.

77. Michael Newton, *The FBI Plot: How the FBI Fought against Civil Rights in America* (Los Angeles: Holloway House, 1981), 162.

78. M. Wesley Swearingen, *FBI Secrets: An Agent's Expose* (Cambridge, Mass.: South End Press, 1995), 116.

79. Memorandum from G. C. Moore to W. C. Sullivan, December 12, 1968.

80. Memorandum from FBI headquarters to Los Angeles field office, June 25, 1970.

81. Judson L. Jeffries, "Local News Coverage of the Black Panther Party: An Analysis of the Baltimore, Cleveland and New Orleans Press," *Journal of African American Studies* 7 (Spring 2004): 19–38.

82. Memorandum from Los Angeles field office to FBI headquarters, February 16, 1970; Memorandum from FBI headquarters to Los Angeles field office, March 5, 1970 (this memorandum bears Director Hoover's initials).

83. Memorandum from FBI headquarters to Los Angeles and San Francisco field offices, May 27, 1970.

84. Memorandum from Los Angeles field office to FBI headquarters, September 10, 1970, 2.

85. Memorandum from Los Angeles field office to FBI headquarters, October 23, 1970.

86. Memorandum from SAC Los Angeles to FBI director, April 2, 1970.

87. Ibid.

88. Memorandum from SAC Los Angeles to FBI director, April 2, 1970.

89. Memorandum from SAC Los Angeles Office to FBI director, June 3, 1970.

Conclusion

A Way of Remembering the Black Panther Party in the Post–Black Power Era: Resentment, Disaster, and Disillusionment

Floyd W. Hayes III

> Each generation must, out of relative obscurity, discover its mission, fulfill it, or betray it.
>
> —FRANTZ FANON, *THE WRETCHED OF THE EARTH*

> Armed with a correct ideology, pursuing all efforts to make sure that the black working class has power and gives direction to the revolutionary struggle, working to develop all forms of popular struggle as well as a network of unknown revolutionaries, preparing for the long-range armed struggle inside the United States, uniting all into a disciplined, centralized, mass party or organization. . . . We will be carrying on the work of all the black sons and daughters who have died in every corner of Africa and the Americas under the whiplash of racism, capitalism, colonialism, and imperialism. And we shall win without a doubt.
>
> —JAMES FORMAN, *THE MAKING OF BLACK REVOLUTIONARIES*

> Knowing and seeing what is happening in the world
> today, I don't think that there is much of anything that
> one can do about it. But there is one little thing, it seems
> to me, that a man owes to himself. He can look bravely
> at this horrible totalitarian reptile and, while doing so,
> discipline his dread, his fear, and study it coolly, observe
> every slither and convolution of its sensuous movements
> and note down with calmness the pertinent facts. In the
> face of the totalitarian danger, these facts can help a man
> to save himself; and he may be able to call the attention
> of others around him to the presence and meaning of this
> reptile and its multitudinous writhings.
>
> —RICHARD WRIGHT, *THE OUTSIDER*

As the chapters in this volume demonstrate, the Black Panther Party represented an indispensable force in the progressive struggle to transform the landscape of American society during the turbulent 1960s. The Panthers voiced the outrage of America's outsiders who resented the hypocrisy of a society that professed the political values of democracy, equality, freedom, and justice, but in every way historically had devalued them. The men and women of the Black Panther Party marched courageously across the nation's chaotic terrain, seeking to leave their footprints on the sands of time. This battalion of soldiers included more than the organization's most famous personalities. For every Kathleen Cleaver there was a Talibah Shakir in Los Angeles, for every Huey P. Newton there was a John Clark in Baltimore and a Larry Little in Winston-Salem, and for every Elaine Brown there was a Barbara Easley-Cox and an Ethel Parish in Philadelphia. For every well-known Panther, dozens more whose names are forgotten voluntarily stood on the front lines in the "War on Black America" that transpired during the 1960s and early 1970s.

Scores of groups dedicated to wholesale political, economic, and social change sprouted up in the United States during the 1960s, but the Black Panther Party was the only one able to attract a substantial following and appeal to a broad constituency. Clearly and unfortunately, much of what is known about the BPP involves the Bay Area. As Judson L. Jeffries and Ryan Nissim-Sabat say in the book's introduction, the Black Panther Party as an organization is often reduced to Oakland, and Oakland is often reduced to Huey Newton, Bobby Seale, and perhaps Eldridge Cleaver. Often over-looked local offices of the Black Panther Party—branches in Baltimore,

Winston-Salem, Cleveland, Indianapolis, Milwaukee, Philadelphia, and Los Angeles have been examined in this book—made significant contributions to the social development of urban Black communities during the period of Black Power radicalism in the late 1960s and early 1970s. In the midst of mounting a revolutionary struggle against the white-supremacist and capitalist American state, the Panthers also created a plethora of community programs designed to inspire popular revolutionary consciousness and to augment grassroots activism among urban working-class Black citizens. Often in conjunction with local social service and health agencies, local Panther branches established liberation schools, free lunch and breakfast programs, free clothing programs, and free health clinics, which were concrete efforts to provide needed educational and medical assistance to impoverished families. Local Panthers also worked to keep cities safe from gangs and gang violence. Because white cops historically had intimidated and murdered Black citizens with impunity, local Panthers confronted the systemic abuse of police power. In the face of political and legal injustices, local Panthers participated in broad coalition politics, seeking to eliminate Black fears and to encourage Black involvement in the electoral political process. In the face of political and cultural domination, the Panthers demanded self-determination for oppressed and impoverished residents in urban as well as rural areas.

These and other developments represented the spirit of the Black Power Movement, especially the Black Panther Party, at a particular moment in American history. Yet, incredibly, so many of today's younger academics, as well as that generation of younger people who were born during or after the 1980s, know scarcely anything about the development, dynamics, and demise of the Black Power Movement generally, or the Black Panther Party specifically. Knowing very little about this history, this younger generation often seems indifferent to learning the lessons of the historic struggle for Black human rights.

This reality is personally troubling, especially when I reflect on the Black Power Movement with my students or write about that period. Often the process of writing about that historical moment is a way of working through certain dilemmas regarding my own perception of the world. These dilemmas are not merely interesting intellectual problems that can be explored with complete detachment and objectivity. Rather, they are dilemmas that I feel caught up in because I am part of the process I am discussing. Writing thus becomes a potential mode of extrication and personal clarification. This is especially true for me because I was a student activist during the turbulent moments of Black Power radicalism.

Hence, in the remainder of this conclusion, I try to make sense of the ultraconservative shift in American political culture as a way of coming to grips with the significance of the Black Panther Party today. Indeed, since the late 1960s, the hopes and aspirations of Black Power radicalism for an antiracist democratic polity in America have been crushed. We live in tragic times. These are not meaningless times, but times that in fundamental ways are distressingly disastrous in the specific sense that the language and struggle of Black liberation are no longer commensurate with an American scene they once sought to comprehend, contest, and transform.

How did this tragedy occur? For me, the answer begins with the Reaganism of the 1980s and the draconian transition of American political culture to the far right. These are the dominant trends and developments in twenty-first-century America. Inspired by Richard Wright's statement above, I am interested in trying to comprehend the meaning of the American political culture's totalitarian shift to the far right since the 1980s and what this transformation has meant to an understanding of the revolutionary moment of the late 1960s and 1970s. Has the rightward transformation of American political culture set in motion the erasure of the meaning and significance of the Black Panther Party?

The 1980 election of Ronald Reagan as president marked the beginning of the end of an era in modern United States political history—the liberal welfare state. The Reagan regime set in motion a draconian assault on the welfare state's politics, policies, and programs, which were established during the Franklin D. Roosevelt administration in the 1930s. The modern liberal policies associated with Roosevelt's New Deal, which developed in response to the Great Depression, reached their zenith with the implementation of President Lyndon B. Johnson's Great Society experiments in the 1960s.

Many of the ideas, policies, and programs that came to be identified with Reaganism signaled an attempt to roll back the kaleidoscope of history and recapture Adam Smith's eighteenth-century classical liberal political and economic design for an emerging modern society. Classical liberalism, however, became contemporary conservatism. Thus, Smith gave to the national government a minimal role in society and the economy—to serve as guardian (not manager or regulator) of business, monetary interests, and fiscal policies. The ultraconservative Reagan revolt against the modern liberal social service state represented the rhetoric of reducing the role of the federal government and shifting social policy and program responsibilities to the states.

Supported by an ultraconservative conception of the federal government's role as night watchman and strengthened by the cynical language of getting government off the people's backs, the Reagan forces moved quickly to slash the budgets of the Medicaid, Medicare, and food stamp programs. The Comprehensive Employment and Training Act also was terminated. In essence, the so-called Reagan revolution sought to interrupt the modern liberal welfare state's policies, principles, and practices and effectively to redirect the American public's social and political attention to the far right. With a public policy agenda that allowed the rich to get richer and that forced the poor to get poorer, the Reagan forces replaced what they took to be bleeding-heart liberalism with a mean-spirited conservatism.

The Reagan ascendancy also dealt a final blow to the politically and intellectually exhausted civil rights coalition, which had been among the primary supporters and beneficiaries of the welfare state. After the mid-1960s, economic, social, and cultural fissures weakened the foundation that held the coalition together. The liberal coalition, composed largely of white political and economic elites and Black civil rights activists and managerial elites, lost its intellectual power and political hegemony. This happened as the fight to end class inequality during the 1930s and 1940s shifted to the struggle to eradicate racial injustice during the 1950s and 1960s. In an obvious move to discredit those struggling against state-supported racism and for racial democracy, Reagan refused even to meet with national Black political and civil rights elites. In a cynical declaration of the end of racism, he supported an emerging assortment of conservative Black and white idea entrepreneurs, political managers, and media elites who embraced the Reaganite dream of recapturing the laissez-faire capitalist state. It has been this new class of right-wing social managers, representing a convergence of knowledge and power, whose ideas and actions have served to forge a new conservative political and policy hegemony in the United States. With the Reagan presidency, white supremacy experienced a new "morning in America." To be sure, George H. W. Bush's conservative administration and Bill Clinton's neo-liberal presidency of the 1980s and 1990s largely carried out the Reagan political and policy "revolution."

What is most significant about the politically reactionary regime of George W. Bush is its so-called war against terrorism, which has discredited America's standing around the world. Going back to the Clinton administration, a cadre of neo-conservative ideologues and war hawks had long advocated the invasion of Iraq and the overthrow of its leader Saddam Hussein. In the aftermath of the Al Qaeda bombings in the United States on September 11, 2001, which killed thousands, the Bush regime misled America into the invasion of Iraq and the overthrow of its leader Saddam Hussein, arguing that Hussein had colluded with the Al Qaeda leader Osama bin Laden. Moreover, Bush gave the impression that Iraq had weapons of mass destruction and intended to use them against the United States. In reality, however, the Bush regime's 2003 invasion and occupation of Iraq was intended to redesign the Middle East in conformity with America's imperialist interests. Yet as American casualties of the Iraq war continue to mount, together with increasing allegations and incidents of the American military's terrorist crimes against Iraqi prisoners and innocent civilians, it is becoming increasingly apparent that America cannot win the war on terror.

History moves, and a thing can turn into its opposite. Since taking office in 2000, an arrogant and overbearing Bush regime has managed to turn the world against America, as former American allies in Europe and Russia have backed away from supporting America's imperialist designs in the Middle East. America will pay a heavy price for decades to come because of the Bush presidency's reckless and ruthless foreign policy. The related domestic impact of a failed war in Iraq is the Bush regime's totalitarian assertiveness. Managed by iron-fisted zealots—vice president Richard "Dick" Cheney, defense secretary Donald Rumsfeld, political hack Karl Rove, and war policy ideologue Paul Wolfowitz are the prominent figures—the Bush regime has sought to dominate the Congress, the Supreme Court, the Pentagon, the CIA, and the media. The Bush forces have allowed little criticism or dissent. Employing a strategy of secrecy and threatening American citizens with state surveillance, Bush forces have fiercely sought to impose popular submission and fear.

However, as the numbers of dead and wounded American soldiers and journalists rise in Iraq, and as Iraq descends into the chaos and suffering of civil war caused by the American military invasion and occupation, many Americans are losing faith in the viability of Bush's war. Increasing numbers of citizens are concluding that the war was a monumental mistake and that America never should have invaded and occupied Iraq in the first place. Significantly, several American retired military generals have criticized Rumsfeld's management of the war and demanded his removal as secretary of defense. There is a growing realization that the Bush regime's unilateral invasion and occupation of Iraq has made Americans increasingly unsafe, uncertain, and insecure. Out of this arrogance, incompetence, and sheer stupidity is the uncomfortable reality that the war in Iraq is a quagmire; it is the twenty-first-century repetition of the war in Vietnam.

It is against this background that I reflect on the life and times of the Black Panther Party. If the social conditions that brought the Panthers into existence were horrendous, they are even more disastrous today. For more than two decades, the ultra–right wing transformation of America has resulted in an increasingly fragmented and crisis-ridden social order and political economy. In an increasingly global postindustrial managerial economy based fundamentally on the investment, production, and distribution of knowledge and advanced technology, those persons caught in the declining industrial-manufacturing economy now face tragic times. Indeed, the social and economic division of American society is pronounced, as advancement for some is accompanied by desperation for so many. Today, urban Black communities suffer more severe crisis-ridden social conditions than during the

1960s. Fewer job opportunities result in permanent forms of agonizing poverty. Family destabilization has reached epidemic proportions. Big-city public schools fail to provide a quality education and to prepare young Blacks to take their place in the postindustrial social order of knowledge. Homelessness is a growing reality. Health care is declining. Demonstrating an abuse of power, police intimidate and murder urban Blacks at will. More and more urban Blacks find themselves incarcerated in America's prison-industrial complex. Significantly, the ruling white American establishment continues a perpetual war against the human dignity of urban impoverished Black people, which began during the holocaust of enslavement.

Yet these desperate and worsening social conditions have been met by relative silence. Why? Are massive Black social protest and political struggles dead? Have Americans become indifferent to people's suffering? Has a historically undemocratic and unjust American society, caught in a monumentally hypocritical war designed to impose democracy in Iraq, lost its moorings? Has America come to a point in its history when there is a growing senselessness of existence? Has a corrosive culture of nihilism overtaken the American spirit? Is America beyond redemption? Living on the margin between totalitarianism and democracy and witnessing the ultraconservative transformation of American society during the period of post–Black radicalism over the past thirty years, it is difficult to avoid becoming increasingly disillusioned and pessimistic about the prospects of authentic democracy and social justice in America's future.

Appendix

Alan Wolfe's Classification of Political Repression in the United States

Category	Definition	Example
1) Legal Repression	The use of laws and or the legal system for the purpose of neutralizing dissent	Loitering, traffic violations
Harassment Laws	When a law that was originally passed with no political purpose is used to repress	Robbery, assault charges
Inclusion Laws	Determine who should be included in society	Restrictive immigration policies
Process Laws	A law that punishes a person for planning to commit a criminal act	Conspiracy charges
Public Order Laws	Actions which create disorder	Disturbing the peace

(Continued)

Category	Definition	Example
Preventive Practices	Practices employed to control the members of an organization and to discourage others from joining that organization	Frequent arrests and long jail sentences
Political Laws	A law which is enacted for the specific purpose of stifling dissent	Smith Act
2) Political Intelligence	The practice of spying on an organization and causing disruption within that organization	Informers, surveillance
3) Violent Repression	Stifling dissent by using the police and other law enforcement to berate, intimidate, and physically rattle dissenters	Raids, National Guard

Source: Alan Wolfe, *The Seamy Side of Democracy: Repression in America* (New York: David McKay, 1973), 93–124.

Contributors

Kevin L. Brooks is a Ph.D. candidate in the College of Education at Purdue University. He earned his B.A. in journalism in 2000 as well as a master's degree in education at historically Black Florida A&M University in Tallahassee. While a graduate student at Purdue University, Brooks completed an additional master's degree in Health and Kinesiology in 2005.

Omari L. Dyson is a Ph.D. candidate in the College of Education at Purdue University. He earned his B.S. in experimental psychology at the University of South Carolina in 2001. He then matriculated at Purdue where he received an M.S. degree in child development and family studies in 2003.

Malcolm Foley, a native of California, earned an M.A. in American Studies from Purdue University. As an undergraduate he attended and graduated from historically Black Southern University in Baton Rouge, Louisiana.

Benjamin R. Friedman received his B.A. in history from the University of Michigan in 1990 and his master's degree in the same field from George Washington University in 1994. He is currently working in the computer networking industry.

Floyd W. Hayes III is a senior lecturer and associate professor in the Department of Political Science and coordinator of programs and undergraduate studies in the Center for Africana Studies at Johns Hopkins University. He is the author of numerous scholarly articles and book chapters in the area of Black politics. His book *A Turbulent Voyage: Readings in African American Studies* is one of the most widely used texts in Black Studies. Presently he is working on a book titled *Domination and Ressentiment: The Desperate Vision of Richard Wright*.

Judson L. Jeffries is Professor of African American and African Studies at The Ohio State University. Prior to matriculating at OSU, Jeffries was an associate professor of Political Science and American Studies at Purdue University. He earned his Ph.D. in political science at the University of Southern California in 1997. His work has appeared in such journals as *Ethnic and Racial Studies*, *Journal of Black Studies*, *Western Journal of Black Studies*, *PS: Political Science & Politics*, and *Radical Philosophy Review*. His books include *Virginia's Native Son: The Election and Administration of Governor L. Douglas Wilder*; *Huey P. Newton, The Radical Theorist*; *Urban America and Its Police* with Harlan Hahn; and *Black Power in the Belly of the Beast*.

Tiyi M. Morris is an assistant professor of African American and African Studies at The Ohio State University. Morris earned her Ph.D. in American Studies at Purdue University in 2002. Her publications include "Women Power Unlimited: Womanist Activism and the Civil Rights Activism in Mississippi" in the *International Journal of Africana Studies* (2003) and two book chapters on women in the Civil Rights Movement.

Ryan Nissim-Sabat is a union organizer with UNITE HERE, organizing casino workers in California. He received his B.A. in political science from Virginia Polytechnic Institute and State University in 1997 and his M.A. in Black Studies from The Ohio State University in 1999.

Andrew Witt is an assistant professor of history at Edgewood College. As an undergraduate he received a B.A. in Afro American History at the University of Wisconsin–Madison. From there he matriculated at the University of Wisconsin–Milwaukee, where he earned an M.A. in history. He earned his Ph.D. at Loyola University of Chicago in 2005. He is the author of *Panthers in the Midwest*.

Index